King Solomon, with his associates and the High Priest, inspects the treasures of the Temple. Many degrees revolve around Solomon and the Temple.

MASONIC
RITES AND DEGREES

Ray V. Denslow

1955
Published by the Author

An Introduction

If you are one of those members of our fraternity who is impressed by the number of degrees which you have received—or hope to receive—then you cannot but be impressed with this volume which we have seen fit to label *Masonic Rites and Degrees,* for herein you will find Rites and Degrees of which you have never heard and, certainly, will never see conferred, for the reason they have been obsolete for years; and many for more than a century. They became obsolete because they added nothing to Ancient Craft Masonry teaching the very same lessons.

The period from 1740-1800 was an open season in Continental Europe for degree peddlers, and the formation of so-called Masonic Rites; Freemasonry was becoming popular and, like today, many organizations were being tied to "the Masonic kite," not being able to stand on their own value. Scientific and religious thought was at the highest ebb in history and some of these ideas crept into Masonic degrees. Swedenborg, with his theories of the New Jerusalem, had a great effect on Freemasonry, especially in the Scandinavian countries; and we have a Swedenborg Rite, colored by the Swedenborg personality.

On the other hand, we find charlatans and degree peddlers, such as Cagliostro, who went from one Royal Court to another, peddling his trashy legends which he dignified by calling "degrees." He offered in his Rite, (the Rite of Memphis), not 3° but 97.°, and gullible brethren flocked to his banner, paying the fees and signing themselves as "Most Powerful and Illustrious Sovereigns," (not overlooking the figures 97°).

The Rosicrucians, the Occultists, and the Alchemists were also busy in an attempt to find the Elixir of Life and to transmit lead into gold. Students of ritual will find many evidences of the occult and Rosicrucian influence in our ceremonies. Many of their theories were in advance of their time.

And while the English, French, Scottish, and Scandinavian brethren were busy with their Rites, we find the Germans perfecting several Rites and degrees, some of which are still being worked in Germany; there we find such men as Zinnendorf, Schroeder, Fessler, Bahrdt, and a host of others.

It seemed as if it were necessary only to attach to their Rite some such names as "Ancient," "Primitive," "Egyptian," "Scottish," "York," and to label the recipients of the degree or order as "Prince of ......," "Knight of ......," "Sublime ......," or apply the name of some historical spot or patron saint to the title of "Knight," whereupon we have "Knight of Jerusalem, Rome, Constantinople, or even the New Jerusalem." It appeared as if all the place names, biographies, and scripture were being exhausted in perfecting some new Masonic degree.

Fortunately, for the fraternity, few of the Rites are being practiced through the world today. Our brethren in Sweden work what is called the Swedish Rite, which is decidedly Christian, but satisfactory in a country where practically the entire population is Christian. This Rite is also practiced in neighboring countries where a similar situation prevails; it is a form of the old Rite of Strict Observance which has many excellencies. Our brethren in the British Isles (and the British Dominion) favor the Craft degrees, which are closely identified with the Royal Arch degree as its completion; they work the Scottish Rite, but under the name of the "Ancient and Accepted Rite" which is probably more nearly correct since the degrees are not "Scottish."

In the United States and Canada, we find two great Rites occupying the attention of the Craft: the American Rite, erroneously called the "York" Rite—and the Scottish Rite, whose title is also a misnomer, since it is not Scottish. Both Rites tell the Masonic story, each in its own way, for after all, Masonic degrees are merely means of teaching lessons and bringing to our attention the value of such virtues as Humility, Charity, Fidelity, Honesty, Toleration, Industry and the like, and stressing the importance of respect for others and their opinions, that we may, as a people, live together in peace and harmony without regard to race, sex, color, or opinion. To some it is given to learn these lessons the hard way; the wise profits by the experience of others, and these experiences have been dramatized in such a way that he who is willing to be instructed may avoid the pitfalls of others.

We began this study of Rites and degrees half a century ago, making occasional notes; the result has been that when we found it possible to compile a volume, we are unable to locate some of the references; this may account for some not being credited with their original material. We have relied little on Mackey, for he wrote a century ago. We have gone to Bro. Harold Voorhis' valuable work on Masonic Organizations; we have combed the New Age Magazine, the volumes of the Allied Masonic Degrees, Nocalore, and made a thorough search of our own 7,000 volume Masonic Library. We have strived to be accurate that we may not be listed as an "irresponsible journalist," yet we do know that it is impossible to produce a volume without some errors, especially one of this type; we will therefore appreciate any note from our readers calling attention to any error, for it may be possible later to issue an "errata."

We have tried to write with only that criticism which we thought to be merited; in our study of original rituals, of which we have some 2,000, we found that if a degree had in it anything of value, it lived; if not, it vanished from the Masonic picture. And in the end, you may sum it all up in our statement that what we know as Freemasonry can be found in the degrees of Ancient Craft Masonry—and all other Rites and degrees are merely elaborations or amplifications of the Symbolic Degrees.

Fraternally,
RAY V. DENSLOW

Trenton, Missouri
August 9, 1955

Masonic Rites and Degrees

Aaron's Band: A degree which appeared in New York City about 1824; it was a social group and an independent body, but its ritual being so similar to that of the Order of High Priesthood, created dissatisfaction to such an extent that it finally became extinct.

Aborigines: An early day (1783) secret society which appeared in England, but which had no particular Masonic significance.

Acacia, Daughters of: In some of the Latin South-American countries, there has been established the "Hijas d'Acacia," or Daughters of Acacia, which is serving the same purpose among the Latins as do some of the juvenile societies in our own country. It seems to have had its origin in Cuba, where it is under supervision of the Grand Lodge.

Acacia Fraternity: The formation of the Acacia Fraternity was due to a desire on the part of a large number of college students to have Masonic intercourse while students in various American universities and colleges.

The first of these organizations was at the University of Michigan in 1904, although there had been a Masonic Club there as early as 1894, but in 1904 a ritual, constitution and by-laws were adopted and the name *Acacia Fraternity* was assumed. Membership at that time was restricted to Master Masons. Later a new ritual was written.

In later years it was discovered that the membership age of students graduating was twenty-one years or less, so that the Fraternity was made up of graduate students. Several efforts were made by representatives of various college groups to admit young men who were members of the Order of De-Molay, but this was violently opposed by those in control and it was not until 1931 that the requirements were changed to admit sons of Master Masons; this, in 1933, was changed to admit Freemasons, sons and brothers of Freemasons, or any person recommended by two Master Masons, thereby throwing it open to practically any protestant student. The Fraternity has an official organ, The Triad. It has held national conclaves fairly regularly since 1904.

Academic Degrees: The Sovereign College, Allied Masonic Degrees, has authority under its laws, to confer various academic degrees, although it has rarely exercised that right. Among the degrees authorized are: Doctor in Universal Masonry; Doctor in Masonic Law; Doctor in Masonic Letters; Doctor in Masonic Theology; Bachelor of Masonic Law.

Academy des Illuminees d'Avignon: A System of Philosophy developed by the Hermetics.

Academy of Ancients and Secrets: Established in Warsaw, Poland, in 1767, modeled after a similar society which existed in Rome; it taught the advancement of natural science and its application to occult philosophy.

Academy Platonic: Founded at Florence, Italy, in 1480; it was supposed to have had a Masonic character, but at that early date it is hardly probable that it was Masonic.

Academy of Sages: A Swedish Order of about 1770; it was said to have been founded originally in London by Elias Ashmole.

Academy of Sublime Masters of the Luminous Ring: This was founded

1

in 1780, in Paris, by members of the French Philosophic Scottish Rite. It devoted itself to the study of the philosophy of Pythagoras, and worked three degrees; the first two of these treated of Freemasonry; the latter of Pythagoras and his school of thought. They believed that Pythagoras was the founder of Freemasonry.

Academy of True Masons: A French Society, established about 1778, conferring six degrees: 1, The True Mason; 2, True Mason in Right Way; 3, Knight of the Golden Key; 4, Knight of Iris; 5, Knight of Argonauts; 6, Knight of the Golden Fleece. One of a long string of Continental degrees; it was established in Montpellier, not far from Avignon and apparently influenced by Avignon groups. Little is known of its history or objective.

Accepted Masons: In 1656, the Company of Freemasons took the modern name of "The Worshipful Company of Masons." Some of the inner meetings of this Company were called "acceptions," from which the word "accepted" comes. This divided the Company into two parts—those who were simply *free,* and others who were *Free and Accepted.* Fees for outsiders were double those of others.

Adept: The word means "one who is well skilled" and appears in many Masonic degrees as part of the title; in other cases it may refer to an individual. All Hermetic Masons were called "adepts." "Prince Adept" is sometimes listed as the 28° of the A.A.S.R.; and the 23° of the Clermont Rite; it is listed as the 4° of the Relaxed Observance Rite; and the 1° of the Rite of Elects of Truth. A second step in the Illuminati. The novice was required to write out his answers to certain questions which were proposed. At this juncture he receives a secret name. Some of the statutes of the order are made known to him, but complete knowledge of the system is withheld. Should he have ever renounced the organization these answers could have been used against him.

Adept of the East: Also known as the "Illustrious Elected of the Fifteen" in the Scotch Rite; it was the 4° of the Order of the Temple.

Adept Master: The 3° in the Order of the Temple.

Adeptus: The word has a meaning similar to that of "adept."

Adeptus Adoptus: Zinnendorf's 7° consisted of instruction in chemicals and pharmaceuticals.

Adeptus Coronatus: The 7° of the Swedish Rite, or "Templar Master of the Key."

Adeptus Exemptus: The 7° of the German Rosicrucians.

Adeptus Junior: The 5° in the Rosicrucian (U.S.A.) Society; it is the first of the degrees given in the II Order.

Adeptus Major: The 6° in the Rosicrucian Society (U.S.A.), and the second of the II Order.

Adeptus Senior: One of the Rosicrucian degrees (U.S.A.), probably same as "Major."

Adonaite Mistress: The Lodge of Mount Tabor published at Paris, in 1812, a ritual of 178 pages, in which the two following degrees are called the "Grades of Perfection, or Assembly of the Grand Mysteries," as such, they were a philosophical explanation of the five recognized grades of the Lodge and Chapter, termed the "Sister Mysteries." Herein the 10° is given as an official grade to the Sis. Inspectress and Depositress, the 11° to the Worshipful Mistress, and the 12° and last degree to the Grand or Provincial Grand Mistress.

Decorations, Clothing, etc. The Apron is green, doubled with black, and having upon it a black rosette. The Jewel is a golden key, which is said to open the words, past, present, and future. The Grand Mistress is called "Supreme Hierophantide," the two next in rank, "First and Second Hierophantides."

Adoniramite Masonry: (See Rite, Adoniramite.)

Adonis, Mysteries of: (See Ancient Mysteries.)

Adopted Masons: Sir William Dugdale, author of the "History of St. Paul's," was acquainted with the paternity of "Adopted" Masons, which he appears to have regarded as derived from a company of Italian Freemasons to whom, according to his statement, the Pope gave a Bull, or Patent, about the time of Henry III, authorizing them to travel up and down Europe while building churches.

In London, certain members of the Mason's Company, who are known to have been Masons by trade, joined the so-called Acception (became Adopted Masons), just as Operative Masons become Freemasons at the present time. The "Accepted" or "Adopted" Mason of the 17th century was an intermediate rank between the mediaeval operative Mason and the present-day speculative Mason.

Adoptive Apprentice: The ceremonies of the several degrees are ordinarily held in the same room, being divided into three parts by means of red, white and blue curtains. The hangings are red, if the blue hangings of an Apprentice are not used. The side of the Wor. Master and Mistress in the back is named the "Climate of Asia"; facing this, the west is the "Climate of Europe"; the Apprentices are in the north, "Climate of America"; the Companions in the south, "Climate of Africa." The Wardens with their corresponding Sister officers are placed respectively in America and Africa. In Asia are two thrones or chairs on one dais. In advance, is an altar upon which is a mallet, a naked sword and a book of statutes. At the sides are placed 8 allegorical figures representing: Wisdom, Prudence, Strength, Temperance, Honor, Charity, Justice, Truth, and distinguished by their attributes. The lodge is lighted by 5 oderiferous vases and by a star of 5 rays placed in Asia. The Brothers and Sisters are ranged in two lines, the Sisters being in advance of the Brothers. Before each officer is a pentagonal table. On the Mosaic pavement is a painting representing the 5 parts of the world by allegorical figures: 1. The Ladder of Jacob. 2. Noah's Ark. 3. Tower of Babel. 4. Sun. 5. Moon. The apron is of white lambskin with a triangular flap and bordered with blue silk. The scarf is of blue moire, worn from right to left. Officers wear the scarf as a collar and suspend therefrom the jewel which is a golden trowel. The jewel of the members represents a heart in flames having an apple in the interior. The garter is worn around the left arm and is of white satin doubled with blue and embroidered in blue with the words "Silence and Virtue." Brothers wear the Masonic insignia to which they are entitled, also a collar of blue moire to which is attached for jewel, a ladder in gold of 5 steps. The dress of the Brothers is a black coat, white vest, trousers and gloves. The clothing of the Sisters is a white apron and gloves.

3

The 1° Rite of Adoption; it was open to Master Masons. (See Rite of Adoption.)

Adoptive Lodge: All societies which accept women whose relatives have a Masonic standing, are known as "Adoptive Lodges." The better known of these groups is the Order of the Eastern Star. Actually, the term applies to those lodges of women which existed in France immediately following the Revolution. This was generally regarded as a measure to relieve the home pressure by giving wives and relatives a place in the Masonic system. In some jurisdictions, Adoptive Masonry is strictly prohibited to Freemasons (Pennsylvania, England, Ireland, Australia, etc.).

The name is not generally used in the United States to describe women's organizations. The French referred to these groups as "Loges d'Adoption" presumably because they were "adopted," or under the wing of some regular Masonic group. French lodges conferred the degrees of: 1, Female Apprentice; 2, Craftswoman; 3, Mistress; 4, Perfect Mistress.

Adoptive Masonry: The *Masonry of Adoption* is the term used in France for a system of Masonry for Women. It would appear that the perfection of character which their husbands had reached, excited a desire in the breasts of some of the other sex to obtain a knowledge of the foundation of Freemasonry.

Those who are admitted bear the appellation of *Sisters*. The Order contains five grades, which are the Apprentice, Companion, and Mistress; these are obligatory—the others are called high grades, High Mistress and Sublime Scottish.

As we might expect, the garden of Paradise, with our first parents and the Temptor, are prominently mentioned, and the dreadful punishment our mother Eve inflicted on her posterity by giving way to curiosity is the first lesson. *Eve* is the password throughout, and *Balba* (Babel), which signifies confusion, is not inappropriate to this mixture of brothers and sisters. The third degree embraces a vast portion of Scripture history, the whole of the events recorded in the Book of Genesis, after the subsidence of the waters of the deluge, being brought to view. The prominent vices of both sexes are dilated on, even to a reference to the crimes which drew down the vengeance of the Most High on Sodom, Lot's wife not being forgotten, of course, to read another lesson to the ladies on the evils of curiosity. Joseph's adventures are related in the examination, but the part played by Potiphar's wife appears unaccountably to be omitted, we suppose because it tells unfavourably to the ladies. Balls and banquets are inseparable from these associations, and they are no doubt the real design of the organization, the ceremonies being merely a pretext.

We are told that, when first organized in France, the institution was acknowledged by the Masonic authorities of the kingdom. The first Lodge, "La Candeur," was opened in Paris on March 11, 1785, a Marquis being the President, and a Duchess acting as Grand Mistress; in the same year the Duchess of Bourbon was installed as Grand Mistress. The Revolution, of course, checked this as well as other associations, but in 1805 there was a revival, and the Empress Josephine presided over the "Loge Imperiale d'Adoption des Francs Chevalieres," at Strasburg.

Advisor's Honor Key: An honor conferred upon Freemasons by the Order of DeMolay; usually given because of exceptional service rendered a subordinate chapter of the Order.

4

African Architects: (See Rite of African Architects.)

African Brother: Not as might be supposed, a member of a colored lodge, but one of those degrees listed under the Rite of Strict Observance; it was not always listed under this title.

African Builders: Name sometimes given to African Architects; they conferred eleven degrees in two divisions—First Temple; Second Temple. The symbolic degrees were all listed under the former, while the latter division included: 4, Apprentice of Egyptian Secrets or Architect; 5, Initiate of Egyptian Secrets; 6, Cosmopolitan Brother; 7, Christian Philosopher; 8, Master of Egyptian Secrets; 9, Squire of the Order; 10, Soldier of the Order; 11, Knight of the Order. At one time this society stood very high, admitting only those of higher education and learning; their object seemed to be to preserve Freemasonry in its original purity. Just where they acquire the title of "African" we are unable to learn.

Afro-American Grand Lodge: Just one of the bogus and clandestine groups of negroes; this was denied incorporation in Missouri when objection was filed by the Prince Hall Grand Lodge of Missouri.

Albions: A pseudo-Masonic society of the 18th century.

Alchemists: Our early-day brethren were filled with occult ideas; for example, the philosopher's stone, and the elixir of life. It was their belief that alchemy held the secrets of the ages. Out of this came such societies as the Alchemists, the Rosicrucians, the Rosy Cross, and, finally, the Royal Society; the latter made a scientific approach to the problem. At one time, danger was attached to those who delved in scientific research, for such matters were condemned by the Roman Church.

Allgemeine Freimauer Liga: A news dispatch from Amsterdam, Holland, in 1929, stated that the organization was formed about 1925 in Basle by a "small congregation of Masons in that place who despatched a message to all Masons of all parts of the world, in which they said that, after the frightful events of the war . . . it was more than ever necessary that the individual Mason of the world should come together and discuss the problems which lay before them in order to come to a mutual understanding."

The International Freemasons' League started with about twenty members and rapidly increased in membership, holding annual meetings until World War II.

Allied Masonic Degrees: (See Rite of Allied Masonic Degrees.)

Amaranth, Order of: (See Order of Amaranth.)

American Federation of Human Rights: (See Co-Masonry.)

American Legion: There are in existence a number of posts of the American Legion composed entirely of Freemasons. The ritual is said to have a Masonic background. Many of the Commanders of the Legion · have been Freemasons.

American Masonic Federation, The: Probably the most troublesome clandestine group which pretended to "confer" Masonic degrees, was the American Masonic Federation which was first heard of in the Northwestern States of the U.S.A. about 1906 and which ended its existence in 1922 when its chief organizer, Matthew MacBlaine Thomson and two of his associates were sent to the Ft. Leavenworth prison for a term of five years, and also assessed a fine of $5,000 each, after which little was heard of this bogus organization.

5

All of the degrees from 1° to 33° were available at a price; and there were elaborate patents which were sold, prepared by a confederate in Scotland; this mailing from Scotland seemed to give regularity to irregularity! Agents were given a commission on all degrees "conferred."

The worst of it was that Thomson had at one time been an active member of the Grand Lodge of Scotland and honored in many ways; he had also served as an officer in the Grand Chapter of Scotland. Just why he changed character so completely is not known—unless it was for the money involved.

His trial was before a jury of non-Masons, the judge being a member of the Catholic church, so his trial must have been a fair one for him. Scottish Masons of high rank came here from Scotland to testify in the case. The case was tried in Salt Lake City, headquarters of the illegitimate organization. Had it not been for prompt action on the part of regular Freemasonry, the Federation might have spread to all parts of the nation.

Hence the necessity of keeping constantly informed as to irregular and spurious groups claiming to confer Masonic degrees.

American Rite of Freemasonry: According to the great Canadian historian, W. J. McLeod Moore, the "Grand Lodge of All England" died about 1790, leaving no subordinates; it never chartered lodges outside of England, and it is therefore an error to suppose that the "York Rite" of the United States of America emanated from it. Moore, rightfully or wrongfully, attributes the establishment of the Rite to Thomas Smith Webb, who, he says, "at the termination of the last century (1797), added degrees and other strange peculiarities to the American Masonic system, revolutionizing, not only the three craft degrees, but the Royal Arch and Knight Templar in an attempt to show that he had adopted the 'true work' of the 'Ancient York Masons,' but it is well known that no such working was known among them." (See York Rite.)

Anchor, Knights and Ladies of the: All of those men and women who were members of the Order of the Anchor.

Anchor, Order of the: An adoptive society, founded in France in 1743; it deals with nautical symbolism; the ladies promise in their obligations: "Not to receive strange vessels in the port she belonged to, as long as a vessel of the Order was at anchor there." Meaning what?

Anchor, Order of Knights and Heroines of: (See Order of Knights and Heroines of the Anchor.)

Ancien de Bouillon: (See Rite, Ancien de Bouillon.)

Ancient, The: The third of the twenty-two degrees of the German Union.

Ancient and Accepted Rite: This is the name used in the British Isles when referring to what is known in the U.S.A. as the "Scottish Rite."

Ancient and Primitive Rite: (See Rite, Ancient and Primitive.)

Ancient Arabic Order Nobles of the Mystic Shrine: In 1871, William J. Florence, a distinguished American actor, returned from a European trip inspired by the pageantry, and Oriental splendor of a private ceremony sponsored by the Arabian Consul at Marseilles, France. From notes and material submitted to him by the actor, Walter M. Fleming—eminent physician, Civil War veteran, 33° Mason, and Knight Templar—contrived a ritual.

On June 16, 1871, Fleming, Florence and eleven Masonic friends, meeting at Knickerbocker Cottage in New York City, endorsed a proposal for the formation of a new fraternal order to be composed of Knights Templar and

6

32° Scottish Rite Masons, based on Fleming's ritual with its background of Oriental glamour, pageantry and mystic splendor. On September 26, 1872, meeting at the Masonic Hall on East 23d Street, the thirteen charter members held their first official session and formally organized "Mecca Temple" of the Ancient Arabic Order, Nobles of the Mystic Shrine. Dr. Fleming was elected Illustrious Grand Potentate. The original ritual, prepared by him in his own handwriting, is now displayed in the Mystic Shrine Rooms of the Masonic National Memorial at Alexandria.

For a number of years Noble Fleming, Potentate of Mecca Temple from its inception, considered the organization of a national body. On June 6, 1876, in New York, the Imperial Council of the Shrine for the United States was finally organized, and on the next day Damascus Temple of Rochester, N. Y., became the second Shrine Temple. By June 20, 1887, the Shrine had 37 Temples, with a total membership of 4,398. On that date the title of "Imperial" was adopted in lieu of "Grand" in designating the Shrine's National Officers, and the title of "Imperial Council for the United States of America" was changed to "Imperial Council for North America," following the chartering of Rameses Temple, Toronto, as the first Canadian Temple.

By July, 1953, the Shrine of North America had expanded to 165 Temples, chartered or under dispensation, with a total membership of 689,678 Nobles in Canada, Mexico, Hawaii, the Canal Zone, every state in the Union, and the District of Columbia.

The Shrine has thus been superimposed on the structure of Freemasonry. Official headgear of the Shrine is the Red Fez; the insignia consists of the scimitar and crescent. The Shrine seeks to keep alive in men the spirit of youth.

Since 1922, over 250,000 crippled children—irrespective of race, creed or color, and without one cent of cost to any child—have been treated and healed in Shrinedom's great Temples of Mercy.

The annual $3,500,000.00 hospital budget is met by an annual $5.00 assessment paid by the Nobility of the Shrine, by the proceeds of Shrine-sponsored feature events, by the income from growing endowment funds, and finally by voluntary gifts and charitable bequests from generous friends of Shrinedom and little crippled children.

The Shrine has seventeen hospitals spread throughout the United States, Canada, Mexico and Hawaii.

The Mother Temple was called "Mecca" after the most holy city of the Moslems; their meeting places are called "Temples." Oriental costumes are worn by officers, bands, drill teams, and chanters.

Ancient Craft Masonry: In the Articles of Union between the Ancients and the Moderns, it was expressly stated:

"Pure Antient Masonry consists of three degrees, and no more, viz: those of the Entered Apprentice, the Fellow Craft, and the Master Mason, including the Supreme Order of the Holy Royal Arch."

The Article further specified that the above was not to prohibit the conferring of the Degrees of Chivalry, but did not prescribe the degrees as a part of Ancient Craft Masonry. It is generally considered that all degrees dealing with the Loss, the Preservation, and the Recovery of the WORD, are ipso facto, degrees of Ancient Craft Masonry. This would include the sym-

7

bolic degrees, the Royal Arch, and the Royal Master. It does not include the commandery orders, which give a Christian interpretation of the Word.

Ancient Egyptian Order of Princesses of Sharemkhu: According to Voorhis, this organization was formed in October, 1925, in Boston, Mass. Its membership was limited to women who have a father, husband, or brother belonging to the Shrine. It appears to have been sponsored by Aleppo Temple, and holds four meetings a year. The initiation is said to be "quite rugged."

Ancient Egyptian Order of Sciots: The Ancient Egyptian Order of Sciots is an organization little known beyond the Pacific Coast. With the exception of three groups, all the Pyramids, as the groups are called, operate in the State of California; the three exceptions are in the neighboring State of Arizona. The organization was originally formed in San Francisco, Calif., in 1905, and at that time bore the name "Boosters." However, it was felt the growth of the Order necessitated a change in name, so, in 1910, it assumed the present designation.

It has held regular sessions since 1905. Any Master Mason in good standing is eligible for membership, and each applicant states in his petition that he will endeavor to visit the lodge of which he is a member at least once a month.

The ritual of the degree, according to a statement issued by them, "is founded upon an event that occurred about 1124 B.C. The Greek inhabitants of Island of Chios, in the Aegean Sea, maintained their government under a democratic organization form known as the League of Neighbors." They were known as Sciots, from which the present organization takes its name. Each group is known as a Pyramid, and the presiding officer is known as Toparch. The State organization carries the title Supreme Pyramid, and its presiding officer is known as the Supreme Pharaoh. The purpose of the organization, as stated in its literature, is "to unite all Master Masons in a closer bond of friendship."

Ancient Free and Accepted Architects: This is an American innovation, the work of the late Henry P. H. Bromwell of Colorado; he was Grand Master of Illinois in 1865; he was widely traveled and during that period unearthed what he thought was most valuable information which should not be issued except through a series of degrees known as "Select Architects," "Most Excellent Architect," and "Royal Architect." The three degrees were published in full in Volume IV of the Grand College of Rites, but have no particular Masonic significance; it is, however, a rather interesting ritual.

Ancient Free and Accepted Masons: Twenty-seven Grand Lodges in the United States use the above title; twenty-one use "Free and Accepted Masons"; one uses "Ancient Free Masons."

Ancient Masons: This group was sometimes termed the "Atholl Masons" after one of their Grand Masters, the Duke of Atholl. It was first established in London about 1751 by Laurence Dermott, an Irishman; he dubbed the older Grand Lodge the "Moderns," and assumed the title of "Ancients" for his own group; he was more aggressive in propagating his rite, laying particular stress upon the Royal Arch as an essential to Ancient Craft Masonry. Not until 1813 was their disagreement settled—and this by consolidation of Ancients and Moderns into the United Grand Lodge of England.

Ancient Master: The 4° of the Rite of Martinism.

Ancient Mysteries: Freemasonry, by some, is believed to have been derived from the Mysteries of Ancient Egypt and Greece; little has come down to us relating to these mysteries, but they must have been of high order; leading men of all nations round about were accepted into membership. No organization is as much interested in the Ancient Mysteries as are the Freemasons. Men have always grasped for Light as to the mysteries of Life and Nature; one or two of our degrees deal at length with the ancient mysteries and their teachings, especially those of Mithras, Egypt, the Essenes, and the earlier sages. It is generally conceded that the mysteries taught the oneness of God, immortality of the soul, and a just reward for a life well lived, the doctrines which fit man to die.

Ancient Order of United Workmen: Not a Masonic Order, although founded by one John J. Upchurch, an active Freemason. Its watchwords are Charity, Hope and Protection; it has three degrees: Junior Workman, Workman, Master Workman. Among its emblems are the All-Seeing Eye, the Anchor, the Holy Bible, and the Square and Compasses. Their emblem is the Square and Compasses—without the "G" but with an arm.

Ancient Order of Zuzumites: The Zuzumites appear to have worked under authority of the Grand Tabernacle of England, Ancient Order of Zuzumites. Whether it still exists we do not know, but we do have a ritual of 1881 which shows they conferred the three degrees of *Neophyte, Graduate,* and *Fellow Zuzumite;* the officers of a "Tent," as they called subordinate bodies, included a Worshipful Master, and a Senior and Junior Warden; they also had a Tyler.

Candidates were in search of "light" and those who broke vows, symbolically, "had their heads cut off and their hearts stabbed through, entrails drawn out and body chopped into minute particles."

In the second degree, the candidate was in search of Truth, and violation of vow brought about "no less a penalty than being considered . . . a shameless vagabond and a lying scamp." The legend of Osiris and Isis is explained.

In the third degree, the candidate sought "higher light" by following "in the footsteps of our worthy Master, Osiris. Violation of a vow resulted in a symbolical (of course) "fire of charcoal lighted on my breast . . . and may life be a curse and burden to me . . . until death."

The rituals bear evidence of one who was acquainted with Freemasonry, although there is no evidence to show the degrees to be in any way connected with the Masonic fraternity.

Ancient Reformed Rite: (See Rite, Ancient Reformed.)

Ancient Toltec Rite: (See Rite, Ancient Toltec.)

Ancient York Masons: Some lodges of Ancient Masons took this title. How says that the authority of the Ancient York Masons was transmitted, viva voce, from individual to individual, the oldest surviving Freemason being considered for the time being, as the Chief Harod of the Order, whose duty it was to seek out some worthy brother to whom he could entrust the keys of the cipher and other documents necessary for the preservation of the Order. It was the duty of that individual to conceal from the world generally the knowledge with which he had been entrusted, but that knowledge was not generally understood or known by other members of the Order.

Androgynous Degrees: These are degrees which are open to membership of both sexes; the Order of the Eastern Star, the White Shrine of Jerusalem, and the True Kindred, are examples of such degrees.

Anointed Kings, Order of: (See Order of Silver Trowel.)

9

Anonymous Society: A German society whose object was Charity and the cultivation of the occult sciences.

Antediluvian Masonry: These degrees deal with matters which occurred before the Flood. Traces are found in some of the Scottish Rite and Royal Ark Mariner degrees.

Antigallic Masons: A pseudo-Masonic organization of the 18th Century which had a short life on the Continent.

Anti-Masonic Order: There have been many organizations which stand opposed to Freemasonry; the Lutheran (Missouri Synod), and the Catholic Church have been outstanding in their opposition. Some regard the Knights of Columbus as an anti-Masonic group; in the Philippines the Knights of Columbus have taken the lead in fighting the public schools and have attacked the Freemasons for their stand on the school question.

In the early days of the fraternity, there were many organizations formed with the idea of ridiculing the fraternity; and during the anti-Masonic troubles (1825-40) there were many organizations formed for the purpose of fighting the society.

Anti-Masonic Party: Such a party was organized for the elections of 1827 in New York; it later spread to other parts of the country. A Convention was held at LeRoy, N. Y., in 1828, and a State Convention at Utica in the same year; it nominated Solomon Southwick for Governor. The anti-Masonic vote by year is shown: 1828, 33,345; 1829, 68,613; 1830, 106,081; 1831, 98,847; 1832, 156,672. A National Convention was held in Philadelphia in 1830, which adopted resolutions attacking the fraternity and urging its dissolution. The last of these Conventions was held in 1836, which nominated General William Henry Harrison for president; the anti-Masonic ticket, headed by one William Wirt, in 1832, actually carried the State of Vermont. Andrew Jackson, a Past Grand Master of Tennessee, was elected president. Anti-Masonry soon fell apart.

Antipodeans: The 60° of the seventh series of the Metropolitan Chapter of France.

Apocalypse, Order of: (See Order of Apocalypse.)

Appendant Orders: These are Orders, or degrees, attached to another; in some jurisdictions the degree of Super Excellent Master is so regarded. When the Supreme Council of the Southern Jurisdiction established themselves, in 1802, they claimed authority to confer most every degree termed Masonic— these were appendant orders, since they were not included in the regular system. The Red Cross and Malta Orders of the Templar system were once regarded as "appendant."

Apprentice: Naturally, the word means "a beginner," or one who set out to learn a trade; it is used in this connection with Masonic degrees, referring usually to the first degree in a rite. When a craftsman desired to apply for work in any of the old building guilds, he was first "entered," and was called an "Entered Apprentice."

The 1° of the Ancient Egyptian Reformed Rite, a Rite of 33°; 1° of the Rite Clerks of Relaxed Observance; 1° in the Rite of Illuminati; 1° in the Rite of Philalethes; 1° in Reformed Rite; 1° of the Swedish Rite; 1° of the Egyptian Rite; the degree has a chamber of reflection; in the center is a large pyramid, at the base of which is a cave. The candidate, after a severe lecture,

10

is introduced as "a Mason, who having passed all the degrees of ordinary Masonry, presents himself to be initiated into true Egyptian Masonry." It shows traces of occultism, and alchemy. The 1°.of the Zinnendorf Rite; one of the degrees of the Illuminated Philosophist; 1° of the Ancient and Accepted Scottish Rite, but not practiced by that rite where grand lodges have control of craft degrees. The first degree of this rite was written largely by Albert Pike.

The 1° of the American or York Rite—or the Freemasonry of the British Isles. As a degree it is one of the most interesting of the craft series, for it explains to the beginner in Freemasonry, the whole plan of organization, the objectives, and the symbolism method of instruction. Most grand lodges require candidates to be examined on this degree before they can advance to that of Fellowcraft.

Apprentice and Fellow-craft of St. Andrew: The 4° of the Swedish Rite.

Apprentice Builder: The 1° of the boy's organization, Order of Builders.

Apprentice Cohen: The 1° of the nine degrees of the Rite of Elected Cohens.

Apprentice of Egyptian Secrets: The fourth of the eleven degrees in the Rite of African Architects; it was the first degree of the Second Temple series.

Archers: The word is thought to refer to those who have received the Royal Arch degree.

Architect: There are many degrees referred to under the above name, for example:

Architect, Free and Accepted.

Architect, Grand.

Architect, Grand Master.

Architect, Little.

Architect of Solomon.

Architect, Perfect.

Architect, Perfect and Sublime.

Architect of All Rites: and Knight of the Philosophy of the Heart: one of the degrees of the Persian Rite.

Architect, Provost and Judge: The Third Grade of the Councils of the Emperors of the East and West. The degree is associated with the mournful events in the traditions of Freemasonry. The Puissant Master represents Solomon on a throne with seven steps; before him is the VSL with compass and triangle; a golden urn plays an important part in the ritual; with it is a golden trowel. The heart of the lost master, the triangle, the blazing star, and the letter "G" are emblems and are carefully explained. The letters "S.V.G." upon the points of the triangle are the basis for the lecture.

Ark and Dove: An adoptive degree once practiced rather extensively throughout the United States; its emblems were the Dove, Olive-branch, Rainbow, and the Ark. Even the distinguished Freemason, Josiah Drummond of Maine, in a letter (1896) refers to having conferred the degree of Ark Mariner, otherwise called the degree of Ark and Dove, upon Bros. . . . In England the degrees are now the property of the Mark Grand Lodge; they have reference to the salvation of Noah and his family from the Deluge.

Ark Ceremony: The Ark Ceremony has survived and may be now con-

11

sidered as the most popular of all so-called "side degrees"; it is controlled in England by the Grand Lodge of Mark Master Masons, which attaches Lodges of the Grade to Mark Lodges and it enjoys wide attraction and numbers its members in nearly every corner of the globe. In Scotland, Lodges of Royal Ark Mariners are attached to Royal Arch Chapters and the membership under the Scotch Constitution is scattered over the world, numbering thousands. In America, today, there are no less than one thousand Royal Ark Mariners, which will indicate to us the importance of the Grade.

Ark Degrees: There are a number of degrees listed as "Ark" degrees, principal of which is that of Royal Ark Mariner. The "Ark and Dove" is an adoptive degree once practiced in the U.S.A. The degrees deal with the Ark of Noah, or Ark of Refuge, and not concerned with the Ark of the Covenant.

Ark Mariners: Usually referred to as "Royal Ark Mariner." This organization existed previous to 1802, for there is in existence a certificate of that date (March 6, 1802) stating "In the year of the flood 3806." The degree, at that time, had no ruling body and was probably worked in lodges; Royal Clarence Lodge at Bristol worked the degree as an additional craft degree. Its members were styled "Ark Mariners, or Ark, Mark, and Link Masons." The fee was five shillings ($1.00). The ritual contains a history of the Order. One has to be a Mark Master in England to receive the degree. In the United States the degree is under the control of the Allied Masonic Degrees.

Ark Mason: Anderson, in 1738, tells us:

"Noachidae, or Sons of Noah, was the first Name of Masons according to some old traditions" (and) that all (Masons) agree in the three great articles of Noah enough to preserve the Cement of the Lodge."

Here is a link with his other statement "well-built arch" and what was subsequently Royal Arch Masonry. The seal was a Dove, often depicted on Irish Red Cross seals, aprons, etc. An early record of the degree appears in the records of Limerick (Ireland) Lodge No. 271. It was usually conferred in a Royal Arch Chapter; at other times it is referred to as "Ark, Mark & Wrestle."

In the Helvetic Rite is a degree which shows traces of the Royal Ark Mariner ritual. There the Master represents Noah, while there are such symbols as the Dove, the Ark, and the Rainbow.

Arras, Chapter of: A somewhat traditional group which it is claimed was chartered by Charles Edward Stuart, Pretender to the Throne of England. Even the date is given—April 15, 1747. The History of Cryptic Masonry states that in that year, twelve months after his return from an unlucky invasion of Scotland and England, Charles Edward issued a charter for the formation of such a Chapter at Arras, in France. In the document he states that he is "substitute Grand Master of the Chapter of H," meaning Heredom, the organization being termed a "Sovereign Primordial Chapter of Rose Croix under the distinctive title of Scottish Jacobite." (See Jacobitism; see Heredom.)

Aspirant: Literally, a "seeker." This is one of the grades in the Order of Amaranth. (See Order of Amaranth.)

Assassins, The: A Persian Society whose history is associated with that of the Templars; the name was derived from that of an oriental drug-hashish—an opium extract which the members used to excite their imagination. The

12

society later split into two sections, the Tunnites, or Orthodox Moslems; the other known as Shi-ites, or Persian Moslems. The date of its origin is given as 1090; the founder was Hassam-ben-Sabah, who became the first Master.

We have said the organization was identified with the Templars and they operated in much the same way, by acquiring castles and property; they used the white dress and the red fillet, while the Templars used the white mantle and the red cross. The Assassins were a branch of the Ishmaelites, the "Illuminati" of the East, and their institution of lodges with various grades of initiation agrees completely with what we have heard concerning many revolutionary societies. The name is a misnomer in that they were not the murderous gang one might suspect; they only sought to slay ignorance and evil. (See Knights Templar.)

Assemblies: The name given to meetings of such societies as the Order of the Rainbow, and Select Masters.

Assembly of Masonic Citizens: The name given to a society formed in Ireland in 1824 to protest the banning of meetings of Freemasons.

Assembly of Princes: The 2° of the Secret Monitor Grade.

Atholl Grand Lodge: (See Ancients.)

Atholl Masons: Members of the Grand Lodge headed by the Duke of Atholl (Antients).

August Order of Light: (See Fratres Lucis.)

Aurori: An association formed at Paris in 1783, being one of a myriad of societies formed on the Continent during the last half of the 17th century.

Auxiliary Degrees: Many rites have, in addition to their regular series of degrees, certain other degrees which bear the name "auxiliary." Such is the case in the Supreme Council of France, which has six degrees in addition to the regular 33 of the rite. These are: 1, Elu de Perignan; 2, Petit Architecte; 3, Grand Architecte (Compagnon Ecossais); 4, Maitre Ecossais; 5, Knight of the East; 6, Knight Rose Croix.

Avignon, The Illuminati of: A French Rite developed at Avignon in 1770, which later became the Academy of True Masons. It had four degrees of Hermetic or Swedenborgian character. (See Illuminati of Avignon.)

Babylonian Pass: Sometimes referred to as the "Red Cross of Daniel," "Jordan Pass" and "Royal Order of Prussian Blue." (See Irish Rite.)

The degree is now conferred under authority of the Irish Grand Council, Knights of the Sword under other names; it is also called "Red Cross Knights." It has an illogical connection with the Templars in Ireland and there have been several attempts to remove it from the system. It was associated with the degrees of Jordan Pass and Royal Order so much they were commonly referred to as "Red Cross Masons." All three degrees are now worked under the Irish Grand Council of the Degrees of Knight of the Sword, Knight of the East, and Knight of the East and West.

Babylon, Red Cross of: In England, the degree of Red Cross of Babylon is worked by the Allied Masonic Degrees; it had been worked as a side degree in Craft Lodges as early as the first part of the 19th century. It deals with the departure of the Jews from Babylon to Jerusalem where they went to assist in rebuilding the Temple after the death of Cyrus, King of Persia, who by decree freed the captives. It is also related to the Illustrious Order of the Red Cross (U.S.A.) in its traditions, legends and attributes.

13

Bahrdt's Rite: (See Rite, Bahrdts.)

Baldwyn Encampment Degrees: One of the oldest chivalric groups exists at Bristol, England, known as Baldwyn Preceptory (or Encampment). Its records go back to 1780, although there are newspaper accounts back to 1772. It conferred seven degrees, three craft, Royal Arch, Knights Templar (St. John of Jerusalem, Palestine, Rhodes, and Malta), Knights Rose Croix of Heredom, and Grand Elected Knights Kadosh. It has a Treaty with the English Templars, as well as the Supreme Council 33°. It derived its name from Baldwyn, King of Jerusalem, who, in 1727, obtained from Pope Honorarius, permission to be formed into a regular order to be known as Knights Templar. It regarded itself as a Supreme Grand Encampment, and December 20, 1780, issued a Charter of Compact, which established laws for the government of subordinate bodies.

Baptism, Rite of: (See Rite of Baptism.)

Bards: The 1° of the Druid Order. (See Druids.)

Bath, Order of: (See Order of the Bath.)

Bayani: The third of the degrees conferred by Katipunan. (See Katipunan.)

Beatitudes, Order of: (See Order of Beatitudes.)

Beauceant, Social Order of the: (See Order of the Beaucant.)

Beloved Daughter: The 1° in the Order of the Sacred Temple. (See Order of the Sacred Temple.)

Berlin: (See Rite of Three Globes.)

Bethels: The name given to groups of Job's Daughters.

Bheremites: The 4° of the Rite of Memphis.

Black Cross, Knight of: (See Knight of Black Cross.)

Black Eagle, Knight of: (See Knight of the Black Eagle.)

Black Eagle or Rose Croix, Knight of: (See Knight of the Black Eagle or Rose Croix.)

Black Mark: The degree is a part of the Templar series in Ireland and was introduced into the Irish ritual (according to our informant) to give color to Templary in Craft lodges; there is a record of its conferment as early as 1765. Little is known of its ritual, except that it was the first degree of Group 4 of the Irish system. The late John Yarker said of it:

"This and the degrees (only the Black Mark will be considered here) which follow are so perfectly inept, that they are quite undeserving of the name of Degrees; they were all, it is understood, brought to Scotland from Ireland, and as they are not recognized by the Grand Encampment of Scotland, nor by the Grand Council of Rites, they are supposed to be the invention of some of the irregular and low Encampments scattered through the interior of that country, probably for the purpose of giving greater dignity and importance to their begging brethren. There is no ceremonial whatever connected with any of them, except the first, if even that can be said to have one. How the *Black Mark,* which is always given as a Christian degree, is connected with the Templarism of Christian Masonry, it is impossible to perceive, as the whole relates to the Old Testament; nor is there any reason why it should be called a "Mark" degree, as the candidate receives no mark. The Encampments in North America and West Indian Islands have however a degree called the *"Christian Mark,"* or *"Knights of the Conclave,"* founded on the circumstance of one of the Popes who distrusted the Italian nobles, choosing his body guards from among the Knights of Malta; in that degree the same passage of the Bible is referred to, and one of the Knights (not the candidate) is provided with a white robe and inkhorn—he represents an angel and marks the

14

forehead of the candidate, so that he and others so marked may be saved from the general destruction about to ensue. This shows that both degrees are founded on the same idea, but in no other point do they accord, the reception and secrets being totally different. It is unnecessary to give the American degree as it is not practiced in Scotland."

Black Masonry: The Wilhelmsbad Congress opens the period of modern-day Templary, or "Black Masonry," so named because the members adopted a black costume as if in mourning for the martyred DeMolay, last chivalric Grand Master, but in reality because the deposed military Templars had joined the Order of St. John of Jerusalem, whose costume is black.

Black and White Eagle: The 30° of the French Rite. In a French Mss ritual of 1780, this degree is said to assert the positive transmission of Free-masonry to the Templars. The history of the Templars and their persecution is minutely described, the Grand Commander declaring in his closing address: "This is, my illustrious brother, how and by whom Masonry is derived and transmitted to us. You are now a Knight Templar, and on a level with them."

Blazing Star, Order of: This Order was established in Paris in 1766. It conferred the degrees of chivalry, following the Templar system of Ramsey.

Blue Brothers: (See Primitive and Original Rite.) The degree was a grade conferred by the Iluminees of Stockholm.

Blue Degrees: A name erroneously given to the three symbolic degrees of Freemasonry—Entered Apprentice, Fellow Craft, Master Mason. They are given that name because blue is said to be the color of Ancient Craft Masonry.

Blue Mason: One who is a member of a lodge of Freemasons.

Blue Masonry: The three degrees of Craft Masonry. (See Blue Degrees; see Early Grand Rite.)

Blue Friars, Society of: The Society of Blue Friars was organized in 1932. The purpose of the organization was to recognize Masonic authors and, up to and including 1954, 29 members had been selected for the organization.

The principal officer is the Grand Abbot, who is elected for life, or at his pleasure. Upon his death or resignation, the Deputy Grand Abbot succeeds. The secretarial duties are attended to by a Secretary-General. Members bear the title "Friar" and are entitled to use the designation "Blue Friar." There are no dues nor fees. One new Friar is appointed each year; additional Friars may be appointed to fill vacancies caused by death or resignation, but no vacancies may be filled when the total membership has exceeded 20.

The names of new members are made known at the annual meeting held in February and suitable certificates and jewels are presented to those selected for this honor. There is usually a representative group of Freemasons at these meetings, which are open to the public, and the programs are of high order. Membership is not limited to Freemasons living in the United States; some have been selected from foreign countries—England, Canada, Scotland, Argentina. Those living Masonic authors, in the order of their selection, who have been thus honored are:

Henry Van Arsdale Parsell (N.Y.)	William Leon Cummings (N.Y.)
Ray Vaughn Denslow (Mo.)	Wallace Everett Caldwell (N.C.)
Harold Van Buren Voorhis (N.J.)	Ward Kent St. Clair (N.Y.)
Carl Harry Claudy (D.C.)	James Fairbairn Smith (Mich.)
Hubert McNeill Poteat (N.C.)	William Moseley Brown (Va.)
Melvin Maynard Johnson (Mass.)	Harry L. Hayword (Ia.)

15

Robert James Meekren (Que.)   George S. Draffen (Scot.)
Richardson L. Wright (N.Y.)   James E. Craig (N.Y.)
Reginald Vanderbilt Harris (N.S.)   Fabian Onsari (Arg.)
Francis Joseph Scully (Ark.)   Edgar A. Guest (Mich.)
Howard Pervear Nash (N.Y.)   Fred L. Pick (England)

Blue Honor Award: (See Order of DeMolay.)

Boards of Relief: In most cities where there exist two or more lodges, there have been organized Boards of Relief; one of these groups describes its activities as follows:

(1) Detection and publication in bulletins of unworthy Freemasons and imposters playing on the fraternity; (2) Co-ordinating the various forms of Masonic relief throughout USA and Canada; (3) Promotion of prompt and effective ways of handling cases of inter-jurisdictional relief; (4) Organization of Masonic relief in times of emergency and disaster when such services are desired or requested by grand lodges; (5) Providing meeting places for discussion of various relief problems; (6) Arranging for Masonic burial service for transients.

These Boards are usually supported by a small per capita tax against the lodges comprising the Board.

Boosters: The original name of the Ancient Egyptian Order of Sciots. (See Ancient Egyptian Order of Sciots.)

Brazen Serpent, Knight of: (See Knight of Brazen Serpent.)

Brazil, Grand Orient of: (Brazilian Rite.)

One of the most confused systems of Freemasonry is that existing in Brazil, where there exists a Grand Orient of Brazil and eleven Grand Lodges which govern the various state lodges. There is no connection between the two groups. As matters now stand, the Grand Orient and Supreme Council of Brazil consist of four grand bodies, heads of rites, as follows:

1. The Supreme Council, which exercises ritualistic control over all Scottish Rite bodies, consisting of 33 active members, chosen by the body itself, from those who have been invested with the highest degree.
2. The Grand Chapter of the Modern Rite, which exercises ritualistic control over the degrees of the French Modern Rite of seven degrees in Brazil. It also has 33 active members who hold the highest degree in that rite.
3. The Grand Chapter of Noachites, which exercises control over the degrees of the Adonihiramite Rite of 13 degrees, and it too is composed of 33 members.
4. The Grand Chapter of York Rite of three degrees, which has control over this rite, which too has 33 members in control, who must be Master Masons.

Out of this arrangement there comes a General Assembly, composed of (1) members of the General Council of the Order; (2) the representatives of the bodies at the seat of the Central Power; (3) the representatives of the bodies away from the seat of Central Power; (4) the representatives of each of the grand bodies, heads of rites above mentioned. This General Assembly is the general legislative body for Brazilian Freemasonry. Judicial powers are invested in a Supreme Tribunal of Justice of fifteen judges, one-third of which are chosen annually for a term of three years. Only one American state recognizes this Grand Orient.

Brethren of the Rose Croix: This may refer to any number of systems but hardly to one by that name. There is the old Rite of Perfection, the Royal Order of Scotland, the Rosicrucians, Rosy Cross, and any number of systems

16

—both of the fraternity and without—which carry Rose Croix as perfection. (A name sometimes given to Rose Croix members.)

Bridge, Knight of: (See Knight of Bridge.)

Brotherhood of the Knights of the Temple: (See Knight of the Temple.)

Brotherly Love: (See Order of Brotherly Love.)

Brothers of Asia: (See Order of Melchizedek.)

Brothers of Light: (See Fratres Lucis.)

Brother Stuart: The 6° of the Swedish Rite.

Bucks: Another of many societies formed in the 18th century of pseudo-Masonic character. This group was founded by the beau-monde group of that day, and was a slang word for the name of the club. Members said their name was derived from the God Bacchus. They were termed "the famous and noble Order of Bucks."

Buffaloes: The Order was officially known as "The Royal Antediluvian Order of Buffaloes" and was regarded as a sort of laboring man's Freemasonry; it was mainly of social character, which later developed into a benefit society in England. The heads of its lodges were "Primos," while the general organization was headed by a "Great Primo." It is an English organization—or was.

Builders, Order of: (See Order of Builders.)

Bunker Hill, Sword of: (See Sword of Bunker Hill.)

Cabin Boy: The 1° of the Order of Felicitares. A French androgynous order of 1743. (See Order of Felicitares.)

Cabiri, The: A Modern organization whose membership is limited to past potentates of the A.A.O.N.M. Shrine.

Cable-Tow, The: A side degree worked in the U.S.A. about 1870.

Calderari, The: A Society formed as a counter-society to the Carbonari; a Spanish society composed of those excluded from the Carbonari. The Spanish rules gave aid to the Calderari in an attempt to put down the Carbonari. Their motto was that of the French populace of revolutionary days—Liberty, Equality, and Constitutional Administration. The society had no Masonic significance. (See Carbonari; see Charbonniers, French, or Communeros, Spanish.)

Callec Patriot: The 1° of the Consecrated Philoclesian Host; "while no reference is made in the ritual, it is self-evident that the author had some knowledge of Ancient Craft Masonry." The degrees are highly religious in nature, with moral teaching and emphasizing of Trinitarian Christianity.

Camel Herders: A Shrine organization, said to be dedicated to "charitable and philanthropic purposes." The only group we know of was reported in the Texas Grand Lodge magazine, August, 1954.

Capitular Degrees: The degrees conferred in a chapter of Royal Arch Masons and having to do with the keystone and Word. The degrees include the Mark Master, Past Master, Most Excellent Master, and Royal Arch Mason. They are sometimes referred to as "Red Masonry," red being the particular color of the Royal Arch. (See Royal Arch Masonry.)

Capitular Masonry: A series of degrees in the Zinnendorf Rite, which included as a III series, called Capitular Masonry, the degrees of 6° Favorite of St. John, and 7° Chapter of Elect Masons. (See Royal Arch Masonry.)

Carbonari, The: An organization which appeared in Italy about the late

17

18th or early 19th century, which emerged as a political force in 1814 when Maghella, Minister of Police, wanted a constitutional government and sought to oppose Murat, one of Napoleon's leaders, by using the Carbonari as his instrument. It became a very strong power, even drilling and arming its members. It came under the ban of the Holy See, but many of the lesser clergy were its supporters. At a trial of conspirators in 1818, the prosecution alleged that they were "offshoots of Freemasonry." It began to lose influence because many joined for mercenary motives; other members looked on them with contempt and reverted to Freemasonry. It practically ceased to exist by 1821, but the movement was carried on abroad by exiles, although sometimes under other names.

Cathedral Masons: Masons who worked on ecclesiastical buildings were sometimes described as such, or as "Church Masons," while the general body of the craft, employed on lay-work were called "Gild" or "Town Masons."

Cedars of Lebanon: A side degree worked in American lodges about 1870. (See Tall Cedars of Lebanon.)

Celebration: The 6° of the Fessler Rite. (See Fessler Rite.)

Cerneauism: A movement which threatened to wreck Masonic harmony in the United States, but which was finally outlawed by grand lodges; it was particularly troublesome to the Scottish Rite bodies who used all their influence with grand lodges to outlaw the movement. Cerneauism is now unknown.

Cerneau Rite: Joseph Cerneau was noted for his attempt to introduce the Scottish Rite degrees into the United States; he was particularly active in New York where bodies existed for several years, and where they were opposed by the Northern and Southern Supreme Councils. The dispute caused feeling to exist among Freemasons. Cerneauism is now unknown.

Chadrath Zereh Aur Boker: An Order of the Rosicrucian type making a special study of the Kaballah and the deeper Hermetics. It was made up of both males and females. Fratres Woodman, Westcott and Mathers of England were members of it and there were some members in the United States, but there were no lodges here. Its membership was, for the most part, cryptic. We have the names of three or four deceased members in the United States and know of at least three living members. It is decidedly inactive, so far as membership in the U.S.A. is concerned. We are not prepared to make an assertion regarding its European status.

Chapters: The name given to subordinate groups, such as Royal Arch Masons, Order of Eastern Star, Scottish Rite bodies, DeMolay, National Sojourners, Acacia, and other organizations. As a rule the governing body is given the name of "Grand Chapter," while national or international organizations are quite frequently referred to as "General Grand Chapter."

Chapter of Clermont: In 1754, according to theory, Chevalier de Bonneville established a chapter of high degrees in Paris, France. It was located in the Jesuit College of Clermont, thereby giving the name *Chapter of Clermont* to this system, which later became known as the Rite of Perfection, or Rite of Heredom. All that is distinctly known of this society or its teaching is that, besides the three ancient symbolic degrees, there were introduced some of the higher ones; all the allegories and symbols of which, *Fessler* asserts, pointed to the establishment of an universal dominion, the desired end and aim of the Jesuit institution. Into this Chapter the famous Baron Hunde, though then a member of the Protestant faith, contrived to gain admission, and upon

18

the Masonic instruction he there received, and the ritual of the new degrees, was formed the nucleus of the system which he introduced into Germany, when a Roman Catholic.

In 1758, the Chapter of Clermont was succeeded by the Council of Emperors of the East and West, the seven degrees of the Clermont grade being expanded to the twenty-five degrees of the Rite of Perfction, which, at Charleston, S. C., in 1801, were still further expanded to the thirty-three degrees of the present Ancient and Accepted Scottish Rite.

Gould believes that the name Clermont was a compliment to the Duke de Clermont, who was Grand Master of French Masonry from 1743 to 1770. It is well to know that the followers of the Stuarts made the College of Clermont their asylum, and being Scotchmen gave the name Scottish Master to one of the degrees; it is also probable that the name Scottish Rite developed in this manner.

The Clermont group confined its privileges to the nobility in higher classes, which resulted in a revival association of a middle class element, which was later instituted under the title Knights of the East, a ten degree system. This act stirred the Clermont faction to greater effort, so that in 1760 they merged into a Council of Emperors of the East and West, with twenty-five degrees.

The controversies of these two groups created so much dissension it became necessary, in 1766, for the Grand Lodge of France to exclude all adherents of both bodies. (Cryptic Rite History.)

Chapter Degree: (See Ancient Toltec Rite.)

Chapter of Elect Masons: The 7° of the Zinnendorf Rite. In one instance it is referred to as "Chief of the Elect." (See Zinnendorf Rite.)

Charbonniers, The: They were known as the "Order of Charcoal Burners," and the origin was in France, later spreading to Italy where they were known as the Carbonari. It had no religious or political aim in France, but became the proponents of the independence of Italy and the reform of the Church. The Carbonari had a ritual, passwords, grips and signs. The Charbonniers were established in France about 1747 by the Chevalier Beauchaine, a prominent Freemason, originally the society was designed for wood-cutters, but spread taking in other classes. (See Carbonari.) (Also known as Fendeurs.)

Charitable Knight of the Holy City: The 5° of the Reformed Rite, which was divided into three sections. (See Reformed Rite.) The three sections of the degree were (a) Novice; (b) Professed Brother; (c) Knight of the Holy City.

Charles XIII, Order of: A Swedish Rite degree. (See Order of Charles XIII.)

Chevalier: A grade in the Order of Amaranth, and in the Order of DeMolay. (See Order of the Amaranth; see Order of DeMolay.)

Chevaliers et Chevalieres de la Colombe: (See Knights and Ladies of the Dove.)

Chevalier de la Palestine: One of the degrees of the Council of Emperors of the East and West. It was the grade of Knights of the Triple Croix, and the third and last grade of the Knight of the Eagle and Perfection; it was conferred only upon a grand officer, who must have been perfect in virtue and thirty-three years of age. It is a grade of nobility and authorizes its holder to wear the "cross of gold and diamonds with a red sash and rose of seven colors." On the sash of the Commander is written "Dieu le Veut," significant

19

of the Templars. The Historical Lecture is a review of the Crusades; such other matters as the Four Elements, the Seven Principal Virtues, and Philosophical matters are treated. (See Knight of Palestine.)

Chief Adept: One of the grades of the Rosicrucian (U.S.A.) society.

Chief Craftsman, or Pledge Degree: One of the degrees of the Order of the Golden Key. (See Order of Golden Key.)

Chief of the Tabernacle: The 23° of the Scottish Rite; in the Southern Jurisdiction the degree is of a philosophical nature; in the Northern Jurisdiction it is a drama whose lesson is, that punishment invariably follows those who attempt by greed and ambition to attain their material desires.

Chief of the Twelve Tribes: One of the degrees in the Rite of Perfection. It was the 11° of the Council of Emperors of the East and West, sometimes called "Illustrious Elect." (See Rite of Perfection.)

Chiefs of Masonry: A name which Scottish Rite Masons give to themselves when they arrive at the 33° of that Rite. The name was once given to those of the degree of Prince of Jerusalem, from which it doubtless derives its name.

Chinese Societies: The Chinese have many societies, such as the Hung League, the White Lotus Society, and the White Lily. They are in no sense Masonic, although frequently some of their emblems would lead one to believe they have traces of symbols which are prominent in Freemasonry. There is a Grand Lodge of China and many grand lodges are represented in that country by subordinate groups.

Chivalric Masonry: The Orders of Chivalry, such as Order of the Red Cross, Malta and Temple, are often referred to as Chivalric Masonry, but the term may equally be applied to any degree, or degrees, having to do with the days of Chivalry and the Crusade period.

Chosen Philanthropist: The 2° of the Consecrated Philoclesian Host. Temperance and Justice are its fundamental principles; "by patience and Godliness we hope to cultivate brotherhood and kindness among our band." The story of David and Jonathan is recounted during the conferring of the degree.

Christ, Order of: After the dissolution of the Templars, many fled to Spain and Portugal, where they united with a new Order which they assisted in creating, based on the same principle as the old one. It was established in 1319 and was called the Order of Christ. The title of Grand Master was vested in the reigning King of Portugal; it was dissolved by order of the Pope in 1854. Its ritual was much on the Order of the Templar Rites. (See Order of Christ.)

Christ, Rite of Knights of: A Rite founded in 1809 by E. de Nunez; it is referred to by Rebold (p. 231).

Christian Fraternity: It is said to have been instituted in 1617-27 by Andrea (See Friends of the Cross; see Order of the Apocalypse.)

Christian Mark: John Yarker states that this degree was at one time conferred in North America and the West Indies by "Encampments," and was often referred to as Knights of the Conclave." (See Black Mark.)

Christian Mark, Knight of: (See Knight of Christian Mark.)

Christian Philosopher: One of the degrees of the African Architects. (See African Architects.)

Church Masons: (See Cathedral Masons.)

Circle of Light, Rite of: The full title was "Sublime Masters of the Circle of Light." Rebold says it existed about 1780.

Clandestine Masonry: Freemasonry which exists without any legal or moral authority, referring particularly to where Masonic degrees are peddled about, with the idea of making money for the peddler. It is the opposite of "Regular Masonry," which is composed of groups that have a legitimate pedigree and are generally accepted throughout the Masonic world as legitimate Freemasons; it may also be opposed to "irregular" Masonry, which is Freemasonry in many ways legitimate, but which has not, for some reason or other, secured the recognition of the majority of Masonic "regular" bodies.

Clerks of Relaxed Observance: A schismatic group of the Rite of Strict Observance. Rebold refers to it as a "Clerical Templar System, founded by Jesuits, which united in 1776 with the Secular Templars." (See Rite of Strict Observance; see Jesuits.)

Clerks of Strict Observance: (See Rite of Strict Observance.)

Clermont, Chapter of: (See Chapter of Clermont.)

Clermont, Council of: This organization was founded by the Chevalier de Bonneville in 1735; it consisted of six degrees, three of Craft Masonry, and three of Templar Masonry. It was named after the Comte de Clermont, a member of the Royal Family of France, who later became Grand Master in France. The Order was Christian in character, having its ritual more like that of the Church than Freemasonry. Many Jesuits were members.

Cloister Degree: One of the degrees of the Ancient Toltec Rite.

Cohens, Elected: (See Rite of Elected Cohens.)

Cohens, Rite of: (See Rite of Elected Cohens.)

College of Builders: The Order was instituted by Numa Pompilius in 715; it was also known as the College of Artisans, at the head of which were the Colleges of Architects or Constructors. Initiates were divided into three classes: Apprentices, Companions or Fellow Workmen, and Masters. Presidents of the Colleges were elected for five years and were named Masters, or Teachers. Labors in their lodges were always preceded by religious ceremonies, and since the membership was composed of men of all countries and beliefs, the Supreme Being necessarily had to be represented in lodges under some general title—and this was the Grand Architect of the Universe, the Universe being considered the most perfect work of a Master Builder. In the beginning there were probably two degrees, later expanded to three: (a) Some religious ceremonies; (b) knowledge of the duties and obligations imparted to the ancients; (c) the explanation of the symbols, signs of recognition, and instruction in the use of the level, square, mallet and chisel. Many students believe that Freemasonry was an outgrowth of these old Colleges of Builders.

College Outside the Bar: (Also within the Bar.) A body of the Sovereign College, Allied Masonic Degrees.

Colleges: Some Rosicrucian Societies (U.S.A. for example) are organized into "Colleges." Membership is limited to Freemasons. (See Rosicrucian Society.)

Collegia, The: In ancient times when Rome was still a republic, men engaged in the crafts, trades, professions and arts began to form themselves into organizations called collegia (the plural of collegium, from which we have our own word "college").

By the time of Julius Caesar this system had spread so widely that there might be a dozen collegia in a community of a 100 population, and the division among them had been carried out to so fine a point that there were collegia of men cooks and of women cooks, of sailors who worked on ships with sails, and of sailors who worked on ships with oars, of men who made shoes for men, and of men who made shoes for women, and of those who made shoes for children—in at least one community there was a collegium of the girls who tended geese on the commons!

A collegium was strikingly like a modern Masonic Lodge. It had a patron, met in its own room, had officers similar to our Masonic officers, used initiations, had a charity fund, cared for its widows and orphans, etc.

Here and there in the larger centres would be a collegium called collegium fabrorum, by which was meant an organization, or guild, of builders and architects.

After Augustus the emperors began to become increasingly arbitrary, tyrannical, despotic. The empire which had begun as a federation of peoples and nations, more or less independent, more or less free to manage their own internal affairs, became in time a single autocratic system absolutely ruled by one man at the top.

Next to the armies the system of collegia was the great instrument by which this tyranny was effected. "He who rules the collegia rules Rome." This was obvious because he who controlled the collegia controlled each man engaged in work, and down to the last detail.

As a result of this despotic control, a vast system of state socialism was established, under which every last vestige of individual liberty was abolished. A baker in a small community was by law compelled to continue to be a baker all his life, and to remain in that same community; and his sons and grandsons after him. Nothing of free thought, free speech, or free association remained.

When Rome was destroyed, the whole collegiate system was destroyed with it. But there are a few general historians, and a certain number of Masonic historians who believe that a few collegia fabrorum survived in southern Italy, that when civilization began to be rebuilt early in the Middle Ages it was out of these collegia that came the guilds of builders and Masons, that out of those early guilds developed the system of builder guilds (or Masons) which spread across Italy into France and finally into Great Britain, and that our own Freemasonry arose within those guilds. If that theory is true we can trace, by however slender a thread, our own history straight back through ancient times to the early years of the Roman republic.—Iowa Masonic Library.

Color Masonry: Black Masonry, refers to the Knights Templar Orders; Blue Masonry usually refers to the three degrees of the lodge; Green Masonry, the Red Cross degrees; Purple Masonry, the Council or Cryptic degrees; Red, or Scarlet Masonry, includes the degrees of the Chapter; White Masonry refers to adoptive Masonry, or the symbolic lodge.

Comacine Brethren: Authentic history affords us little concerning this mysterious fraternity "belief in which seems to have been based on imagination and incorrect entomology."

Comacine Masters: Derived from the Latin, Magistri Comacini. (See Comacines.)

Comacines: Tradition says there was a brotherhood under this title at Lake Como, Italy, which had for its objective the building of churches, and that out of this grew the present-day Freemasonry. There is little evidence to prove this statement, although the word "comacinus" has in it the idea of a *Brother Mason.*

22

Co-Masonry, International Order of: Co-Masonry in the United States is largely centered in Larkspur, Colorado, where it carries on under the name of the American Federation of Human Rights.

From an official pamphlet issued in 1936 by the association, we learn:

In Co-Masonry, the degrees of the Ancient and Accepted Scottish Rite are worked, from the first to the thirty-third inclusive. The governing authority is invested in a Supreme Council. The Order was founded in 1893 and there are lodges in every part of the world. The word *Co-Masonry* was adopted to distinguish the Order from the exclusively masculine obediences, and to indicate that both men and women are admitted to membership.

Another pamphlet tells of the origin:

During the latter half of the 19th century, several French Masons who were interested in the feminist movement, urged the admission of women into Masonry . . . in 1883 this agitation resulted in the application for membership in the Lodge *Les Libres Penseurs,* at LePecq, near Paris, of Marie Deraismes, a writer and lecturer in behalf of women's rights. This Lodge working under the recently formed Grand Lodge of France (Symbolic), asked authorization to enter this woman and was refused. The Lodge then withdrew from the Grand Lodge . . . and proceeded to carry out the innovation . . . Marie Deraismes was made a Mason . . . in the presence of a large number of visitors (Ed. Note: naturally!)

In 1893, Dr. Georges Martin, a French Senator and ardent feminist who had been present at the initiation . . . persuaded the Master of the Lodge . . . to start a new organization to be open to men and women equally. *Human Rights Lodge,* Co-Masonry (La respectable Lodge Le Droit Humain, Maconnerie Mixte) was opened in Paris . . . it became the mother lodge of the Co-Masonic Order.

Other Lodges followed in France and Switzerland (1896) and in London (1902). Then came Cayenne, South America, Benares, India, and Charleroi, Pennsylvania. In 1905, Lodges were opened in Holland, Italy and the Argentine; finally, in 1914, a General Assembly was called for Paris but was postponed until 1920, when an International Constitution was adopted. The pamphlet further states that since that time, Federations have been established in England, Holland, France, India, Australia, South Africa, Portugal, Mexico, Finland, Belgium, Scandinavia, Argentina, Brazil, Costa Rica, Dutch Indies, and New Zealand. The Association was later divided into the Western and Eastern Federations (1934) and at that time there was claimed 700 lodges of the "Order."

Lodges in the United States are said to be located in Massachusetts, New York, Pennsylvania, Maryland, District of Columbia, Ohio, Indiana, Illinois, Michigan, Missouri, Nebraska, Kansas, Oklahoma, Minnesota, Montana, Texas, Arizona, Wyoming, Washington, California—and presumably—Colorado.

Inasmuch as it claims to confer "Masonic" degrees, it is purely clandestine and looked upon with disfavor by regular Freemasonry.

Commander, Knight: (See Knight Commander.) (See Knight Commander Court of Honour.)

Commander of the Temple: The 27° of the Scottish Rite in England. In the United States it is Knight Commander of the Temple; the English also use "Grand Commander of the Temple."

Commandery: The name applied to a body of Knights Templar once referred to as "Encampment" or even "Grand Encampment"; the latter title is now applied only to the national (U.S.A.) body of Templars.

Commodore: The 3° of the Felicitares, or Rite of Adoption.

Communeros: This was a Spanish society which resembled closely that of the Carbonari; it was organized about 1820, and believed that the social and philanthropic ideals of Freemasonry were insufficient. Women were admitted, and at one time it claimed a membership of 40,000. The penalty of their obligation was a gentle (?) one: "I swear to put to death whoever shall be pointed out as a traitor to this society, and if I am found wanting in carrying out this promise, may my head fall under the axe, my remains consumed by fire, and my ashes be thrown to the winds."

Compagnonage: This was originally a French trade-guild, and was known as the "Compagnons de Devoir." They provided free board and lodging for fellow traveling craftsmen, and held burial ceremonies for their deceased. The Council of Avignon, 1376, prohibited the order because of its attitude toward liberty of thought and religious toleration.

Compagnonage, French: A widespread society embracing many trades and a well developed ritual which contains a legend and secret methods of recognition. It was for journeymen only, and was started to combat the French guild system under which a Master could employ whom he pleased provided he did not instruct them in the mysteries. There was a small chance of a journeyman ever becoming a Master, a station reserved for the privileged classes, friends, and relatives. After the 1789 Revolution, this resulted in the formation of Journeymen or Compagnons, differing from the Steinmetzen who included Masters. Four Crafts originally formed the Compagnonage: stonecutters; locksmiths; joiners; carpenters. They were first called "Sons of Solomon" and had a legend about the building of the Temple; they also bore the name "Companions of Liberty and of Wolves." Maitre Jacques was said to have been one of the first Masters of Solomon, and was born in the south of Gaul; he was a son of Jacquin, celebrated architect and stonecutter. In Greece he was associated with Pythagoras (?), who may have taught him sculpture. He went on to Egypt where he constructed two columns with such skill that he was accepted as a Master. When the Temple was completed he started home and was attacked by one of his companions (Maitre Soubise) and his followers, who assassinated him, inflicting five wounds. Sons of M. Jacques called themselves "Werewolves" and those of M. Soubise, "Foxes." Howling was a part of their ceremonies; feuds often led to pitched battles. "Enfants of Solomon" were limited to Catholic members.

Companion: A grade in the Order of Amaranth. A degree of the Egyptian Rite; it has a chamber of reflection in the degree; there is a representation of Minerva, Goddess of Wisdom, and the whole degree teems with philosophic and natural philosophy. (See Ancient Reformed Egyptian Rite.) The title is applied to members of the Royal Arch Chapter.

The 2° Rite of Adoption: The lodge is arranged as in the First degree. The part reserved to the right is named the Garden of Eden, and filled with flowers and fruits. In the centre is an apple tree bearing fruit and around the trunk is an artificial serpent with an apple in its mouth; it represents the Tree of Knowledge of good and evil. Upon the altar before the W. Mistress, is a lighted wax taper and a gilded tray containing apple jelly. Near the door of

24

Europe is a burning lamp fed with spirits of wine, on which a little salt has been thrown. Near the door of entrance is a table covered with a black cloth, above which is a transparency picturing the death of Abel. On the floor is a picture representative of the five parts of the earth as in the 1°. Also there is represented: (1) An apple surrounded by a serpent; (2) Adam; (3) Eve; (4) A river watering the tree of knowledge; (5) The Sun; (6) The Moon; (7) The Star in the East. The clothing is the same as that of the 1° with the addition of a gauze veil for the Sisters. The dignitary officers have black gloves, the rest of the Brothers and Sisters have white gloves.

Conclaves: Many organizations, instead of "meetings" hold "conclaves." Among such are the Knights Templar and the True Kindred. The word is derived from the Latin "conclavo" which means a calling together.

Confidential Knight: The 6° of the Ancient Egyptian Reformed Rite.

Consecrated Philoclesian Host: A Rite of three degrees; not Masonic, but it shows evidence that it had been written by a Freemason. Its three degrees included: Patriots; Chosen Philanthropist; Devoted Brother. The entire ritual appears in *Collectanea* Vol. IV, part 1. The rite was patriotic and Trinitarian.

Conservators of Masonry: The name given by Rob Morris to the group which he organized "to preserve the purity of Masonic ritual" (?). Many grand lodges disagreed with Morris and for a period of ten years there raged quite a dispute. Members received a degree prepared by Morris. The movement died a natural death. Morris was at all times the Chief Conservator. (Read Masonic Conservators for the complete story.)

Consistory: The name applied to one division of the Scottish Rite.

Constantine, Red Cross of Rome and: Tradition says the Order was founded in 312 A.D. by the Emperor, Constantine the Great. Eusebius, the historian, tells us that in that year, Constantine, who was a pagan, was marching with his army on Rome, when the sign of a cross shone out among the stars, under which appeared the motto "In Hoc Signo Vinces" (In This Sign Thou Shalt Conquer). Constantine immediately embraced Christianity, adopted the Cross as his emblem, and founded the society "Red Cross of Constantine." The Order was revived in 1190 by the Emperor Comnenus, whose family retained the Grand Mastership until 1699, when the rights were transferred to the Duke of Parma. The Rite was brought to England in 1798 by the Abbe Giustianini, a member of the Venetian Embassy, at which time several new members were admitted. It was brought to the United States, via Canada, about 1870, under the authority of the Earl of Bective, who delegated his authority to William J. McLeod Moore. At this date (1955) two large groups and one smaller one exist in the U.S.A.

Constantinople, Knights of: In England and in the U.S.A. the degree is listed among those held by the Allied Masonic Degrees. (See Knight of Constantinople.)

Constellation of Junior Stars: This organization is sponsored by the Grand Chapter, Order of the Eastern Star of New York for teen-age girls, and is one of the most recent innovations in youth organizations. Sons of Master Masons, sons of Eastern Star members, and DeMolay members may be admitted to witness the ceremonies after taking an obligation of secrecy. The climax of the esoteric work, according to their statement, is "conferring what is known as the *Degree of Perfection* and transmitting the *secret word*." Their circulars

25

say "The Key opens the door, symbolizing that through Vision, Knowledge, Wisdom, Understanding, Faith, Hope and Love, Man may solve all the mysteries that surround him.

Constellations: One of the early forms of Adoptive Masonry. Rob Morris was active in the dissemination of this rite; it had as officers:

Men: Heleon; Philomath; Verger; Herald; Warder.
Women: Luna; Flora; Hebe; Thetis; Areme.

It was organized in 1855; families were organized in 1861, and by 1868 it turned into "Chapters" of the Order of the Eastern Star.

Constructor Masons: (See Order of Constructor Masons.)

Continental Masonry: The name applied to the type of Freemasonry on the Continent of Europe, especially French, German, Italian, etc. It is largely of the Ancient and Accepted type, although Royal Arch Masonry is making inroads.

Convent General: The name given to a governing body—such as the Convent General of the Knights of the York Cross of Honour. The original "Convent General" was a reform movement intended to restore the original Order of the Temple, so far as modern conditions would permit. There was a Convent General of the Order of the Temple.

Corks: (See Order of Corks.)

Cornerstone: Freemasonry has a ritual for use in laying the cornerstones of public buildings; it is not a secret ritual.

Cosmopolite: A degree of the Rite of African Architects.

Council: The use of the word "Council" is quite common among Masonic groups and their associated bodies. We find it in the Council of Royal and Select Masters, the Scottish Rite, Job's Daughters, the DeMolay, Council of Deliberation, Grand Imperial Council of the Red Cross, the Order of Builders, and the Shrine.

Council Degrees: The degrees conferred in a Council of Royal and Select Masters, or those conferred in Councils of Princes of Jerusalem of the Scottish Rite; other bodies also have "Councils," which is just another way of naming a group. (See Cryptic Masonry.) (See Ancient Toltec Rite.)

Council of Emperors of the East and West: Also referred to as "Sovereign Prince Masons." (See Emperors of the East and West.)

Council of Nine Excellent Masters: Some of the degrees now conferred in the Ancient and Accepted Rite were practiced about 1840 at the Crown Tavern in London; this association was termed a Council of Nine Excellent Masters, analogous to the Supreme Council; they probably conferred the degrees of Royal Ark Mariner, Noachite, and Rose Croix.

Council of the Trinity: (See Rite, Council of Trinity.)

Counselor: One of the grades in the Order of Amaranth. (See Order of Amaranth.)

Courts: The term applied to an Amaranth organization.

Cowan: A Masonic term, meaning one who is not regularly apprenticed. Knoop and Jones, in their history, say that originally the term meant a "dry-diker" or builder of dry stone walls; later, it was applied to one who did the work of a Mason without being properly apprenticed. The Mason Word was given to qualified Masons to be able to prove themselves as such.

Craft: The name applied to the Masonic Fraternity, particularly those of the

26

symbolic degrees. The Royal Arch Mason refers to himself as a member of "The Royal Craft," because the ritual of the chapter deals with King Solomon and his Royal associates. The term was applied to members of the Zinnendorf Rite.

Craft Clubs: Organizations, social or otherwise, whose members are Freemasons.

Craft Masonry: (See Ancient Craft Masonry.)

Crata Repoa: The name of a book published in Germany in 1770, translated by Ragon and republished by him in 1821, purporting to reveal the Egyptian Mysteries—that being the name of the volume—Initiations of the Egyptian Priests. There is a question as to its accuracy; it included the six degrees of Pastophorus, Neocoros, Melanophoros, Kistophoros, Balahate, Astronomos.

Cross and Crown: An adoptive degree which originated in the U.S.A. Its emblems were devices alluding to the Life, Death and Ascension of Jesus. Little is known of it today.

Cross, Knight and Lady of the: The 3° of the True Kindred.

Cross of Christ: (See Christ, Order of.)

Cross of Honor: (See Order of DeMolay.)

Cross, Order of Holy: (See Knight of the Holy Cross.)

Crowned Princess, or Sovereign Mistress. 12° Rite of Adoption: This honorary degree is the last of the various systems of the Masonry of Adoption and was worked at Saxe in 1770. The Sanctuary represents the Council.Hall of King Solomon. The hangings are red ornamented with garlands of flowers and crowns. There is a magnificent throne raised on seven steps covered by a canopy. To the right of the throne is the rich footstool of the Grand Master, to the left is a table upon which are three lights, a cup and some bread. Near the throne on one side is a large male and female statue. There is an ornamented altar for receiving the oath of the Aspirant. The hall is lighted by twenty-one lamps.

The scarf is of sky blue, terminated by a silver fringe, and tied upon the shoulder with a white rosette and bands of gold. The jewel of the degree is attached to it by a rose colored rosette. It is a circle of gold, which encloses a sceptre and the hand of justice and in the centre is an antique crown on which are the three attributes of Royalty.

The degree refers to the virtues of Solomon and the circumstances accompanying the reception of the Queen of Sheba when she journeyed to Jerusalem to inspect the Temple. The Grand Master represents King Solomon and is termed Very Wise King. The Grand Mistress represents the favorite wife of Solomon, daughter of the King of Egypt, and is termed Very Wise Queen. Each has two Councillors, (Brother and Sister First and Second Wardens) who are termed Favored Favorites. The other officers are termed Favorites.

The altar is at the steps of the throne, and has upon it the Bible, and an antique mural crown. Near this is a table on which is a vase of wine; a dish of cakes; a pot of honey; a salt cellar. There is also a cup or flask for each member; an incense pot; a jar of scent; and several embroidered napkins.

Cryptic Degrees: The Masonic degrees which deal with a crypt or vault. In the U.S.A., the degrees include the degree of Super Excellent Master, although it is not strictly speaking a "vault" degree. Actually, the degrees of the Council which should be termed "Cryptic" are those of Royal and Select

27

Master. In England, Ward says the Cryptic degrees are Most Excellent Master, Royal Master, Select Master, and Super-Excellent Master. They are under control of a Grand Council which is in close alliance with the Grand Lodge of Mark Master Masons of England, whose offices are also those of the Cryptic degree.

Cryptic Masonry: Cryptic Masonry is the name usually applied to the degrees conferred in a Council of Royal and Select Masters; yet, technically, one of those degrees cannot well be called a "cryptic" degree.

"Cryptic" refers to a "crypt" and well applies to the degrees of Royal and Select Master, the scene of each being laid in an underground crypt. The degree of Super Excellent Master, while forming a part of the Council system, has for its background an entirely different age, characters, and setting.

There are many other degrees in other rites which represent underground scenes, but we do not know of any reference being made to them as Cryptic degrees.

There are no more beautiful degrees in all Freemasonry, nor are there any more explanative of Ancient Craft Masonry, than those of the Cryptic Rite, a Rite, which in recent years has been "coming into its own."

The degree of Royal Master portrays an incident in which our ancient Masonic forbears explained to one of the principal architects of the Temple why the Word could not at that time be communicated; this section constitutes one of the finest bits of ritual in Freemasonry. The lecture of the degree is quite explanatory of the vessels used in the Temple.

The degree of Select Master portrays an incident in the lives of our three ancient grand masters, wherein clemency was shown to one who had trespassed into parts of the Temple which had been forbidden him. It is a highly dramatic degree when properly presented, and is said to "round out the circle of perfection in Ancient Craft Masonry."

Subordinate bodies are called "Councils." These form into state organizations known as "Grand Councils," and they in turn become members of the General Grand Council—at least most of the American states do so. There are more than one-third million members of councils in the United States.

Dame Ecossais: The 6° Rite of Adoption; these degrees are entirely honorary, and rank with the third series of Ancient and Primitive Rite. There are several of these Rites of Adoption consisting of ten degrees, which vary somewhat in the arrangement; this is 7° in one, 5° in another, etc.

The hangings are yellow. There are four lights, one at each corner. The tableau represents: (1) The Star of the East; (2) a Square figuring the March by four red cyphers; (3) Four Candlesticks; (4) Mount Ararat; (5) The Ark of Noah; (6) Noah and his family setting out from the Ark, conducted by a star, to the abode of felicity. The Apron is white, doubled and bordered with yellow, upon the lapel, in a square, is a silver star. The Sash is yellow. The Jewel is a Silver Star suspended from the neck.

Dames of Malta: A Protestant group, but not thought to be Masonic.

Dames of Mt. Tabor: An androgynous degree current about 1818 and under sponsorship of the Grand Orient of France; its idea was to give relief to destitute females of Masonic connection.

Dames of the Order of St. John: One of the androgynous degrees conferred about 1820; probably the same as the "Dames."

Dark Vault, The: The 4° of the Melesino (Russian) Rite.

Daughters of Bethany: The junior Order of True Kindred.

Daughters of Bethlehem: Mentioned in 1866 in the magazine "Ladies' Friend" (Mich.).

Daughters of the Eastern Star: A New York organization which is known as "an organization for girls of Masonic families." It accepts girls between the ages of fourteen and twenty, and is now sponsored by the Grand Chapter of the Eastern Star in New York. It was formed October 15, 1925, although the first "Triangle" did not function until May 7, 1927, in Rochester. It has three degrees: (1) Initiatory introduced; (2) Honorary Majority (conferred at the age of twenty-one); (3) Public Degree (known as Membership, parents, etc.). Local groups are called "Triangles" and are presided over by a "Beloved Queen." Each "Triangle" has an Advisory Council of seven members which meets annually. Recent reports showed 79 Triangles, with 3,460 members.

Daughters of Isis: A women's organization which serves as an auxiliary to the A.A.O.N.M. Shrine.

Daughters of Mokanna: The Mystic Order of Veiled Prophets of the Enchanted Realm has an auxiliary known under the above title; it was perfected as an organization June 5, 1919, at Rock Island, Ill. Membership is limited to wives, widows, mothers and daughters, as well as sisters of members of the Grotto. It has one degree—the Admission Degree. Subordinate bodies are known as "Cauldrons"; it has a "Supreme Cauldron" over which presides a "Supreme Mighty Chosen One." Cauldrons exist in twenty-three states and the Canal Zone.

Daughters of the Nile: An auxiliary for women whose husbands are members of the Shrine. It was established February 20, 1913 (or 1914), in Seattle, Wash. According to Voorhis, the original organization was known as "Ladies of the Nile Club," or "Shriners' Ladies." On October 30, 1913, there was formed a Supreme Temple, first called the "Club of 22" because of the 22 members who composed it. Groups are called "Temples." The ritual was written by Charles Whaley in August, 1913. It is presided over by a "Supreme Queen" and its membership is limited to relatives of Shriners. There is said to be 93 active Temples.

Daughters of Osiris: This is an auxiliary group of ladies, attached to the Order of Rameses, and was limited to relatives of members of Royal Arch Chapters. It was first introduced in Louisville, Ky., but a few years later ceased to function.

Daughters of Zelophadad: This organization was mentioned in the Michigan "Ladies' Friend" (1866), but we find no further mention. Nor have we discovered just who Zelophadad was, or whether he had any daughters. It was a women's organization.

David and Jonathan: One of the degrees under control of the Allied Masonic Degrees in England. Its ritual carries out the story of David and Jonathan. It is said that the Odd Fellows utilize the same story in their ritual. In England there is a "Brotherhood of David and Jonathan" which has a ritual similar to that of Secret Monitor.

Death: (See Knight of Death.)

Decoration of Aliddee: The second of the decorations awarded by the Ancient and Primitive Rite.

Decoration of the Grand Commanders: The third of the decorations awarded by the Ancient and Primitive Rite (third series).

29

Decoration of the Libyan Chain: (Also Libian) The fourth of the decorations awarded by the Ancient and Primitive Rite; it was probably conferred without ceremony.

Degrees: It is quite generally believed that as late as 1717 there were no systems of degrees; that, originally, there was but one degree which contained the elements of the three degrees now practiced of E.A., F.C., and M.M., the names being merely the designation of the class of workmen. The actual Masonic society may have been composed largely of those who had received the secrets—and were Fellow Craft, or Fellows.

DeMolay Medal of Honor: One of the awards given by the Order of DeMolay.

DeMolay, Order of: (See Order of DeMolay.)

De Secta Massonum: Literally, "the Sect Masonic." The title applied to Freemasons by various popes in the Bulls issued against the fraternity. It could hardly be deemed a title of respect!

Desert, Knights of: Probably the same as "Masons of the Desert," which Rebold says existed in 1781.

Desoms, Order of: Masonic law does not permit the initiation of those who are deaf, dumb or blind. In order to provide an organization for those who are deaf, and who are sons of Freemasons, the above Order was established in 1946 in Seattle, Wash., "to further the spirit of friendship, and lend a hand when needed" among those who were deaf and dumb and who were related to Freemasons. The Order derives its name from the words "Deaf Sons of Master MasonS (D-E-S-O-M-S). At the present time, chapters exist in Seattle and Hollywood. They issue a Desomic News which began publication in March 1952. The head of each group is a "Master Councilor" and its object is "to unite all able-bodied white deaf men over twenty-one years of age, who are of good moral character, and who are relatives of Master Masons . . . to perpetuate fraternal unity."

Devoted Brother: The third of the degrees in the Consecrated Philoclesian Host; it is a strictly Trinitarian degree, composed largely of lectures.

Dignitary of the Chapter: The 11° of the Swedish Rite. (See Swedish Rite.)

Diocesan: One of the degrees in Bahrdt's Rite.

Dionysian Mysteries: The Grecian type of the Ancient Mysteries, which some think to have been the forerunner of Masonic degrees. Most of these mysteries portrayed the slaying of a God—in this case. Dionysius or Osiris, for they were the same. In the mysteries the doctrine of immortality appeared to be uppermost. They had a Sacred Word, *Konx Ompax.*

Disciples of Memphis: (See Ancient and Primitive Rite.)

Disciplina Arcani: The secrets of the Mystery of Christianity were communicated only to *initiates;* the initiates were first made Christians, then advanced, and, finally, *raised* to a knowledge of all its Aporrheta.

There were three steps, or degrees, in Christianity, and its religious system was known as the Disciplina Arcani—discipline of the secret. There was an exoteric and an esoteric doctrine. The three classes in the primitive church were: "Catechumens; Competente; Illuminati. In the first degree, the candidate was baptized. The secret doctrines were taught in the several degrees which followed; they were "Trinity in Unity," the "Incarnation of the Logos, or Son of God," the "Crucifixion," the "Resurrection," and the "Secret of the Liturgy."

30

While baptism initiated the candidate, a participant in the Eucharist, or Lord's Supper, marked the raising to the highest degree. Initiates were forbidden to cut, paint, carve, or make any reference to the mysteries, hence little has come down to us as information.

Discreet Master: The 4° of the Rite of Memphis; it is the same as 4° of A.A.S.R.; 4° of Rite of Mizraim, and corresponds in a way to the Royal Arch degree. (See Rite of Memphis.)

Doctors of Universal Masonry: A degree conferred by the Sovereign College of Allied Masonic Degrees for U.S.A. There is no record of its conferral in recent years.

Dove, Knights and Ladies of: (See Knights and Ladies of the Dove.)

Druid: The 3° of the Ancient Order of Druids. (Also Sanctified Authorities.)

Druids, The: The society was founded in 1780 as a benefit society (England). It is to be distinguished from the Ancient Druids. Its lodges are called "Groves," recalling the early days in Britain when the Ancient Druids met in their glades in the forest to perform their rites. There are some who claim, without proof, that Freemasons inherited some of its forms from the Ancient Druids.

The Order was established in 1781 in London; it was a benefit society and conferred three degrees: Bards, Evates, Druids (or Sanctified Authorities). A ritual of the Order appears in Lux Vol. II, and in Nocalore, Vol. IV; it is unimpressive. Officers wear white robes and long beards. The password is that of a famous Roman general, who it is said, drove the Druids out of Britain.

Druses, The: A Syrian fraternity existing during the time of the Crusades; Lawrie thinks they were the forerunners of the Order of the Temple.

Dublin Preceptory: It is a matter of record that in 1779, the Lodge at Kilwinning, though practicing only Craft degrees, granted a Warrant for a Knight Templar Preceptory at Dublin. This has been denied.

Dublin Union Band: Once known in Ireland, from whence it came, as the "Sacred Band Royal Arch Knight Templars after the Order of Melchizedek," but in recent years it has become the "Knight Templar Priests," and as such has been introduced into America.

Ducks: An organization formed for those who are engaged in handling the scenery for the Scottish Rite degrees; it is confined to the States of Kansas, Oklahoma and Texas. It has no ritual or secret work; it was formed in Dallas, Texas; local units are called "flights." Its objective is—good fellowship. The emblem of the Order is a Mallard Duck (in flight). Members give their assent to matters presented them by giving three "quacks."

Eagle: There are many Masonic degrees which include in their title the word "Eagle." It may be added that the Eagle is the Christian symbol of St. John. Some of the degrees are:

Knights of the Eagle, Knight of American Eagle, Knight of Black Eagle, Knight of the Golden Eagle, Knight of the Prussian Eagle, Knight of the Red Eagle, Knight of the White and Black Eagle, Knight of the Two-Crowned Eagle, etc.

Early Grand Encampment of Ireland: This organization existed between 1770-1826; it granted 14 charters to "encampments" in Scotland (Knights Templar). It claimed control of the Red Cross of Constantine as did the Royal Conclave of 1819. It granted a Charter to the Early Grand Encampment of

31

Scotland (1822), and the latter changed its title in 1880 to the "Grand Encampment of the Temple and Malta in Scotland," later uniting with the Great Priory of Scotland. It was said to be the first governing body over a miscelleaneous group of degrees unrecognized by the grand lodges of the British Isles. Scottish lodges worked any degree they pleased until 1800 when the Grand Lodge forbid it.

Early Grand Encampment in Scotland: This group was chartered by the E. G. Enc. of Ireland (See above) in 1822. It changed its name to the "Grand Encampment of the Temple and Malta in Scotland" in 1880, and in 1909 United with the Great Priory of Scotland. Under the Grand Encampment any subordinate encampment worked the Red Cross of Constantine. But in 1880 it split up into (a) Early Grand Supreme Chapter, (b) Grand Encampment of Temple and Malta in Scotland, and (c) Scottish Council of Rites.

Early Grand Rite of Scotland: (See Rite, Early Grand Rite.)

Early Grand Scottish Rite: This Rite was divided into five series, of which rituals were published in several books, as follows:

1. Blue Masonry, 10 degrees.
2. Red Masonry, 12 degrees.
3. Black Masonry, 9 degrees.
4. Green Masonry, 9 (or 12) degrees.
5. White Masonry, 7 (or 9) degrees.

Thus it will be seen that approximately 62 degrees were available to the Scot Freemason. Blue Masonry was largely that of the symbolic degrees; Red Masonry was applied to the Chapter degrees (They had four Mark degrees, The Fellow Craft Mark, the Master's Mark, the Fugitive Mark, and the Christian Mark). Black Masonry was that of the chivalric degrees (Temple, etc.), while Green Masonry related to the Babylonian Pass or Red Cross Mason, or Knight of the Sword. White Masonry was the governing degrees, principal of which was the Priestly Order of the Temple, complement of the Irish Rose Croix.

Early Grand Supreme Chapter of Scotland: It united in 1895 with the Supreme Grand Chapter Royal Arch Masons of Scotland. (See E. G. Enc. of Scotland.)

East, Knight of the: (See Knight of the East.)

East and West, Knight of: (See Knight of East and West.)

Eastern Star: (See Order of the Eastern Star.)

Eclectic Masonry: (See "Eclectic Rite".)

Eclectic Rite: (See Rite Eclectic.) (See Knight of Eclecticism.) Some time between the years 1779-1883, German lodges engaged in a movement to restore Freemasonry to its original purity by separating the high degrees from symbolic Freemasonry. The title of "Eclectic" applied to the Rite conveyed the idea of "universal"; its headquarters were at Frankfurt/am/Main, and at Hamburg (says Rebold); it rejected all high degrees and resembled the primitive English Rite. In the preamble to its constitution, it stated that:

without deciding against, for or against any of the regular systems, but by taking from each what was good"

whence came the name "Eclecticism" thus avoiding all struggles between sects which had divided the fraternity.

Eclectic Union: The German lodges which united in 1783. (See Eclectic Rite.)

Ecossais Apprentice and Companion: The 4° of the Zinnendorf Rite. (See Zinnendorf Rite.)

Ecossais Degrees: A list of these might cover as many as eighty separate degrees. The word "Ecossais" means literally, "Scottish Master." The French refer to Ecossism as the Masonry of the Scottish Rite. We find listed as Ecossais degrees:

Perfect Architect; English; French; Grand; Grand Architect; Grand Master; Knight; Master; Novice; Clermont; Franville; Hiram; Messina; Montpellier; Naples; Perfection; Prussia; St. Andrew; St. George; of the Forty; Sacred Vault of James VI; Toulouse; Triple Triangle; Parisian; Perfect.

Very few of these degrees need further explanation. (See Rite Ecossais Rectifie.)

Egyptian Knight: The 7° of the Ancient Egyptian Reformed Rite. (See Ancient Egyptian Reformed Rite.)

Egyptian Masonry: Most of the degrees referred to as Egyptian have had their origin elsewhere than Egypt. Giving the name Egyptian to a degree would tend to make the reader believe in its antiquity.

Egyptian Mysteries: The Egyptian Mysteries dealt with Osiris, Isis and Horus, and it is thought the teachings were in the form of a drama, in which the death of Osiris by violence was represented. The candidate was required to perform various mysterious wanderings, such as were attributed to the Goddess Isis; these wanderings were accompanied with frightful scenes, and he was conducted through dark and mysterious labyrinths, over involved paths and chasms, in darkness and in terror; at length he arrived at a stream of water, where he was assaulted by three men disguised in grotesque clothing and forced to drink of water from the stream. This was symbolic of the water of forgetfulness through which he was to take his former crimes, and prepare his mind to receive new instruction in truth and virtue. During the initiation, the Judgment of the Court of the Dead was represented, and according to Apulius, "when all was concluded, I beheld the sun rising in full power at midnight." These ceremonies were veiled in allegory and illustrated by symbols, teaching doctrines fit only for the highest development of the mind.

Egyptian Reformed Rite: (See Rite, Egyptian Reformed; see Rite of Misraim; see Rite of Memphis.)

Egyptian Rite: (After Cagliostro) A ritual of the rite as used by Cagliostro appears in *Collectanea,* Vol. V, part 2, but gives only the three degrees of Apprentice, Companions, and Master.

Egyptian Sphinx: (See Fifth Order of Mechizedek.)

Elect: There are many Masonic degrees listed under the title "Elect" or "Elected." The French refer to the "Elu" degrees, which, of course, means "elected." The name also conveys the idea of "selected" as in Elu of Nine, Fifteen, etc. We find among Elu degrees, the following:

Brother; Elected Cohens; Commander; Grand; Grand Prince of the Three; Irish; Sublime Lady; Master; Elect of 15; Elect of 9; of London; Elect of Nine and Fifteen; of Perignan; of New Jerusalem; of the Twelve Tribes; of Truth; of Twelve; Perfect; Perfect and Sublime; Philosopher; Secret; Sovereign; Sublime; Supreme; Symbolical, and probably a dozen or more others. A degree in the Rite of Mizraim. (See Rite of Elected Cohens.)

Elect of Fifteen: A degree in the Right of Perfection; 10° in the A.A.S.R.; 2° in the Rite of Elect of Truth (Elus de la Verite); a degree of the Helvetic

33

Rite, similar to that of the 15° of the A.A.S.R. It is another of the so-called "vengeance" degrees.

Elect of First Order of Rose Croix: A degree in the Modern French Rite.

Elect of the Mystic City: The 29° of the Ancient and Primitive Rite.

Elect of Nine: The 9° of the English Accepted Rite; 6° of A.A.S.R.; a degree of the II Class of the Rite Elected of Truth; one of the Adonhiramite Rite degrees. It is one of the so-called "Vengeance" degrees. Its principal officer represents King Solomon. The degree teaches prudence in judgment.

Elect of Perignan: A degree of the Adonhiramite Rite.

Elect of Truth, Rite of: There seems to be a difference of opinion as to the division of the Classes of this Rite. One writer states there were two classes, superimposed upon the craft system: The First Class including: Knights Adept, and Perfect Master; the Second Class: Elected of Truth, Master Elect, Grand Architect, Elect of Nine, Architect, Knight of the East, Elect of Fifteen, Second Architect, and Prince Rose Croix. (See Rite, Elect of Truth.)

Elect of Twelve: (See Knight Elect of Twelve.)

Electa, or Martyrs Degree: Electa is the fifth point of the Star in the Eastern Star ritual; it is not in itself a degree, but a section of the degree.

Elected Brother: A degree in the Zinnendorf Rite.

Elected Cohens: (See Rite of Elected Cohens.)

Elected Knight of Kadosh: Sometimes called the "Knight of the White and Black Eagle." It is the 2° of a Consistory of Princes of the Royal Secret, Scottish Rite, and the 30° in the catalog of that system. The historical allusions in the degree are to the ancient order of the Templars and its downfall. There are five apartments. Officers include Frederick the Great as Grand Commander. The double-headed Black Eagle appears as a symbol, its gold beak and claws holding a golden sword.

Elected Priests, Rite of: The Martinist Order. (See Martinism.)

Electrical Craftsmen: An organization of Freemasons composed of men engaged in electrical engineering.

Eleusinians, Mysteries of: The Mysteries of Eleusis were first established at Eleusis in Greece, but headquarters were later removed to Rome, where it ceased to exist about 450 A.D. The Egyptian Mysteries were the envy of the Greeks, and the Mysteries at Eleusis developed as a result of this rivalry; they were established about 3150 B.C. and existed for more than 1800 years. Every five years, in September, they held their ceremonies in the greatest secrecy, lasting nine days; both sexes participated. It was a celebration in honor of Ceres, Goddess of Corn and Harvest, and her daughter, Proserpine.

Eleusis, Rite of: The practice of the Eleusinian Mysteries. These are mentioned in Virgil in his Sixth Book of the Aeneid. While the Egyptian Mysteries dealt with Osiris, Isis and Horus, the Greek Mysteries dealt with Pluto, Persephone, Demeter, Zeus, and Hecate. Part of the myth was the story of Venus and Adonis. The Rites at Eleusis were founded in 1356 B.C. by Eumolpus. The office of Hierophant was hereditary. He, during the initiation, was clad in a regal robe and sat on a throne brilliant with gold; over the throne was a rainbow in which were to be seen the moon and seven stars. From his neck hung a golden disc, symbol of absolute power and universal dominion. There was a peculiar form of interlaced triangles in the disc, much like those found afterward in Italian lodges.

34

These Mysteries were divided into parts—Esoteric and Exoteric, or the Greater and Lesser Mysteries. The general public were admitted to the Lesser one, which dealt with symbolical representations of the history of Demeter and Persephone; the Greater ones were confined to the elect. They are said to have taught the doctrine of one God. Nine days were devoted to the Greater Mysteries. One who had passed through the Mysteries received the title of *Epoptae*.

Elu Apprentice: A French degree, similar in character to that of "Enduring Apprentice." The candidate was presented with a white apron and gloves.

Elu Degrees: (See Elect.)

Elus Cohens: A degree of the Rite of Elected Priests. (See Elected Priests.)

Elysian Knight: The Irish Lodge of Research CC (1923, p. 274) says:

"Br. Georges Mervyn Irvine (who had been "Templed" and "Malted" in 1820) received the Degree of Elesian (sic) Knight from Br. Dolan of Lodge No. 700 Cushendall." (April 25, 1823.)

Dolan was from Antrim, Ireland.

Emperors of the East and West: Under this pompous name was established, about 1758, in Paris, an authoritative body, the members of which at first assumed the titles of "Sovereign Prince Masters, Substitutes General of the Royal Art, Grand Superintendents and Officers of the Grand and Sovereign Lodge of St. John of Jerusalem." Ragon, in his "Orthodoxie Maconnique," asserts that this is the parent of the Ancient and Accepted Rite, which was established by Frederick II at Berlin in the same year. This rite had twenty-five degrees, the first nineteen being the same as the Ancient and Accepted Rite, the others: Grand Patriarch Noachite; Key of Masonry; Prince of Lebanon; Knight of the Sun; Kadosh; Prince of the Royal Secret. In the year in which it was formed, the degrees and part of the ritual were adopted by the Grand Lodge of the Three Globes in Berlin, but the actual working of the degrees of their Inner Orient differs very materially from the Ancient and Accepted System.

Emulation Ritual: One of the popular forms of ritual used in England for the Craft degrees; there is no proscribed or uniform ritual for English lodges. Other forms are known as Stability, Logic, Oxford, etc.

Encampment: The title once given to a commandery of Knights Templar. The term was once used by Templars and Royal Arch Masons alike, convocations of chapters being often referred to as "encampments." (See Grand Encampment.)

Enduring Apprentice: The French used the word "souffrant," which means "ill" or "suffering." It constituted, as a degree, some very rough tests for an aspirant for Masonic degrees and contains a portion of ritual reminiscent of a portion of Templar ceremony. In the end the candidate is received as Knight, Apprentice, Mason, and Brother.

Enfants of Solomon: Literally, "Children of Solomon." (See Compagnons, French.) A Society of the Compagnonage which was limited to Roman Catholics.

Enemies of Freemasonry: Several societies have been organized in times past which had for their objective the overthrow of Freemasonry. Today, the enemies seem to have given up their organization of "anti" societies, their work being carried on through "religious" channels, such as Roman Catholics and Lutherans of the Missouri Synod.

English Rite, The: The United Grand Lodge of England, in 1813 proclaimed the Rite to consist of the three Craft degrees of Entered Apprentice, Fellow Craft, Master Mason, and the Holy Royal Arch. There should also be included the degree of Installed Master, limited to Masters of Lodges, and the three Installation Degrees of the Royal Arch Chapter. The Rite is sometimes referred to as Rite of York.

Enlightened Phreemason: Known as Green Brother; the 4° of the Primitive and Original Rite.

Enoch, Rite of: A French Rite of 1773, but died out. It had four degrees: Apprentice, Fellow Craft, Master, and Architect.

Enoch, Royal Arch of: The 13° of the A.A.S.R. It differs materially from a similar degree, Royal Arch, of the English Rite.

Entered Apprentice: Practically every Masonic system has an Apprentice degree as the beginning of the series. It is a degree in the Rite of Strict Observance, Elected Cohens, Adonhiramite, Elect of Truth, Fessler, Modern French, Zinnendorf, Perfection, all regular Freemasonry throughout the world, and in the Scottish Rite at one time, when they claimed control of symbolic Masonry.

Epopt: The first of the Little Mysteries of the Illuminati and known as "Illuminated Priest." The degree was conferred only upon Scotch Knights; knowledge of its existence was withheld from those of a lower degree, and was conferred with pomp and ceremony unknown to other degrees. For example, there was a hall "with a thousand lights, rightly adorned with draperies, and a shining throne . . . on one side they offer a candidate a Sceptre, a Crown, and a Royal Mantle, and all sorts of riches; on the other, they present to him a single simple linen tunic with a girdle of scarlet silk; he must choose which he prefers. (To our readers: which one would you take?) If he determines upon the throne, he is turned out of the membership; if he prefers the simple garment of priesthood, he is received."

Esoteric Masonry: That portion of Masonic ceremonies which usually appears in our monitors and which does not include the means of recognition.

Esquire: Once a degree in the Order of the Temple; also a degree of the African Architects.

Essenes, The: The Essenes were a peculiar sect which existed in Judea; their code of living required poor and simple lives; most of them were celibates, although the lower grade were permitted to marry. They held community property, took no oaths, and were scrupulously strict in their observance of the Sabbath; they held firm to the faith of One God, ruler of heaven and earth, and believed in the immortality of the soul. Josephus says they taught

"to the soul of the good, there is reserved a life beyond the ocean, and a country oppressed neither by rain, nor sun, nor heat, but refreshed by a gentle west wind blowing over the seas. But to the wicked a region of wintry darkness and of unceasing torment."

The society existed from 200 B.C. until 100 A.D. in Palestine; Josephus was an initiate, but did not complete his education in the rite. One had to undergo a probationary period of one year, during which he was given a spade and a linen apron (used as a towel), and a white apron (for use at mealtime).

36

At the expiration of a year, he became a Novice and underwent a baptismal ceremony; if after two years he was accepted, he was elected a member, first as Josphus says, "after undergoing tremendous oaths." These required piety to God, Justice to fellow-men, Faithfulness as a citizen, respect for authority, and secrecy to the order. They rejected all the pleasures of the flesh, living a monastic life, avoiding riches and poverty. Some believe that Jesus was a member of this group which never exceeded 4,000 members.

Esteemed Sister: A degree in the Order of the Sacred Temple.

Esther, or Wife's Degree: Not strictly speaking a degree, but a portion of the initiatory ceremony of the Eastern Star; Esther is the third point of the Star.

Eureka Hiatus: A little heard of side-degree; it has to do with the discovery of the 47th Problem of Euclid and the Successor to Hiram the Architect.

Evates: The 2° of the Druid Order.

Excellent and Super Excellent Mason, Arch Mason: These subsidiary degrees are incorporated in the present working of the Veils of the Irish Royal Arch. The legend referred to by Pennell (1730) says "Till Moses, Master Mason rose, and led the Holy Lodge from thence" contains the essential features of the ceremony. One seldom finds a reference to "Arch Mason" except in Fowler's Table; it was a brief ceremony describing the building of an arch. The trowel was said to have been the working tool, but the trowel is not used in Irish Masonry today. The Keystone was the emblem of the degree; its history may be traced to D'Assigny who said: "Like the working of an arch of stone, etc." The jewel had the initials HTWSSTKS in a circle which enclosed Three Axes.

Excellent Degree: In the United States and probably elsewhere, the degree of Past Master was once so listed; it had nothing to do with the degree of Most Excellent Master.

Excellent Mason: A Helvetic degree which contains much of the material found in the American system of "passing the Veils." Carlile refers to it in an exposure of 1826; it was followed by the degree of Super Excellent Mason.

The 20° of the Early Grand Rite; it is held in a Royal Arch Chapter, and "is one of the Royal Arch degrees proper under a Royal Arch Chapter." The scene represents a Grand Lodge at Babylon, discussing the return of the captives to Jerusalem; the candidate is prepared as for a journey and acknowledges that he has "been marked as a Master, sat in the chair of King Solomon, and desires to assist his brethren to rebuild the House and City of God." Then follows a passing of the veils. The degree is conferred in Scotland today as a preparation for the Royal Arch; in the U.S.A. the degree is regarded as a part of the Royal Arch.

Excellent Master: The Grade of Excellent Master, or Excellent Master as it was known in its earlier working, is of such age as to confuse us in estimating just how old it is. It is almost safe to state that it is as old as Royal Arch Masonry, because it has always formed a part thereof. Even in America it is mentioned as early as 1769, when in St. Andrew's Chapter, Boston, a Brother was "made by receiving the four steps, that of an Excellt., Sup-Excllt., Royll. Arch and Kt. Templer."

Until quite recently, the Excellent was never worked alone; it was always with the Super Excellent and Royal Arch. Later, when this most beautiful method of work was abandoned almost everywhere, the title was changed to "Excellent Master," the ritual reworked and in Scotland was placed as the immediate predicant to the Royal Arch. It is not worked elsewhere today, save in the Allied Councils of America. Ireland has preserved some of both the Excellent and Super Excellent in her veil-working in the Royal Arch, but the formal ceremonies are a thing of the past.

The origin of the American Royal Arch did not cause a wide swept discontinuance of the older form of working. The Grand R. A. Chapter of Virginia used the old form, and even chartered Chapters as "Excellent Super Excellent" well into the 19th century. The very abundance of early records and Minutes makes unnecessary its transcription as we are all familiar with the antiquity of the Excellent Master and its significance to Royal Arch Masonry.

The Ritual used in America is the Scotch work, unchanged. It is a beautiful ceremony and almost necessary to the Royal Arch. Having passed the three Veils in Babylon, there is necessity at Jerusalem only to enter the fourth, or White, Veil. It is a simple and beautiful method of working.

Exceptional Service Cross: One of the awards given by the Order of DeMolay. (See Order of DeMolay.)

Exoteric Masonry: That portion of Masonic ceremonies which usually appears in our monitors and which does not include the means of recognition.

Expert Master: The scene of this degree is laid in one of the outer courts of the Temple. The legend is built around a deceased Grand Master whose body had been brought to Jerusalem by order of King Solomon to be burned; he had selected seven Chosen men to take the place of his late architect and to whom he confided with the greatest secrecy the Ancient Sacred Word.

The seven thus chosen were: Adoniram, Stohim, Joaben, Hamatec, Moaban, Bengade, and Zabud. To this group he added one for each of the Twelve Tribes of Israel. When arrangements had been completed for the funeral ceremonies, Solomon appeared at their head, dressed in violet-purple, directing the Prefects to wear over their black clothing a long scarf of violet color, and at the end of the scarf a triangular medal, divided into seven smaller triangles to indicate that "seven of them had replaced one." Each bore a torch; Solomon, with his torch, set fire to the funeral pyre. When the ashes had been collected it was discovered that the heart of the Architect had not been burned, but was whole and entire. The heart was taken, wrapped in a rich cloth, placed in an urn with the ashes, and borne by Solomon in a procession to the monument which had been prepared to receive it.

Faithful Companion: A degree in the Order of Sacred Temple; 3° of the II Temple.

Faithful Scottish Freemason: This so-called Rite appears mythical. (See Veille Bru.) Also known as "Faithful Scots."

Fatherland: A degree of the Fessler Rite.

Favorite Brother of St. Andrew: The 9° of the Swedish Rite.

Favorite of St. John (or Favorite Brother of): The 8° of the Swedish Rite; 6° of Zinnendorf Rite.

Favorite of Solomon: Sometimes known as Favorite Brother of Solomon. The 7° of the Swedish Rite; one of the degrees of the Chapter of that Rite.

Felicitares: (See Order of Felicitares.)

38

Felicity, Order of: An androgynous order established in France in 1743. (See Felicitares.)

Fellow Craft: Throughout the world the degree of Fellow Craft is almost universally the second degree of the Masonic system. It was a degree in the Rite of Illuminated Theosophist; 2° of the Persian Rite; the Adonhiramite Rite; Clerks of Relaxed Observance; Fessler Rite; Illuminati; Modern French Rite; Zinnendorf Rite; Rite of Perfection; Philalethes; Reformed Rite; Rite of Strict Observance; Order of the Temple Swedish Rite; Rite of Elect of Truth; Rite of Elected Cohens; A.A.S. Rite, when they claimed control of symbolic degrees.

Fellow Craft Adept: A degree of the Persian Rite, sometimes called Esquire of Benevolence.

Fellow Craft Cohen: A degree in the Rite of Elected Cohens.

Fellow Craft Mark: The 5° of the Early Grand Scottish Rite; it was conferred on Fellow Crafts. The degree was much the same as that now worked as "Mark Master Mason" in English and Scotch lodges; but in the modern version are several anachronisms, alterations and omissions. There is a substitution of the word "keystone" for "capstone." The stone used has characters and emblems on all four faces. Around the figure of the 47th Problem are letters which read "May Jehovah Finish This Building With Great Joy."

Fellow Craft Perfect Architect: The 26° of the Rite of Misraim.

Female Masonry: The title is erroneously used to refer to degrees conferred on women; there is no such thing as "Female" Masonry. The use of the word is intended to apply to those organizations, membership to which is limited to relatives of Freemasons. Adoptive Masonry, while not exact, is a better term. There are however, groups, even in the U.S.A. which pretend to confer Masonic degrees; all such are illegitimate and clandestine.

Fendeurs, The: (See L'Ordre des Fendeurs, and Charbonniers.)

Fessler Rite: (See Rite of Fessler.) Ignatius Fessler was born at Czarendorf, Hungary, May 81, 1756; from his earliest years he revealed a rather religious character. He entered a monastery and came out again after a sad experience. He was received as a Freemason at Leipzig in 1783, and having removed to Berlin in 1796, he founded the "Society of Friends of Humanity," and although very enthusiastic as a Freemason, he became affiliated with the lodge, Royal York, but left it in 1802. He reformed Masonic usages by taking for his models the English rituals.

The Rite named for Fessler was that used in the Grand Lodge Royal York of Berlin; it had six higher degrees, taken from the rituals of the Rosy Cross of Gold, the Strict Observance, the Illuminated Chapter of Sweden, and the Ancient Chapter of Clermont. Fessler added to the three symbolical degrees an intimate or "interior orient," in which one might attain complete Masonry through six degrees. The Rite originated in Prussia during the 18th century and the degrees were extensively worked. An irregular German lodge in New York worked a modification of the Rite in New York as late as 1857.

The nine degrees of the Rite were: the three symbolic degrees; 4. Holy of Holies; 5. Justification; 6. Celebration; 7. Knight of the Passage; 8. Fatherland, and 9. Perfection.

Fidelity, Order of: This Order was established about 1742; Rebold refers to it; it is also mentioned in the Fendeurs.

39

Fifth Order of Melchizedek and Egyptian Sphinx: A secret society for both men and women; its last known appearance was at Boston in 1894. It was also known as "The Solar Spiritual Order of the Silver Head and Golden Star," a name which in itself denoted short life. It set forth claim as established several thousand years B.C., which might signify ante-Melchizedek or after-Melchizedek. The Order of Brothers of Asia, now extinct, had a Rite of Nine degrees, one of which bore the name Order of Melchizedek.

Flaming Heart: A Ritual of the last century, written by Albert Pike.

Flaming Star, Order of: The ritual for this society was written by Baron Tschoudy in 1756; he was a student of occultism and alchemy, and his ritual bore witness to that fact. It referred to the Templars at the time of the Crusades.

Foresters, Order of: Not a Masonic Order, but one which has traces of Templary in its ritual. It was registered in England under the Friendly Societies Act; it had signs, passwords, initiatory ceremonies, and at one time numbered more than a million members, admitting both sexes and juvenile members. Its meetings were known as "courts," which were presided over by a Chief Ranger. The first known organization was at Old Crown Inn, Leeds, in 1790. There was also a "High Court" in which the government of the Order was vested.

A part of the ritual is said to have been based on the promise of a Grand Master of the Templars that they would be ever ready to depart for the recapture of the property seized by Pope Clement and Philip the Fair; they wore long white robes; officers wore crowns. A section of the ritual deals with the Four Elements. The Master is called "Noble Arch."

Founders Cross: One of the awards given by DeMolay (See Order of De Molay).

Franc Macon: The name of "Freemason" in the French language.

Frankmason: The word appears in a statute of 1494 which fixes the wages of Frankmasons and Roughmasons.

Fratres Lucis: Literally, "Brothers of Light"; a ritual published a few years ago in the "Theosophical Review" (1899). It has no connection with the "August Order of Light." The ritual is said to have been used in 1780 by Freemasons gathered together from all those Rites with a Hermetic basis; it was published by the Grand College of Rites (Vol. I). The Rite is divided into five degrees: 1, Knight Novice of the Third Year; 2, Knight Novice of the Fifth Year; 3, Knight Novice of the Seventh Year; 4, Knight Levite; 5, Knight Priest.

Freestonemasons: A Mason who worked in free stone. A name given to any fine grain sandstone, or little stone that can be easily worked in any direction and sawn with a toothed saw. There is a possibility that "Freestonemason" may have been abbreviated to "Freemason." Freestone is par excellence for carving.

Freimaurer: In Germany the Masons were known as the Freimauer-from "Frei" meaning "free" and "mauer" meaning "stone."

French Dame: One of the degrees of the French Rite of Adoption. It was the Grand Elect 7°.

French Rite: (See Rite, French.) The French Rite, which is practiced in Brazil, was founded in 1786 under guidance of the Grand Orient of France.

40

It comprises seven degrees, three being the symbolic degrees, the others being: 4, Elect; 5, Scotch Master; 6, Knight of the East, and 7, Rose Croix.

French Rite, Modern: (See Rite, French.) This Rite was created in Paris in 1761 and constituted December 24, 1772, proclaimed March 9, 1773, and modified in 1786 as it now exists.

It comprises the three symbolic degrees and four Capitular degrees: Elected, Scottish, Knight of the Orient, and Rosicrucian. The introduction of these four degrees at the time of modification in 1786, and welcomed by the Grand Orient of France, brought regretful consequences; the Rite was proscribed in England, Holland, Denmark and Germany, and entrance into all lodges was declined to French Masons who practiced that system; circumstances caused a modification of the Rite and it gained in importance. It is now practiced by French lodges and is to be found in Belgium and South America. A Grand College of Rites, within the bosom of the Supreme Council, with seat in Paris, has the task of supervising the Chapters and Philosophic Councils. In 1918 there were 472 symbolic lodges, 75 of which had a chapter; there were 31 Councils.

Freres Pontives: A community of operative and speculative Masons, who, as a religious house of brotherhood, established themselves at Avignon, at the close of the twelfth century; they devoted themselves, as the name denotes, to the construction and repair of stone bridges. It is on record, that the community existed as late as 1590; John de Medicis, who was Master in 1560, may perhaps have been a son of Cosmo, Duke of Florence, who died 1562, and was made a cardinal shortly before.

Friend of St. John: The 6° of the Swedish Rite.

Friend of Truth: The 5° of the African Architect Rite.

Friendly Societies: In England there are a number of organizations known as "Friendly Societies," among which are the Foresters, the Oddfellows, Buffaloes, Druids, and others. Most of them have social features, an initiation, and in many instances, have developed into benefit associations. An Unlawful Societies Act of 1799 hindered the activity of these societies for a time; this was followed by a Seditious Meetings Act of 1817, which set forth that meetings of fifty or more members were unlawful.

Friends of the Cross: An article appearing in A.Q.C., Vol. V, refers to this Order as a religio-civil order which united with an "originally operative Dutch lodge" in which Count Sporck was initiated. On page 187, Vol. IV, is a photograph of the medal of the lodge; on one side is Sporck; on the other side is the New Jerusalem, a symbolism which might seem to connect this grade with the 19° of the Chapter of Clermont. The name is derived from that of a much older order. (See Militia Crucifera Evangelica.)

Fugitive Mark: This was the 12° of the Early Grand Rite of Scotland; it had no particular ceremony, except an obligation, and an explanation; the latter involved the use of a piece of paper which could be folded so as to carry a message to another member when they were not in a position to communicate otherwise. The ritual referred to "Noah presiding in a Mark Ark Lodge." We are told that "this degree was much used in ancient times when brethren suffered persecution at the hands of priestly or secular authority."

Funeral Master: The 4° of the Early Grand Rite of Scotland.

Garter, Order of the: (See Order of the Garter.)

41

Gebalites: Men of Gebal; they were the "stone-squaring Phoenicians," far advanced in the arts and sciences.

General Grand Chapter: The name applied to the organization composed of American, Canadian, Mexican and Philippine Grand Chapters, controlling Royal Arch Mason policies and traditions. In 1955 it included 46 American Grand Chapters, three Canadian, one Mexican, one Alaskan and one Philippine Grand Chapter, as well as subordinates in Cuba, Puerto Rico, Isle of Pines, Canal Zone, Chile, Nicaragua, Guatemala, China, Germany, Costa Rica, and Hawaii.

There are other organizations which bear the same name but are not Masonic.

General Grand Masonic Congress, A. F. & A. M.: One of the multitudinous clandestine groups composed of negroes.

Gentlemen Masons: Freemasons made by Scottish lodges of English travelers in Scotland, later known as "accepted" Masons. Or it may refer to Freemasons created at a distance from their lodge, with or without authorization.

German Guilds: There were at one time many guilds existing in Germany, formed along the lines of English guilds, which later developed into Freemasonry.

German High Degrees: Several of the old German, and some of the present, grand lodges, work the "higher" degrees; for example:

Grand National Lodge: 10 degrees.
Grand Lodge of Three Globes: 7 degrees.
Grand Lodge Royal York: 3 degrees, with a virtual 4° known as "Schottischer Meister" (Scotch Master).

The Grand National Lodge refers to these degrees as "higher degrees"; the Three Globes term them "steps to knowledge"; Royal York practices a pseudo Royal Arch; The Grand National Lodge transacts all business of the five degrees; the Chapter transacts business from 6° to 10°, and has supervision over all ritual and dogma matters. There are four types of Chapters—those who work the 6-7°; 6°, 7° 8°; and 6°, 7°, 8°, 9°; and there is a Grand Chapter Indissolulibilis at Berlin; at the head is the "Ordenmeister." In Royal York, the members of the "Inner Orient" are selected from members of the 4° and control ritual and dogma.

German Grand Lodge, Royal York of Friendship: This Grand Lodge confers the three Craft degrees, and the 4° "Schottischer Meister," which is a pseudo Royal Arch degree. From this 4° is formed a committee which controls the Rite, its dogma and rituals. Only Christians are eligible and by agreement with three other Prussian Grand Lodges, its members may visit the other groups. These high degrees in Germany constituted a serious obstacle in attaining unification.

Gild (or Guild) Masons: (See Cathedral Masons.)

Glaire's Helvetic Rite: The name applied to the Grand Orient of French Helvetia; it was formed at Lausanne in 1810 and lasted only twelve years.

Golden Branch of Eleusis: Fifth and last of the "decorations" awarded by the Ancient and Primitive Rite.

Golden Chain: (See Order of Golden Chain.)

Golden Cord, The: A New York organization of which little is known although it is supposed to have some Masonic and religious connection.

Golden Dawn, Order of: A Rosicrucian body which is quite different from its parent. In 1910 an injunction was refused some who wished to prevent the publication of its ritual. The ritual has been printed in the U.S.A. and is available to students.

Golden Fleece: Masonic ritual refers to the "Golden Fleece." Greek writers tell of Medea, who accompanied Jason on his journeyings in search of the Golden Fleece, and having killed her brother, cut his body in pieces and strewed the limbs about the sea. Her father, who was in pursuit of Jason, had to wait in order to collect the scattered Aetes and give them burial, during which the fugitives managed to escape. In Europe we find the Order which has become a religious decoration.

From the story of Jason and the Golden Fleece comes the name of this celebrated order of knighthood, founded by Philip III in Austria and Spain in 1429. It was formed to commemorate his marriage to Isabella of Portugal. Its chief aim was the protection of the Roman Catholic Church, and the fleece was assumed as its emblem because it was the chief product of the Low Countries. Of course, Philip became the first Grand Master; at first there were 24 knights, later increased. Spain and Austria competed for rights in the Order and a schism occurred, each country having its Golden Fleece. In Austria, the Emperor could create any number of knights, even Protestants if the Pope gave permission; in Spain, only the nobility were eligible. The search for the Golden Fleece may well be compared with Freemasonry's search for the Lost Word.

Golden Key, Order of: (See Order of Golden Key.)

Golden Links: Voorhis says that "contact with offices brought response that no information would be given out." It is thought to be a Hebrew organization.

Golden Star: The Fifth Order of Melchizedek.

Good Samaritan: The 3° of the Supreme Conclave True Kindred; also called "Knight and Lady of the Cross." It was also an Adoptive degree formerly in much vogue in the U.S.A. Its origin is unknown; it had no emblem or means of recognition except its medal, which had displayed on one side the letters "G.S." (Good Samaritan), and on the other side were eight lines of letters engraved upon the arcs of circles:

L.t.t.   O.n.a.o.s.   T.i.m.i.t.w.   S.i.i.t.c.   (Lots)
W.i.i.c.n.   I.t.m.s.i.w.g.i.u.   F.w.n.o.w.i.t.s.d.   E.l.a.f.l.   (Wife)

The ritual story was that of the Good Samaritan "who stopped at the wayside to relieve the distressed; who walked that a stranger might ride his beast; who, with his own money, paid others for providing for the wants of the distressed."

"Collectanea," organ of the Grand College of Rites, refers to three degrees conferred under the above title. One was used in the State of Georgia about 1897, the second was an Arkansas version, while the third was one found in Alfred Creagh's notebook.

There is a decided similarity in each of the rituals; all deal with the Biblical story of the Good Samaritan; all appear to have been conferred only upon Royal Arch Masons and their immediate relatives

upon no person beneath the dignity of a Royal Arch Mason, his wife, his widow, his mother, or unmarried daughter or sister.

43

The penalty for failure to fulfill the vow had reference to Lot's wife who turned to a pillar of salt. And one of the principal signs was to place the hands on the hips, akimbo, turning the back, and looking over the left shoulder —just as "Lottie" did before she turned to salt. The sign was to draw a handkerchief through the left hand raised about the height of the shoulder.

The Signet contained letters, reading L-O-T-S-W-I-F-E (Lot's Wife). But these initials were cabalistic for the words

Light of the Seraphic World Inspires Fraternal Excellence.

What a wonderful thought!

Gormogons: A rival society to the Freemasons in England; it ridiculed Freemasonry by having imitative (mock) processions. It is said to have consisted of many who had been rejected by Masonic lodges; it was definitely anti-Masonic.

Grain of Mustard, Order of: A German organization founded upon Mark IV, 30-32. There is some doubt as to whether it was Masonic. (See Order of Mustard Seed.)

Grand Adept of the Black Eagle of St. John: This was at one time a degree in the Order of the Temple, sometimes referred to as "Elected Knight of Nine."

Grand Architect: A degree of the Helvetic Rite in which the candidate is listed among the Grand Master Architects, and prepared for advancement. It is in the list controlled by the Allied Masonic Degrees. It is the 12° of the A.A.S.R.; the 6° of the St. Martin Reformed Rite; 14° of the Rite of Elected Cohens; 23° of the Rite of Misraim; it appears in the Rite of Elected Truth; in the Martinism Rite; in the Adonhiramite Rite; and the Early Grand Rite of Scotland; here it is also called the Scotch Fellow Craft.

It was worked in the Councils of Emperors of the East and West as a third section; candidates were examined as Ecossais; the principal emblem was a brilliant triangle enclosing a well-known Hebrew letter. The candidate was crowned with laurel at the conclusion of the degree.

Grand Chapter: The name given to a parent organization, most prominent of which are the Grand Chapters of Royal Arch Masons; the O.E.S. has a Grand Chapter.

Grand Chapter of Harodim (or Herodem): An institution revived (it is supposed by Brother Preston) in 1787. He says:

"Though this order is of ancient date, and had been patronized in different parts of Europe, there appears not on record, previously to this period, the regular establishment of such an association in England. For some years it was faintly encouraged, but after its merit had been further investigated, it received the patronage of several exalted Masonic characters. The Grand Chapter is governed by a Grand Patron, two Vice-Patrons, a Chief Ruler or Harod, and two Assistants, with a Council of Twelve Companions. It was a school of instruction, organized upon a peculiar plan, and the lectures were divided into sections, and the sections into clauses. Its teaching embodied the whole art of Masonry."

It was in reality a Lodge of Instruction, and nothing more.

This appears to have been a combination of the Ancient York Masons with other degrees imported from France, as arranged by Ramsay and others, but there is evidence that it was started as a Craft lodge of instruction. Harodim

44

is a Hebrew word, signifying "princes" or "rulers." There is a reference in II Chronicles 11, 18, where the three hundred Chief Overseers appointed by Solomon, set the people to work. We hear nothing of the Harodim Chapter after Preston's day.

Grand Chapter Prince Masons of Ireland: The only body of its kind in the world. It is a continuation of the Grand Council of Rites, which was established in 1838 and controls the degrees of Rose Croix (Prince Mason), and Most Wise Sovereign, a degree conferred upon a brother who has been elected to a chair in the Rose Croix Chapter.

Grand College of Rites: (See Rite, Grand College of.)

Grand Commander, Knight: (See Knight Grand Commander.)

Grand Commander of the Eastern Star: Not the Order of the Eastern Star, but a degree in Pyron's Collection.

Grand Commander of the Orient: A degree in the Fifth Grade of the Rite of Seven Degrees, or Councils of the Emperors of the East and West. A lecture of this degree refers to Aristides the Just, the first to take the title of Knight of Rose Croix, and who joined with Godfrey de Bouillon and other Crusading Knights; the tracing board showed a well, situated west of Jerusalem, with other emblems of the grade. Esdras conducts the candidate, using six Blessed Names; there is a six-fold word—one Assyrian, one Chaldean, three in Hebrew, and the final word is pronounced jointly.

Grand Commander of the Temple: The 27° of the A.A.S. Rite.

Grand Consecrator: The 22° of the Ancient and Primitive Rite (See Ancient and Primitive Rite.)

Grand Council: The term is used in many ways; it refers primarily to the controlling body of Royal and Select Masters, usually a state organization. The national body is the "General Grand Council," the words "Royal and Select Masters" is usually added to it, but not always. The term sometimes applies to the three principal officers of an organization, as in the Royal Arch, or in the Order of the Red Cross in the commandery. It is also found in other rites, including the A.A.S.R.

Grand Council of Allied Masonic Degrees: (See Rite, Allied Masonic Degrees.)

Grand Council of the Degrees of Knight of the Sword, Knight of the East, and Knight of the East and West (Ireland): This is an Irish group which controls the degrees of Babylonian Pass, or Red Cross of Daniel (now called Knight of the Sword). The latter is a recent revival of the old Red Cross Mason degrees, having nothing to do with the Scottish Rite; they are founded upon the rebuilding of the Temple by Zerubbabel, and no doubt once formed a part of Royal Arch Masonry. The old "Jordan Pass" became the "Knight of the East"; the "Royal Order, Prussian Blue" is now known as "Knight of the East and West." There is a "chair degree" conferred upon those elected Great Chief of a Council of Red Cross Masons.

Grand Council Princes of Jerusalem: It confers the 16° of the A.A.S.R., known as "Prince of Jerusalem."

Grand Cross: The honor of "Grand Cross" is usually awarded by an organization as its highest gift. We find such in the following orders:

Amaranth, highest grade; Order of Rainbow, Cross of Color is a degree; Red Cross of Constantine, highest honor, given only to those who have ren-

45

dered unusual service to Freemasonry; Knight Templar Priests, 25° of the Rite; Knight Templar Priest, 17° is Grand Cross of St. Paul.

As a rule, the word "Knight precedes that of 'Grand Cross' "—Knight Grand Cross, sometimes abbreviated to "K.G.C."

Grand Defender: The 31° of the Ancient and Primitive Rite. (See Ancient and Primitive Rite.)

Grand Elect (or Grand Elected Knight Kadosh): There are a number of degrees listed as "Elect" degrees; sometimes the title is changed to "elected." We find:

The 4° of the Rite of Elected Cohens.

The 30° of the A.A.S.R. is the "Grand Elect Knight Kadosh," sometimes called "Knight of the White and Black Eagle." In Latin countries the degree is strongly Templar in tone, and has acquired sinister significance because some of its rituals stress the avenging of the death of DeMolay. The England ritual has been purged of all vengeance themes. Only the Supreme Council in England may confer the degree. The word "Kadosh" is Hebrew and means "separated" or "consecrated." The object of the degree is to teach that "the quest of the Lost Word ends, not at the Temple of Jerusalem, but on Mount Calvary."

The 14° of the A.A.S. Rite is known as "Grand Elect, Perfect and Sublime Mason."

In the Rite of Perfection is the degree "Grand Elect Perfect Ancient Master."

The Helvetic Rite has the "Grand Elect Perfect Mason." The ritual of the degree has a ceremony in which wine is drunk and bread is eaten, much after the ceremony of the Order of High Priesthood. The ceremony also includes the presentation of a ring, much like that of the 14° of the A.A.S.R.

The 7° Rite of Adoption (Grand Elect, or French Dame). The hangings are white, and the throne is red. There are five lights, of which one is a transparent star of eight points, with the S.W. in the centre. The brothers dress in black and the sisters in white. The W. Master and Mistress wear a hood from which the Jewel is suspended by a long black ribbon. The Apron is white, doubled and bordered with black and having the star of eight points embroidered in the centre. The Jewel is of mother of pearl in the form of an eight pointed star, with rim and points of gold; in the centre is the S.W., it is worn over the heart by a black ribbon. The Sash is black. The titles are Sovereign Grand Master and Sovereign Grand Mistress.

Grand Encampment: The name given in the U.S.A. to the governing body of the Knights Templar. It comprises all Grand Commanderies of the various States and subordinate bodies in several foreign countries and colonies. It meets triennially and is presided over by a Grand Master. In England, Scotland, Ireland and Canada, the organization is called a Great Priory, which is better adapted as a name. In the early days of the organization, commanderies (as now known) were called "Encampments," probably because of the semi-military character of the Order. Over a century ago there was in Germany a Grand Encampment, Knights of St. John, which had among its membership many of the crowned heads.

Grand Encampment of Temple and Malta: This was the name of an early day Templar Order in Scotland; it grew out of the group known as "The Early Grand Encampment, or Early Grand Encampment of Scotland." It united, in 1909, with the Great Priory of Scotland, now the governing body of Templars in Scotland.

Grand Eulogist: The 23° of the Ancient and Primitive Rite; the aspirant was entrusted with the ritual of the burial ceremony; it was an official degree and taught the doctrine of the immortality of the soul, stressing the Egyptian opinions.

Grand Haram: The 73° of the Rite of Mizraim. (See Rite of Mizraim.)

Grand High Priest: While this is the name of the highest officer of a Grand Chapter of Royal Arch Masons, it is also the name of a degree controlled by the English Allied Masonic Degrees, similar to the Order of the High Priesthood in the U.S.A.

Grand Imperial Council: The name applied to several national organizations, particularly the Grand Imperial Council of the Red Cross of Constantine, and the Grand Imperial Council of the Nobles of the Mystic Shrine. The former organization, of which there are at present at least three bearing the name, control the conferring of the degrees of the Red Cross of Rome and Constantine. (See Red Cross of Constantine; also Shrine.)

Grand Initiates: The 6° of the Rite of Memphis.

Grand Inquiring Commander: The 66° of the Rite of Mizraim. (See Rite of Mizraim.)

Grand Inquisitor (or Grand Inquisitor Commander): The 31° of the Ancient Reformed Egyptian Rite.

The A.A.S.R. confers the degree, calling it Grand Inquisitor Commander, Sovereign Tribunal of the 31°. (See Ancient and Accepted Scottish Rite.)

Grand Inquisitor Commander: (See Grand Inquisitor.)

Grand Inspector: The 18° of the Rite of Memphis; it teaches toleration, love and charity, to those who are to become leaders in Freemasonry. In England, the 31° is that of Grand Inspector, Inquisitor, Commander. The 9° of the Philosophic Scotch Rite; it is also termed "Grand Scotch Mason." (See Philosophic Scotch Rite.)

Grand Inspector General: The 32° of the Ancient Egyptian Reformed Rite. The words are also applied to a Scottish Rite degree, and to individuals.

Grand Inspector, Perfect Initiate: The 8° of the Philosophic Scotch Rite. (See Philosophic Scotch Rite.)

Grand Installator: The 21° of the Ancient and Primitive Rite; the candidate is entrusted with the ritual used in installing officers and is taught lessons in symbolism.

Grand Lodge of Antients: The Dermott (Irish) organization, established in 1751, in London, as opposed to the older Grand Lodge of the "Moderns." Both united in 1813 to make the "United Grand Lodge of England."

Grand Lodge of Berlin: (See Rite, Grand Lodge of the Three Globes.)

Grand Lodge of Mark Master Masons: The body, which, in England, controls the degree of Mark Master, and certain other associated degrees, including the Royal Ark Mariner.

Grand Lodge of the Three Globes: (See Rite, Grand Lodge of Three Globes.)

Grand Lodges: England had at least five such in the early history of the fraternity:" The "Moderns," the "Antients," the "Grand Lodge of All England," the "Grand Lodge South of the River Trent," and the "Wigan Grand Lodge." The "Antients" were known as "Atholl Masons," after the Duke of

Atholl, who was their Grand Master. Wigan Grand Lodge hardly deserved the title of a Grand Lodge.

Grand Lodge of South Africa: Is a bogus negro organization; there is no such Grand Lodge except in the imagination of the organizers.

Grand Maitre Ecossais: One of the degrees listed by Moses Cohen in his capacity as Grand Inspector General, in a certificate given, November 9, 1790, to Abraham Jacobs in Jamaica.

Grand Master Ad Vitam: Sometimes called "Grand Master of All Symbolic Lodges." The 20° of the A.A.S.R.

Grand Master Architect: The 12° of the Ancient and Accepted Rite; one of the "Architect" degrees; in this degree instruction is given as to the Five Orders of Architecture. (See A. A. S. R.)

Also one of the degrees of the Helvetic Rite, where it follows the degree of "Grand Elect Perfect Master and Royal Arch Mason."

Grand Master of All Symbolic Lodges: This is a misnomer; there is no one who is Grand Master of *All lodges.* (See Grand Master Ad Vitam.)

Grand Master of the Key of Masonry: A degree in the Rite of Perfection. (See Rite of Perfection.)

Grand Master of Light: The degree of Knight of St. Andrew. (See A.A.S.R.)

Grand National Lodge of Germany: This Grand Lodge confers ten additional, or "higher" degrees, and is very much like the Swedish system:

1°-3° Craft degrees in a St. John's Lodge.
4°-5° Conferred in a St. Andrew's Lodge.
6°-9° The Chapter.
  10° Apprentice of Perfection, an honorary degree conferred only by the Grand Lodge, and in Berlin. Its distinctive mark is a red cross worn around the neck; members are styled "Knights of the Red Cross."

Grand Orient of Brazil: (See Brazilian Rite.)

Grand Orient of France: In many Latin countries the word "Orient" is used in lieu of the word "Lodge." The Grand Orient of France is only one of several Grand Lodges in France, but it controls several Masonic degrees. Its failure to place the Bible on its altars has removed it from the pale of Masonic recognition; it is said to have united with the Ancient and Primitive Rite in 1862.

Grand Patriarch: A degree in the Rite of Perfection.

Grand Patriarch Noachite: A degree of the Councils of Emperors of the East and West.

Grand Patriarch of the Order: The 33° of the Ancient Egyptian Reformed Rite.

Grand Pontiff (or Sublime Ecossais): One of the degrees of the Rite of Perfection. The 19° of the Ancient and Accepted Rite of England.

Grand Priest of Spiritual Knighthood: The 7° and last degree of the Melesino (Russian) Rite.

Grand Prince of Jerusalem: The 16° of the Ancient and Accepted Rite in England.

Grand Scotch Knight: The 14° of the Ancient and Accepted Rite in England.

Grand Star of Sirius: The Ancient and Primitive Rite confers five "decorations" of honor; the first is the "Grand Star of Sirius."

Grand Tiler of King Solomon: The degree appears under several names; under the above name it is conferred by the Allied Masonic Degrees; Hartley Carmichael of Virginia, as head of the A.M.D. in the U.S.A. conferred it upon the Earl of Euston in 1892, with "power to propagate it in England," which he did (including India).

It is also similar, if not the same, as the degree of Select Master; the degree relates the story of the accidental intrusion of a craftsman into the secret vaults of King Solomon; its jewel is the Triangle of the Preserver, its points downward, with Hebrew letter in gilt on an enamel background. The degree also appears in the Scottish Rite.

This interesting Grade was formerly known under the title of "Masons Elect of the Twenty-Seven," or "Select Masons of the 27," and is found in many different countries, although records are by no means abundant. There can be little doubt that this Grade and the Grade of "Select Master" owe their origin to a common source. In his "Masonic Orations," published in 1803, Frederick Dalcho mentions (appendix) that in addition to the regular degrees of the Scottish Rite, they possessed many detached degrees and among those mentioned is "Select Masters of 27." Elsewhere there is mention of "Select Masons of the 27," etc., indicating that the Grade which we now work as "Grand Tilers of Solomon" is of very close resemblance to the present-day "Select Master."

Early evidence of the Grade is contained at page 1305 "History of the Cryptic Rite," where is reproduced a diploma issued by Moses Cohen to Abraham Jacobs, dated November 9, 1790, which in addition to some of the regular Grades of the Rite of Perfection, mentions the "Select Mason of Twenty-Seven." There are also other references to such a Grade at an early date.

The Jamaica Ritual, purporting to have been used by Morin in the West Indies in the 18th century, is yet available for study and indicates a close adherence to the present working of the Allied Grade, while at the same time it indicates a direct line to the Select Master. However, following the trend of thought here introduced, the origin of the one Grade would be the birth of the other and the two Grades, while somewhat different today, indicate formerly one Grade. The Allied Grade merely holds to older working and has not been amplified and changed by too many hands. It appears to be old work.

It appears that the entrance of this Grade into the Allied System of England came in 1892, during which year Bro. C. F. Matier (who was at that time P.D.G.M. and Grand Secretary of the Grand Council of England and Wales) received the Grade from America. He also received authority to confer the Grade. The records of this are contained in the archives of the Grand Council here. Thus, it is evident that the Grade is an American product and our records here are earlier than have yet been found elsewhere.

The Ritual now used by Grand Council is the same as that used by England and is a product of late 19th century American ritualists. The Ritual is of deep interest to those who really understand early Ritual and the environs in which it was created. Many lessons may be found in simple and easily explained ceremonies of last century.

The Jewel of Grand Tilers of Solomon is a black delta, edged with gold, containing in the centre "27" in Hebrew characters. On the reverse appears the Tetragrammaton in the Kabalistic Order. The Jewel is suspended from a scarlet ribbon, edged with pale grey, on which is a hand grasping a sword and surmounted by three crowns.

49

The Sash is approximately four inches in width; scarlet in the centre, with pale grey on either side thereof.

The Apron of the Grade is black, with gold border. In the centre is a gold crown, while on the flap in gold, is a hand grasping a sword.

Grand Trinitarian Knight of St. John: The 24° of the Knight Templar Priests Rite. (See Knight Templar Priests.)

Great Priory of Ireland: This body controls the degrees of Knight Templar, Knight of Malta, Eminent Preceptor, and Eminent Prior; the latter two are conferred upon a brother who has been elected to a chair in the Preceptory.

Great Priory of the Temple: The controlling body for the Order of Malta and Knight Templar orders in England; they have headquarters at Mark Masons' Hall, Great Queen St., London.

Green Brother: (See Rite, Early Grand; see Enlightened Phreemason.)

Gregorians: An imitative Masonic society, formed in England as early as 1730; the Duke of Wharton is said to have organized it, although once a Grand Master. It had a regular initiatory ceremony for "men of honor, sound morals, and true loyalty"; it was a convivial group but ceased to exist in 1805. Prince William Frederick of Glocester was "Grand of the Order" at one time.

Gregs: One of the pseudo-Masonic societies of the early 17th century.

Grotto: (See Order Mystic Order of the Veiled Prophets of the Enchanted Realm.)

Happy Folks: An androgynous degree of 1743. Now extinct. (No happy folks?)

Harlequin Freemason: Not a member or degree, but a pantomime produced at Drury Lane Theatre in London, by Charles Dibdin. It consists of a dialogue with songs, followed by a pageant and must have been quite a show for that day (1780). The advertising read:

"This day will be presented the Suspicious Husband . . . which will be added (first time) a new Pantomime call'd Harlequin Free-Mason. To conclude with a procession of Principal Grand Masters, from the Creation of the World to the present century, dressed in the habits of their respective Ages and Countries. (We wonder about Adam?) With New Music, Scenes, Dresses, Pageants, and Decorations. Books of the Songs, with an Explanation of the Pageant, to be had at the Theatre." (They had a good press-agent.)

Harodim (or Harodem): (See Rite of Perfection or Harodim.)

Harodim, Grand Chapter of: A society formed in London in 1787, under the auspices of William Preston, which has served as a model for our Schools of Instruction. The term signified "Princes and Rulers." There was once a side-degree in the U.S.A. called "Harodim." (See Rite of Haredom.)

Hasidim, Sovereign Prince of: The 75° and 76° of the Rite of Mizraim. (See Rite of Mizraim.)

Hatchet, Order of: (See Order of Fendeurs.)

Heberemites: The 2° of the Rite of Memphis. (See Rite of Memphis.)

Hedge Masons: The name by which certain irregular groups of Masons in Ulster were known. These groups met by what was termed "inherent right" before a grand lodge was firmly established. The lodges frequently organized and conferred degrees without a regular warrant.

Hell Fire Club: An infamous society founded by Philip, Duke of Wharton;

50

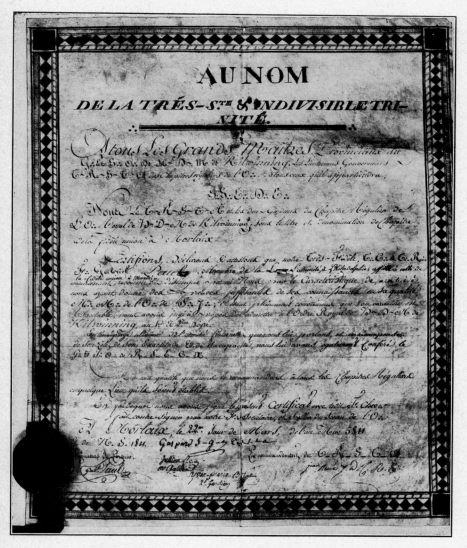

Diploma of Gabriel Paul, early day Freemason in St. Louis; it is in French and issued by Chapter Rose Croix in Morlaix (1811).

he was an Irish peer, born in 1698; married at 16; bankrupt at 24; indicted for high treason at 31; dead at 33. He had an inane desire to head organizations. He organized the "Hell Fire Club," his object in doing so not being known.

Helvetic Reformed Rite: (See Rite, Reformed Helvetic; see Glaire's Helvetic Rite.)

Hen Masonry: A name humorously applied to some of the women's organizations which have a Masonic connection.

Hercules, Order of: (See Order of Hercules.)

Heredom: We are indebted to the Stuarts for the word *Heredom,* which is today found in the language of Freemasonry. The word is variously spelled Herodom, Heredom, Heroden, Heredon.

Some writers say it was taken from the Greek, meaning Holy House or Temple. Ragon thinks it is from a Latin word meaning Heritage. In a catechism appearing in the degree of Grand Arch, there is a reference to the Mountain of Heredom, which states that it was "a mountain situated between the West and North of Scotland, at the end of the sun's course where the first lodge of Masonry was held; in that terrestial part which has given name to Scottish Masonry."

Heredom of Kilwinning: One of the degrees in the Early Grand Rite of Scotland. Also appears in the Royal Order of Scotland.

Heredom, Royal Order of: (See Order of Heredom and Red Cross.)

Hermetic Brotherhood of Atlantis, Egypt and India: Organized in Chicago, Ill., in 1883, by Dr. W. P. Phelon (died December 30, 1904), with the object of expounding Hermetic philosophy. It published annual proceedings in octavo pamphlet form, as well as some reprints of papers read at their meetings. A serial *Temple Lectures* was also published for the members. At least six volumes of these appeared. The superior teacher was called the "Elder Brother." Francese I. Rogers was the second Elder Brother.

Hermetic Brotherhood (or Brothers) of Luxor: A group which originated in England, the membership, however, being about equally divided between that country and the United States. It is not known just when it started, but in 1888 it was reorganized after disruption by internal dissentions. The newly organized group quickly died out. M. Theon was Grand Master of what was known as the Exterior Circle. Nine degrees, divided into three grades were given before one arrived at Adeptship. The United States Council consisted of seven members. It published a 52-page quarto, called "The Mysteries of Eros," for advanced students. The adytum was located in Denver, Colo.

Hermetic Rite: (See Illuminati of Avignon.) In 1760, (Rebold says 1772) there was founded the Hermetic Rite; it existed in Avignon, France; its ritual dealt with the Elixir of Life and the Philosopher's Stone, which might indicate a Rosicrucian connection.

Hermetic, or Sublime Masters of the Luminous Ring: One of the degrees of the Philosophic Scotch Rite. (See Philosophic Scotch Rite.)

Hero of Jericho: The 2° in the Supreme Conclave True Kindred, sometimes called "Royal Companion."

Heroes of '76: Under the National Sojourners there is listed the "Heroes of '76" as one of the degrees conferred by that organization. As a matter of fact, it is not conferred within the body of the National Sojourners, but as a side degree, and in local "Camps" which are attached to Sojourner Chapters.

It has a humorous ritual, written by a distinguished Kentucky Freemason, Thomas J. Flournoy.

In June, 1922 a side degree, auxiliary to National Sojourners was instituted in Chicago Chapter. The degree is called "Heroes of '76," and was originally founded by Past Grand Master Jones of Kentucky and handed down to Brother Christopher VanDeventer, 33°, who saw in it the important teachings and history of our country and felt it was especially appropriate for the Sojourners, the membership being both Master Masons and Officers. The first Camp of Heroes was organized at Chicago and is called Bonhomme Richard Camp. This was followed by camps in practically every Chapter in this country and its possessions. This innovation has aroused a much keener interest in other chapter activities.

A National organization was formed in 1930, and today there are approximately 130 Camps existing under sponsorship of the National Sojourners. No records of admission are kept and the total membership is unknown. Annual meetings are held and have been held since 1930.

There is no fee for membership into a Camp of Heroes and its founders never intended that it should ever have any fees or dues, its sole purpose being to give enjoyment and innocent pleasure to Master Masons and Sojourners.

Heroine of Jericho: An androgynous degree conferred upon Royal Arch Masons, their wives and daughters; it was very popular during the period 1840-60; it was founded on the scriptural account of the Fall of Jericho, the faithfulness of Rahab, and its reward. The story is recorded in Joshua II. The recognition signet had the word ARHAB (Rahab) within a heart, with the letters ML FY IYUN TOB within a circle, which contained the letters BF R PNWTTEN. The colored folks have a degree of the same name. When conferred upon a Freemason, his title was "Knight of Jericho." The degree seems to have been unknown elsewhere than in the U.S.A. It is said to be conferred at this date by chapters organized under Prince Hall Grand Lodges, and one of the noted members of a Prince Hall lodge was the author of an "improved ritual" for the degree.

It had for its object the protection of relatives of Royal Arch Masons by giving them certain signs and words which would enable them to make themselves known to the craft. In an old volume published at Independance, Mo., in 1847 or later, it is told that the degree was conferred upon several wives of Royal Arch Masons about to leave in a caravan for California.

The degree recounts an instance of friendship extended to the whole family of a benefactress by those whom she had benefited, and of the influence of a solemn contract in averting danger, such as referred to in the case of Rahab, the woman of Jericho, from which character the Order derives its name. Read the second chapter of the Book of Joshua for further details; this chapter is read to the candidate during the degree. The sign of the degree is sometimes referred to as the "plumb-line sign."

Hetairia: A Greek society organized in 1814; its ritual was the work of a Freemason, Xanthos of Patmos. The degrees conferred were: Brothers, Batchelors, Priests of Eleusis, Prelates, Grand Arch. The organization was under control of the last named group.

Hiccubites: A pseudo-Masonic group of the early part of the 18th century.

High Degrees; High Grades; Hautes Grades: The latter term is the French. (See comment under "Higher Degrees.")

Higher Degrees: The name is improperly applied to all of those degrees beyond the three craft degrees. The degrees are not "higher," but are "associated" with those of Craft Masonry and afford additional instruction.

High Egyptian Masonry: Cagliostro, the Masonic fraud, used this term in speaking of his Rite (1784), and especially of the Adoptive Rite.

High Knight Templar: Referred to in the old Wigan Ritual, and conferred in a Chapter and Royal Encampment. It is said to date from 1740 to 1760. The ritual is Christian in character and has ceremonies similar to those of the Templars. The candidate was first created a "Knight of the Order of St. John of Jerusalem," then presented with a White Stone; among the emblems of the degree were the skull and cross-bones, a ladder of five steps, hour glass, scythe, and similar emblems.

High Knight Templars Lodge of Ireland: The forerunner of the Early Grand Encampment. (See Early Grand Rite of Scotland.)

High Priest: In the U.S.A. this represents the highest officer of a chapter of Royal Arch Masons, but in England it is a degree, to be conferred upon a Freemason who has attained the station of Third Principal (corresponding to Scribe in U.S.A.). It deals with the Priesthood after the Order of Melchizedek, and is much the same as the Order of High Priesthood. Its jewel is the Triangle with the point upward, which is imposed on a mitre.

High Priests, Rite of: The Rite of High Priests, or Cohens, was founded by Martinez Paschalis; it had nine degrees. (See Rite of Elected Cohens.)

High Priesthood: An Order conferred upon those who have been elected High Priest, or First Principal of a Royal Arch Chapter; a meeting of such is called a "Convention." It is sometimes referred to as "The Anointed Order of High Priesthood." Each state has its own convention; the presiding officer is termed "President." It consists of but one degree, beautiful in ritual and teaching Monotheism. It is founded on the Blessing of Abram.

High Twelve: (See International High Twelve.)

Holy and Illustrious Order of the Cross: The 11° of the Knight Templar Priests Rite. It was also a degree in the Early Grand Rite of Scotland.

Holy and Thrice Illustrious Order of the Holy Cross: The 3° of the Council of the Trinity.

Holy City, Knights of: The 5° of the Rectified Rite of Strict Observance, founded, says Rebold, about 1768 by an emissary of the Jesuits. (See Rite of Strict Observance.)

Holy City, Knights Beneficent: (See Knights Beneficent of the Holy City.)

Holy Cross, Order of: According to Arthur Edward Waite's Encyclopedia, the Order, which was the 27° in the Early Grand Rite, was invented in America, and found its way into the Early Grand Rite of Scotland. In a printed ritual, 1890, Ayr, Scotland, it is stated: "The 27° of the E. G. Rite is called the Holy and Illustrious Order of the Cross. It is worked in connection with a conclave of the Red Cross of Rome, a Constitution held under the authority of an encampment of Knights Templar."

The ritual is short and uninteresting, but its control is vested in the Priestly Order of the Temple at this date. In 1828, a Masonic magazine in New York referred to the institution of a "Grand Council of Knights of the Holy Cross" at Rome, N. Y. Nocalore (Vol. VI, p. 205) gives a complete story of the group.

Holy Grave, Knight of: (See Knight of Holy Grave.)

Holy Land, Knight of: A Deputy Grand Master of England wrote to a Dutch brother, that in discussing the matter with three foreign visitors, he discovered a Masonic Order known as "Knight of the Holy Land" (1757).

Holy of Holies: A degree in the Rite of Fessler. (See Rite of Fessler.)

Holy Order of Wisdom: The Holy Order of Wisdom is one of the finest and most impressive degrees in Masonry, according to a circular sent out by its Sovereign College. The qualifications provide that a candidate must be a Knight Templar, or a Knight Rose Croix; the degree is essentially Christian and Trinitarian, and the reported fee was $10.00.

Holy Royal Arch: The name often applied to the degree of Royal Arch Mason. (See Honourable Fraternity of Ancient Freemasons.) The 22° of the Early Grand Rite; three candidates are required and the ceremony starts with the admission of the three sojourners into the presence of the Grand Council. The degree bears resemblance to the American Royal Arch, but the candidates discover three keystones, the Crown of Solomon and Hiram of Tyre, and (believe it or not?) the embalmed heart of Hiram Abif.

Holy Royal Arch Knight Templar Priest: The 33° of Knight Templar Priests.

Holy Sepulchre: (See Sepulchre, Order of.)

Holy Virgin: An Adoptive degree composed by Rev. William Leigh, about 1851; he was a past grand master of Alabama and prepared an ingenious monitor to go with it; eligibles were wives, widows, sisters, daughters, and mothers of Master Masons.

Honorable Distinction Cross: (See Order of DeMolay.)

Honorary Degrees: Degrees conferred without petition, and usually given for some special service to Freemasonry.

Honorary Legion of Honor: (See Order of DeMolay.)

Honorary Members: A means of recognizing active Freemasons; election as such carries no financial or other responsibility.

Honorary Thirty-Thirds: The Ancient Accepted Scottish Rite makes a distinction between its 33° members; all who receive the 33° are said to be "Honorary 33°." Those who become active members in the Supreme Council are said to be "33° Active," and it is they who carry on the business of Scottish Rite Masonry. Honorary members are not admitted to executive sessions.

Honored Mother: The 4° in the Order of Sacred Temple.

Hope, Knights of: An androgynous degree of 1820.

Honourable Fraternity of Ancient Freemasons: An irregular group, composed of women, and claiming to be "the only women's Masonic Order in the World, conferring the Craft degrees, the Holy Royal Arch, and the Rose Croix." (See Women's Lodges of Freemasons.)

Hospitallers of St. John of Jerusalem: We are indebted to this Order, founded in 1096, during the First Crusade, for the transmission of Templar precepts and usages; it sprang from a secular body instituted in Palestine in 1058, and which included both sexes; it was devoted to the succor of the poor and sick in Jerusalem. Their dress was a plain black robe having a white cross on the left breast. Later it assumed a religious character, and added to their vows the defense of the Christian religion, at which time they became a military group, and began wearing a red tunic or surcoat with a plain Greek Cross in white on the breast, back and upper part of the sleeve, over the armor. The civil branch retained the black habit and the eight-pointed cross.

55

In the American Masonic system, they are today known as the Knights of Malta. (See Knights of Malta.)

Hour Glass Club: A club composed of Master Masons, which reported, in 1955, as holding its thirty-first annual dinner.

Hurlothumbrians: One of the many pseudo-Masonic orders founded during the early part of the 18th century.

Hutten: A fraternity formed by Freemasons in Strasburg, Vienna, Cologne, Zurich, and Freburgh. Strasburg was recognized as the Haupt-Hautte—the High Chief Lodge. On April 25, 1459, chiefs of these lodges assembled at Ratisbone and drew up the act which established the fraternity, fixing headquarters at Strasburg.

Illuminated Prince: The 2° of the Little Mysteries of the Order of Illuminati; it follows that of Epopt; in this degree the candidate is queried as to his attitude toward government and secret societies. He is confronted with several "horrors," among which are "blood, some poniards, instruments of torture, and a skeleton raised upon several steps, trampling upon the attributes of royalty." He is later presented with shield, boots, spurs, a mantle adorned with feathers, and receives the embraces of his fellows.

Illuminated Theosophists: A part of the Swedenborg Rite, which included such degrees as Apprentice, Illuminated Theosophist, Fellow Craft, Blue Brother, Master Neophyte, and Red Brother.

Illuminati, The: There were several groups known as "Illuminati," those of Bavaria (1776); Avignon (1779); Stockholm, founded in 1621; resuscitated in 1750. There was also a group known as "Illuminati of the Zodiac," founded in 1783.

In 1776, the Chair of Canon Law at the Bavarian University of Ingolstatt was occupied by a young man, Adam Weishaupt, educated by the Society of the Jesuits, but who fell away from their teachings and became an advanced thinker in politics and religion and the bitter enemy of his former instructors. He became regarded as an apostate Catholic. He had the desire to sweep away all existing monarchies and creeds, and to establish republics in which the desire to do good to one's fellow-man would take the place of all natural and revealed religion. To find suitable material for membership, it was necessary to enlist young men; with this in view, he sought admission to the Freemasons, and was initiated in the Lodge of Good Council in Munich; soon afterward he organized the Illuminati. There were a number of degrees, divided into groups:

The Nursery: 1, Preparation; 2, Novice; 3, Minerval; 4, Illuminated Minor.
Group II, known as Masonry: 1, Apprentice; 2, Fellow-Craft; 3, Master; 4, Illuminatus Major, or Scotch Novice; 5, Illuminatus Dirigens, or Scotch Knight.
Group III was divided into two parts, Lesser and Greater: 1, Presbyter, or Priest; 2, Prince, or Regent. 1, Magus; 2, Rex.

In a charge to candidates, it was said: "Since the great strength of the Order lies in its concealment, let it be always covered by another name; Freemasonry is a useful cloak to borrow."

And that probably explains how Freemasonry was brought into the Illuminati picture; it entered into the political life of the United States, then recovering from the Revolution; George Washington was charged with being a member—which he vehemently denied in several letters still in existence.

Webster classifies the Illuminati as follows:

56

1. (Eccles) Those who had received baptism in which a lighted taper was given them. (Enlightened.)
2. (Eccles) A sect in Spain, 1775, those who "by means of prayer had attained so perfect a state as to require no sacraments."
3. The Weishaupt group.
4. An obscure sect of French Familists.
5. Hesycharts, Mystics, and Arielists.
6. The Rosicrucians.

The Order had a ritual ceremony comprising the several degrees noted, and was governed by an "Unknown Superior" to whom implicit obedience was pledged; Freemasonry has been charged with being under control of an "Unknown Superior," a charge made by the Church. This system of the Illuminati probably furnished the idea for use of our critics. Let it be understood that Freemasonry has no unknown officers; in fact we have too many officers trying to be the head which constitutes one of our troubles. (See Rite of Illuminati.)

Illuminati of Avignon: (See Rite, Illuminati; see Avignon, Illuminati of.) The Rite bore a resemblance to the doctrines of Swedenborg; it had a system of confession and formed a secret spy system, each member spying on the other. In 1785, Weishaupt quarreled with an influential supporter, a noble, who banished Weishaupt from the kingdom—and the Illuminati folded up its tents. The word in the French language is "Illumines." Goethe, Herder, and the Dukes of Weimar and Gotha were at one time members.

Illuminati of Bavaria: (See Illuminati.)

Illuminati of Stockholm: (See Illuminati.)

Illuminati of the Zodiac: Founded in 1621; resuscitated in France about 1750.

Illuminatus, Dirigens: Known as "Scotch Knight." (See "Illuminati.")

Illuminatus Major: Known as "Scotch Novice." (See "Illuminati.")

Illuminatus Minor: (See "Illuminati.")

Illuminism: The practice of the doctrines taught by the Illuminati. (See Illuminati.)

Illustrious Elect of Fifteen: A degree of the Rite of Perfection, sometimes called "Illustrious Elect." (See Rite of Perfection.)

Illustrious Knight Commander of the Black and White Eagle: (See Rite of Perfection.)

Illustrious Knights of the Honorary Order of the Garter: (See "Garter" or "Order of the Garter.")

Imitative Societies: Practically all secret societies are copies of Masonic organizations, since it was first in the field. The rituals of most imitative societies have been written by Freemasons, who utilized their knowledge of Freemasonry in framing new rituals. Most imitative societies have altars in the center of the room; most officers are stationed in the South, West, East (and sometimes to break the style) and North. Most rituals demand a preparation, a historical explanation, a lecture, and a charge. In this sense they may be said to be "imitative."

Independents, Rite of: Rebold refers to this organization as being organized in 1776; it was connected in some way with the "Perfect Initiates of Egypt."

Indian Freemasonry: That Indians practiced certain ceremonial rites is quite well known; that they could be called "Masonic" is quite questionable. Indians have been generally accepted among the fraternity in the U.S.A. when

57

their education was such as to make them eligible. Several Cherokees became Grand Masters of Oklahoma.

Induction: The I Grade of the Secret Monitor. (See Secret Monitor.)

Ineffable Degrees: Those degrees dealing with the Ineffable Name of Deity, particularly the 4°-14° of the Rite of Perfection and the Scottish Rite.

Inflamed Heart: This degree is referred to as "Le Coeur Enflame" (French), "The Ardent (or Fervent) Heart," the "Fiery Heart," and the "Inflamed Heart." Our copy of the ritual is taken from one written by Albert Pike which he says was copied from a manuscript in possession of the Grand Lodge of Louisiana (1858). He tells us that the history of the degree which appears in the manuscript was "written with a distinct purpose to say and mean nothing." Pike refers to it as the 34th degree. Undoubtedly it followed the 33° for it has in its obligation a restriction on conferring the degree upon any who are not "Princes of the Royal Secret, or Grand Inspectors General of the 33°, whose moral and civil and Masonic abilities are perfectly well known."

The figure of Napoleon is frequently brought into the ritual; in fact the name Napoleon is one of the significant names mentioned. The object of the degree was stated to be "to reform the grave abuses which exist in Masonry." The degree is decidedly Christian in character, but shows traces of Hermeticism and Occultism.

Initiate: (E. C.) A degree in Order of the Temple.

Initiate in the Egyptian Secrets' Cosmopolitan Brother: (See Rite of African Architects.)

Initiate in the Mysteries: The 21° Metropolitan Chapter of France.

Initiate in the Profound Mysteries: The 62° Metropolitan Chapter of France.

Initiate into the Sciences: The 2° of a system founded on the teachings of Pythagoras.

Initiate of the Interior: A degree in the Order of the Temple.

Initiated: A degree in the Rite of Philalethes. The word means "a beginning."

Initiated Brothers of Asia: The 6° of Initiated Knights and Brothers of Asia.

Initiated Knights and Brothers of Asia: Established in 1780 by members of the German Rose Croix, as a result of a schism; they studied the natural sciences and prolonging life. It had as its basis the three symbolic degrees and the following nine others: 4, Seekers; 5, Sufferers; 6, Initiated Knights and Brothers of Asia in Europe; 7, Masters and Sages; 8, Royal Prince or True Brothers of the Rose Croix; 9, Melchizedek.

Initiatory: A degree of the Order of the Rainbow; the Order of DeMolay; in the Order of Golden Key; of Job's Daughters.

Inner East (or Orient): Part of the German "High" degree system. (See Rite of Perfection of Harodim.)

Inspector of the Works: (See Expert Master.)

Inquisitor: One of the degrees of the Ancient and Primitive Rite. The Scottish Rite has a 31° called by that name.

Installation of a Supreme Ruler: The III grade of Secret Monitor.

Installed Excellent Chief: A degree of the Knight Masons of Ireland.

Installed Mark Master Mason: The degree is conferred upon those who have been selected to preside over a Lodge of Mark Master Masons. It is very similar in general form to the degree of Past Master, including a seating in the Oriental Chair, an obligation, and a reading of the Keystone in reverse—Hiram, the Whole Structure Showed to King Solomon. The legend of the degree is that it was necessary to select a presiding master to fill the place of the late architect; it was difficult to select from 12 competent brethren; it was agreed that on the following morning they should all go to a certain spot and watch for the rising of the sun, and he who saw the first rays would become the Master and take the architect's place. One of them saw the light strike the top of the Temple and he was the winner. (See Mark Master Installed.)

Installed Sovereign Master: A degree of the Installed Masters. The scene of the degree is laid shortly after the completion of the Temple. Ambassadors from all over the world came to behold the magnificence of the Temple; the Queen of Sheba was among the group. The incident around which the degree is built has to do with Solomon, the Queen of Sheba, and Hiram Abiff.

Instruction, Lodges of: Lodges of Instruction do not confer degrees; they only exemplify and discuss degrees. The study of ritual in Freemasonry is essential in preserving its dignity, purity and character. They serve a different purpose from Lodges of Research, which are organized to study the history of the fraternity.

Intendant of the Buildings: The 8° of the Ancient and Accepted Scottish Rite; the legend of the degree is that it was instituted to supply a successor to the architect, Hiram; Adoniram was finally selected. (See Rite of Perfection.)

International Assembly: World Conferences of Freemasonry have never been successful in the main; the Supreme Councils of the A.A.S.R. attempt to get together occasionally, but usually without representation from some of the larger Supreme Councils. The International Masonic Association once tried such a convocation; and the International Masonic League still attempts to promote international gatherings. They encounter the same difficulties as the League of Nations, and United Nations—too much diversity of opinion, and too little desire to promote International Harmony.

International Bureau for Masonic Affairs: Founded in 1902, and in August 1914, devoting itself to the aid of World War I victims and soldiers missing in action. It was headquartered in Switzerland.

International High Twelve: A Masonic dining club, imitative of Rotary, Kiwanis, Lions, etc., but requiring Masonic membership. It is very active in certain parts of the country, and holds national meetings.

International League of Freemasons: The International League of Freemasons is almost exclusively a European group of Freemasons, known also as the Universala Freemasona Ligo (Universal Freemasons League). This name came to it because of its early connection with the spread of Esperanto, a universal language. Because of some of the elements which retain membership in the League, the Scandinavian and British Dominions have abstained from having anything to do with it.

Yet if we are to judge the League according to its intentions we can hardly find criticism of it for it would promote unity and universal world peace, which are Masonic ideals. We have little information to guide us as to recent actions of the League because World War II changed the Masonic picture to a great extent.

Membership in the League is open only to members of lodges belonging to regular obediences, or of lodges which acknowledge and conform to the Ancient Landmarks. Its Constitution requires it to abstain from all intervention in matters concerning Grand Lodges to which its members belong and it observes the most rigid neutrality in political and religious matters.

It originated in 1905 as an Esperantist Masonic group out of an Esperantist Congress which convened that year in Boulogne, France. It assumed its present form in 1913 when Esperanto passed from the scene.

We have a record of one of the Congresses (4th) held in Holland in 1929; the President of the League at that time, and who presided, was Dr. Fritz Uhlmann of Basle, Switzerland, Grand Master of the Grand Lodge Swiss Alpina; the Congress was officially opened by the late Dutch martyr, Col. H. von Tongeren, Grand Master of the Grand Lodge of the Netherlands; Col. von Tongeren gave a welcome to the group of 608 representatives in German, French, and English, showing the make-up of the languages represented. Bro. Plantagenet of France and Bro. Dudley Wright of England spoke, their remarks being translated into German by Brother Bing. Senator LaFontaine of Belgium gave an address in French (he was the winner of a Nobel Peace Prize). Then followed sectional meetings of the medicos, writers, and journalists—all attempting to find some practical way of serving the fraternity, and especially in counteracting the anti-Masonic propaganda circulated in Europe. Both Eugene Lenhoff of Austria and the venerable A. F. L. Faubel of Holland spoke. The symbolic ritual was exemplified according to the Dutch ritual which has many beautiful and impressive sections. At the conclusion all rose and sang Bro. Mozart's "In diesen heil'gen Hallen." Then followed the Dutch, Belgium, French, English, and German national anthems.

International Order of Co-Masonry: (See Co-Masonry.)

International Order of Oddfellows: While the "Oddfellows" is not a Masonic Rite, nevertheless it had its beginnings in Freemasonry and the character of its ritual is very much like that of Freemasonry.

It is primarily an English society, although like Freemasonry, it found fertile soil in the United States of America. It was established in the latter part of the 18th century and grew out of a schism in a Masonic lodge at Manchester, England, caused by a controversy over the dispensing of charity to its members. The result was the formation of a new lodge which soon took the name of the Manchester Unity Odd Fellows; in London there was formed the Patriotic Order of Odd Fellows, using the Manchester ritual; the organization spread throughout England and became a power for good.

The Manchester body was composed largely of workingmen who desired to make the lodge a beneficiary society; however, they did not form an irregular Masonic lodge in so doing, but made it an organization for giving mutual assistance in times of distress; they were known as "unities" instead of lodges.

The rituals and ceremonies were quite distinct from those of Freemasonry, but contained many of the old Masonic expressions; there are three degrees as in symbolic Masonry.

In 1819, Thomas Wildey and some of his associates, members of the Manchester group, established in Baltimore, Maryland, the Independent Order of

60

Odd Fellows of the United States. The society has some higher degrees or honors but these are seemingly unimportant.

Interparliamentary Group of Defense Against Masonic Activities: A French group organized in Paris in 1935, which sponsored the "Anti-Masonic Union of France." It is thought the organization supported the printing and distribution of Anti-Masonic literature.

Intimate Initiate: The 4° of the Order of the Temple.

Intimate Secretary: The 6° of the A.A.S.R. and the Rite of Perfection. Its ceremony and legend intend to commemorate an instance of unlawful curiosity, punishment being averted by reason of previous fidelity. The degree is comparable with that of Select Master of another Rite. The degree is also found in the Helvetic Rite, built around a legendary dispute between Solomon and Hiram of Tyre as found in the scripture.

Invincible Order: (See Order of Garter.)

Invisible Lodge: An organization of Magicians, its full name being "Grand Diet of Master Adepts." It is said to be a global organization composed of Freemasons, and members are found in all civilized countries. Houdini, Thurston, and many others were famous Freemasons and magicians.

Ireland: Ireland was the birthplace of many Masonic rites and degrees. The brethren of Grand Lodge in Ireland insist they do not have an "Irish Rite of Freemasonry," hence in deference to them we shall call it the Irish *System*.

Iris, Knight of: (See Knight of Iris.)

Irish Systems:

Arch Mason: Embraced some of the essentials of a degree now conferred. under another name.

Ark Mason: Obsolete degree.

Excellent Mason: Worked in the Veils of the Irish Royal Arch.

Grand Lodge of Ireland: Controls the degrees of Entered Apprentice, Fellow Craft, Master Mason, and Installed Master. The latter is conferred only upon a brother when elected to the Chair in a lodge. The requirement of the Installed Master degree, requiring as a pre-requisite the degree of Royal Arch Mason, was abolished in 1850.

Grades Not Worked: Royal Order of Scotland; Red Cross of Constantine; the Cryptic Degrees; Rosicrucian degrees. The following degrees are said to be obsolete: Ark Mason, Mark Fellow Mason, Mark Master, Link Mason or Wrestle.

Grand Chapter (Royal Arch Masons): Controls the degrees of Mark Master Mason, Royal Arch Mason, Very Worshipful Master, Chief Scribe, High Priest, and Excellent King. The latter degrees are "Chair" degrees. In the Royal Arch is embodied the old workings of the Excellent and Super Excellent (not the degrees as conferred in the U.S.A.). The legend of the Royal Arch is that appertaining to the "repair" of the Temple and the finding of the Book of the Law by Hilkiah, the High Priest. They do not use the Zerubbabel legend.

Super Excellent Mason: Worked as a part of the Veils of the Royal Arch.

Supreme Council Ancient and Accepted Rite: Works a peculiar form of the Scottish Rite.

Irish Freemasonry seems to have been divided into at least three separate periods:

The *First Period* was characterized by the briefness of the minutes of lodges, and covered the period 1775-1797. The degrees were our present 1°, 2°, and 3°, but the 1° and 2° embraced all including the Hiramic legend. The 3° probably had the Installed Master, Royal Arch and Red Cross Mason. About 1785, the Royal Arch degree appeared. Crossle states that it included much already had. There is no Templar reference during this period.

The *Second Period* covered from 1800-1827. The three degrees were maintained, but some names were changed. The 1° and 2° were one degree, references being "entered and crafted." Then came the 2° which was the same as Master Mason. The 3° was the Master's Part, or Royal Arch. In 1801 it was stated "that any Fellow Craft (commonly called Master Mason) of approved conduct as a man and Mason wishing to be exalted to this sublime degree (of Royal Arch) must be proposed," etc.

The *Third Period* was from 1866-67, when the 1° and 2° of the First and Second Periods were expanded into the present 3°. The 3° of the Second Period elaborated and expanded into the Past Master, Excellent Mason, Super Excellent Mason, Arch Mason, Royal Arch Mason, and an addition of group 4. In group 3 were the Ark, Mark Fellow Mason, Mark Master, Link Mason (or Wrestle), Babylonian Pass or Red Cross of Daniel, Jordan Pass, Royal Order of Prussian Blue. Group 4 had the Black Mark, Templar; and the four grades of Mediterranean Pass, Malta, Red Cross of Constantine and Knight of Patmos.

Most of these degrees have now disappeared from Irish Freemasonry and are known only to students.

I. Secreti: The name given to the Academy of Sciences, membership to which was limited to those who had made advancement in the sciences. (See Templar Rite.)

Ish Sodi: An organization formed in Iowa in recent years as a method of giving recognition to those who had served the Freemasons of the Cryptic Rite in some outstanding manner. It means "Man of My Choice," or "Select Man," a very proper name for an award by Royal and "Select" Masters.

Italian Architects: In the 12th and 13th centuries we find in Italy a College of Architects, or as some think, Freemasons, who settled on the shores of the beautiful Lake Como, in Northern Italy. They were the guiding spirit of European Architecture. It is said that the Pope once gave them authority to travel over Italy, building churches. They had pass-words, signs, and an oath of secrecy. Some see in the Architects the lineal ancestors of Freemasons.

Italian Philosophical Rite: This Rite had its seat at Florence, Italy, and is the center of the Federated Orthodox Rites; it is generally regarded as irregular.

Jacobin Rite: Rebold says it was first known in 1736 and that it was created by the Pretender to the Scottish Throne about 1747. (See Jacobitism.)

Jacobites, The: Followers of the Stuarts in their claim for the throne. There was a Lodge of Jacobites in Rome as early as 1735-37.

Jacobitism and Freemasonry:

(A lecture delivered at Glasgow, January 9, 1872, under the auspices of St. Andrew's Royal Arch Chapter No. 69.)

In studying the popular Masonic accounts of the Order, the student's attention is arrested by manifold historical absurdities, and, to use a mild term, gross perversions of the fact. Personages are dragged in, either as Grand Masters or patrons, who never heard of our Society, and an importance is given to it, during the pre-Christian and the Middle Ages to which it can lay no claim. Indeed, till the beginning of last century, our Society, as it at present exists, was unknown; and the operative Masons neither possessed the organization, nor the public consideration, which the speculative now do. This, I believe, is the received opinion of all candid Masonic students. In fact, this is amply proved from a Crown charter granted in the 15th century, during the reign of Henry VI, wherein the Masons are styled "laborers." We also know that their position among the Serving Brethren, the third class of the Knights Templars was insignificant, and not to be compared with the smiths, farriers, or even the cooks. But, while denying that speculative Freemasonry is older than a couple of centuries, it must be kept in mind that much of the peculiar philosophy and doctrines adopted by its founders are as old as the first institutions of society. Among the Jewish Essenes, among the Ancient Egyptian and Greek mystagogues, among the Roman sodalities, and the societies of the Middle Ages, both Moorish and Christian, such as the Rosicrucian, the principles of brotherly love, relief and truth were well known and practiced. But it was when, by the progress of civil and religious liberty, the conservatism of guilds became dissolved, and the fetters which, under the feudal law, bound the different grades of society in iron bands, became loosed, that those principles settled in the building fraternity, and became the noble spirits which inhabit the temple of Freemasonry.

We find the name of Prince Charles Edward Stuart figuring among the votaries of Masonry, and preceding the rules of the Scottish Knights Templars an interesting, but most fallacious account of his connection with that Order. But this account was penned as a squib by the late Bro. Professor Aytoun, who always acknowledged it as an excellent piece of fooling, and no one was more surprised than he that such a manifest fable should have been accepted by any one as fact. The statement of Athole having robed him in the white cloak of the Templars is absurd, as that nobleman was far distant from Edinburgh at the period in question, and we suspect that the Prince had other business to attend to at that particular time than in attending meetings of the Freemasons or of a chivalric order. It must also be borne in mind that the Prince's proceedings while in Edinburgh are perfectly well known, and from the circumstances which I am about to lay before you, the proof is positive that he had no connection in 1745, either in Scotland or elsewhere, with any such secret society.

(If the account of the reception of Charles Edward Stuart, at Holyrood, into the *real* order of Knights Templars, and of his immediate election as Grand Master, in the stead of the Earl of Mar, was a *squib*, penned by Professor Aytoun, we would be glad to be furnished with the acknowledgment of the Professor that it was so, or the proof of the fact, if either acknowledgment or proof was published; for, on *this* side of the Atlantic, we have supposed the account to be a statement of actual facts, and we fail yet to see the wit or point of such a "squib" or practical joke.

We did not, indeed, suppose that the *true* Order of Templars had been continued in Scotland, nor that the Earl of Mar was legitimate Grand Master of the *real* Order of the Temple; and, being at a loss to know whence he derived what right he might have claimed, thought that he might have had somewhat such a title as the Duke of Sussex got from Paul, Emperor of Russia, when that crack-brained Monarch declared himself Grand Master of *all* the Templars.

And we never imagined that the supposed investiture at Holyrood was the reception into the Order of *Masonic* Knights Templars. No such Order was at that time known in Scotland or England.)

In 1717 the Grand Lodge of England was instituted, and, in 1736, that of Scotland. A complete account of the proceedings which led to the foundation of the latter will be found in the minutes of the Canongate Kilwinning, in which lodge William St. Clair, of Roslin, was initiated, and owing to the connection of his ancestors with the operative Masonry of the midland counties of Scotland, his claim to be the first Scottish Grand Master was pressed to a successful issue by the brethren of his mother lodge. Now, turning to the minutes of the Grand Lodge, during the year 1736 to 1750, the only events of importance mentioned are, the starting of a charity fund for the relief of distressed brothers; the interest which the Craft at large took in the Edinburgh Royal Infirmary; a claim on the part of Mother Kilwinning to have the first, instead of the second, place on the roll of daughter-lodges; and the foundation of a Provincial Grand Lodge in Turkey. Not one single statement appears relative to Jacobitism, and even the officers appear to have been Hanoverians, with one exception. It may be advanced that, in the doubtful circumstance of the Prince making good his father's claim to the crown, it would have been imprudent to have minuted anything, which, in the case of defeat, would have brought the Order into peril with the powers. The argument is sound, had the Order been at all Jacobitical; but this it never was. It held firmly by its principles of non-interference with Church and State; and so well was this established, that, when, in 1779 and 1817, acts were passed for the suppression of secret societies, a special clause was inserted in these, specially exempting the Freemasons from the penalties. But although the Freemasons, as a body, held loyal to the House of Hanover, many members joined the Stuart cause, and attempted, by their connection with Freemasonry, to make it a vehicle for the propagation of their favourite views. One of these brethren was Murray, of Broughton, a member of the Canongate Kilwinning, the brethren of which lodge, to a man—so far as can be known—were Jacobites.

(We have never supposed that the Grand Lodge of Scotland was a Jacobite body. But the fact is indisputable that Charles I was originally represented by Hiram. The names of the assassins in the ineffable degrees of the Rite of Perfection, prove that positively, and there is other evidence of it besides. Whether that degree was used during the exile of Charles II, by his adherents in France and Scotland, as a means of combined action, and mutual recognition, or whether it was invented and used in the latter part of the 17th century, by the adherents of the legitimate King of England (the Pretender), it may never be possible to know. It is very certain that the first lodge established in France, after 1717, was a Jacobite body, for the exiled Jacobite, Charles Radcliffe, brother of the last Earl of Derwentwater, was its first Master.)

I have stated that Prince Charles had no connection with the Freemasons, nor could he, with his religious bias, have had any sympathy with them. Although their interests pointed to an adherence to the Protestant faith, the last Stuarts were staunch and rigid Papists. From James II of Great Britain and Ireland—of whom Louis XIV, of France, was accustomed to say, with a sneer,

64

that he was a man who had given three crowns for a mass—down to Henry, Cardinal-Duke of York, who died in the present century, a pensioner of the British crown, not one would abandon his religion, even for the throne of these islands. In 1738, Clement XII published the first of those Papal bulls, of which we have heard so many thundering from the hand of the gentle Pius IX in these days, about our Masonic and anti-Papistic ears. As a Roman Catholic, Prince Charles could not have been a Freemason, for, although in the Romish creed the end justifies the means, it is questionable whether the Pope, even in the peculiar circumstances of the case, and though from the Roman exchequer funds were provided for the conquest of Britain, would have granted a dispensation in the Prince's favor. Doubtless Rome was profoundly interested in the success of the Stuart cause, and which she only abandoned on the dawning prospect of religious equality being permitted her votaries in these isles; but the spread of free thought in Italy and other Romish countries, now triumphant, touched her to the quick, and made her wary of seeming anyways the friend of so redoubtable an ally of civil and religious anti-papistical liberty. It has also been said that the Chevalier Ramsay, a devoted adherent of the Stuarts, was not only a Freemason, but the inventor of several Masonic degrees. Mr. William Pinkerton, in *Notes and Queries,* demolished this theory, for Ramsay, like his Prince, became a Roman Catholic, and died one. The Knights Templars, by a process most illegal and unjustifiable, conducted with a barbarity unparalleled in history, were dissolved by Papal warrant in 1312. The members of the Order entered that of the Hospitallers of St. John, and ceased to have any independent existence. In Scotland, by the form of legal documents, in deeds relating to Temple Lands, in possession of the Maltese Knights, the Templars are mentioned as conjoint with the Hospitallers, but never alone. But, even admitting, although it is an absurdity, that Templars existed in the days of Queen Mary, we know that the Maltese Order became then extinct in Scotland; and I defy any one to produce evidence of the meeting of a preceptory, commandery, or chapter of either of the Orders of the Temple or Hospital, between the date of the erection of Torphichen into a temporal barony, and the end of last century. Prince Charles could not have belonged to the Templars any more than to the Freemasons, and those who make such rash statements display, not only their ignorance of the commonest of historical studies, but a self-instructed credulity, or an atrocity of falsehood scarcely to be conceived. We are to believe that the Church of Rome, the infallible, had quietly broken through the decrees of the past, and without explanation, by permitting the Prince to become a Freemason and a Templar, acknowledged the errors of opinion of former Popes and Councils. This is absurd. It is, perhaps, an ungracious task to disabuse the fond dreams of many Masons of the truth of such stories; but, in a Society such as ours, founded upon the pillar of truth, the less we have to do with falsehood the better.

(That Prince Charles Edward Stuart, and the Chevalier Ramsay, were *Catholics,* is rather a thin foundation on which to rest a positive assertion, otherwise unsupported, that they *were* not Masons because they *could* not be. The writer forgets that at that day, the Pope had denounced Masons and Masonry, the first Bull having been issued in 1738, and that still the Order was *full* of Catholics, as, indeed, it has always been since, and is yet; dignitaries of the Church being members of it in France, as some are in Spanish countries at this day. There is no doubt that the Young Pretender was a Rose Croix, nor that Ramsay was a Mason of the High Degree.) (A.A.S.R. Bulletin, Vol. I.)

Jepthah's Daughter: A portion of the initiatory ceremony of the Order of the Eastern Star, traditionally known as "Adah" Point of the Star, and rehearsing a portion of the story of Jepthah and his Daughter.

Jericho, Heroine (or Hero) of: (See Heroine of Jericho.)

Jerusalem, Knight of: (See Knight of Jerusalem; see Prince of Jerusalem.)

Jerusalem, Order of: It is claimed that the Order came to England from America, but there are no available records to prove the statement. It was probably born on the Continent about 1791.

Jesters, Royal Order of: An organization composed of members of the Shrine and noted for their conviviality.

Jesuits: Active in the formation of the Chapter of Clermont. They are given some credit for the establishment of a 33° system to commemorate the thirty-three years of the life of the Saviour. (See Chapter of Clermont.)

Job's Daughters: (See Order of Job's Daughters.)

Johannite Masonry: Most of the regular lodges are "dedicated to two eminent patrons of Freemasonry, St. John the Baptist and St. John the Evangelist," hence lodges so dedicated are referred to as "St. John Lodges," and the practice of the Rite as Johannite Masonry.

Jordan Pass: One of the legends in Irish Masonry.

Junior Constellation of Stars: "Intended for teen-age girls; has a ritual, and is incorporated in New York as a sorority sponsored by the Order of the Eastern Star members" says the Muskogee Masonic Monthly.

Justification: One of the degrees in the Rite of Fessler.

Kabalah, The: Many of our Masonic degrees derive some of their doctrines from the Hebrew Kabalah (or Cabala). It is a sort of religious treatise not generally recognized by the Jewish people.

Kabalistic Companion: A degree of the French Philosophical Rite.

Kaditri, Order of: An Arabian secret society which is said to be formed along Masonic lines.

Kadosh: Among the Kadosh degrees are to be listed: Knight Kadosh, 30° of the A.A.S.R.; Kadosh, 10° of the Martinist Rite; Kadosh, Grand Elect Knight, 65° of the Rite of Misraim; Kadosh, Philosophic, a degree of the Grand Orient of France; Kadosh, Prince, one of the Pyron Collection; Kadosh, Prince of Death, 27° of the Rite of Mizraim. (See Knight Kadosh; see Council of Emperors of East and West.)

Kaes, Knight of: (See Knight of Kaes.)

Katipunan: A Philippine revolutionary organization headed by some who were active in Freemasonry during the Spanish ownership of the Islands. Emilio Aguinaldo, the great insurrectionist, was most active in the organization which contributed greatly to Philippine Independence. It taught Liberty, Equality, and Fraternity—three great Masonic principles. The Katipunan was a three degree system: 1°, Katipunan; 2°, Kawal; 3°, Bayani.

Kawal: The 2° of the Katipunan.

Key of Masonry: One of the degrees of the Council of Emperors of the East and West.

Kharbarites: A rival Masonic society (1730) in England. About the time it came into being, there was published an "Ode to the Grand Khaibar," which poked fun at the legendary history of Freemasonry.

66

Kilwinning, Knights of: One of the four degrees worked by the Baldwyn Encampment at Bristol, England; the date was 1802. The degree was founded in memory of a Scotch Knight who fought in the Crusades at the Battle of Ascalon, and who led his men to victory with the battle-cry "For the honor of Kilwinning, to the rescue."

Kilwinning Masonry: One of the most ancient lodges was that of Kilwinning, in Scotland. For many years it functioned as a supreme authority, long before a grand lodge for Scotland had been proposed. Just how many daughter lodges she had established prior to November, 1736, may never be known; there is definite evidence of eight. From the very first there was friction between "Mother" Kilwinning and the Grand Lodge of Scotland, and, although one of the founding lodges, she seceded in 1744 and the difference was not healed until 1807, when she returned to the Grand Lodge and was assigned "No. 0." During that period, Kilwinning had chartered at least 37 lodges. Kilwinning is a prominent name in Freemasonry, and many lodges proudly bear the title "Kilwinning."

Rebold says that the lodge at Kilwinning subsequently became the "Royal Grand Lodge and Chapter of the Order of Herodim of Kilwinning," and abandoning the administration of the first three degrees to the Grand Lodge of Scotland, reserved the right to confer the degrees of Templar and Scottish Master.

Kindred Degree: An androgynous degree based upon the Biblical story of Ruth and her gleaning in the fields of a Jewish gentleman named Boaz. The signet of recognition was composed of the letters: A.H.R.M.P.C.A.S.D.E., encircling the letter Ruth, arranged:

U
T H
R

The degrees were conferred upon Master Masons and their female relatives.

King David's Grand Lodge of Select and Most Excellent Architects: The governing body of the Ancient Free and Accepted Architects.

King of the Sanctuary: A degree in the Priestly Order of the Temple. It was also an old-side-degree requiring the presence of five Past Masters.

King of the World: A degree of the Philosophical Rite.

Knife and Fork Degree: Actually there is no such degree conferred in Freemasonry; the name is given to those social activities which follow the conferring of degrees; it is that portion of the ceremonies which has to do with luncheons, banquets, or outside activities, the Knife and Fork being, as might be supposed, the indispensable emblems. The letter "G" in the center of the crossed knife and fork is supposed to represent the word "Grub."

It is too bad that there are many who regard this as the supreme degree (?) conferred by the fraternity, yet it is around the banquet table that we enjoy the wholesome companionship of our brethren and rub shoulders with those with whom we like to associate.

Knight: One of the degrees of the African Architects.

Knight Adept: A degree in the Rite Elect of Truth. (Elus de Verite). The 3° of the Order of Christ.

Knight of the Alliance: The 14° of the Ancient Egyptian Reformed Rite.

Knight of the Altar: The 12° Rite of the East.

Knight of the American Eagle: An honorary degree in American midwest.

Knight of the Anchor: An androgynous degree; the 21° Metropolitan Chapter of France.

Knight Architect: The 12° of the Ancient Egyptian Reformed Rite.

Knight of the Argonauts: A degree of the Philosophic Scotch Rite, 6°.

Knight of Athens: The 52° of Mizraim; Fustier Rite; Philosophic Rite.

Knight of Aurora: Rite of Palestine (Knight of Palestine).

Knight of Banqueting Table of Seven Sages: Philosophic Scottish Rite.

Knight of Beneficence: The 49° of Metropolitan Chapter of France; Knight of perfect silence.

Knight Beneficent of the Holy City: In Europe the organization of Knights Beneficent of the Holy City is given the title *Chevaliers Bienfaisants de la Cite Sainte,* from which it derived the initials C.B.C.S., by which it is best known in the United States.

Practically, it is the old Rite of Strict Observance which at one time had Provinces scattered throughout Europe. In the beginning it maintained the right of conferring the symbolic degrees, but in recent years has retained no such claim because of the Grand Lodge system which has grown up throughout the world.

Its origin was due to one Baron Carl G. von Hund in 1754. In the beginning it had six degrees, but later a seventh was added, although never officially adopted. There are now four Great Priories in the world—Switzerland, France, England and the United States. Its character naturally differs in each country. In England it is regarded as the highest honor given in the Great Priory K.T. of England, and membership is strictly limited. In Switzerland, it is the Great Priory of Helvetia which is on a par with the Grand Encampment of the United States.

The literature of the organization states its purpose is to

"maintain and strengthen among its members the following principles: Attachment to the spirit of Christianity and belief in the Supreme Power as designated under the name of the Supreme Architect of the Universe; Devotion to Country; Individual Perfection by the work which every man must do within himself for subduing his passions, correcting his faults and making intellectual progress; the exercise of an enlightened charity toward all mankind without regard to nationality, political opinions, religious convictions or social status."

The peculiar degrees of this Order are known as (a) Scottish Master of St. Andrew and Perfect Master of St. Andrew; (b) Squire Novice; (c) Knight Beneficent of the Holy City.

The presiding officer of a Great Priory is known as the Great Prior; the term of office is two years. Membership is by invitation, requiring the approval of each member.

The Great Priory of America was established in 1934 at Raleigh, N. C., by Dr. William Moseley Brown and J. Raymond Shute II, both of whom had received the various grades on a visit to Geneva, Switzerland. Other names were added until there were fourteen founders. Annual meetings are held in Washington, D. C., in February each year. Under an agreement with the Great Priory of Switzerland, the number of members may not exceed 81.

Knight of Bethany: The 6° of the Knight Templar Priests.

Knight of the Black Cross: The 5° of the Knight Templar Priests.

Knight of the Black Eagle: The 5° of the Order of Christ; 76° Metropolitan Chapter of France; 38° Rite of Mizraim.

Knight of the Black Eagle or Rose Croix: A degree of the Philosophic Scotch Rite; it is divided into two parts.

Knight of the Brazen Serpent: The 25° of the A.A.S. Rite.

Knight of the Bridge: The 19° of the Ancient Egyptian Reformed Rite.

Knight of Brightness: The 7° and last Clerks of Strict Observance.

Knight of the Burning Bush: Theosophic degree of the Philosophic Scottish Rite.

Knight of Chanuca: The 69° Rite of Mizraim.

Knight of Christ: Spanish successors of the Templars.

Knight of the Christian Mark: The 1° in the Order of Knight Templar Priests. A degree in the Early Grand Rite of Scotland. It was one of the four Mark degrees worked by that body. It is usually worked in a conclave of Red Cross of Constantine; a candidate represents one of the guards supplied by the Grand Master of the Knights of St. John to Pope Alexander. It is the 1° of the Council of Trinity, where it is referred to as "Knight of the Christian Mark and Guard of the Conclave." It was once conferred in the U.S.A. on Templars.

Knight of Columns: The 7° Rite of the East.

Knight of the Comet: In the Hecart Collection.

Knight Commander: A grade in the Order of Amaranth; a grade in the Rite of Elected Cohens; a grade in the Priestly Order of the Temple; 9° Rite of Elect Cohens. A degree in the Early Grand Rite of Scotland.

Knight Commander Court of Honor: Commonly referred to as the "KCCH" as distinguished from the "KYCH." It is an honor conferred by the Supreme Council of the Scottish Rite of the Southern Jurisdiction for meritorious service rendered by 32° Freemasons. It is not a degree, but an investiture; the ceremony was written by Albert Pike, but was never adopted by any other Supreme Council. Members wear a red cap; when advanced to the 33°, it is replaced by a white cap.

Knight Commander of the Temple: The 27° of the A.A.S.R.

Knight Commander of the White and Black Eagle: The 80° of the Metropolitan Chapter of France.

Knight Companion: Appellation given to members of the Red Cross of Constantine. The 2° Rite of Adoption; degree in the Early Grand Rite of Scotland.

Knights of the Conclave: (See Christian Mark.)

Knight of Constantinople: The degree is associated with the Emperor Constantine, and inculcates universal equality. The jewel is a cross surmounted by a crescent moon, not exactly a Christian symbol, for it infers the Crescent has overcome the Cross.

The degree is in the repertoire of the Allied Masonic degrees, but it is seldom conferred. Mackey's statements constitute the earlist reference we have to the degree; it was unknown in U.S.A. as far back as 1831; at that time, Avery Allen in his expose gives an outline of the ritual which has been changed little; there it was said to have been an honorary degree which one Mason might confer on another after the regular business of a lodge or chapter had been completed. This latter antedates Mackey's reference by 20 years.

This degree often referred to as above, but should more properly be called "Knight of Constantine." It is a side degree, the legend with which it is connected going back to the time of Constantine Porphyregenitus, who became

69

Emperor in 911 A. D. It may be conferred upon any Master Mason by those in legal possession of it, provided five other Knights are present at the time.

Bodies of this group are called "Preceptories." Its presiding officer is an "Eminent Preceptor." The dress is black coat and trousers, hat, sword, and spurs.

The ritual teaches a fine lesson in Equality and Humility—that Masonic honors should be given only as a reward of merit; another lesson taught is Justice, that we should be assured of the truth of an accusation before condemning.

And there is a very extensive lecture which has no historical or Masonic background, attempting to connect the legendary Constantine with the Masonic Fraternity—statements which no student of Masonic history will support.

In 1865, Major F. G. Irwin introduced this Grade to several English Brethren in Devonport, England. Amongst those who received the ceremony at that time was Brother W. J. Hughan, the noted Masonic writer. Hughan states that Brother Irwin received the Grade in Malta and organized it in Devonport and Plymouth, in both of which places it was worked many years after the England Grand Council A.M.D., was formed. Therefore, the year 1865 may be assigned as the date of its Masonic foundation (see p. 46, Transactions of Lodge of Research No. 2429, Leicester, 1906-08).

In America, records are available as early as January 14, 1892. There is no doubt that still earlier records will some day be uncovered.

There is a bare possibility that the Knight of Constantinople is traceable, in legend, to the same source as, or directly from, the Red Cross of Constantine. This is stated in face of the fact that the two Grades have nothing in common save the characters found in each. Yet, it appears likely that a knowledge of these two characters in a Masonic setting would be necessary for the invention of the Knight of Constantinople.

The jewel of the Grade is a Maltese Cross, surmounted by a Crescent, in gold, suspended from a green ribbon, on which are three poniards, in gold. This Jewel, like the others, is to be worn as a breast Jewel.

The Apron of the Grade is white, trimmed with green, having a Maltese Cross surmounted by a crescent in the centre, while on the flap appears the three poniards, all of which is in green.

The name was also given to a side degree invented some say, in America. We are told it could be conferred by any Master Mason, who is possessed of its secrets, on another; but there is a ritual for its full performance, though, as a degree.

Knight of the Cork: An androgynous Italian society.

Knight of the Courts: The 3° Rite of the East.

Knight of the Crown: Pyron collection.

Knight of the Crusades: The 17° of the Ancient Egyptian Reformed Rite.

Knight of Death: The 4° in the Knight Templar Priests. It was also a degree in the Early Grand Rite of Scotland.

Knights of the Desert: (See Desert, Knights of.)

Knight of the Door: The 4° Rite of the East.

Knight of the Dove: Androgynous French degree of 1784.

Knight of the Eagle: The 30° of the Ancient Egyptian Reformed Rite; it also appears in the Clerks of the Relaxed Observance; 1° Chapter of

70

Clermont; 56° Metropolitan Chapter of France; Grand Lodge Royal York of Berlin; 37° Rite of Mizraim.

Knight of the Eagle and Pelican: Sovereign Prince Rose Croix of Herodom: The name by which the 18° is known in the A. A. Rite of England.

Knight of the Eagle Reversed: Conferred by Lodge St. Louis des Amis.

Knight of the East: The 11° Adonhiramite Rite; degree in the Knight Masons of Ireland; 5° Rite of Philalethes; degree in the II Class in the Rite of Elected of Truth (Elus de Verite); third Order of the Rose Croix of the Modern French Rite; 15° A.A.S.R.; 6° French Rite; 6° Royal York Berlin; 15° Chapter of Emperors of East and West; 52° Metropolitan Chapter of France; 41° Rite of Mizraim.

One of the most popular degrees of Continental Freemasonry, known in France as "Chevalier d'Orient," and appearing in various rites, such as the Adonhiramite Rite; the Knight Masons of Ireland; the Rite of Philalethes; in the II Class of the Elected of Truth; the third order of the Rose Croix of the Modern French Rite; the Rite of Royal York of Berlin; Rite of Mizraim; Chapters of Emperors of the East and West; Metropolitan Chapter of France, and here in the United States where it appears as the 11° of the American Rite under the title of "Illustrious Order of the Red Cross," the legend being the same in each of the above rites. It is to be found in the Ancient and Accepted Rite in a different form as the 17° of that rite.

Knight of the East, Victorious: From the Hecart Collection.

Knight of the East, White: The 40° of Mizraim.

Knight of the East and West: The 17° A.A. Rite in England; a degree of the Rite of Perfection or Harodom; a degree in the Knight Masons of Ireland; 17° of the Chapter Emperors of the East and West.

Knight of the Eastern Star: The 57° Metropolitan Chapter of France.

Knight of Eclecticism and of Truth: The 5° of the Persian Rite.

Knight of the Elect: The 9° of the Ancient Egyptian Reformed Rite.

Knight Elect of 12: The 11° of the A.A.S.R.

Knight Elect of 15: The 10° Ancient Egyptian Reformed Rite; 16° A.A.S.R.; 10° Emperors of East and West; 11° Mizraim.

Knight of Election: The 33° of Mizraim.

Knight of Election, Sublime: The 34° of Mizraim.

Knight Evangelist: Conferred by Lodge St. Louis des Amis at Calais.

Knight of the Garter: Probably another name for one of the degrees invented by the Early Grand Scotch Rite. (See Order of the Garter.)

Knight of the Golden Circle: A semi-military secret society which appeared in the U.S.A. between 1851-54, whose object was to "restore the Union"; it was organized by Democrats in opposition to Republican policies; its name was changed in 1863 to the Order of American Knights, and in 1864 to Sons of Liberty; it was not Masonic. At one time it had between 250,000 and 300,000 members.

Knight of the Golden Eagle: Pyron Collection.

Knight of the Golden Fleece: The 7° of the Philosophic Scotch Rite; 6° Hermetic Montpellier Rite; (See Golden Fleece).

Knight of the Golden Key (or Initiatory Degree): One of the grades in the Order of the Golden Key.

Knight of the Golden Star: Peuvret Collection.

71

Knight of the Grand Arch: Conferred in Lodge St. Louis des Amis.

Knight Grand Commander: An honorary title conferred by the Priestly Order of the Temple.

Knights Grand Cross: Those who have been created Knights Grand Cross; the appellation appears in the Red Cross of Constantine and is an award given by Supreme Councils of the Scottish Rite. The Allied Masonic Degrees controls such a grade and it is conferred upon Sovereigns of that Order following their installation. A degree in the Early Grand Rite of Scotland.

Knight Grand Elect Kadosh: (See Kadosh.)

Knight Grand Inspector: The 20° of the Ancient and Primitive Rite; it is the last of the series conferred by the Senate (2d Class). Its emblem is the double-headed eagle with the Hermetic Cross on its breast. The candidate takes five obligations, one to the flag of his country; second, to the banners of the Rite; third, fidelity to the secrets; fourth, duty to his brethren; and, lastly, general obligation, being crowned with a civic crown, a wreath of cypress and a crown of roses. The lecture is a eulogy upon ancient and modern Freemasonry and the blessings which it has conferred upon mankind.

Knight of Harodim: The 13° of the Knight Templar Priests.

Knights and Heroines of the Anchor: Replaced the Felicitares. (See Anchor, Order of.)

Knight Hermetic Philosopher: The 17° of the Ancient and Primitive Rite, its ceremonial embracing a description of the cross and the cabalistic signification of the letters I.N.R.I., to which a moral application was assigned in the degree of Rose Croix. The lecture is a Hermetic explanation of nature's mysteries.

Knight of the Holy City: (See Knight Beneficent of the Holy City.)

Knight of the Holy Cross: The 28° of the Knight Templar Priests.

Knight of the Holy Grave: The 21° of the Knight Templar Priests. This is not the same as Knight of the Holy Sepulchre; it may have once been a part of another degree.

Knight of Holy Land: (See Holy Land, Knight of.)

Knight of the Holy Sepulchre: A degree in the Early Grand Rite of Scotland; the 2° of the Council of Trinity; 5° Metropolitan Chapter of France. There is a ritual of this degree in the Histoire des Ordres Militaires ou des Chevaliers, printed in Amsterdam in 1721. According to that, the degree, or Order, was instituted by St. James, first Bishop of Jerusalem. The 9° of Knight Templar Priests.

Tradition says that it was instituted by St. Helena after her discovery of the true cross; she was the mother of Constantine. It is distinctly a Christian degree and religious ceremony, the obligation requiring defense of the church. (See Sepulchre, Order of.)

Knight of the Holy Virgin Mary: The 22° of the Knight Templar Priests.

Knight Hospitaller: Sometimes called "Knight Hospitaller of St. John of Jerusalem." It is said to have been organized about 700-760, and was one of the great monastic orders of the Crusade period. (See Knight of Malta; see Hospitaller of St. John of Jerusalem.)

Knight Illustrious or Elect: The 13° of Misraim.

Knight of the Interior: The 5° of the East.

Knight of Intimate Initiate: The 4° of the Order of the Temple.

72

Knight of Iris: The 4° in the Philosophic Scotch Rite, Hermetic Rite of Montpellier.

Knight of Israel: The 8° of the Ancient Egyptian Reformed Rite.

Knight of Jericho: A male member of the "Heroines of Jericho."

Knight of Jerusalem: The 16° of the Ancient Egyptian Reformed Rite; 65° Metropolitan Chapter of France.

Knight of Jupiter: The 78° of Peuvret Collection.

Knight of Justice: Knights Hospitaller so-called.

Knight of Kabbala: The 8° Metropolitan Chapter of France.

Knight of Kadosh: The 30° of the A.A.S.R.; a degree in the Martinist Rite; 14° Rite of Memphis.

Knight Kaes: The 7° of the Order of Christ.

Knight of Kilwinning: (See Kilwinning Masonry; see Rite, Kilwinning.)

Knight and Ladies of the Cross: It is the degree of "Good Samaritan"; 3° of the True Kindred.

Knights and Ladies of the Dove: In 1784 a secret society of both sexes was framed on the model of Freemasonry; its meetings were held at Versailles under the title of Chevaliers et Chevalieres de la Colombe. Its existence, we believe, was of brief duration.

Knight Levite: (See Fratres Lucis.)

Knight of Libanus: The 22° of the Ancient Egyptian Reformed Rite.

Knight of Lilies of the Valley: A Templar appendage.

Knight of the Lion: The 20° Metropolitan Chapter of France.

Knight Mahadon: Conferred by St. Louis Lodge des Amis.

Knight of Malta: The Knight of Malta as a Masonic grade, was, under the old constitution, an appendant to that of the Knights Templars. This is the second degree (or Order) of the Templar chivalric system. Its ritual is decidedly Christian and deals with the story of the Knights of Malta from the time they left Jerusalem until they reached their final home on the Island of Malta. The ceremony of initiation contains many Christian references and is full of Christian symbolism. The present day ceremonies follow those of the original Order so far as is possible; but in the ancient order those in charge were priests and officials of the Church.

There is a Catholic organization of Knights of Malta, plainly not a part of the Masonic Order, and in nowise connected. There is still another group in Pennsylvania which is not Masonic. (See Knights Templar.)

Knight of Masonry: LePage Collection.

Knight Masons of Ireland: The Order of Knight Masons of Ireland is, as may be inferred, an Irish organization. Its headquarters are at Freemasons Hall, Dublin. There are four Provincial Grand Superintendents governing different areas—three in Ireland and one in the United States of America. The chief officer is known as Great Chief. The Grand Council of the Order meets four times a year in Dublin, and there carries on the business of the organization.

The present organization was formed in Dublin June 18, 1923, and reached the United States May 20, 1936, when it formed a Council in North Carolina. There are, in 1954, fifty-six Councils working under the Grand Council of Knight Masons. There are four Councils in the United States of America— St. Patricks in America No. 26, at Monroe, N. C.; Shamrock, Thistle and

Rose No. 27, at Raleigh, N. C.; Harp, Cross and Eagle No. 28, at Warrenton (Voorhis history says Wilson), N. C.; Paumanok No. 32, Garden City, L. I., N. Y.; Gateway of the West No. 58, at Pittsburgh, Pa. Recently a Council was constituted at Lagos, in Nigeria, Africa.

The degrees were once the property of Knights Templar in Ireland and were referred to as "The Grand Degrees." They are four in number; (a) Knight of the Sword; (b) Knight of the East; (c) Knight of the East and West; (d) Installed Excellent Chief. The fourth degree might be considered similar in character to that of the Order of High Priesthood.

In 1937, the Deputy Great Chief, Sir Edward Burne, with associates, came to the United States and constituted a Provincial Grand Council. With the formation of two Councils in the northern jurisdiction, it was thought necessary to establish two jurisdictions, one for the northern territory and one for the southern territory, but in 1950 they were again combined into one jurisdiction. Since membership is by invitation, the number is necessarily small, not exceeding 150.

The Order seems to bear the approval of the Grand Lodge of Ireland since its official list of Councils and other material appears in the annual directory of that Grand Lodge.

Knight of the Mediterranean Pass: An honorary degree conferred on Knights Templar as Knights of Malta, under the old constitution. The degree is said to have originated from the following circumstance: In an excursion of the Knights of Malta into the Kingdom of Naples, while crossing the river Offanto (the ancient Aufidus), they were attacked by a very superior force of Turks. However, notwithstanding the disparity of numbers, the Knights succeeded in obtaining a complete victory, the Moslems being entirely routed, and the river dyed with their blood. As a reward for the valour displayed by these Knights, they had granted to them free permission to pass and repass at every port in the Mediterranean in possession of the Christians. The legend of the degree relates that this event occurred in 1367, nearly 200 years before the Knights of St. John, or Rhodes as then called, obtained Malta. At this period the Knights, headed by the Grand Master Raymond Berenger, with a large naval force attacked the Ottoman corsairs in the Mediterranean and chased them into the port of Alexandria, but were compelled at last to retire before the superior force of the Sultan of Egypt.

Knight of the Morning Star: Philosophic Rite. (See Knight of Hope.)

Knight of the Ninth Arch: The 13° A.A.S.R.

Knight Noachite: The 21° of the Ancient Egyptian Reformed Rite.

Knight of the North: The 14° of the Knight Templar Priests. Conferred in Lodge St. Louis des Amis Reunis.

Knight Novice: Degrees of the Fratres Lucis, which include Novice of the third, fifth and seventh years.

Knights and Nymphs of the Rose: An order of Adoptive or Androgynous Masonry, invented towards the close of the 18th century by M. de Chaumont, the Masonic Secretary to the Duc de Chartres. The only establishment known was in Paris; the place of meeting was called the Temple of Love. It was ornamented with garlands of flowers, and hung round with escutcheons, on which were painted various devices and scenes of gallantry. There were two presiding officers, the man being styled the Hierophant, the female the High Priestess. The former initiated men, the latter women. The Conductor Assistant of the men was called Sentiment, that of the women Discretion. The Knights wore a crown of myrtle, the Nymphs a crown of roses. The Hierophant and High Priestess wore in addition a rose-coloured scarf, on which were embroidered two devices within a myrtle wreath. One dull taper was the only light during the initiation; at the closing business the hall was illuminated by numerous wax candles. When a candidate was to be initiated, he or she was taken in charge by Sentiment or Discretion, divested of all weapons, jewels, or money, hood-winked, and loaded with chains, and conducted to the door of the Temple of Love, where admission was demanded by two knocks. When admitted and presented, the candidate was asked his or her name, country, condition in society, and having answered these questions was asked: "What are you now seeking?" To this the answer was "happiness." The interrogatory then proceeds a little further, "What is your age?" and the candidate has, if a male, to reply "The age of love"; the female, "The age to please and to be loved." The candidate's feelings and opinions on matters of gallantry are further probed, and all being satisfactory, the chains are removed and replaced by garlands of flowers, which are called "the chains of love."

After some probationary exercises of a like character, the O.B. is administered:

"I promise and swear by the Grand Master of the Universe never to reveal the secrets of the Order of the Rose, and should I fail in this my vow, may the mysteries I shall receive add nothing to my pleasures, and instead of the roses of happiness may I find nothing but thorns of repentance."

The candidates were then conducted to the mysterious groves in the neighbourhood of the Temple of Love, and during the time there spent, slow and delicious music in march style is played. These trials ended, the novice is next conducted to the altar of mystery, placed at the foot of the Hierophant's throne, and there incense is offered to Venus and her son Cupid; a brief space spent there, and after some more ceremonies of a like character, the bandage is removed from the novitiate's eyes, and with delicious music and in a brilliantly lighted apartment, the signs and secrets are communicated.

All the information here given is gathered from Clavel, "Maconnerie Pittoresque."

Knight of the Order of Christ: The 8° of the Order of Christ.

Knight of the Orient: The 10° of the Ancient Primitive Rite. (See Ancient and Primitive Rite; see Knight of the East.)

Knight of Paisley Abbey: In 1810 the Knights at Paisley Abbey petitioned membership in the Grand Imperial Council of Scotland, and were received— the last of the Grand Encampment Conclaves to join.

Knight of Palestine: The 27° of the Knight Templar Priests; 63° of Mizraim; 9° Reformed Rite of St. Martin; in the Baldwyn Encampment list. (Also called Chevalier d'Palestine-French.)

Knight of the Palm Tree: (See Order Knights of the Palm Tree.)

Knight of the Passage: A degree of the Fessler Rite.

Knight of Patmos: The 3° of the Knight Templar Priests. It had a place in the Irish Templar system.

Knight of the Pelican: The 18° of the Ancient Egyptian Reformed Rite.

Knight Perfect: Ancient Chapter of Clermont.

Knight of Perfumes: The 8° of Rite of the East.

75

Knight of the Phoenix: The 4° of the Philosophic Scotch Rite.

Knight Priest: (See Fratres Lucis.)

Knight Priest of Jerusalem: The 26° of The Knight Templar Priests.

Knight of the Propaganda: The 29° of the Ancient Reformed Egyptian Rite.

Knight Prussian: The 35° Rite of Mizraim.

Knight of the Prussian Eagle: Recart Collection.

Knight of Pure Truth: A Jesuit society.

Knight of the Purificatory: The 7° and last degree of Clerks of Strict Observance.

Knight of the Rainbow: The 68° of Mizraim.

Knight of the Red Cross: The first of the degrees conferred in a commandery of Knights Templar, where it is referred to as the "Illustrious Order of the Red Cross." It is a case of an Order being conferred within the body of a degree. The degree is not used in England or Scotland as a part of the Templar system. The story is the same as that of the 15° of the Ancient and Accepted Scottish Rite. It is not the Red Cross of the Constantine group.

Knight of the Red Cross of Constantine: (See Constantine, Red Cross of.)

Knight of the Red Eagle: The Order was said to have been instituted in 1705 by a Prince of Beyreuth; the symbol of the Red Eagle was taken from the coat of arms of the Brandenburgs; it began as the 39° of the Rite of Misraim and was later placed in the Prussian group of degrees. In the French it was referred to as the "Chevalier de l'Aigle, Rouge."

Knight of Redemption of the Road: The 30° of the Knight Templar Priests.

Knight of Rhodes: In 1309 these knights seized the Island of Rhodes, which they held for more than two centuries, until driven out by Soliman the Magnificent, of the Ottoman Empire; ultimately, they occupied the Island of Malta which was ceded them by Spain in 1530. In their new location they were called "Knights of Malta." (See Knight of Malta.) The Order gave the first idea for forming hospitals in England, where they were called "stranger houses," affording comfort to the sick and weary traveler.

Knight of the Road: An illiterate rendering of Knight of Rhodes and Malta; a tramp is sometimes referred to as a "Knight of the Road."

Knight of Rome: (See Constantine, Red Cross of.)

Knight of the Rosae Cross: The 19° of the Knight Templar Priests.

Knight of the Rose: An androgynous degree.

Knight of the Rose Croix: (See Rose Croix.)

Knight of Rose Croix (Cabalistic and Hermetic): (See Rose Croix.)

Knight of Rosy Cross of St. Andrew: A degree of the Early Grand Rite of Scotland.

Knight, Rosy and Triple Cross: Conferred by Lodge St. Louis des Amis Reunis.

Knight of the Round Table: The name "Knights of the Round Table" has a very distinct appeal to the average person, bringing to our minds the stories of Knighthood and such Knights as Sir Galahad, the Holy Grail, and the Great Crusades. It is not at all surprising to find the counterpart in the Masonic rites and degrees of the 17th and 18th centuries.

There are many versions of the ritual. Moses Holbrook, whose note-book supplies so many of these side-degrees has been the source of one ritual whose date is supposed to have been about 1809-17. In the Masonic Monthly, Vol. III, page 524, is another, taken from a manuscript of Benjamin Gleason, early day teacher of Masonic ritual, whose date is about 1827. A third ritual appears in the History of Cryptic Masonry (Hinman, Denslow, Hunt) Volume II, page 1186. This latter ritual was conferred in Columbian Council No. 1 of New York City in 1810.

"Collectanea" refers to the degree appearing in the Lodge St. Louis des Amis Reunis (Calais) and a *Knight of the Round Table of King Arthur* in the Primitive Rite.

The second of the rituals refers to the birth of the Order of England about 500 A.D. in a refectory at Glastonbury Abbey. There are seven officers: (1) Abbot of Glastonbury; (2) Prelate; (3) Standard Bearer; (4) Verger; (5) Sword Bearer; (6) Recorder-Treasurer, and (7) Warder or Guard. Templars will note the similarity to present day names. Members carry banners, arms, and emblems to form a pageant. It is a degree of Hospitality, commemorating the beneficence of the Great Prince Arthur. The East is vacant.

Among the emblems are the English arms of King Arthur's day; a banner with the Emblems of Mortality; the Hour Glass, and the Cross. The degree is a rich and beautiful pageant, ending with the table of Hospitality in allusion to the Round Table in Glastonbury which was always supplied with meat, food and drink.

In the third ritual is found much of the above ceremonies; there are five banners (Templars note similarity to Malta Order). A procession was divided into five sections each headed by a Banner:

1. Arthur the Good, yellow banner, born 486.
2. Arthur the Valiant, red banner, fought the Saxons, 515.
3. Arthur the Just, blue banner, Crowned King, 510.
4. Arthur the Charitable, white banner, established the Order, 516.
5. Arthur died at Winchester, black banner, buried 542.

The obligation of a Knight of the Round Table was a series of questions:

Will you help and assist a worthy poor Knight with your purse and counsel?
Will you tender him meat, drink, and lodging to the best of your abilities?
Will you defend him in danger and vindicate his character?
Do you swear on the Holy Missal to defend your country against any invader, to protect our Sovereign and the Holy Mother Church, and do you promise not to be concerned in heresy, schism, and rebellion, under the penalty of being dishonored and despised by every worthy Knight?

The novitiate responds:

I do promise all this in the name of God. Amen.

(He kisses the Mass Book; the Sovereign presents sword.)

Valorous Knight of the Round Table, take this sword, defend your Honor, keep it untarnished, fight for your King, your Country, and the Holy Mother Church, by so doing you will obtain honor here and happiness hereafter.

Arise, Sir Knight A. B. of the Most Honorable Order of the Round Table.

All then sit around the Round Table, partaking of food and drink, then forming in Procession, move around the table singing an Ode which completes the ceremony.

This degree was conferred in Columbian Council No. 1, New York, during the first eight years of its existence. With it was associated the degree Knight of the Honorable Order of the Garter. See "Order of the Garter."

According to tradition, the Order of the Round Table dates from 516 A.D., and that happens to be the date of King Arthur's greatest exploit.

The story of the Round Table is one of the legendary myths connected with King Arthur, the traditional British King of whom many marvelous stories have been told. Many stories connect King Arthur's Court with Freemasonry, particularly those which deal with the search for the Holy Grail. Mackey says: "When the Knights of the Round Table were established, King Arthur told them that the San Graal should be discovered by one of them, but that he only could see it who was without sin. One day when Arthur was holding the high feast with his Knights, the San Graal suddenly appeared to him, and as suddenly disappeared," whereupon all the Knights took a solemn vow to seek the holy dish and the quest became one of the myths of what has been called the "Arthuric Cycle." It reminds Freemasons of their quest for the Lost Word, for the symbolism is identical, the loss and the recovery being but the lesson of death and eternal life.

Knight of the Rower: Androgynous French, 1738.

Knight of the Royal Arch: A degree of the Helvetic Rite in which the candidate discovers the Sacred Word upon a triangular delta. It follows the Enoch legend. The degree contains complete instructions as to the history of the arches and Solomon's suggestions about the Temple. It is understood that such a degree, or honor, is being conferred in at least one Grand Chapter of Royal Arch Masons as an award for service to the rite.

Knight of the Royal Axe: The 22° A.A.S.R. (See Prince Libanus.)

Knight of the Royal Mystery: The 17° of the Rite of Memphis.

Knight of the Royal T of King Arthur: (See Ancient and Primitive Rite.)

Knight Royal Victorious: Chapter G.O. Bologne.

Knight of St. Andrew: The 29° of the Ancient and Accepted Rite; a degree of the Clerks of Strict Observance.

Knight of St. John: The 8° of the Knight Templar Priests. (See Constantine, Red Cross of.) A degree in the Early Grand Rite of Scotland.

Knight of St. John the Baptist: The 18° of the Knight Templar Priests.

Knight St. John the Evangelist: Of Asia, 1786.

Knight of St. John of Jerusalem: The ceremonial for this Order appears in Vol. V, part II of *Collectanea,* as copied from a manuscript in the British Museum; it closely resembles the Order of Malta ceremonial.

Knights of St. John and Malta: An English organization which came to America about 1874. It is not Masonic. It has twenty-one degrees, four of which are conferred in "encampments," and seventeen in a "College of Ancients." The latter degree is awarded for merit.

Knight of St. Paul: The 2° of the Knight Templar Priests.

Knight of St. Paul or the Mediterranean Pass: A degree in Early Grand Rite of Scotland. (See Knights of Mediterranean Pass.)

Knight Sage of Truth: The 16° of the Knight Templar Priests.

Knight of the Sacred Arch: The 6° of the Ancient and Primitive Rite; its scene is laid in the audience chamber of King Solomon. Its ceremonial refers to the preparation for Solomon's Temple, when the workmen discovered the Temple of Nine Arches erected by Enoch before the flood; reference to the tradition is to be found in the "Book of Enoch," but this is curious, as the degree is far more ancient than the rediscovery of the lost Book of Enoch. The degree explains the assistance which Solomon received from the Mysteries of Egypt. The moral is that labor in the Nine Arches of the Great Cause is necessary to those who would know the Truth. There is a possibility that the degree of Select Master may have been derived from this degree.

Knight of the Sacred Delta: The 26° of the Ancient Egyptian Reformed Rite.

Knight of the Sacred Fire: The 27° of the Ancient Egyptian Reformed Rite.

Knight of the Sacred Mountain: Conferred by Lodge St. Louis des Amis.

Knight Sacrificing: Conferred by Lodge St. Louis des Amis.

Knight Sage of Truth: The 16° of the Ancient and Primitive Rite; the ceremonial teaches that God and Truth are One, and that man's happiness is a matter of his own creation; the lecture treats of the knowledge of the Chaldean and Egyptian Magi.

Knight of the Sanctuary: The 16° of the Knight Templar Priests; 11° of the Rite of the East.

Knight of the Scarlet Cord: (See Order of the Scarlet Cord; see Secret Monitor.)

Knight of the Secret: The 4° of the Ancient Egyptian Reformed Rite.

Knight of the Secret Vault: The 13° of the Ancient Egyptian Reformed Rite; 7° of the Ancient and Primitive Rite.

Knight of the Sepulchre: Royal York of Berlin.

Knight of the Serpent: The 15° of the Ancient and Primitive Rite.

Knight of the Serpent of Sinai: The 25° of the Ancient Egyptian Reformed Rite.

Knight of the South: The 15° of the Knight Templar Priests. Pyron Collection.

Knight of the Sun: The 28° A.A.S.R. Old Kent Lodge No. 15 (England) had a warrant empowering it to confer seven degrees, among which was the Knight of the Sun; it was the 3° of the Philosophic Scotch Rite; also the 28° of the Ancient Egyptian Reformed Rite. A degree of the Council of Emperors of the East and West.

Knight of the Sword: A writer in 1789, alluding to the legend of the Knight of the Sword degrees, of the then French Rite of Perfection says: "It is the same as the Irish Royal Arch and lately, with some enthusiasts, the Red Cross." While similar to the Irish Red Cross, in many respects it is quite different. (See K.T. of the East.) The 15° of the Ancient Egyptian Reformed Rite.

Knight of the Sword of the East: The 15° of the Ancient and Accepted Rite. A degree of the Rite of Perfection.

Knight of the Tabernacle: The title was used in lieu of that of "Knight Templar." The 29° of the Knight Templar Priests.

Knight of the Tabernacle of Divine Truths: Fustier system.

Knight Templar: The 29° in the Early Grand Rite of Scotland. (See United Religious and Military Orders of the Temple and of St. John of Jerusalem, Palestine, Rhodes, and Malta.)

Knight Templar of Jerusalem: One of the Helvetic degrees (?) said to be "Primitively Hospitaller and now Knights of Malta." The candidate is

79

given a pilgrim's robe, sandals, leather cap, script, and long staff. The words Alpha and Omega are used, as well as words found in the present day Templar ritual. The penalty closes with a threat of "excommunication of ye Roman Church."

Knight Templar Priest: The Holy Royal Arch Knight Templar Priests Order is comparatively new in American Freemasonry, but its records go back to at least 1806, and probably many years previous to that, for there is on file in the Lodge of Research CC, in Ireland, a certificate of the Dublin Union Band, which was the precursor of the Templar Priest Order. This certificate listed among its virtues, "Wisdom, Strength, Beauty, Truth, Power, Glory, Light." There is also contained in the certificate the expression:

"He that overcometh will I make a Pillar in the Temple of my God." Another quotation says: "Wisdom has builded her house. She hath hewn out her Seven Pillars. The light that cometh from wisdom shall never go out."

The first reference we have to the organization is in Ireland, and there are numerous certificates issued by the Order still in existence. Later it was organized in England by the well known John Yarker, and still later, 1933, introduced into the United States by the late Sydney C. Bingham, of New Zealand, who came to the United States that year and organized three Tabernacles, the number necessary to establish a Grand Tabernacle. Twenty-four Tabernacles were established in the United States up until 1953, these were in Arkansas, Illinois, Indiana, Iowa, Kentucky, Maryland, New Jersey, New Mexico, New York, North Carolina, Ohio; Oklahoma, Oregon, Pennsylvania, Texas, Virginia, West Virginia, Wisconsin; one Tabernacle is located in Nova Scotia.

Meetings are referred to as *Ingatherings*. Membership is limited to those who have been installed Commanders of Commanderies of Knights Templar. In the United States, annual proceedings are issued and the total membership, in 1953, was slightly more than 300. It is ruled by a Grand College, within whose bosom there is a Chapter General consisting of not more than 12 Knights Grand Commanders and 144 Knights Commanders; the presiding officer is known as a Grand Preceptor.

Thirty-three degrees are listed in the category of the Order, but so far as we know none of them are actually conferred; the degrees listed in their Constitution and By-Laws are:

1. Knight of the Christian Mark
2. Knight of Saint Paul
3. Knight of Patmos
4. Knight of Death
5. Knight of the Black Cross
6. Knight of Bethany
7. Knight of the White Cross
8. Knight of Saint John
9. Knight Priest of the Holy Sepulchre
10. Holy Order of Wisdom
11. Holy and Illustrious Order of the Cross
12. Priest of Eleusis
13. Knight of Harodim
14. Knight of the North
15. Knight of the South
16. Knight of the Sanctuary
17. Grand Cross of Saint Paul
18. Knight of Saint John the Baptist
19. Knight of Rosae Cross
20. Knight of the Triple Cross
21. Knight of the Holy Grave
22. Knight of the Holy Virgin Mary
23. Knight of the White Cross of Torphichen
24. Grand Trinitarian Knight of Saint John
25. Grand Cross of Saint John
26. Knight Priest of Jerusalem
27. Knight of Palestine
28. Knight of the Holy Cross

29. Knight Priest of the Tabernacle
30. Knight of Redemption
31. Knight of Truth

32. Knight of Rome
33. Holy Royal Arch Knight Templar
Priest

Knight of the Temple: The 8° of the Rite of Philalethes; 69° Metropolitan Chapter of France; 6° Clerks of Strict Observance; 9° Rite of the East; 36° Rite of Mizraim. It is the 13° and final degree of the American Rite of Freemasonry; it bears a similarity to the Knight Kadosh, 30° of the Scottish Rite. The Order is strictly Christian and depicts the travels of a poor and weary pilgrim on his way to visit the Holy Sepulchre; it constitutes one of the most impressive of all Masonic degrees, although much could be done in the United States to improve its ritual and methods of conferring. (See Knights Templar.) The 23° Ancient Egyptian Reformed Rite.

Knight of the Three Kings: A side degree worked in the U.S.A. about 1870. Membership requires that one be a Master Mason; tradition is that the circumstances on which the degree was founded were that at the dedication of the Temple, Solomon invited all the Eastern Kings and Princes to attend; it so happened that two of the Kings were at war, and Solomon attempted a reconciliation but without effect; he determined to do with force what he could not accomplish by argument, so he invited them into a small apartment, locked the door and left them in silence, informing them that when they were agreed, they would be liberated, but until that time their diet was bread and water. Two days later, Solomon returned to find how they were faring; he returned again on the third day to find them agreed. Solomon advanced toward them with a lighted taper in each hand, saying: "If you can agree in the dark, you can agree in the light."

Knight of the Throne: The 2° Rite of the East.

Knight of the Triple Cross: The 20° of the Knight Templar Priests; 66° Metropolitan Chapter of France; 3° of the Order of Christ.

Knight of the Triple Period: Conferred in Lodge St. Louis des Amis.

Knight of the Triple Sword: In the Pyron Collection.

Knight of the True Light: 1785.

Knight of Truth: The 31° of the Knight Templar Priests.

Knight of the Two Crowned Eagles: The 22° of the Metropolitan Chapter of France.

Knight of Unction: The 51° of Metropolitan Chapter of France.

Knight Victorious: Hecart Collection.

Knight of the West: 64° Metropolitan Chapter of France; 47° Rite of Mizraim.

Knight of the White Cross: The 7° of the Knight Templar Priests.

Knight of the White Cross (of Torpichen): The 23° of the Knights Templar Priests.

Knight of the White Eagle: The 64° of Mizraim.

Knight of the White and Black Eagle: The 30° A.A.S.R.; 24° Emperors of the East and West; 2° Order of Christ.

Knights of the York Cross of Honour: According to a historical sketch appearing in the Quaternion, the official organ of the Convent General of the United States of America, Knights of the York Cross of Houour, the organization was established first in Monroe, N. C., March 13, 1930, by J. Raymond Shute, Walter C. Crowell, J. Ed. Stewart, Lee Griffin and S. Henry Green.

81

Two months thereafter, May 20, 1930, Lily of the Valley Priory No. 1 was formed, to hold jurisdiction over North Carolina, and on June 6, 1930, the Convent General of the United States of America was formed to superintend the subordinate Priories; J. Raymond Shute II was named Grand Master General.

The next to organize was Virginia (1934), followed by New York, (Feb. 27, 1935). Knickerbocker Priory No. 3, of New York, was organized out of an older association, the Past Officers' Association No. 4. There are now more than fifty Priories in 42 states, one in Canada and one in Mexico.

Membership in the Order is limited to those who have presided in lodge, chapter, council and commandery. Those who have been honored by any of the four American Rite Grand Bodies are entitled to be recognized as Knight York Grand Crosses. The emblem is divided into four quadrants, and those who have presided in one Grand Body are referred to as having one quadrant, etc. Only one honorary Knight Grand Cross has ever been bestowed, and that upon the late John J. Ray, Sr., of Texas, who had lived to be more than one hundred years of age and at the time was the oldest Mason in the world in point of membership.

Only two degrees, or honors, are conferred: (a) The reception as Knight (KYCH); (b) Knight York Grand Cross (KYGC), the latter being those who have presided in one or more Grand Body.

The Convent General, the governing agent, has seven officers, the principal officer being the Most Eminent Grand Master. Local bodies are known as Priories, have eight officers and are presided over by an Eminent Prior. A membership tabulation, December 31, 1949, shows 2,960 living members. At that time there were forty-five Priories located in the North American Continent, including one in Mexico City, Mexico, and two in Canada. Annual conclaves have been held since 1930.

The Order has a ritual of initiation and a ceremony of installation, the latter of which includes the so-called "secrets of the chair," given to all Priors who have been elected and installed as head of a Priory.

Knight York Grand Cross: A degree in Knights of the York Cross of Honour.

Ladder, The Golden: Referred to in Lux IV, p. 23 as "The Golden Ladder of Charity" but not strictly speaking a degree.

Ladies' Oriental Shrine of North America: One of the larger groups attached to the Ancient Arabic Order of the Mystic Shrine is that known as Ladies' Oriental Shrine of North America. The organization was the result of a meeting held at the McLure Hotel, Wheeling, W. Va., where the visiting ladies were being entertained by the ladies of Isis Temple. We quote an interesting feature of its origin:

"One of the ladies, in a spirit of fun, came upon a rope which the men had used in their parade and carelessly thrown on the floor. They joyously began to trail it through the halls of the hotel; other ladies grasping the rope and joining others already holding on to it; a parade followed; then someone asked 'Why should we not organize a ladies' shrine?'"

The result was the formation of Isis Court, Isis being the wife of Osiris. For many years the membership was restricted to members of a single Shrine Temple; later, other Courts were established and on June 24, 1914, at a meeting of these Courts there was established the Grand Council of the Ladies' Oriental Shrine of North America. Fifty-seven Courts have been chartered in the United States and Canada, four of which are dormant. In 1950, there were 15,592 members.

Lady Masons: Freemasonry does not recognize women as members. There are many organizations composed of relatives of Freemasons, and because of that relationship regard themselves as semi-Masonic. Among these are the Order of the Eastern Star, the White Shrine of Jerusalem, Order of the Beauceant, Order of the Rainbow, Job's Daughters, the Amaranth, True Kindred, Daughters of Isis, Daughters of the Nile, Daughters of Zelophadad, and a host of others not so active.

Lady of the Cross: Mentioned in connection with the "Ladies Friend" (Michigan 1866).

Lady of the Dove: The 8° Rite of Adoption. The hangings are red and green. There are seven lights of which three are East, two South and two West. The throne is reached by five steps, above which is the transparency of a dove. Upon the altar, which is covered with green, are three flambeaux containing wax candles. There is also a mallet, an olive branch and a Bible. Near the altar is a cup containing a Dove with a written scroll attached to its neck. The Tableau represents: (1) The Ark of Noah on Mount Ararat; (2) A Dove with an olive branch flying towards the Ark, at the foot of the mountain and the edge of the water where the verdure commences, amphibious animals are seen sporting. The insignia of "Father Noah" is a red and green ribbon worn on the baldric, to which is suspended a trowel and the Jewel. The Apron is white, doubled and bordered with green taffeta; upon the lapel is a dove with an olive branch in its beak. In the middle of the Apron is a mountain emerged in green water. The Jewel is a Silver Dove, with an olive branch in its beak. The Ill. Grand Master represents "Father Noah." The Senior Warden only ranks as "Dear Eldest Son," the Brothers and Sisters he calls "his children." All "thee" and "thou" each other. (This degree is derived from the "Chevaliers and Chevalieres de la Colonite," founded at Versailles in 1784.)

Lady of the Rosy Cross: The 9° Rite of Adoption. The Sister Officers wear a scarf from left to right made of black ribbon embroidered with red, and have a rosette of poppy red. The scarf of a Sister is violet, to which is suspended the Mallet, emblem of command. The Apron is of violet taffeta bordered with a ribbon of the same color; in the middle of it is a pocket fixed with two green rosettes. The Jewel is a Cross of Gold having rays at the four angles; it is suspended by a green ribbon worn in the saltire. The Garter is of violet ribbon, bordered with gold, on which is embroidered the three letters F.H.C. (Faith, Hope, Charity), it is worn on the left arm. The President is called "Brother Commander," the Wardens, "Commanders," or "Generals," the Brothers and Sisters, "Chevaliers" and "Chevalieres" Battery 9—9.

Langue: The Order of Malta (ancient) was divided into "langues" and not "languages" as Grand Encampment ritual states. The division was geographical and according to languages. In the Order of St. John of Jerusalem, subordinate bodies under a Grand Master were called "priories" or "commanderies," divided when they became Knights of Malta, into eight "languages" or "tongues," and ruled by "Bailies" who were Grand Crosses of the Order; each house, or priory was governed by a Commander.

Lausanne, International Congress: One of the most important of the Congresses held by Supreme Councils of the Scottish Rite, though marked by the absence of certain large jurisdictions. A Conference of English-speaking Supreme Councils was held in Toronto, Canada, in 1954.

Lax Observance, Rite of: Substantially the same as the Rite of Strict Observance, being an off-shoot of that Rite; it was limited to Germany where the lodges refused to submit to the regulations, and as they said "innovations" of the Strict Observance Rite.

League: (See International League of Freemasons.)

Leg of Mutton Masons: The name given in complaint made in a Craft Lodge in England in 1752, where "certain leg of Mutton Masons" pretended to confer the mysteries of the Royal Arch in return for a dinner; the irregular group knew nothing of Freemasonry.

Legion of Honor: A degree in the Order of DeMolay.

Les Illumines d'Avignon: The Illumines of Avignon were in sharp contrast with those of Weishaupt in Bavaria. They lacked the elaborate ritual and ceremony and the vulgar boasting of Weishaupt's group. Don Pernetty was the inspiration for the Avignon society and he regarded it as an adjunct to Freemasonry, and a spiritualizing of the broad principles which form the foundation of a brotherhood. Pernetty propagated a rite known as the "Rite Hermetique," sometimes called the "Rite de Pernetty," honoring its founder, Pernetty, who died in 1796.

Levit, Der: The 4° of the Order Knights of True Light.

Levite, Knight: The 7° of the fourth section of the Clerks of Strict Observance.

Libanus, Knight of: (See Knight of Libanus.)

Liberte, Ordre de la: An androgynous French degree of 1740.

Libian: (See Decoration of the Libyan Chain.)

Light, Knight of: (See Knight of Light.)

Link and Chain: The 13° of the Early Grand Rite of Scotland. The Link and Chain followed that of Fugitive Mark; it was conferred in a regular Royal Arch Chapter; the degree was presided over by Noah, and during which initiation the candidate was tested as to his five senses: Hearing the lodge prayer, seeing the Holy Bible, feeling the points of the compasses, tasting the pot of manna, and smelling the pot of incense.

The legend is connected with an event which happened during the building of the Temple; Solomon, while inspecting the work, lost one of the jewels from his crown, one which formed the emblem of Deity; this was a bad omen; it was found and Solomon ordered the workman to place on the keystone the name of this jewel which was an amethyst—Amasaphus.

Link and Wrestle: This degree is often referred to as "Link and Chain," or "Jacob's Wrestle," and in one instance as "Link of the Wilderness." It utilizes a story in Genesis xxviii, and its emblem is depicted as a seven-stepped ladder. The legend was applied to predict the efforts of Daniel and Zerubbabel in the cause of Truth, to prevail on Cyrus and Darius to preserve the City of Jerusalem for the chosen people of God. Link and Wrestle is not now worked and the passing of the Early Grand Rite of Scotland a few years ago saw the Grade Pass into the list of unworked ceremonies.

84

Lion, Chevalier du: The 20° of III Series of the Metropolitan Chapter of France.

Listening Apprentice: The 1° of the Persian Rite.

Livery Companies of London: These organizations were the outgrowth of the old guild system.

Lodge of Perfection: Bodies of the 14° are frequently referred to as Lodges of Perfection. There was also a Rite of Perfection. The name is given to a degree of the Helvetic Rite, which follows that of Grand Master Architect. The ceremonies follow those of the Royal Arch in style, and the degree is sometimes called the "Sublime Degree of the Royal Arch Grand Elect." It contains the story of a secret vault and its ritual refers to "brother Royal Arch Masons."

Lodge of Perfect Truth: We had always believed Truth to be perfect, but here is a degree conferred as the Elect of Truth. (See Elect of Truth.)

Logic Ritual: The name applied to the ritualistic working of the Craft degrees in England, in contradistinction to the *Emulation* working and *Oxford* ritual.

London Mason's Company: Craft guilds commonly sought to preserve the monopoly of trade in a town by preventing "foreign" artisans (those who were not Freemen) from carrying on their trade in the town. This was not the policy of the London's Mason's Company, although it later became so. It was connected with the "Acception," or lodge of Accepted Masons, and had a copy of the 1665 Constitutions and manuscripts.

Lovers of Truth: Little is known of this degree.

Lumiere la Vraie: Translated, it means the "True Light," and it was a degree conferred by the Royal York Grand Lodge in Berlin.

Lusitania, Grand Orient of: The name given to the Grand Lodge of Portugal (probably extinct in recent years).

Lybic Chain: The 85° of the Rite of Memphis (old style). The fourth of the decorations awarded by the Ancient and Primitive Rite.

Malta: (See Order of Malta.)

Malta, Knight of: (See Knight of Malta.)

Mariner's Club: The Mariner's Club is an organization of active York, or American, Rite Freemasons, resident of Dayton, Ohio. Its formation was due to some half dozen Freemasons who journeyed to Windsor, Ontario, where they received the degree of Royal Ark Mariner in International Lodge No. 4 of Royal Ark Mariners. Because the Canadian group were invading the jurisdiction of the Grand Council of Allied Masonic Degrees, U.S.A., which exercised control of the degree in this country, the Canadian group were forbidden to continue the conferring of degrees upon American citizens. The Dayton group, thereupon dropped the name of Royal Ark Mariner and organized themselves into a *Mariner's Club;* the membership is small; membership is by invitation and extended only to those who are actively identified with Royal Arch Masonry. It engages in many social activities and at the conclusion of York Rite Reunions gives a dinner for the Grand Officers. It presents, annually, an award to the outstanding Royal Arch Mason of that area.

Its emblem derived from the Royal Ark Mariner degree, is a steering wheel enclosing the seal of the Club, which is the Ark, the Rainbow, and the Dove of the Royal Ark Mariner degree. Its presiding officer is known as "Captain."

Mark Master Degree: One of the oldest and most interesting degrees in any Rite of Freemasonry is that of the Mark Master; there is nothing in any other than the American or English Rite which approximates it and its origin has been a study for all interested Masonic students.

It would appear from the information available that the degree grew out of an ancient ceremony where each Craftsman selected for himself a Mark, which was then duly registered with the constituted authorities. The ceremony of presenting the Mark was very important in the life of a craftsman because it showed that he had passed the stage of an apprentice, and was now qualified to receive wages as a true and faithful craftsman. Scotland was undoubtedly the home of the Mark degree, from whence it filtered into England and Ireland, and later to the United States and other sections of the world.

It is usually found as the 4° of the American or English Rite, following immediately that of the Master Mason of the Lodge. In point of chronology the degree would follow that of the Fellowcraft—and this it does in Scotland, where it is open to all Fellow Crafts; but in the event a candidate does not receive it at that time under lodge supervision, he may receive it in a Chapter of Royal Arch Masons when assembled as Mark Masters. In England, the degree is independent of either Grand Lodge or Grand Chapter, for there is a Grand Lodge which controls the degree—the Grand Lodge of Mark Master Masons.

There are a number of degrees called "Mark" degrees, but most of them have become obsolete and some of the features of these degrees have been incorporated into the present Mark Master degree.

The grade of "Mark Man" (or Mark Craftsman) was an extension of the Craft Mason, or Fellow Craft degree. The Craft Mason, who by diligence and excellence of work, had earned the distinction of Mark Man, had that distinction conferred upon him in his Craft Lodge, and after years had elapsed, he could hope to be advanced to the higher status of a Master Mason; this higher degree was reserved for brethren who had been Masters of a Craft Lodge; again, it was conferred in the Craft Lodge, which was duly opened in the Mark Master Mason degree, all below that rank being excluded. No brother was styled a Master Mason until he had been installed as a Master of a Lodge (See Ancient Charges IV). Later, it became customary for non-operatives to be admitted to the fraternity; the Master Mason degree, as we know it today, was conferred on Fellow Crafts, and one Mark ceremony only was retained. For this degree, only Master Masons were eligible, and the ceremony was still worked as from the Craftman's degree. Sir Lumley-Lumley Smith says that lodges illegally worked the degree from 1813-1856. The Lodges Bon Accord and Royal Cumberland were active in forming the Grand Lodge of Mark Master Masons.

The Marked Master degree was one of those in the Early Grand Rite of Scotland; and there was the Mark Fellow Mason, not to be confounded with the present Mark Master degree, but which was placed between the Ark and Wrestle. Its legend was taken from Genesis and had to do with the rebuilding of the Temple by Zerubbabel.

The degree has now become one of the most popular of all degrees, its homely lessons of honesty, industry, and charity, offering a popular appeal to all classes; its historical connection with Craft Masonry and the legends of which it tells, combine to make the Mark Master degree an outstanding one in the system to which it is attached.

Martinists: (See Rite of Martinists; see Order of Martinists.)

Masonic Congresses: The average member of the fraternity looks forward to a time when Freemasonry may be truly said to be universal in form and brotherhood; this hope has been in the heart of all Freemasons since the very beginning. Undoubtedly, some good is attached to these Congresses; but on the other hand they fail to bring the desired end and many grand lodges, largely through jealousies and clinging to obsolete rules which they call "Landmarks," fail to participate.

The first of these Masonic Congresses was the *traditional* one held at *York* in 926, convoked by Edwin, son of King Athelstan, which had for its object the reconstruction of the Masonic corporations. A new constitution based upon ancient laws, was at that time promulgated.

A Masonic Congress was held at *Strasburg, Germany* in 1275, convoked by Erwin of Steinbash, for the continuation of the work on the cathedral in that City. A great number of architects and workmen from Germany, England, and Lombardy were assembled there. At the suggestion of the English groups, they constituted themselves under the rule of the Freemasons, and each took oath to faithfully observe the ancient laws and regulations of the fraternity.

Another Congress was called in Extraordinary convention at *Strasburg* in 1564 by the Grand Lodge of Strasburg, its objects being (1) to harmonize disputes in lodges by submitting them to the grand lodge, and (2) to continue the customary reports.

In the meantime, other Congresses were being held, the first at *Ratisbonne* in 1459, convoked by Job Dotzinger, working master of the Cathedral at Strasburg, to discuss the affairs of the fraternity generally, and sanction new laws and regulations prepared at the 1452 meeting in Strasburg. Five years later (1464) another convention was held at Strasburg to (1) discuss general affairs and receive reports on edifices being constructed with the idea of rushing their completion, and define more precisely the rights of the four grand lodges in Cologne, Strasburg, Berne, and Vienna, and (3) the nomination of Conrad Kuyn, working master, to the Grand Mastership of the Grand Lodge of Cologne.

In 1469, the Grand Lodge of Strasburg convoked a Congress to meet at *Spire,* to (1) receive and act upon religious edifices in process of construction, and (2) to hear reports on the situation in England, Gaul, Lombardy, and Germany.

In 1535, a Congress was convoked by Hermann, Bishop of Cologne, to meet in *Cologne* to take up measures for facing the dangers which menaced Freemasons. The so-called "Charter of Cologne" is said to be the offspring of the Congress.

At *Basle,* Switzerland, in 1563, was held another Congress, called by the Grand Lodge of Strasburg, to (1) receive reports of the general condition of architecture, (2) discuss differences arising in 22 of the subordinate lodges, and (3) to sanction revised statutes.

While the meeting of the four London lodges in 1717 may not have been regarded as a general congress of Freemasons, yet the results had a great effect on present day speculative Masonry. It was the turning point marking the official change from Operative to Speculative Freemasonry. Briefly, the result was to specify:

That the privileges of Masonry shall be no longer confined to operative Masons, but be free to men of all professions, provided they are regularly approved and initiated into the fraternity.

Thereupon, they constituted themselves into the Grand Lodge of England, of Free and Accepted Masons, the first ever to be organized, and controlling but three degrees of Apprentice, Fellow Craft, and Master Mason.

In Ireland, we find the lodges of Dublin, imitating the English by convoking the lodges to organize Freemasonry upon the English basis. Viscount Lord Kingston was elected Grand Master.

And the Scotch, not to be behind their English and Irish brethren, were convoked to meet in *Edinburgh* in 1736, by Baron Sinclair of Roslyn, whose family had held the hereditary Grand Mastership since 1439. They were organized on a new basis and were recognized by both England and Ireland. There were present at this convention, members of 32 lodges, who elected Baron St. Clair as Grand Master in the year 1737.

A Masonic Congress was held at the *Hague* in 1756, called by the mother lodge, "Royal Union," with the object of instituting a national grand lodge for the United Provinces, under the auspices of the Grand Lodge of England. It was consummated by act of the 13 lodges assembled, and the Baron Aersen-Beyeren was elected Grand Master.

Three Congresses were held in the years 1763, 1764, and 1765, at Jena and Altenburg, in Germany. Johnson, who called himself the "Unknown Superior" assembled the lodges at Jena in 1763, to reorganize the lodges of Strict Observance, that they might recognize him as Superior; he held a second convention there the following year; Baron von Hund was invited to represent his Rite, but discovering Johnson's mission, he declared him to be an impostor, and at a third convention, in Altenburg, von Hund was elected Grand Master of all the lodges of the system.

At *Kohlo,* in 1772, a convention was called by lodges of the Strict Observance to oppose the new Rite established by Zinnendorf. The Duke Ferdinand of Brunswick was elected Grand Master of Strict Observance lodges.

Ferdinand called a convention to meet at *Brunswick* in 1775, to discover what Rites pretended to hold the true Masonic science. Baron von Hund was present along with members of 23 lodges. Although fifteen days were spent in discussing the matter, no decision was reached.

The lodges of the Strict Observance, convened a Congress in *Leipsic* in 1777 to discuss a compact of union among all the lodges of the system, both in Sweden and Germany, and to nominate a Grand Master, for which they proposed the Duke of Sudermania. Nothing was done.

Frederick, Duke of Brunswick, called a convention in *Brunswick* in 1778, which lasted 37 days, where it was decided to make a general appeal to all Masonic bodies to convoke a convention at Wilhelmsbad to discuss the chaos caused by the many systems of Freemasonry. Previous to this, Frederick had held another Congress in 1782 at Wilhelmsbad to discuss the general reformation of Freemasonry and which resulted in the exposure of a number of mystical systems, a remodeling of the Rite of Strict Observance, and in the creation of the Eclectic Rite.

The Wilhelmsbad Congress was one of the most important ever held for it resulted in a complete change of the Masonic picture by bringing to the attention of the fraternity the conditions which it faced.

In 1778, a Congress was held at *Lyons,* France, called by a lodge of the Benevolent Knights at Lyons; its pretext was to throw light upon Masonic "obscurity" and to correct the rituals. The real object was to establish the Martinist Rite over that of the Templars. They did change the rituals.

In 1785, the Rite of Philalethes called a Congress to meet in Paris; it was hoped to assemble all of the learned Masons in France to "clear up the fog produced by the different Masonic systems and determine the actual situation which confronted the fraternity. It was to the French what the Wilhelmsbad Conference was to the Germans. There were no direct results.

A Masonic Congress was held at *Zurich,* Switzerland, in 1836, in an attempt to fuse the Masonic groups of Switzlerland and to abolish certain high degrees by founding the Alpine Grand Lodge; a second Congress was held at *Berne* in 1838, and a third at *Basle* in 1840; the fourth Congress was held in *Locle* in 1842. A Constitution of Union was signed at Locle in 1842, and ratified in 1843, becoming the law of the fraternity in 1844.

At Paris, in 1848, another Congress was held, following the Revolution; it was called by the "Supreme Council for France" to constitute a new power, to elaborate on the Constitution based upon democratic principles, and to adopt the English Rite exclusively. Out of this came the National Grand Lodge of France.

Prince Lucien Marat, called all of the Grand Orients and Grand Lodges of the World to meet in Paris in 1855, to a Universal Masonic Congress, with the object of cementing more closely the bonds of the fraternity. Very few grand lodges responded and the results accomplished were nil.

Since that date there have been several Masonic Congresses but none marked by a representative attendance. In the Western Hemisphere there are held Conferences of Grand Masters of Masons in U.S.A. and Canada, which hold annual meetings in Washington, D.C., but which accomplish little except to know each other better. In our neighbor to the south, Mexico, we find an annual conference, called the Supremo Consejo (Supreme Council), which while it bears what might seem to be a title of Scottish Rite authority, is an organization much like that of the Conference of Grand Masters, U.S.A.

And there is the Inter American Masonic Conference which includes all of the Latin-American countries of South and Central America, which held its Third triennial Conference in Havana, Cuba in 1955. The first one was at Montevideo, Uruguay in 1949; the second at Mexico City, Mexico in 1952.

Masonic Employment Bureaus: This is Freemasonry in practice; such organizations are to be found in all the larger cities, usually coupled with Bureaus of Masonic Relief. As a rule, there are no fees, the Bureau being supported by lodges of the area, and supported by a small per capita tax levied against each lodge.

Masonic Librarians: While there is no society of such a name at this time, occasional meetings are held of Masonic students and librarians for the discussion of Masonic topics.

Masonic Posts of American Legion: In most all larger cities there are Posts of the American Legion made up of Master Masons.

Masonic Relief Association: Such associations are to be found in the larger cities, associated with the Employment Bureau (see Masonic Employment Bureau) ; they afford relief to the indigent, arrange for burial services for transients, and such other duties as may fall to their work.

Masonic Service Association, U.S.A.: This Association serves as a clearing house for all the Freemasons in the United States, Philippines, and elsewhere. Only thirty-six American Grand Lodges are members at the present time. It was organized immediately following World War I, when American Grand Lodges failed to unite in Masonic relief ; it was an attempt to prepare the fraternity for later service, which came during World War II. Its work in military and naval hospitals has become outstanding. Its work in sending relief to brethren in Europe in 1945 is well known, and its work in reviving Freemasonry in Italy and Holland during that period, and in rejuvenating Freemasonry in Germany will ever stand to their credit.

Masonic Veterans: There are a number of states which have organizations of the above named ; in one or two instances there is to be found a short ritual. Membership is limited to length of membership in the fraternity, usually twenty-five years.

Masonry of Adoption: (See Adoptive Masonry.)

Mason's Company: One of the first titles ascribed to the Society of Operative Masons.

Mason's Daughter: An androgynous degree which had for its foundation a legend connecting Mary, sister of Lazarus, with Jesus' triumphal entry into Jerusalem ; it had certain modes of recognition and a signet in which the letters AMRY (Mary) were encircled by the letters F.N.D.O.Z., B.T.K.C. (Fear Not, Daughter of Zion, etc.) Membership was limited to relatives of Master Masons.

Mason's Wife: Once conferred upon the wives of Master Masons; later, it included other relatives. It is now extinct; it was of American origin.

Master: There are many rites and degrees labelled "Master." Among these are the following :

Egyptian Rite: To each candidate is assigned the name of a prophet which he retains permanently. There is a chamber of reflection; the degree teaches regeneration. It contains nothing of Ancient Craft Masonry. It is the 3° of the Rite.

Elect of Truth: The degree is included in this Rite.
Felicitares: It was the 2° of this Rite.
Fessler: It was one of Fessler's degrees.
Illuminati: The degree appears in this Rite.
Persian Rite: It was the 3° of the Rite.
Philalethes: It was a Philalethes degree.
Reformed Rite: It appears in this Rite.
Swedish Rite: It is the 3° of the Swedish Rite.
Temple: It constituted a degree of the Templar Rite.
Zinnendorf Rite: The 3° of the Rite.
U.S.A.: The degree of Master Mason is sometimes referred to as the "Master's" degree, and as such it appears as the 3° in all lodges throughout the world. (See Master Mason.)

Master, Degrees with the name of:

Master Ancient: 4° of Martinism.
Master Architect, Grand: (See Grand Master Architect.)

90

Master Architect, Perfect: Philosophic Scottish Rite.
Master Architect, Prussian: (See Royal Order of Prussian Blue.)
Master of the Blue: 9° Early Grand Rite of Scotland.
Master Cohen: Philosophic Scotch Rite.
Master Crowned: Lodge St. Louis des Amis.
Master, Egyptian: Philosophic Scotch Rite.
Master, English: 8° Rite of Mizraim.
Master, Hermetic: Lemanceau Collect.
Master Hermetic Architecture:
Master, Illustrious Symbolic: Fustier Col.
Master, Irish: 7° Rite of Mizraim.
Master, Israel: Intendant of the Building.
Master, Perfect English: Le Rouge Col.

Master of All Symbolic Lodges: The 10° of Early Grand Rite of Scotland.

Master of Black Eagle of St. John: A degree in the Order of the Temple.

Master of the Blue: The 9° of the Early Grand Rite of Scotland.

Master Builder: A degree of the Order of Builders.

Master Cohen: A degree of the Rite of Elected Cohens.

Master of the East: A degree in the Order of the Temple.

Master Ecossais: The 5° of the Zinnendorf Rite.

Master of Egyptian Secrets: A degree of the African Architect Rite.

Master Elect: A degree of the Rite of Elect of Truth.

Master Elect of Fifteen: (See Elect of Fifteen.)

Master, Good Shepherd: The 6° of the Persian Rite.

Master, Knight of the Sun: A degree of the Persian Rite.

Master of the Little Elect: A degree of the Helvetic Rite, akin to that of the Elu of 12 in the A.A.S.R. It is one of the so-called "venergance" series.

Master Mason: A degree of the Modern French Rite, and Adonhiramite Rite; a degree of the Clerks of Relaxed Observance; a degree of the Zinnendorf Rite; a degree in the Rite of Perfection and Rite of Elected Cohens; a degree in the Rite of Strict Observance; the 3° of practically all organized Freemasonry.

Master Mason, Irish System: The degree once comprised the essentials of the present Irish Installed Master, Royal Arch and Red Cross Mason, the Entered Apprentice and Fellow Craft containing the ceremonies up to and including the present Hiramic legend. A candidate was "entered and crafted" (before 1797) on the same occasion as one degree.

Master Neophyte: A degree of the Rite of Illuminated Theosophists.

Master of the Ninth Arch: The 13° of the Ancient and Accepted Rite.

Master Perfect: (See Expert Master.)

Master of the Royal Secret: A term applied to those who receive the 32° of the A.A.S.R.

Master of the Secret: A degree of the Rite of Martinism.

Master of St. Andrew: The 5° of the Swedish Rite.

Master of Tyre: A degree of the Allied Masonic Degrees series.

Medal of Appreciation: An award given by the Order of DeMolay.

Medal of Heroism: An award given by the Order of DeMolay.

Mediterranean Pass: Known as Knight of the Mediterranean Pass. An honorary degree conferred on Knights Templars as Knights of Malta, under the old constitution. The degree is said to have originated from the following circumstances:

In an excursion of the Knights of Malta into the Kingdom of Naples, while crossing the river Offanto (the Ancient Aufidus), they were attacked by a very superior force of Turks. However, notwithstanding the disparity of numbers, the Knight succeeded in obtaining a complete victory, the Moslems being entirely routed, and the river dyed with their blood. As a reward for the valour displayed by these Knights, they had granted to them free permission to pass and repass at every port in the Mediterranean in possession of the Christians. The legend of the degree relates that this event occurred in 1367, nearly 200 years before the Knights of St. John, or Rhodes as then called, obtained Malta. At this period the Knights, headed by the Grand Master Raymond Berenger, with a large naval force attacked the Ottoman corsairs in the Mediterranean and chased them into the port of Alexander, but were compelled at last to retire before the superior force of the Sultan of Egypt.

Melchizedek: (See Order of Melchizedek.)

Melesino Rite: In 1765, the Rite of Melesino, consisting of seven degrees was founded by Melesino, a Greek by birth, and a Lt. General in the Imperial Army; it flourished for a time, and, according to the Freemason's Calendar for 1778, established its first Lodge in 1771 at St. Petersburgh, which was composed largely of English merchants. Not including the three craft degrees of the English system, it conferred: (4) The Dark Vault; (5) Scots Master; (6) Philosopher's degree; (7) Spiritual Knighthood, or Grand Priest. It was a mixture of Kabbalistic doctrines, Magic, Gnosticism and Hermetic Philosophy. The 7° was said to be Rosicrucian, was Christian, and taught the doctrine of the Trinity and the Messiah.

Member of the Chapter: The 10° of the Swedish Rite.

Memphis Rite: (See Rite of Memphis.)

Men of Desire, Society of: (See Order of Martinists.)

Mere Loge d'Adoption de le Haute Macconerie Egyptienne of Cagliostro: It was a part of the Rite of Adoption. Its first degree was that of Apprentice; here we find King Solomon instructing the Queen of Sheba in the mysteries of divine religion. In the 2° she cuts off the serpent's head; in the 3°, called the Master's degree, we find the Queen, this time with a Dove.

Merit: (See Order of Merit.)

Merit Medals: (See Order of DeMolay.)

Mesmerian Masonry: Founded by Mesmer, based on the science of magnetism, and which many writers claim to have been known by the initiates of the Ancient Mysteries. This legend is based upon the science of Mesmerism, popularized by Friedrich Anton (or Franz) Mesmer, the German physician who was raised for the priesthood but took up the study of medicine. His investigations began about 1772. Mackey says he founded, at Paris in 1782, the "Order of Universal Harmony"—that it was Masonic few will allow.

Mesopolyte: A degree of Bahrdt's Rite.

Methodist Craftsmen Club: A club composed of Methodists who were also Freemasons. It was disapproved when approval was asked of the Grand Lodge of Texas in 1953.

Metropolitan Chapter of France: In the beginning this body constituted the Council of Emperors of the East and West and Knights of the East; in 1786 it united with the Grand Orient, thereupon assuming the above title.

Mexican National Rite (Rito Masonico Nacional): (See Rite Nacional Mexicano; see Rite, Rito Nacional Mexicano.)

Military Lodges: These are lodges which have been established in connection with military units, and in the early days of the fraternity Freemasonry was spread to all corners of the globe through these lodges. In recent years, Grand Lodges have been rather careful in establishing lodges with military units because of the difficulty of keeping records and the rapid change in personnel. The English, Irish and Scotch have been very free in granting charters to military units until recent years. There were lodges in the Revolutionary Army, in the Mexican War Army, the Spanish-American War Army and both World Wars.

Militia Ecclesiastic Evangelica: (See Order of Militia Ecclesiastic Evangelica.)

Minerval: (See Illuminati.)

Minor Architect: (Or Scotch Apprentice.) A degree of the Elect of Truth.

Minor-Illumined: The third step in the Order of the Illuminati; candidates were examined as to their capacity, knowledge, rank, finances and their means of propagating the Order. It was the 4° of the Illuminati of Bavaria.

Misraim, Rite of: (See Rite of Misraim.)

Mistress: The 3° of the Rite of Adoption. A ladder of five steps covered with flowers; upon the steps are inscribed names of the five senses. A rainbow transparency over the altar. In the African quarter is a small spiral tower about sixty centimetres high, solid enough to bear a man's weight. Upon it is written in large letters "Tower of Babel monument of the pride of man." Near the Inspectress is a small joiner's bench lighted by two lamps, upon which lie a mallet and chisel, and a small box made to imitate a stone, in such a way that at the first blow on the chisel it opens and discloses the emblem of a flaming heart. The temple is lighted by thirteen other lights of which seven are placed to the right and six to the left; also by a chandelier of three branches placed upon the altar, and one each upon the table of the Inspectress and Depositress. If these should not sufficiently light the room others are added, but they do not count in the mysterious number of 15 or 3 x 5. The painting represents: 1, The Ladder of the Mistress; 2, The Tower of Babel; 3. The Pit of Joseph; 4, The Dream of Jacob; 5, Lot's Wife as a pillar of salt; 6, The Burning of Sodom; 7, The Sacrifice of Noah; 8, Two flaming lamps; 9, Ark of Noah upon Mount Ararat; 10, Eleven Stars; 11, Sun; 12, Moon; 13, Rainbow; 14, Door; 15, Raven. Clothing same as in 1°. A crown of myrtle upon the head. The jewel is a golden trowel. Opening is same as 1°, except that the duty of the Mistress is as follows: To love, protect and aid the Brothers and Sisters.

Mithra (Mithras), Mysteries of: Credit is given to Zoroaster for instituting the Ancient Mysteries in Persia; they were celebrated in caves and the number of degrees has been estimated as from seven to twelve. From what has come down to us, it would seem that candidates were given tests of air, fire and fasting, which were terrifying; eventually he emerged in full possession of the Mithraic doctrines, which seemed to revolve around the solar symbolism. It is said that the mysteries were taken to Rome where one of the Roman Emperors became a candidate.

Mizraim, Rite of: (See Rite of Misraim.)

Mock Masonry: In 1747, certain London Freemasons organized a mock procession to ridicule that procession which occurred during Grand Lodge meetings.

Moderns, The: While the old, and original, Grand Lodge of England, was first established in England, a later group referred to them as "Moderns," and to themselves as "Ancients" (See Ancients). In 1813, both groups united to form the United Grand Lodge of England.

Modern French Rite: (See Rite, French Modern.)

Mokanna, Daughters of: (See Daughters of Mokanna.)

Mopses: An organization established by Roman Catholics as a travesty on the Masonic ceremonies; a pug-dog was used as one of the features in the ritual, hence the name "Mopses" from the German word meaning "dog." Ladies were permitted to membership; an old print shows a lady being required to kiss the tail of the dog. It was largely a German group. It was oldest of the Adoptive group. The name, from the German "mops," signifies a young mastiff, is intended to indicate the mutual fidelity and attachment of the brethren—those virtues being characteristic of the noble animal. This Order originated in the following manner:

In 1738, Pope Clement XII issued a bull condemning and forbidding the practice of the rites of Masonry. Several brethren in the Catholic States of Germany, unwilling to renounce the Order, yet fearful of offending the ecclesiastical authority, formed, in 1740, under the above name, what was pretended to be a new institution, devoted to the papal hierarchy, but which was, in truth, nothing else than Freemasonry under a less offensive appellation. It was patronized by the most illustrious persons in Germany, and many of the princes of the Empire were its Grand Masters.

Mormons: The leaders of the original group which formed the Mormon Society were Freemasons, receiving their degrees in a lodge at Nauvoo, Ill. Because they used no care in selecting their candidates, the Grand Lodge of Illinois took away their charter, but they kept on conferring degrees—irregularly; when they removed to Salt Lake City, Utah, they continued their ceremonies, adopting certain sections for their church ritual. They are not accepted for membership in Utah.

Most Excellent Architect: (See Ancient Free and Accepted Architects.)

Most Excellent Master: One of the degrees of the Early Grand Scottish Rite, the only one of the old Rites which contains a grade celebrating the completion of the first Temple; it was the 19° of the Rite; its ritual is similar to the ritual of the same named degree in the U.S.A.

In Scotland the degree is worked, but must not be confused with the Excellent Master; there the degree is under control of the Grand Council of Cryptic Degrees. Its legend is that of the completion and dedication of the First Temple; a candidate is required to be a Mark Master.

It is the third, and one of the most spectacular of the American system; its ritual portrays the celebration of the completion of the Temple and its dedication by Solomon. It has reached its highest development among the Chapters of the Midwest and Pacific Coast.

Most Illustrious Sovereign Prince of Masonry, Grand Knight, Sublime Commander of the Royal Secret: A degree in the Rite of Perfection.

Mother Lodge of St. John of Scotland: Organized in 1751 at Marseilles by a Scotsman. (See Chapter of Clermont.)

Mother Word, or Royal Secret: A degree in the Early Grand Rite of Scotland.

Mouzehemites: The 3° of the Rite of Memphis.

94

Mustard, Order of the Grain of: (See Order of Mustard Seed.)

Mysterious Rose: The climax of the degrees conferred in the Council of Clermont (1758). It was probably the source of the 18° Rose Croix. The degree was known as the "Mysteries of the Mysterious Rose." At least it had a *mysterious* title.

Mystic Body: The group of seven members who constituted the Sovereign College of Allied Masonic and Christian Degrees. The Grand Master was the eighth member.

Mystic Order of Veiled Prophets of the Enchanted Realm: (See Order, Mystic Order of Veiled Prophets of the Enchanted Realm.)

Mystic Shrine: (See Ancient Accepted Order Nobles of the Mystic Shrine.)

Mystic Tie: Not a degree, but the name given those of the Masonic fraternity who are united by one common tie—their obligation—which is to them a Mystic Tie.

Napoleonic Masonry: (See Order of French Noachides.)

National College of Masonry: About 1920, one Reuben Clark mailed out literature urging the establishment of a great National Masonic College, to be financed by a 1c per capita tax on every Master Mason. There is no evidence that the "college" was ever established. Few Freemasons would vote a 1c per capita tax on themselves for education.

National Federated Craft: This is an organization of Freemasons engaged in the trades.

National Grand Lodge: The Great Desideratum of all Freemasons, but probably never to be formed, because of sectional jealousies and the fear that it might assume domination or dictatorship. Washington was once proposed to head such an organization.

National Grand Lodge of German Freemasons: This Grand Lodge has, or had, ten degrees; the first three constituted the Lodge of St. John; the 6°-9° the Chapter; the 10° was an honorary degree called the Apprentice of Perfection. Its badge was the Red Cross hung around the neck, the holders of the degree being called "Knights of the Red Cross." It had a special interest in the first five degrees; at its head were the Grand Master and Associate Officers who settled all questions concerning the degrees 6°-10°. There are four Chapters: Those working the 6°, 7°; the 6°, 7°, 8°, 9°; and lastly the Grand Chapter at Berlin, with a Master of the Order at its head (Ordenmeister).

National League of Masonic Club: The formation of this Association grew out of a desire to secure closer cooperation between Masonic Clubs which had been established throughout the United States, and to set up certain objectives. Out of this agitation there was formed, in 1905 in Syracuse, N. Y., a League of Masonic Clubs, which, at that time, was limited to the State of New York. In 1906, at an annual convention, the name was changed to the *National League of Masonic Clubs,* a constitution and by-laws were adopted, and, in 1952, the Association was incorporated in the District of Columbia. The first President was S. R. Clute, of Syracuse, N. Y. Annual meetings have been held since 1905.

National Masonic Research Society: Founded in 1914 at Anamosa, Iowa, it promised to be one of Freemasonry's greatest assets, but the demon "commercialism" entered into the picture and it passed away about 1927. It had been removed to St. Louis about 1923 and came under private ownership;

financial difficulties wrecked the organization. During its better days, it was the most outstanding Masonic publication in the world; it had at one time, 12,000 subscribers.

National Sojourner: The experiences of Grand Lodges in the establishment of subordinate lodges in military units has never been entirely satisfactary, although there are certain exceptions. Because of this fact, members of the fraternity who are in military or naval service, discovered that the same fellowship might be obtained through a group formed within their own organization, and this resulted in the formation in 1921, in Chicago, Ill., of the society known as National Sojourners, whose membership is limited to commissioned officers serving in the armed forces of the United States, all of whom are members of a recognized Masonic Grand Lodge. Brigadier General Samuel C. Stanton was elected the first National President.

The claim is made that the organization grew out of a former organization known as "The Sojourners Club," which met in Manila, P.I., during 1900 and 1901. Out of this early organization was formed Manila Lodge No. 342, chartered by the Grand Lodge of California in 1901. With the formation of the lodge in the Philippines, there was no further need for the organization, but in 1907, there was organized in Manila the Masonic Sojourners Association, which is said to have been a continuation of the former Club, but its members had become scattered to all parts of the earth.

Late in the year 1917, numerous officers of the Army, Navy and Marine Corps of the United States who were on duty in the Chicago area discovered a mutual and fraternal understanding and felt that some form of society should be organized where the officers of Masonic affiliation could meet and pass pleasant and educational time. Master Masons who become officers in our armed forces too rarely visit their home lodges or other lodges where they may be stationed or sojourning. This is understandable but regrettable.

This Chicago group gathered onto themselves a nucleus of qualified officers and formed a club calling it the Sojourners Club of Chicago and it was chartered under the laws of the State of Illinois.

At present active chapters are located in nearly every large city in practically every Army camp and Post and at practically every Naval Station and Marine Corps base. A Sojourner from one chapter may visit and fraternize with Sojourners from other chapters wherever a chapter may be located.

To become a member one must be a Master Mason in good standing and a commissioned officer or warrant officer, past or present of the uniformed forces of the United States. The various chapters are not lodges but they acknowledge the sovereignty of the various Grand Lodges in whose jurisdiction they operate. A great many of the present and past Grand Masters are Sojourners.

The purposes of National Sojourners to organize commissioned officers and warrant officers of the uniformed forces of the United States who are Master Masons into Chapters, are for the promotion of good fellowship among its members for assisting such as may be overtaken by adversity or affliction, for cultivating Masonic ideals, for supporting all patriotic aims and activities in Masonry, for developing true patriotism and Americanism throughout the nation, and for bringing together representatives of the uniformed forces of the United States (past and present) in a united effort to further the military

96

needs of National Defense and for opposing any influence whatsoever, calculated to weaken our National security.

Out of this group came the organization formed in 1921. On June 20, 1931, it was incorporated in the District of Columbia as National Sojourners. It holds annual meetings, elects national officers, and confers the Reception degree and Heroes of '76. In 1953, there were more than 150 active chapters. However, since its inception 306 chapters have been established.

Ne Plus Ultra Templar: There is in evidence a certificate from the Royal Arch Grand Chapter of Scotland, 1812, naming one Louis Charles Tissot, 43, France, a Royal Master Mason, as being:

received in our camp and was duly and properly initiated and instructed in all the mysteries of our religious and military Orders of K.T. and Holy Sepulchre of St. John of Jerusalem; also that we have made him a Knight Templar of Malta and Sovereign Prince Rose Croix, after having subjected him to all the mysterious and (to him) surprising trials necessary for his admission, etc."

It was signed by officers of the "Royal Arch Lodge No. 5812; Lodge No. 3212 of the Knights Templar, and Lodge No. 612; also Lodge No. 712 Knights of Malta." It can be seen that the numbers of lodges as given are not actual dates but the "year of the Order."

Nescherites: The 5° of the Rite of Memphis.

New Templars: A Rite of five degrees introduced into France, conferring the degrees (1), Iniati; (2), Intimi Initiati; (3), Adepti; (4), Orientales Adepti and as a climax—(5), Magnae Aquila Nigrae Sancti Johannes Apostoli Adept. (The Great Black Eagle of the Holy St. John Adept.)

Noachite, or Prussian Knight: (See Prussian Knight.) The 2° of the Illuminati of Bavaria. The 5° of the Rite of Strict Observance.

Anderson, in his Constitutions, tells us that "the first name of Masons, according to some traditions, was Noachidae." There was a tradition that Masonry was established at the building of the Tower of Babel, and that its architect journeyed to Prussia where he established a Masonic Order known as the Noachites. In the A. & A. Rite it is the 21°.

Noah, Rite of: We have Rebold's statement that it was Masonic; it is now extinct. It was known as the "Order of the Noachites" in 1735.

Novice: The first step taken by a candidate in the Illuminati (1°). He was required to submit to unknown superiors—which was distasteful to Freemasons. Candidates for the Shrine are called novices. The degree was the 5° of the Rite of Strict Observance.

Novitiate: A grade in the Order of Amaranth. A "Novitiate Cross" was conferred by the Red Cross of Constantine.

Odd Fellows: (See International Order of Odd Fellows.)

Old Man, The: A degree in Bahrdt's Rite.

Operative Masons: Freemasonry was once composed of operative Masons only—laborers. Traveling through various countries, they became closely associated, developing ideas and plans of architecture which they kept closely concealed from outsiders. Wherever they worked they set up "lodges" in which to live and keep their tools; in this place it was explained, in due time, to the apprentice, the secrets of the Craft. This was undoubtedly the origin of the word "LODGE." In time, men were "accepted" into the society

97

who were not operative workmen. They were called "Accepted Masons," and in due time they gained control over the Craft, so that today, Freemasonry is a Speculative society, engaged in building only "spiritual temples."

Orange Society: This Society was formed to glorify the acceptance of the English throne by William III, Prince of Orange; it was an Irish Society which grew out of the "Peep of Day Boys." The title was no double taken from the Masonic fraternity which had an *Orange Lodge of Belfast No. 257.* It was a Protestant society and resulted in a counter-order established by the Catholics—"The Defenders," later known as the "United Irishmen." Daniel O'Connell, made a Freemason in 1799, and who later left the fraternity, referred to the Orange Society as "a feeble imitation of Freemasonry which lent something of mysticism and much of regularity to the Orange lodge."

Order of Adoption: (See Rite of Adoption.)

Order of African Architects: (See Rite of African Architects.)

Order of Amaranth: This is an American organization with a Swedish background. The Degree (or Order) was the work of Brother James B. Taylor, musician and song writer (1860). Just where Taylor received the inspiration for writing the ritual is not known but he must have had access to a ritual used in Sweden.

At this juncture, Robert Macoy, a New York publisher, took over and revised the Taylor ritual; it was his intention to set up a series of "high degrees" for the wives of Master Masons—a Rite of Adoption—which would have included the following:

1°. Order of the Eastern Star.
2°. Queen of the South.
3°. Order of the Amaranth.
4°. Administrative Degree for Matrons.

Rob. Morris, founder of the Order of the Eastern Star, favored the project because it would end for the ladies "the monotony of the endless repetition of one degree," and adding "Why should the ladies be less favored than the men?"

Macoy became the first Supreme Royal Patron at the organization in 1873; the degree was conferred in the body of the Grand Chapter of the Eastern Star. Rob. Morris accepted the station of Supreme Secretary.

The Order was reorganized in 1897, having become independent of the Rite of Adoption. In the beginning membership was predicated upon membership in the Eastern Star, but in 1921, the Amaranth was asked to abolish that requirement at the request of the General Grand Chapter of the Eastern Star; this was done, and at the present time wives, widows, daughters, granddaughters, mothers and sisters of Master Masons are eligible to membership, as well as Master Masons in good standing.

There are "Courts" of the Amaranth in the United States, Canada, Scotland, Philippine Islands, and Australia.

The ancient and original Order of the Amaranth (Amaranther Order) was established in Sweden in 1653 by Queen Christina of Sweden; at that time it consisted of fifteen ladies and fifteen gentlemen, with the Queen at the head; it began as a social group and its magnificent balls created great interest in Sweden. The list of membership constituted the aristocracy of the country, while visiting dignitaries were created honorary members.

But Queen Christina gave up her Lutheran faith, joined the Catholic church and the Amaranth disappeared for a century, until reorganized in 1760 by a group of young people. We are informed that the initiation "is dignified, without the slightest trace of other worldliness or romanticism." There are two grades—companion and novitiate. The highest grade is the "Grand Cross." The various grades are termed (1) Amaranth, (2) Aspirant, (3) Counselor, (4) Chevalier, (5) Knight Commander, (6) Grand Cross Commander. The motto is *Sempe Idem* and *Memoria Dulcis (Always the same* and *Of sweet memory).*

Order of the Anchor: (See Anchor, Order of.)

Order of Apocalypse: A degree, or degrees, founded on the Revelation of St. John; it was established in the 17th Century, and is said to have been a precursor to the Templar system. It was connected with the 17th° of the Chapter of Clermont; it was probably a branch of the Christian fraternity, and was instituted by Gabrano. The Scottish Rite's 17° (Knight of the East and West) is an Apocalyptic degree. Our dictionary says that the word describes "any writing professing to reveal the future, such as in early Christian or Hebrew circles." The Last Book of the New Testament is called the "Revelation of St. John the Divine."

Order of Bath: The Order of the Bath of the United States is a New Jersey organization, founded June 21, 1921, in Red Bank, N. J. Originally it was known as "The Wahoo Band" and its members were taken from Mystic Brotherhood Lodge No. 21 F. & A. M., of Red Bank, N. J. It was established to secure greater interest in the ritualistic work of the lodge. In 1930, it assumed the name "Order of the Bath." It has no connection with the English historic Order, but is a humorous diversion for brethren accustomed to the serious side of conferring degrees.

When it became the Order of the Bath, its presiding officer, who was formerly "King" became "Commander General," and he holds the office for life. There are four sections of the degree: (a) Outer Band; (b) Middle Band; (c) Inner Band; (d) Order of the Bath. Meetings are held in Washington, D. C., in February each year when Masonic brethren meet in that City for the purpose of attending other Masonic functions. In 1953, it was reported there were more than 300 members.

Order of the Beatitudes: Organized in 1925 by the Grand Chapter of the Eastern Star of Florida and under its control, it accepts girls from twelve to eighteen when recommended by members of the Star or Master Masons.

Order of the Beauceant: The Social Order of Beauceant is an adoptive organization whose membership is limited to wives and widows of Knights Templar in good standing, or who were in good standing at the date of their decease.

Denver, Colo., was the home of the first assembly, which was established February 20, 1890, previous to the holding of the triennial of the Grand Encampment, K.T., in that city in 1892. It has 23 charter members, all of whom were residents of Denver. It was apparently designed for the purpose of raising money and assisting in the entertainment of representatives to the twenty-fifth triennial, for a bazaar held in 1891 raised over $1,000.00, later increased to $2,500.00, from which they were enabled to contribute money to the triennial committee and pay expenses for ladies headquarters.

The first ritual was short and unimpressive; two years later another ritual was adopted, and finally, in 1913, when the Grand Encampment again met in Denver, a third ritual was adopted. January 9, 1913, the name S.O.O.B. was changed to Social Order of the Beaceaunt; the Beauceant was the ancient banner of the Order of the Temple, and this tends to show the relationship of the organization with Knights Templar. There are approximately 130 assemblies meeting in twenty-nine States and the Territory of Hawaii, extending from Massachusetts to California, and from Montana to Texas.

Order of the Black Eagle: The Order of the Black Eagle was founded in the old Prussia which later became a part of Germany; the date was 1701, at the time of the coronation of their King. The number of knights was first limited to 30, not including members of the Royal Family; they were required to be thirty years of age, of noble descent through both parents for at least four generations. No member of the Court was allowed to travel more than twenty miles without permission. (See Knight of Red Eagle.)

Order of the Blazing Star: (See Blazing Star, Order of.)

Order of Blue Friars: (See Blue Friars, Society of.)

Order of Brotherly Love: The 16° of the Early Grand Rite, and the "cast of characters" includes Noah and his sons, Shem and Jafeth. Samuel I, Chapter xx is read for instruction. The ceremony is short; the obligation is short and refers to a "heart pierced with an arrow," the lecture referring to the love between David and Jonathan which continued throughout their lives.

Order of the Builders: January 12, 1922, a committee connected with the Van Renssalaer Lodge of Perfection, in Chicago, arranged a constitution and by-laws for an organization made up of young men to be known as the *Order of the Builders.*

The ritual was adopted January 21, 1921, and consists of two degrees: Apprentice Builders and Master Builder. At that time only sons and brothers of Master Masons, between the ages of fourteen and twenty-one, were admitted; later this requirement was abolished and members were admitted regardless of Masonic affiliation. In the first year more than sixty chapters were constituted, most of which were in the Chicago area. The Constitution states:

"The object of the voluntary organization in promoting the Order of the Builders for Boys (now the Order of the Builders) is to aid in advancing the mental, moral, physical and spiritual upbuilding and development of the boys in its membership."

The ritual treats of great Americans of the past, and officers wear robes in keeping with the lessons to be taught. The Order is governed by a central Council of Master Masons. A Board of Grand Examiners surpervises instruction in the ritual; each chapter elects or appoints fifteen officers, the principal officer being Master Builder. When a member becomes twenty-one, he becomes an honorary member of the chapter of which he had been a member; he may attend meetings, but does not take part in the business of the meeting and pays no dues. Those who become distinguished by their activities in the Order are made Legionaries of the Sovereign Council.

Order of Charitable Knights of the Holy City: (See Knights Beneficent of the Holy City.)

Order of Charles XIII (Karl or Carl): Although, properly, it does not

100

Diploma issued by the Grand Lodge of England in 1774 to Brother Jean Paul Marat, French Revolutionist.

directly bear upon the subject we have in hand, still, as a solitary instance of the honours paid to distinguished Masons by a sovereign in modern times, we must notice the *Order of Charles XIII,* an order of knighthood instituted by the King of Sweden in 1811, which he intended to be conferred only on the principal dignitaries of the Masonic institution in his dominions. In the manifesto establishing the Order, the King decreed:

"To give to this (the Masonic) society a proof of our gracious sentiments towards it, we will and ordain, that its first dignitaries, to the number which we may determine, shall, in future, be decorated with the most intimate proof of our confidence, and which shall be for them a distinctive mark of the highest dignity."

The number of Knights in the Order is twenty-seven, all Masons, and the King of Sweden is the perpetual Grand Master.

Order of Christ: When Rome broke up the Order of Templar Knights, the Order continued in Portugal under the title "Order of Christ." Many attempts to gain recognition therefore on the part of spurious French Templar bodies were unsuccessful. Finally, in 1807, a Portuguese-Nunez appeared in Paris with a concocted system which he foisted upon many under the pretext that it was the original Order of Christ, the titles of the grades being: (1) Knight of the Triple Cross; (2) Knight of the White and Black Eagle; (3) Knight Adept; (4) Sublime Elect of Truth; (5) Knight of the Black Eagle; (6) Sovereign Grand Commander; (7) Knight Kaes; (8) Knight of the Order of Christ.

The jewel of the Order is worn on a ribbon around the neck; it has two eagles, one black, the other white. The ritual of the degree is in *Collectanea* Vol. I, part 2. The Order is sometimes referred to as the "Nec (sic) Plus Ultra Templar." It is a degree thought to be one of those conferred by the "Order of the Temple of Christ."

Order of Co-Masonry: (See Co-Masonry.)

Order of Consecrated of the Philoclesian Host: (Consecrated Philoclesian Host.)

Order of Constantine, and Red Cross of Rome: Few degrees have so won the Masonic Craft as those connected with the Red Cross of Rome and Constantine. About a dozen years ago it was scarcely known, save to students of our ancient history, unless indeed it was erroneously classed with the Red Cross of Babylon. Now there are about 100 conclaves working under authority of the Grand Imperial Councils of England and Scotland, and many Grand Councils have been formed under its auspices, such as those now working most vigorously in Scotland, Pennsylvania, and other states in America, Canada, etc. Indeed, wherever these conclaves are flourishing, their origin is due to the revived Grand Imperial Council of England. It is somewhat singular that in this respect the modern Masonic Lodges throughout the world are in like manner indebted, directly or indirectly, to this country, as Brothers Hughan and Gould have clearly demonstrated.

The revival of the degrees occurred in this wise. The Red Cross of Rome and Constantine was given by Major Charles Shirreff and others from about 1780, and was patronized during the 17th century by Brothers James Heseltine (Past Grand Secretary), and William White (Grand Secretary from 1780), and other well-known Masons. Lord Rancliffe was Grand Master in

1796, as also of the Knights Templars, and was succeeded by Judge Waller Rodwell Wright in 1804, after which H.R.H. the Duke of Sussex was installed as "Grand Master for and during his natural life." In proof of these facts, we have but to point to the records of the Society for this period, which are happily still preserved. Some have advocated its being conferred *after* that of the Templar Degree, considering such was the custom during the period alluded to, but it is quite an error, the only prerequisite Masonically being then as now, viz, a duly certified Royal Arch Mason.* As an instance of this, we may remark that Brother William Henry White (who succeeded his father as Grand Secretary) was entrusted with this Red Cross Degree on the 13th of March, 1809, before he received either the Royal Arch or Knight Templar. The prefix *SIR* was used, not *Sir Knight* as now. The signature as Grand Master, by H.R.H. the Duke of Sussex, is carefully treasured by the present authorities, bearing date 22 November, 1813, being a resolution of the "High Council" approved by their illustrious Grand Master. The MS. ritual of the ceremony observed on the installation of the Duke of Sussex as G.M., lately discovered amongst certain papers in the Grand Lodge, has been duly forwarded to the Grand Imperial Council for custody. The ritual of the Grand Cross is still kept, and is in Brother W. R. Wright's own hand-writing. The ritual of the Red Cross is that sent by Col. M'Leod Moore (the Knight Templar historian), as executor of Brother Wright, to Brother Henry Emly, 33° Grand Chancellor, K.T.), by whom it was given to one of the three members who revived the degree. These three members obtained the *"Novitiate Cross"* from Brothers Henry Emly, William Henry White, and Sir J. Doratt, who were all at one time active in their support of the Grand Council. Permission was given by the High Council early last century to grand officers to confer the degree, and it is clear therefore that an unbroken line of descent has been preserved in the manner noted. One of the three *original* members named was elected Grand Secretary of the revived order (Brother W. H. White), who was succeeded by the Earl of Bective (then Lord Kenlis); afterwards Brother Sir Frederick M. Williams, Bart., M.P., occupied the chair. The body in England comprises a Grand Imperial Council and Grand Senate, and Intendants-General are appointed correspond-ing to the Inspectors-General of the Ancient and Accepted Rite. The *Knights of the Grand Cross* comprise the foregoing and about twenty others. There is likewise a "Patriarchal Council" for the control and working of the *Knights of the Holy Sepulchre and St. John,* the Grand Sovereign being the Grand Commander. Sanctuaries and Commanderies are warranted separately, about twenty having been issued in England.

Granting the desirability of degrees of Christian knighthood in connection with Freemasonry, the Red Cross of Rome and Constantine has clearly proved its legitimate descent from the Council worked in the last century, and that we apprehend is all that any can do of the kind. Its votaries will not soon forget their indebtedness to the late Brother R. W. Little for the excel-lent management displayed by him on its revival.

A Declaration of the Principles of the Order, written in 1806 by the late Judge Waller Rodwell Wright, the M.I.G. Master of the Order, and R.W. Prov. G. Master for the Ionian Isles, under the G. Lodge of England. (Bro.

---

* (In England, a Master Mason.)

103

Waller Rodwell Wright is said to have formed the present elaborate ritual of the Order.)

This Declaration stated:

The Order of Red Cross is one of those numerous branches of chivalry which had their origin in the Holy Wars, and the distinction won by its knights was the original badge of the Crusaders in general.

As this Order never was endowed with particular revenues, its members were for the most part persons of independent condition, or associated with one of the great Sovereign Orders of the Temple, or St. John of Jerusalem.

As, however, the distinguishing characteristics and constitutions of this Order, though existing only in unwritten tradition, have been partially preserved to the present age, some Knights Templars, zealous in the united cause of Masonry and Chivalry, have thought it expedient to revive it, on the footing of its ancient establishment, and that for various reasons:

First: Because the original intent of the Masonic Institution has been greatly frustrated by the indiscriminate admission of persons of every description and character.

Second: Because it unfortunately happens that the sublime branch of our system known by the denomination of Christian Masonry has fallen into still worse hands, whereby the Test of Faith originally required of the candidates for initiation has been dispensed with, the rites and mysteries of the Order degraded, and selection rendered indispensably necessary.

Thirdly: And this, indeed, is the most powerful reason which has induced them to bring forward this ancient Order—They earnestly wish to counteract the evil designs to which the privileges of the Masonic System have been perverted by men of unprincipled character, and to combat the enemies of Christianity and social order by the same secret and powerful means which they have made use of to effect their purposes.

The objects of the Red Cross are these:

"To draw closer the bond of Masonic union, purify the system of Masonic science, extend its limits, and increase its influence by combining such of its professors as are best qualified, by character and principle, respectability and influence, genius and talent, to effectuate this great purpose.

"To prevent the perversion of its institutions and privileges to objects contrary to, and abhorrent from, its original intent.

"To combat infidelity and treason under whatever form existing, and promote, by every humble means, the social happiness and eternal welfare of our fellow-creatures."

It is therefore necessary:

"That we observe the greatest circumspection in the choice of our members and associates.

"That we adhere inviolably and scrupulously to the principles and constitutions of our Order.

"That we cultivate a strict and fraternal union among ourselves.

"That we on all occasions give our decided preference to intellectual and moral excellence over every other consideration whatsoever."

HISTORICAL ORATION

(In the Ceremony of Reception)

The founder of our Chivalric and Illustrious Order was Constantine the great Roman Emperor, by whom it was instituted, A. D. 313, as a memorial of the Divine miracle which effected his conversion to the Christian faith,

104

and also as a reward for the valour of certain of his soldiers. Our Order is therefore not only the most ancient, but the most honourable institution of Christian Knighthood recorded in the pages of history; and it behooves us, beloved Sir Knights, to prize the privileges which we have obtained as descendants of these worthy men, ever remembering the watchwords of our Conclave—"Faith, Unity and Zeal." Before proceeding to relate the circumstance of Constantine's conversion, which produced such momentous results, I may first observe, that in tracing the influence of this great event upon the world in general, it is more particularly our duty, as Masons, to remember that our Royal Founder had been at an early period of his life initiated into the mysteries of the "Collegium Artificium" at Rome, and had attained the position of Magister or Master, of the College of Architects; and it was doubtless this early training which had sufficiently enlightened his mind to perceive the errors and absurdities of paganism, and caused him eagerly to desire a more complete knowledge of the unknown deity worshipped in those ancient mysteries. When he arrived at the Imperial dignity, not even the cares of empire or the responsibilities of command could erase those ideas, or restrain his profound researches after truth and wisdom. The manner of his conversion is thus described: One evening, the army being on its march towards Rome, Constantine—reflecting upon the fate of sublunary things and the dangers of his approaching expedition, and sensible of his own incapacity to succeed without Divine assistance—meditating, also, upon the various religious opinions which then divided mankind—sent up his ejaculations to Heaven for inspiration and wisdom to choose the right path to be pursued. T.G.A.O.T.U. heard his prayer, for as the sun was declining, there suddenly appeared a pillar of light in the heavens, in the shape of a cross, with this inscription: *In hoc signo vinces*—In this sign thou shalt conquer. So extraordinary an appearance created the utmost astonishment in the mind of the Emperor and his whole army. The Pagans deemed it a most inauspicious omen; but Constantine, being reassured by the visions of the night, at dawn of day caused a royal standard to be made like that which he had seen in the heavens, and commanded it to be carried before him in his wars, as an ensign of victory and ecclesiastical protection. Several Christian Masons among the soldiers, no longer fearing persecution, then came forward to avow their faith, and the Emperor, in order to commemorate the event, directed them to wear upon their armour a Red Cross with sixteen stars, denoting the sixteen letters of the mystic words. On returning to his capital, Constantine, with the assistance of Eusebius, opened a Conclave of Knights of the Order, and these valiant and illustrious men became afterwards the body-guard of their sovereign. The rose and the lily were adopted by our Royal Founder as emblems of the Divine Being he had learned to adore— mystically representing the Rose of Sharon and the Lily of the Valley. Among the acts of Constantine, his encouragement of learning is conspicuous; he commanded the Scriptures to be carefully kept and frequently read in all churches; he also devoted the fourth part of his revenue towards the relief of the poor and for other pious purposes. His tomb, of grey marble, continues at Constantinople to this day, and even its present possessors retain a veneration for the memory of the illustrious Constantine. Three hundred years had the persecution of our brethren continued, when it ceased with this great Emperor, who laid a lasting foundation for the honour of the Christian name. Upon this account his memory will flourish in the minds of all good men and Christian Masons until time shall be no more.

Order of Constructor Masons: Visitors to a recent Inter-American Conference in Mexico City heard much of an organization formed for the purpose of promoting a better feeling between the nations of the Western Hemisphere. The organization is known as the *Order of Constructor Masons* —Builders. But they are not engaged in the work of temporal building, but in the building of Unity among the Americas.

It is not a new organization, for it was founded in 1777. Its founders were men of distinction in their day—Pierre Francois Charles Augereau, Duke of Castiglione—Armando Charles Augustin, Duke of Castries, and Charles Axel Guillaumont of Paris. The first named brother was a member of the Lodge *Les Enfants de Mars* (Sons of Mars), and was a Chief of the 27 Regiment of Infantry and an official of the Grand Orient of France. The Duke de Castries was a distinguished Freemason of the Lodge *Les Bon Ami* in Paris. In civic life he was a General of the Army and a Deputy of the States General for Paris.

Guillaumont was a member of the Royal Academy of Architecture and Managing Director of Gobelin Tapestry industries; as did the two former brethren, he too occupied high Masonic station.

These three Founders of the Order celebrated their first reunion in the Lodge *Les Bon Ami,* December 17, 1777. In that session they devised the Statutes which governed the new institution and designated Hon. Charles Augereau as Sovereign Grand Commander. That illustrious Freemason governed the Order without interruption until 1816.

The institution showed quick growth among Freemasons, but in the few years which followed, the period of the Revolution, it suffered a series of setbacks. But the Chief Founder reunited the dispersed elements and with great enthusiasm sought to reestablish its ancient prestige.

In 1817, Juan Bautista Vermay de Beame was elected Grand Commander, a famous French artist, who in that same year removed to Havana, Cuba, resulting in the offices of the Order being moved to that city. Beame ruled until 1837. The Order thereafter declined in Europe but grew in the Antilles, Mexico, and Central America. It thereafter became a strictly American institution.

In 1838, Francisco O'Donnelly Bastion headed the Order and moved it to the City of Mexico, his permanent residence. Here it exercised its functions until 1858; in 1859 Juan Francisco de la Serna became Grand Commander and moved the headquarters to Guatemala City, Guatemala. The following year, Manuel Bonilla succeeded to the office and served until 1886, when in 1887, he too was succeeded by Francisco Eleazaro Asturias who governed for 36 years uninterruptedly. During a part of this period Bro. Asturias served as Grand Commander of the A.A.S.R. for Central America. Then in 1924, Juan Clausel of Caracas, Venezuela was made Chief, serving until 1939. Then came a removal to Havana, Cuba, with the selection of Ramon Gonzalez de la Gandara; he was an active member of the Supreme Council of Cuba.

The list of members numbers some of the most distinguished Freemasons of the Western World—at least the Latin-American section. The late Porfirio Diaz, President of Mexico was one of the members.

From the very beginning the objective has been to give active collaboration with the Masonic Fraternity; it accentuates the American character of the institution, an objective which has grown little by little since its removal to the Western hemisphere. It would unite all of the republics of the new world.

It was General Simon Bolivar, who advised: "Unite, unite, or otherwise you will be destroyed."

The organization is not, properly speaking, a Masonic organization; it has no desire to invade the field of regular Masonry. It has but twenty-one nations listed on this continent. Its mission is to create better relations between these various countries.

Members of the Order—known as *Knights*—are supposed to carry on correspondence with each other in the hope of forming closer friendships.

In 1948, General Miguel Orrico de los Llanos of Mexico City was elected Grand Commander and the headquarters removed to Mexico City. Grand Commanders are elected for a period of five years. Other officers are a Lieut. Grand Commander, a Secretary General, a Treasurer General, and a Chancellor General.

Membership is limited to nationals of each country; one must be 25 years of age; he must be an active member of some Masonic lodge, possessing the third degree; he must be one of good report in the community in which he lives; he must respect the laws of his country, obey the orders of the Grand Commander which are of high moral or patriotic dictum; he must agree to carry on correspondence with his fellow Knights.

The Badge of the Order is a Maltese Cross suspended from a bar by a black ribbon. In the centre of the Cross are the initials O.C.M.

Order of Corks: This "Order" was established October 12, 1933, in Washington, D.C., by the late Marquis of Ailsa; he was at the time visiting the General Grand Chapter of Royal Arch Masons, being the First Grand Principal of the Grand Chapter of Scotland. Ten brethren were created "Corks," and these were the nuclei for the formation of "Ye Antient Order of Corks." The U.S.A. constitutes a Province of the Scotland order; meeting places are called "cellars." Only Royal Ark Mariners are eligible. The degree is now under the control of the Allied Masonic Degrees. The object is to promote good fellowship; needless to say it has a humorous ritual. The fee is 25c, which goes into a charity fund.

De l'Ordre Macconique de Misraim: (See Rite of Misraim.)

Order of DeMolay: One of the fastest growing youth organizations has been that of the Order of DeMolay, whose growth has been phenomenal, was established on March 18, 1919, in Kansas City, Mo. The object of the organization, as set forth in its advertising pamphlets, is "encouragement and development of good citizenship and sound character among youth, teaching clean and upright living by inculcating and practicing the virtues of comradship, reverence, love of parents, patriotism, courtesy, cleanliness and fidelity. It is governed by a Grand Council which meets annually in the month of March. Its head is known as the Grand Master Councilor, but the Secretary-General (Frank S. Land, who is the founder) acts as administrative officer, assisted by the seventy-five members and deputies of the Grand Council. A local body is known as a *Chapter* and is presided over by a *Master Councilor*.

In 1955, there were more than 1600 active chapters, with more than 130,000 members. It confers a number of degrees, orders and awards. Any young man between the age of fourteen and twenty-one is eligible.

The Order derives its name from Jacques DeMolay, Grand Master of the Order of Knights Templar, who was burned at the stake on an Island in the Seine River in Paris in 1314, following seven years of imprisonment and torture, for refusal to identify other members of his organization.

There are two classes of degrees and awards: (1) For DeMolays; (2) For Freemasons. They are listed as follows:

DeMolays:
1. Initiatory and DeMolay degree
2. Order of Knighthood
3. Representative Award
4. Legion of Honor
5. DeMolay Medal of Honor
6. Chevalier
7. Medal of Heroism
8. Blue Honor Award
9. Merit Medals

Freemasons:
1. Advisor's Honor Key
2. Zerubbabel Key
3. Exceptional Service Cross
4. Honorable Distinction Cross
5. White Honor Key for Freemasons
6. Cross of Honor
7. Medal of Appreciation
8. Honorary Legion of Honor
9. Founder's Cross

The headquarters of the organization are at Warwick and Armour Blvd., Kansas City, Mo. Chapters of the Order have been established in many foreign countries.

Order of Desoms: (See Desoms, Order of.)

Order of Ducks: An organization formed for those who are engaged in handling the scenery for the Scottish Rite degrees; it is confined to the area of Texas, Oklahoma and Kansas. It has no ritual or secret work. It originated in Dallas, Texas; local units are called "Flights." It was recently given approval by the Grand Lodge of Texas. Its object is said to be "to further cooperation, good fellowship and harmony among its members." There is a Flight Commander, who presides over the flights; a Flight Leader, who executes his orders; a Chief Quacker, who is the Orator; a Chief Hatcher, "who examines the egg" (candidate) and has charge of the "incubation." The Quill Driver is the Secretary, and a Sky Pilot does the "spiritual duties," whatever they may be. The "emblem of the Order" is a facsimile of a Mallard Duck in flight; the colors are green, white and red. Members give their assent to any proposition presented them by giving three "Quacks."

Order of Eastern Star: An organization for women, founded by Rob. Morris in 1850; it began as an American organization, but has since spread to other Continents; it is the foremost of the adoptive rites. Morris went about the country lecturing to Freemasons and took advantage of such tours to confer the degree in homes and lodge rooms; he gave the groups thus formed the name "Constellations." This was followed by a "Supreme Constellation." In 1867, the group assumed the name now in use. The first Grand Chapter was formed in Michigan in 1867, and in 1876, at Indianapolis, Ind., the General Grand Chapter came into being; today every state in the union has a Grand Chapter. Two states saw fit not to enter the national body— New York and New Jersey. In Pennsylvania, Freemasons are forbidden to join; in New York, any Freemason, after assuming an obligation of secrecy, is permitted to sit in their meetings.

It is said to have five degrees, although, actually, they constitute only sections of a degree. These are the Star Points of Adah, Ruth, Esther, Martha, Electa, representing the daughter, widow, wife, sister, and a Christian martyr, to whom was given the name Electa.

Order: Ethiopian Hebrews, Royal Order of: A negro organization which claims to be made up of "Jewish" negroes.

Order of Felicitares (L'Ordre des Felicitares): This was one of the adoptive systems in vogue in France about 1745.

Order of Fendeurs (L'Ordre des Fendeurs): The Order existed in France about 1747, where it was established by one of the Paris lodges. It imitated the Society of Carbonari, or Charcoal Burners. Their meeting places were termed "wood-yards" and represented a forest. The most distinguished people in France joined and it became very popular for a time. It was one of the androgynous degrees. Its object was said to be the protection of those who lived in the woods, and who might, through such a life, meet with dangerous characters (?). Candidates were "lost in the woods," cleansed, purified, taught to give charity. The penalty of the obligation was: "May the axe of the woodcutter separate my head from my body if I ever perjure myself."

Order of Fratres Lucis: Literally, Brothers of Light.

Order of French Noachidae: Dr. Anderson, in his 1723 Constitutions, stated: "A Mason is obliged by his tenure to observe the moral law as a true Noachida," which probably gave rise to the name of the Order. They are descendants of Noah. It became a French Rite.

Order of the Garter: The Order of the Garter is of British origin and is still being conferred; most of the Grand Masters of the United Grand Lodge of England have received the decoration. It is said to have been instituted by King Edward III, and there are many stories extant as to the occasion for its institution. It was at first dedicated to the Virgin Mary, St. Edward the Confessor, and St. George, the latter being the patron saint of England. Members were known as *Knights of St. George;* its religious headquarters were in the Chapel of St. George at Windsor; at first there were but 26 members, which always includes the Sovereign, who is the constitutional head of the Order. In 1786 it was decided to name all princes of the realm as members. Most recent additions were Sir Winston Churchill and Anthony Eden. The insignia is distinctive; a garter of dark blue ribbon is worn on the left leg below the knee; on the Garter is the motto "Honi soit qui mal y pense" (Evil to whom, who evil thinks"). The mantle is of blue velvet with a Star on left breast; then comes a hood of crimson velvet, lined with white; a black velvet hat has a white ostrich plume in the center of which is a black heron plume; a pendant bearing the figure of St. George slaying a dragon is worn on a collar of dark blue ribbon, with a lesser "George" on the left shoulder. Freemasonry antedates the Order by many years, hence the expression "More ancient than etc."

American Order of the Garter:

This was the second of the degrees conferred in Columbian Council No. 1, New York, during the first eight years of its existence. It was known as *Knight of the Honorable Order of the Garter,* although it bore various titles. In one instance, November 3, 1811, "Illustrious Knights of the Honorable Order of the Garter"; at other times it is called "The Invincible Order." In some instances the minutes convey the information that candidates who had received the Order of the Garter were installed "Knights of the Order of St. George of Capidosia." Some think that the Order of the Garter and the Order of St. George were one and the same.

In 1811, it was stated that the year of the Order of the Garter was 454,

109

which would give the date of its origin as 1357 A.D., that happens to be the date of the founding of the Order of the Garter by King Edward.

Winston's Encyclopedia states:

"The common title of the order was the Order of St. George, and it still bears this title, as well as that of the Garter. The original number of knights was twenty-six, including the sovereign, who was its permanent head; and this number is still retained, except that by a statute passed in 1786 princes of the blood are admitted as supernumerary members. The peculiar emblem of the order, the garter, a dark-blue ribbon edged with gold, bearing the motto and with a gold buckle and pendant, is worn on the left leg below the knee. The mantle is of blue velvet, lined with taffeta, the surcoat and hood of crimson velvet, the hat of black velvet, with plume of white ostrich feathers, having in the center a tuft of black heron's feathers. The collar of gold, which consists of twenty-six pieces, each in the form of a garter, has the badge of the order called the George, pendant from it. This consists of a figure of St. George on horseback fighting the dragon. The lesser George is worn on a broad blue ribbon over the left shoulder. The star formerly only a cross, is of silver, and consists of eight points, with the cross of St. George in the center, encircled by the garter. A star is worn by the knights on the left side when not in the dress of the order. The officers of the order are the prelate, the Bishop of Winchester; the chancellor, the Bishop of Oxford; the registrar, Dean of Windsor; the garter king of arms and the usher of the black rod. There are a dean and twelve canons, and each knight has a knight-pensioner."

The Order of the Garter had twenty-four knights, with the King and Black Prince—26 in all, as distinguished from the Order of the Round Table with 24 knights with the King at the head. The collar of the Garter has 26 pieces, one for each member, which with the badge of "George" numbers 27. The number of members cannot be increased; they were a select company of 24, to which three leaders were added making the whole number 27—one of Freemason's symbolic numbers.

The Robe of the Order has a Star and Garter on the left shoulder and is a source of our Masonic expression "The Star and Garter."

A special patron of the Order is St. George, who has been identified with George of Cappadocia, although some believe that St. George was another character. St. George is the patron saint of England, Aragon and Portugal; St. George of Cappadocia was the patron saint of the Caucasian countries. (Cryptic Rite History.) (See Order of the Round Table.)

Order of the Golden Chain: The Order of the Golden Chain is a New Jersey organization, established August 5, 1929, at Asbury Park, with the idea of assisting in the maintenance of a 145 acre camp, and a 10 acre lake, in Warren County, N. J. The camp is primarily for underprivileged children and has a capacity of 150 campers. The investment in this camp is over $100,000.00. There are thirty-seven "Links" located in the States of Connecticut, Delaware, Massachusetts, New Jersey, New York, Pennsylvania and Rhode Island.

Order of the Golden Fleece (See Golden Fleece.)

Order of Golden Key: The Order of the Golden Key was formed March 21, 1925, in the Masonic Temple, Norman, Okla., and apparently grew out of Sigma Mu Sigma Fraternity, an organization of Master Masons at the University of Oklahoma. On that occasion the President of the University, the Deans of several departments, and some distinguished Oklahoma Freemasons received the Order.

In 1929, when there appeared to be a lack of undergraduates who were Freemasons, the fraternity was forced to admit sons of Freemasons, and Sigma Mu Sigma was absorbed by Tau Kappa Epsilon. Several hundred candidates were initiated in the nine chartered chapters.

In 1930, there was formed a Sovereign Preceptory, which was reorganized in 1932. At the present time (1953) its headquarters seem to be in Joliet, Ill. Membership is by invitation, and is limited to Freemasons. There are two degrees: (a) Chief Craftsman, or Pledge Degree; (b) Knight of the Golden Key, or Initiatory Degree. There appear to be four divisions, Honorary Knights being members of the Order of the Pentalpha; Sovereign Knights, who are officials, belong to the Order of the Golden Circle; those who have been pledged belong to the Order of Chief Craftsmen; and those who have been initiated as Knights belong to the Order of the Golden Key.

There are, on occasion, open meetings. The Order is under control of a Sovereign Preceptory, headed by a Sovereign Preceptor.

Order of Grain of Mustard: (See Order of Mustard Seed.)

Order of Harmony: In 1783, a society was established in Paris whose object was to carry on experiments in Mesmerism; it was a quasi-Masonic order and bore the title of "Order of Universal Harmony."

Order of Hercules: According to Voorhis, the Order was organized within the body of Cincinnati Lodge No. 1, Cincinnati, Ohio.

Order of Heredom: In 1764, the Prince of Clermont was Grand Master of this Rite; the Duke of Chartres was his deputy. It has twenty-five degrees, nineteen of which were the same as the A.A. Rite; others were Grand Patriarch Noachite; Key of Masonry; Prince of Lebanon; Knight of the Sun; Kadosh; and Prince of the Royal Secret. The Kadosh was a mixture of Templary, Knight of the Sun, Philosophical, etc., and was called "Knight of the Black Eagle."

Order of Heredom and Red Cross: Said to have been founded by King Robert Bruce at Kilwinning. After the Battle of Bannockburn, on June 24, 1314, the King created the Order of St. Andrew of the Thistle, to which was afterwards united that of Heredom, for the sake of the Masons who formed a part of his troops. The King established the Royal Grand Lodge of Heredom at Kilwinning, reserving to himself and his successors the office of Grand Master. The Order is, we believe, largely confined to Scotland and is given only to those who, by exaltation or affiliation, are registered in the books of the Grand Chapter of Royal Arch Masons. The historical tradition relates that after the dissolution of the Templar Order, several of the Knights placed themselves under the protection of Bruce, and greatly contributed to gain the victory of Bannockburn; these were the Masons, it is said, for whom he instituted the Order of Heredom. All Masonry declined during the 16th and 17th Centuries, and this Order was in abeyance until the middle of the last Century, when its functions were resumed at Edinburgh. In order to preserve a marked distinction between the Royal Order and Craft Masonry, which had formed a Grand Lodge in that city in 1736, the former confined itself entirely to the two degrees of Heredom and Rosy Cross. Dr. Oliver says the Heredom was not originally Masonic, but appears to have been connected with some ceremonies of the early Christians, which are believed to have been introduced by the Culdees, whose principal seat was at I-Colm-Kill, during the second and third centuries of the Christian era. The Rosy Cross,

111

which in French was termed *Grade de la Tour,* is honorary, the tradition being that it was an Order of Knighthood first conferred on the field of Bannockburn.

Its seat is in Edinburgh, the Governor being (if a Mason) the King of Great Britain and Ireland. Otherwise it is never filled, but a Deputy Governor is appointed. It is worked in England and abroad by authority of the Scottish Grand Lodge of the "Royal Order."

Order of High Priesthood: In the old ceremonial of the Royal Arch in England, the government was vested in the Three Chiefs: High Priest, King, Prophet—and this form is preserved in the United States. An honorary degree was conferred on the retiring first officer, as we now confer one, on the Past First Principal. When the ritual was performed in ample form, the presence of nine High Priests was required. (See High Priesthood.)

Order of the Holy Cross: (See Knight of the Holy Cross.)

Order of the Holy Sepulchre: (See Sepulchre, Order of.)

Order of Jerusalem: (See Jerusalem, Order of.)

Order of Jesters: (See Jesters, Royal Order of.)

Order of Job's Daughters: The Order of Job's Daughters is an auxiliary, limited to daughters of Master Masons, or daughters of marital relatives of Master Masons. It is an enthusiastic organization, and has greatly spread throughout the United States, having 768 Bethels in thirty-one States. Its membership is past the 70,000 mark. It was established October 20, 1920, by Mrs. Ethel T. Wead Mick, of Omaha, Nebr. It limits membership to girls between the ages of thirteen and twenty, providing honorary membership for those who attain their twentieth birthday. It has one degree—the Initiatory Degree—which was written by Mrs. Mick, its lessons being taken from the 15th verse of the 42d chapter of the Book of Job.

Local groups are Bethels, and each is headed by an Honored Queen; each Bethel has a Guardian Council, with five adults, one of whom must be a Master Mason. The Supreme Guardian Council of the World has jurisdiction over all Bethels; each State may form itself into a Grand Guardian Council, and twenty-two have done so.

Order of Kaditri: (See Kaditri, Order of.)

Order of Knighthood: A degree given in the Order of DeMolay. (See Order of DeMolay.)

Orders of Knighthood: Technically speaking, Orders of Knighthood are those conferred by Kings, or Sovereigns, upon their lesser nobles. Freemasonry apes the custom by conferring degrees (and not Orders) on candidates, and giving them titles hardly in accord with the great principles of the fraternity, which stress equality and fraternity. The great mass of people like titles, and the longer the title the better they seem to enjoy them. The only Order of which we have knowledge, which has a Masonic connection, is the Order of Charles XIII of Sweden. The Templars, Knights of Malta, and Knights Hospitaller, have connection by only the widest stretch of imagination. Our Masonic brethren have built some of their degrees around these ancient knights, forgetting that most of these were rival Orders in their heyday. The Scottish Rite stresses the Teutonic Knights, even to the adopting of a Teutonic Cross. The Order of Malta assisted the Church in driving Freemasons from Malta, and today exists as a Catholic Order with apparently the same antagonism to the fraternity.

112

Order of Knight Masons of Ireland: (See Knight Masons of Ireland.)

Order of Knights Templar: (See Knights Templar; see United Religious and Military Orders of the Temple and of St. John of Jerusalem, Palestine, Rhodes and Malta.)

Order of Knight Templar Priest: (See Knight Templar Priest.)

Order of Knights and Heroines of Anchor: Sometimes called "Knights and Ladies of the Anchor," an androgynous order of 1745, referred to by Clavel as a schismatic group which grew out of the Order of Felicitares. (See Anchor, Order of.)

Order of Knights and Nymphs of the Rose: (See Knights and Nymphs of the Rose.)

Order of Knights Beneficent of the Holy City: (See Knights Beneficent of the Holy City.)

Order of Knights of the East: (See East, Knight of.)

Order of Knights Grand Cross of Constantine: During the early history of the Red Cross of Constantine, an attempt was made to set up the above organization, which would have established a "super control" over the national organization. It failed and was frowned upon by the Grand Imperial Councils of other countries. In recent years it was consolidated with the Grand Imperial Council U.S.A. (Western Empire).

Order Knights of the Palm Tree: Among the several variants of the *Order of the Palm* (the best known of which is *The Palm and Shell*), one of the most interesting is that which forms the title of this paper.

This was originated by Robert Morris, LL.D. Its membership was confined to those who had contributed to his "Holy Land Expedition Fund."

Morris conceived the idea of a Masonic Expedition to the Holy Land in the early '50's, but did not succeed in accomplishing it until 1868. It was financed by contributions from individual Masons and Masonic Lodges. A complete account of the expedition is given in Morris's "Freemasonry in the Holy Land; or Handmarks of Hiram's Builders," a work of more than 600 pages, which met with a considerable sale and which can be found in almost all Masonic libraries.

According to Morris, the whole number of contributors to the fund was 2,782, the aggregate of the contributions being $9,631. Each contributor was to receive certain souvenirs or specimens from the Holy Land, these varying according to the amount of the contribution.

The idea of a special Masonic "Degree" or "Order" to be confined to those who had assisted in financing the expedition probably originated during the late 60's.

So far as can be ascertained the Order was never very widely disseminated, but was communicated by Morris (and possibly by others) upon individual Masons in various parts of the country. There seems never to have been any regular organization of the Order, and *The Royal Solomon Mother Lodge at Jerusalem,* referred to in the ritual, was doubtless a purely imaginary institution.

The ritual is rather well written and is far more elaborate than that of most of the "side degrees" of the period.

The badge of the Order was a Palm-tree with twelve branches, about one inch high and slightly less than one-half inch at its widest point. (Wm. L. Cummings.)

113

Order of Knights York Cross of Honour: (See Knights of the York Cross of Honour.)

Order of Liberty: Masonic research has failed to reveal material on this Order.

Order of Light: (See Fratres Lucis.)

Order of Malta: According to A. S. Hall-Johnson, there are today, three separate organizations which are of especial interest to Freemasons. They are:

(a) The "Sovereign Military Order of Malta," in Rome.
(b) "The Order of St. John of Jerusalem," in the British Empire.
(c) The "Masonic Order of St. John of Jerusalem, Palestine, Rhodes, and Malta," which is the one in which we, as Freemasons, are interested.

These organizations are also referred to as (a) the Papal Order, (b) the Order of St. John, and (c) the Masonic Order.

The President and his wife, Eva Peron, of Argentina received the Papal Order in January 1949; the Order has diplomatic representatives to certain countries. In 1949, the Argentine postoffices used a cancellation stamp showing the Malta Cross.

The British Order is always headed by the King, or a member of the nobility, who is the Grand Prior.

The Masonic Order was conferred in Malta even before the Knights were banished from the island. In England, March 22, 1791, Thomas Dunckerly accepted the Grand Mastership of the Masonic Knights Templar of Jerusalem. And in Edinburgh, Scotland, December, 1778, the Edinburgh Royal Arch Chapter recorded in their minutes that "Knights of Malta" was one of its "steps."

It is often wondered why a Templar system should include in it such a degree as Knight of Malta, when they consider the fact that the Templar and Hospitaller were, in the past, often rivals, and sometimes enemies. In England today the Order is known as the "Great Priory of the United, Religious, and Military Orders." In the United States and Canada, the Order is attached to, and made a part of the Templar system, and is conferred previous to that of Knight of the Temple.

The ritual of the degree is an elaborate ceremonial of which "passing the banners" constitutes a large part, during which the history of the Order is given during its various residences in Palestine, Rhodes, Cyprus, Candia, and Malta. The degree is Trinitarian in character. (See Order of the Temple; Knights Templar; Knight of Malta.)

Order of Marquis St. Martin: (See Rite, Grand College of.)

Order of Martinists: The Rite of the Elus-Cohenim (Elected Priests) was organized in France about 1750 by Martinez de Pasqually, a contemporary of the Rosicrucians of England. Pasqually went to San Domingo in 1772, and died there two years later. Louis Claude de Saint Martin, a disciple of Pasqually, remodeled the society under the name of *Men of Desire,* but it was not successful. Martinism continued, however, to be the repository of many of the sacred traditions of the Rosicrucians and Freemasons.

The Order was introduced into Germany in 1782, being revivified by J. B. Willernoz. In 1886 it appeared in the United States, confining its membership to Master Masons. In 1900 the Superiors in France authorized some innovations desired by a few of the American brethren, allowing membership to profanes. A group, with headquarters in Sandusky, Ohio, met for a short time and became dormant.

A Convention of the Martinists of the United States was held in Cleveland, Ohio, June 6-7, 1902, and adopted the name *American Rectified Martinist Order,* with initiates to the School of Martinism being selected from the Masonic Fraternity exclusively. Martinism, like Rosicrucianism, being a guide into the labyrinth of arcane Masonic symbolism, both fraternities are adjuncts to it. One of the points stressed in the reconstructed order was the quality of its membership, rather than the quantity.

Dr. Edouard Blitz, of New York City, was closely connected with this group, although he was the head of another group called the *Universal Idealist Union of Fraternity of Initiates.* Attempt has been made to determine if Dr. Blitz is still living, but nothing has been found.

Order of Melchizedek: No doubt this Order was the forerunner of the present Order of High Priesthood.

Order of Merit: A Canadian group of limited membership, established by Lt. Col. Alexander Gordon in 1854, to commemorate the revival of Templary in Canada; it was limited to 12 members, all of whom had to be members of Hugh de Payens Encampment. It died early because the members could not agree on their successors. The number symbolized the number of the Apostles. (See Ancient and Primate Rite.)

Order of Militia Ecclesiastica Evangelica: This group claims a descent from an Order organized by Simon Studion in 1527, called *The Soldiers of the Crucifixion,* which followed the teachings of Paracelsus to a great extent. The first Manifesto was issued in 1530 and the first general convention was held in 1598. Introduction into the United States is claimed in 1902, with a Manifesto issued in that year, followed by another in 1903. It published an official organ called *The Initiates.* As a separate Order it is not active, but is now listed under the heading *Subordinate, Auxiliary, Ritualistic, Preparatory Order of Degrees,* controlled by *The Confederation of Initiates,* whose head in the United States is Dr. R. Swinburne Clymer, Quakertown, Pa.

Order of Misraim: (See Rite of Misraim.)

Order of Mustard Seed (or Grain of Mustard): Order of Mustard Seed, or The Fraternity of Moravian Brothers of the Order of Religious Freemasons, was instituted at Halle, in Germany, about 1720, by Count Zinnendorf, and was the origin of the Herrnhutters or Moravian Brethren. Its mysteries were founded on the parable in St. Mark's gospel, where our Lord said:

"Whereunto shall we liken the kingdom of God; or with what comparison shall we compare it? It is like a grain of mustard seed, which, when it is sown in the earth, is less than all the seeds that be in the earth; but when it is sown, it groweth up, and becometh greater than all herbs, and shooteth out great branches; so that the fowls of the air may lodge under the shadow of it."

The description which our Lord has given of the mustard tree occasioned much conjecture, and Lightfoot cites a passage from the Talmud, in which a mustard tree is said to have been possessed of branches sufficiently large to cover a tent, while Schkuhr describes and represents a species of the plant several feet high, and possessing a tree-like appearance.

The jewel of the Order, suspended from a green ribbon, was a cross of gold surmounted by a mustard plant, with the words, "What was it be-

115

fore? Nothing!" The brethren wore a ring on which was inscribed "No one lives for himself." This Order is obsolete, and is now represented by the rite named after its originator, Count Zinnendorf.

Order of the Mystic Star: An organization, now extinct, for women, which for a time threatened to be a competitor of the Eastern Star. It was formed in New York about 1873.

Order: Mystic Order of Veiled Prophets of the Enchanted Realm: The official name of the Grotto is the *Mystic Order of Veiled Prophets of the Enchanted Realm.* Its membership is limited to Master Masons, members of regular lodges. Its object is "to benefit the symbolic lodge," although the organization does not claim to be a Masonic Order. It confers a degree whose ritual, adopted in 1940—

"Is founded on a very ancient Persian manuscript, discovered in a secret vault in one of the sacred temples of Teheran, the City of Mystery."

Local groups are called Grottoes, presided over by a Monarch. The national organization is presided over by a Grand Monarch. Annual sessions of the Order have been held since 1890, although at that time it was conferred in the body of Hamilton Lodge No. 120, F. & A. M., Hamilton, N. Y. Until 1904, charters were granted only to groups in the City of New York, but by 1953 Grottoes had been established in forty-one states, the District of Columbia, the Canal Zone, and two Canadian Provinces. There are more than two hundred active Grottoes; they no longer bear numbers, simply names.

Order of Noachidae: (See Order of French Noachidae.)

Order of Odd Fellows: (See International Order of Odd Fellows.)

Order of Palm and Shell: The *Masonic Order of the Palm and Shell,* which enjoyed considerable popularity during the decade from 1875 to 1885 was an outgrowth of *The Masonic Order of the Knights of the Palm-Tree,* the complete ritual of which was published in Parts 10 and 11, Vol. I, of *Miscellanea.*

It is doubtful if any official ritual of this Order was ever published. In 1879, Rev. Henry R. Coleman published *The Pilgrim Knight, a Guide to the Ceremonies and Lectures of the Oriental Order of the Palm and Shell.* Coleman was then Supreme Chancellor of the Order. He claimed that the Order was conferred upon him by some Sheik in Egypt, who commissioned him, under seal, as Master for the Western Hemisphere.

This book of 96 pages is really a monitor rather than a ritual, the esoteric portions being represented by asterisks. From a careful comparison of it with the ritual of *The Masonic Order of the Knights of the Palm-Tree,* and from a number of brethren who received the Order, either from Coleman or from Rob Morris, it is evident that it was created by taking the original ritual of *Knights of the Palm-Tree* and engrafting upon it some additional matter.

According to Bro. Harold V. B. Voorhis, Grand Supt. in N. J., Brother Coleman was a paralytic in the Old Masons' Home at Shelbyville, Ky., where he died in 1924. While there he conferred the grade on a number of brethren, including Bro. W. H. McDonald, then editor of the "Masonic Home Journal" of Kentucky, to whom he left all the regalia, paraphernalia and the chiefship of the Order. Bro. McDonald died March 31, 1925, leaving the chiefship and regulation to someone in Atlanta, Ga., who has not yet been traced.

116

Like the *Knights of the Palm-Tree,* the *Order of the Palm and Shell* was intended to encourage the researches commenced in the Holy Land in 1868, under the personal lead of Robert Morris.

The idea of the "Shell" portion of the degree probably had its inception in the fact that from a very early date the scallop-shell was the recognized badge of a pilgrim. While originally those who had made a pilgrimage to the Holy Land wore a palm-branch, the scallop-shell being the peculiar emblem of pilgrims to the shrine of St. James of Compostella (in Spain), it became the custom for pilgrims from Palestine to wear the shell also, sometimes sewn on the cloak, but more frequently on the hat. (Dr. W. L. Cummings.)

Order of the Palm Tree: (See Order of Knights of the Palm Tree.)

Order of Perfect Happiness: (See Felicitares; Order of Felicity.)

Order: Priestly Order of the Temple: At one time Priories of Knights Templar in Scotland were authorized to confer the grade of "Priest of the Order of the Temple." We are uncertain as to whether this is the present degree known as Knight Templar Priest or not, but we are inclined to believe that it is.

The Holy Royal Arch Knight Templar Priests, ofttimes called the *Priestly Order of the Temple,* is generally recognized as one of the highest, if not indeed the highest, honor that can be bestowed upon a Freemason. Its history, like all ancient and meritorious orders, is lost in the hoary past. In Ireland its appearance was contemporary with the Templar Order, with which it is so inextricably associated. Records of the two Orders appear throughout the Emerald Isle at an early date and at the turn of the nineteenth century, the Priestly Order was exceedingly popular with the Irish, where it was worked by so-called *Union Bands.* The History of Freemasonry in Ireland, by Crossle & Lepper, is replete with references to The Order and therein are many illustrations of charters and membership diplomas.

In Scotland, the Priestly Order was called *White Masonry* and was jealously controlled by the Early Grand Rite. In England, it has been mothered and nourished at Newcastle-on-Tyne, the seat of the Grand College of England.

Here in America it was known and conferred by the title of the *Holy Order of Wisdom* during the last century.

John Yarker, an English writer, in his Mysteries of Antiquity, says that the Order formed the system used by York Grand Lodge, and consisted of seven degrees:

1, 2, 3, Symbolic; 4, Past Master; 5, Royal Arch; 6, Knight Templar; 7, Knight Templar Priest, or Holy Wisdom.

The latter degree was conferred in a place referred to as a Tabernacle and was governed by seven officers known as Pillars. Another eminent English writer, William J. Hughan, doubts the York origin of the Order.

The original Great Priory of Americas used the Latin "Ordo Sacerdotalis Templi," which at present, in order to conform with our English Grand College nomenclature, has been changed to H.R.A.K.T.P.

The High Priest of a Royal Arch Chapter is honored by being anointed, consecrated and set apart in the Order of High Priesthood. The Master of a Council may receive the degree of Thrice Illustrious Master. It remains for

117

the Priestly Order of the Temple to honor the installed Commander of a Commandery of Knights Templar by consecrating him a Holy Royal Arch Knight Templar Priest.

Tabernacles of the Order, which are located in numerous states and in Canada, are limited to thirty-three Knights Priests, in commemoration of the number of years which Jesus, our Blessed Emmanuel, spent on earth. Following the same symbolism, Tabernacles control the following thirty-three Orders:

Knight of the Christian Mark, Knight of Saint Paul, Knight of Patmos, Knight of Death, Knight of The Black Cross, Knight of Bethany, Knight of The White Cross, Knight of Saint John, Knight Priest of the Holy Sepulchre, Holy Order of Wiscom, Holy and Illustrious Order of The Cross, Priest of Eleusis, Knight of Harodim, Knight of the North, Knight of the South, King of the Sanctuary, Grand Cross of Saint Paul, Knight Priest of Jerusalem, Knight of Palestine, Knight of the Holy Cross, Knight of Saint John the Baptist, Knight Rosae Crucis, Knight of the Triple Cross, Knight of the Holy Grave, Knight of the Holy Virgin Mary, Knight of the White Cross of Torphichen, Grand Trinitarian Knight of Saint John, Grand Cross of Saint John, Knight Priest of the Tabernacle, Knight of Redemption, Knight of Truth, Knight of Rome, and Holy Royal Arch Knight Templar Priest.

Obviously, these orders are not actually conferred, but a blanket obligation is administered which covers them all. The Holy Royal Arch Knight Templar Priest is occasionally worked in extended form by some of the Tabernacles.

Grand College confers two honoraria: *Knight Grand Commander,* the number of which is restricted to twelve, and *Knight Commander,* which is limited to twelve times twelve, in conformity to the ancient customs of the Order.

The liturgical procedure of the Priestly Order of the Temple is, unquestionably, the most beautiful extant, and throughout its ritualistic movements are contained the most sublime symbolism and philosophy to be found anywhere in Masonic ritual. At the same time, however, its procedure is simple, intensely Trinitarian, easily understood and appreciated.

The insignia of the Order is a purple Salem cross, superimposed on a scarlet delta, edged in gold. (J. Ray Shute, III.)

Order of Prussian Blue: (See Order: Royal Order of Prussian Blue.)

Order of Rainbow: The Order of Rainbow for Girls is an International Order for the daughters of Master Masons or Order of the Eastern Star, between thirteen and eighteen years of age. It has assemblies in forty-one States, the Canal Zone, Canada, Guam, Philippine Islands, Mexico, Cuba, Australia, Japan, Alaska.

The first assembly was convened in McAlester, Okla., April 6, 1922, by Rev. Sexson and 11 adults, who comprised the first Supreme Assembly of the Order of Rainbow for Girls. It has two degrees: (1) Initiatory; (2) Grand Cross of Color. The ritual, written by Rev. W. Mark Sexson, of McAlester, Okla., is based on Faith, Hope and Charity, as referred to in the 9th chapter of Genesis. It has seven colors—those of the rainbow—symbolizing life, religion, nature, immortality, fidelity, patriotism and service. Local bodies are called *Assemblies* and are sponsored by Chapters of the Order of the Eastern Star or associate organizations; there is a Supreme Assembly, which meets biennially. Each assembly is governed by a group of advisors. At the present time, there are 1900 assemblies in the forty-one States and other countries mentioned, with approximately 150,000 members.

118

Order of Rameses: Louisville, Ky., was the scene of the formation of this Order, which is a social group whose membership is limited to members of Royal Arch Chapters. It was later introduced into Ohio, but at the present time (1953) has apparently ceased to exist. It had as an auxiliary organization the "Daughters of Osiris," composed entirely of ladies.

Order of Red Cross of Rome and Constantine: (See Order of Constantine.)

Order of the Red Eagle: The Order of the Red Eagle was founded in 1734 and was a subordinate degree to the Order of the Black Eagle. Candidates were required to be members of the Order of the Red Eagle before becoming members of the Black Eagle; both Orders are now extinct. (See Knight of the Black Eagle.)

Order of Rose Croix and Elected Cohens: (See Rose Croix Degree; Ancient and Primitive Rite.)

Order of the Rose: An androgynous society, established in Germany about 1778, with two degrees: (1) Female Friends; (2) Female Confidants. Its ritual has been published.

Order of Roses: A French androgynous order of 1784.

Order of Rosicrucians: (See Rosicrucian Society.)

Order: Royal Order of Heredom (and Red Cross): (See Heredom.)

Order: Royal Order of Prussian Blue: This was an illogical association of Red Cross Masonry with Templarism; it attained great popularity in Dublin. The words "Libertas" and "Veritas" were engraved on its seals. It may have been the Red Cross of Daniel, because "Daniel was an instrument in God's hands by which Cyrus was urged to restore the Temple at Jerusalem."

Order: Royal Order of Scotland: One of the popular organizations in Scotland is the Royal Order of Scotland, with its two degrees—Heredom of Kilwinning and Rosy Cross. The former, according to tradition, originated in the reign of David I in the 12th century, while the second is said to have been instituted by Robert Bruce, who revived the former and combined both into one organization, of which the King of Scotland was to be forever the head. This, however, is mere tradition without documentary proof.

David Lyon, Scottish historian says:

"The paternity of the Royal Order is pretty generally attributed to a Jacobite knight named Andrew Ramsey, a devoted follower of the Pretender and famous as a fabricator of certain rites inaugurated in France about 1735-40, and through the propagation of which it was hoped the fallen fortunes of the Stuarts would be retrieved."

A Provincial Grand Lodge of the Royal Order of Scotland was established in Washington, D. C., May 4, 1878, by thirteen members.

The organization has 17 officers and is presided over by a Provincial Grand Master; Albert Pike was the first of the line, serving 1877-1891. The Order consists of two sections—the Provincial Grand Lodge of the Rose Croix, and the Provincial Grand Chapter of Heredom of Kilwinning. Originally there was a membership limit of 150, and eligibility requirements included that of the degree of Royal Arch Mason. In recent years the requsite has been made a 32° Scottish Rite Mason and with no limit as to number. Annual meetings of this body are held during the sessions of the Supreme Councils of the Northern and Southern Jurisdictions in alternating years.

119

The Royal Order of Scotland really embraces two degrees, the H.R.D.M. (Heredom) and the R.S.Y.C.S. (Rosy Cross), the latter being the Order of Knighthood. How long the degrees have been worked it is impossible now to state, save approximately; but undoubtedly there is abundant evidence of the *Royal Order* being worked in England as early as any degree other than the Craft. Brother Hughan, the well-known Masonic historian, who visited Edinburgh in order to examine the records in the custody of the Order, was able to trace the degree back to the first half of the last century, there being four *time immemorial* Chapters in operation in the City of London, and the 5th bearing a date, was warranted December 11, 1743. No. 6 was issued for Deptford, December 20, 1744; and the 7th for the Hague, empowered to act as a Grand Lodge on July 22, 1750. At this time a Grand Lodge was held in London, and the one for the Hague was really constituted in London, giving the authority to a Brother William Mitchell. The list of Grand Lodges, &c., of the degree from "Time Immemorial" (still in existence) being silent as to Edinburgh, would tend to prove that this city was the headquarters of the Rite about 1740, as so many have long claimed. Bro. D. Murray Lyon (Gr. Sec. of Scotland), historian of No. 1 Edinburgh, evidently favours an English origin for this quaint rite. Notice was given in 1750 that

"The nine clauses and additions, or extra characteristics, belonging to the Grand Chapter termed the Grand Lodge of the Royal Order at Edinburgh, to meet every last Friday at six."

When the several lodges and chapters became dormant has not been stated, but several of the foreign lodges (now styled Prov. Grand Lodges) have continued regularly to meet from their constitution, such as that at the Hague of 1750, and others; and of late years warrants have been granted to India, France, Norway, New Brunswick, Shanghai, London, Manchester, Canada, and the City of Washington for the United States. The most of those chartered during the last century have however ceased to exist for many years past; but whilst in an active condition there must have been many initiations, for the various rolls still preserved in Edinburgh contain a great many names both from home and foreign sources. In 1750 the list of officers comprised Pro. G.M., Deputy G.M., two Grand Wardens, G. Secretary and Treasurer, Sword Bearer, Banner Bearer, and others; but later the title of Deputy G.M. and Governor was substituted for the acting chief officer, as now prevails, the Throne being always kept vacant, unless filled by the King of the United Kingdom. This regulation applies only to the headquarters of the Royal Order, and not to Provincial Grand Lodges and Chapters, as their Chairs are necessarily filled by the Prov. G. Master for the time being. When the degree was "re-established by King Robert Bruce, and until the union with England, the King of Scotland was the hereditary Grand Master," according to the traditions of the Order. One of the oldest prayers used in connection with the ceremonies is to be found in one of the ancient minute books as follows:

"The might of the blessed Father of Heaven, the wisdom of His glorious Son, and the fellowship of the Holy Ghost, being the glorious and undivided Trinity, three persons in one God, be with us at this our beginning, and so guide and govern our actions in this life, that at the final conflagration, when this world and all things therein shall be dissolved, we may be received with joy and gladness into eternal happiness in that glorious everlasting, and heavenly kingdom which never shall have an end. Amen."

It will be noticed that it was Christian in character then as now, the first portion of the ceremonies being really Freemasonry in a purely Christian aspect, and by many considered to be the relics of the old Third Degree as worked prior to the advent of the Royal Arch. Most of the language (as Dr. Mackey states) is couched in quaint old rhyme, retaining sufficient about it to stamp its genuine antiquity. The choice also of characteristics is one of the peculiarities of the Order, as also these being spelled by members in ordinary usage without the vowels; e.g., Geometry would be represented as G.M.T.R.Y., and wisdom as W.S.D.M. Every member is known by one of these characteristics, typical of a moral virtue. The Order is said originally to have had its seat at Kilwinning, but of this there is no evidence, and by many it is believed that the R.S.Y.C.S. is the same as the most ancient *Order of the Thistle,* containing the ceremonial of admission formerly practised in it. This may be true, but at present we are without any facts to guide us to that conclusion. Since its revival in Edinburgh in 1839, the Royal Order of H.R.D.M. Kilwinning and R.S.Y.C.S. has been very popular with the adherents of the "hautes grades." It embodies much that is common to the Rose Croix, and it is perhaps as well that it should be kept select as to members, and given as a special privilege to Rose-Croix Masons.

Order of Sacerdotalis Temple: (See Order of the Sacred Temple.)

Order of the Sacred Temple: About 1866-69 this organization was active in Michigan, being organized at Hillsdale in 1866 by Mrs. Mary Adele (Brown) Hazlett. Mrs. Hazlett was active in the formation of Eastern Star Chapters and the *Women's Right* movement. The degrees of the Sacred Temple were open to daughters, sisters, wives and mothers of Master Masons.

The first ritual includes an obligation requiring obedience to the laws and regulations of the Supreme Sacred Temple, which was organized at Sturgis, Mich., October 26, 1867. There appeared to be four degrees: Beloved Daughter; Esteemed Sister; Faithful Companion; Honored Mother.

Mrs. Hazlett soon ran afoul the Grand Master of the Grand Lodge of Masons in Michigan, who threatened to declare her and her sisters clandestine; the "Sacred Temple" folks declared that Grand Master Coffinbury had "communicated our sacred mysteries to many gentlemen" and "has violated the trust reposed in him." But Mrs. Hazlett's "Temple" was too elaborate a ceremony; we read in *"Collectanea,"* which published the ritual of the Order:

"Her chapter room was furnished with officer's chairs of crystal, gold and silver. Elaborate robes for officers and candidates, silver platters of fruits, a fountain of running water—all made the services 'something to see.' "

There are no records after 1870. The first degree ritual provides stations for such officers as Faithful Companion, True Sister, Justice, Mercy, Charity, Temperance, Wisdom, Peace, and Beauty "the Beloved Daughter of Wisdom." Passwords were "Unity" and "Fidelity." Candidates were invested with white robes and wore a white veil.

The ritual was rather puerile and full of high sounding phrases with little meaning; this, with the competition of a rival order—the Eastern Star— led to its dissolution after an uneventful life of not more than three years.

Order of the Scarlet Cord: The 15° of the Early Grand Rite of Scotland. There is a sister organization of the degree of Secret Monitor; it is called the "Royal Order of the Scarlet Cord," and it is said to have been "discovered in a book printed in Amsterdam in 1770." Its meetings are "conclaves," held quarterly at the time the sun enters the constellations of Aquarius, Taurus, Leo and Scorpio. There is no special ceremony, but Chapter II of Joshua is read; the degree was once known as Knights of Jericho; it is founded upon incidents pertaining to the siege and capture of Jericho by Joshua, and the assistance given him by Rahab, an inn-keeper, who had a house of refreshment on the city walls.

Order of Secret Monitor: (See Secret Monitor, Order of.)

Order of Service to Masonry: In 1945, the Grand Master of the United Grand Lodge of England was authorized to "confer on brethren who have rendered special service to the craft, a distinction, to be known as the Grand Master's Service to Masonry."

The decoration carries with it a rank above the Grand Deacons, and the right to the title "very worshipful." Holder of the title may place after his name the letters "O.S.M." The collars and aprons worn by the holders may have the emblem. Only twelve brethren are eligible to hold the honor.

Order of the Silver Trowel: At a meeting of the Grand Council, Royal and Select Masters of North Carolina, held at Asheville in 1932, a resolution was adopted authorizing appointment of a committee to prepare a ritual for the degree of Thrice Illustrious Master. Grand Master McKeel appointed J. Ray Shute and J. Edward Allen as a committee to prepare the ritual, but charged with the responsibility of obtaining the right to its use from the Supreme Grand Chapter of Scotland, the only authority pretending to hold jurisdiction over the degree.

The degree was exemplified at the annual assembly in 1933 and a committee was ordered to prepare the ritual, see that it was conferred at ach annual assembly, and collect a fee of $5.00 for each candidate, candidates being limited to those who had been elected as Masters of their respective Council.

We find the matter had been brought to the attention of the Grand Council of North Carolina in 1931. There was an effort on the part of some to insist that the degree be conferred upon a Master of a Council before he should be qualified to proceed. The first council in North Carolina was formed May 10, 1932. This was followed in rapid succession by Illinois, Indiana, Maryland, Nebraska, New Jersey, Ohio, Oregon, Tennessee and Virginia. Then came the triennial meeting at Salt Lake City, Utah, in 1942, which gave an added spur to the formation of new councils, so today there are at least thirty-two councils operating throughout the United States. In some States the Order is referred to as The *Order of Anointed Kings;* in others, the *Order of the Silver Trowel;* and in other instances *Order of Thrice Illustrious Masters.*

Membership is limited to those who have been elected as Masters of Councils, and the degree is rapidly gaining the popularity to which it is justly entitled. The principal character is King David, and the ritual of the degree refers to events connected with the closing years of King David's life.

Order of the Star: The Order of the Star is of French parentage; it was founded by King John II in 1350, in imitation of the then recently organized Order of the Garter in England; it chose as its emblem the Star of Bethlehem. It never became as prominent as its English rival.

Order of the Sword: (See Sword of Bunker Hill.)

Order: Ordre du Temple: This is a non-Masonic organization, formed in Paris between 1805-10, basing its claims on the forged doctrine of transmission—the Charter of Larmenius. In 1810, a manual was published, declaring to the world its authenticity and the Grand Mastership of Bernard Raymond Palaprat. Nothing is heard of the Order after 1840, when Admiral Sir William Sidney Smith, then head of the Order, died. At one time there existed four convents of the Order in British Dominions—Scotland, India, London, Liverpool. The ritual of the Order appears in *Nocalore,* Vol. VI, p. 148.

Order of the Temple at Paris: An organization by this name appeared in Paris about the dawn of the 18th century; it had in its possession the so-called Charter of Larmenius, and had a series of six (later eight) degrees. At one time the membership was limited to Roman Catholics. Candidates were required to take the preparatory degrees which belonged in reality to Freemasonry. These were:

House of Initiation:
Initiate, E. A. with the same sign, sacred word, symbolic age, emblems, etc.
Initiate of the Interior, the degree of Fellow Craft.
Adept, the Master's degree, with its legends and characteristics.
Adept of the East, 4°, Elu of Fifteen of the A.A.S.R.
Grand Adept of the Black Eagle of St. John, 5°, the Elu of the Nine of the A.A.S.R.
House of Postulance:
Postulant of the Order, 6°, Perfect Adept of the Pelican, or Rose Croix.
Council:
Esquire, 7°
Knight of Levite of the Interior Guard, 8°

The latter two degrees are properly but one, the Philosophical Kadosh. The story of this Order is told in the Official Bulletin I of the A.A.S.R., p. 497.

Order of Teutonic Knights: A German organization of knighthood, closely resembling those of the Templars and Hospitallers. The Order was abolished by Napoleon in 1809. The Teutonic Cross of the organization has been adopted by the A.A.S.R.

Order of the Thistle: Thory, in a brief mention of the origin of the Royal Order of Scotland, says:

"On the 24th June, 1314, Robert Bruce, King of Scotland, instituted, after the Battle of Bannockburn, the Order of St. Andrew of the Thistle, to which was afterwards united that of H.R.M. for the sake of the Scottish Masons, who composed a part of the thirty thousand men with whom he had fought the English army consisting of one hundred thousand. He formed the Royal Grand Lodge of the Order of H.R.M. at Kilwinning, reserving to himself and his successors forever the title of Grand Master."

Order of Travelers: In 1944, there was reported the formation of a society known as the Order of Travelers. The first chapter had been organized in 1941, at Camp Roberts, Calif.; No. 2 was at Camp Hood, Texas; No. 3 at El Paso, Texas. Its membership was confined to Master Masons serving in the armed forces as enlisted men, and similar in characteristics to the National Sojourners, which confines its membership to commissioned officers. The Sojourners played an active part in forming this group.

Order of True Kindred: An adoptive degree popular at one time in the

123

south and west; it is still active in the United States and holds national meetings. Its origin is unknown, although it is said it came from the family of Degeer Gilmore, of Toronto, Ont., Canada. Date of establishment was June 29, 1894, when it became "The Supreme National Conclave of True Kindred." At that time it elected a Supreme Commander and other national officers. The meeting was in San Francisco, Calif., during the World's Fair held in that city. Those who are eligible are wives, widows, mothers, sisters and daughters of Master Masons in good standing.

It confers three degrees—(a) True Kindred; (b) Hero or Heroine of Jericho (Royal Companion); (c) Good Samaritan (Knight or Lady of the Cross). The degrees are founded upon the teaching of the piety, submission and filial tenderness of Ruth, the gleaner, as recorded in the biblical account in the Book of Ruth.

Its purpose, according to its statement, is

"to encourage the practice of the principles of fraternal love, relief and truth; to promote the moral and intellectual advancement of its members; to administer relief and furnish clothing for needy babies and orphans . . . among the true kindred of the Masonic fraternity whose wives, widows, daughters, mothers and sisters we are."

Recent regulations permit the admission of Master Masons.

A local body is called a Conclave; State organizations are Grand Conclaves; the National organization is a Supreme Conclave. Conclaves are located in the States of Illinois, Missouri, Kansas, Michigan, Ohio, Wisconsin, and the Provinces of Ontario and Quebec. There are more than seventy conclaves at the present time, with a membership in excess of 6,000. The degree Heroine of Jericho is conferred by State organizations, while the Good Samaritan degree is conferred only at national conclaves.

Order of True Masons: A former monk of the Benedictine Order, Antoine Joseph Pernetty, is said to have founded, in 1760, the Rite of the Illuminati of Avignon, which, when its headquarters were moved to Montpellier, assumed the title of Academy of True Masons. In this Christo-theosophical group of Grades was *Le Vrai Mason,* an early ritual of which mention is made in Pike's Morals and Dogma, p. 782, et seq. Pike translated this ritual from the French between the 21st and 26th of July, 1858, and secured it from the archives of the Grand Lodge of Louisiana. The original bore the following in French:

"In our character of Grand Master of the Provincial Sovereign Chapter of Rose Croix d'Heredom de Kilwinning of Edinburg, we refrain from certifying this degree of V.M. Still, it is curious and leads to investigations which cannot fail to increase knowledge; which ought to be the object of a good Mason. Everything in Masonry ought to be known to a Rose Croix d'Heredom. He should weigh both the evil and the good.

"This Cahier is taken from the collection of a most worthy Mason. We can certify no more. In faith whereof we do hereunto set the Seal of our arms, impressed on black wax.

"At the Orient of Port-au-Prince, this 18th day of the 4th Month (Masonic), the year of the True Light 5796.

"A(chille). Huet de la Chelle
"Gd. Mtre. Provl."

Thus, using the French dates of the period, this grade is older than the date of the certifying, i.e., 18 June, 1796.

In this degree the Lodge is styled "Academy," The Master is Most Wise Expert; the 1st and 2d Wardens, Sages; and all the other brethren, "Wise Academicians."

The Order was an offshoot of the "Hermetic Rite of Pernetty," and was formed at Montpellier, in France, in 1778, by Pernetty's pupil, Boileau. This rite had six degrees beyond the three symbolic degrees of Ancient Craft Masonry, which were essential for admission, but not practised. The degrees were: The True Mason; The True Mason in the Right Way; Knight of the Golden Key; Knight of the Rainbow; Knight of the Argonauts; Knight of the Golden Fleece.

Order of the White Rose: According to literature published by this group it was a spiritual, mystic and Rosicrucian Order. It had two branches, the Spiritual Order of the Red Rose, which was the exoteric branch, and the Spiritual Order of the White Rose, which was the esoteric branch, both of which formed, or led to, the Order of the White Rose, which was celestial and the main branch of the Order. Its period of activity was about 1900. It was stated that "Chapters or members of chapters can be found in nearly every center of civilization in the Western World," but this is most certainly an exaggeration. There were nine objects in the Order, all outlined in their literature.

The President was listed as J. C. F. Grumbine, 1718 W. Genessee St., Syracuse, N. Y., who was, no doubt, the mainstay of the organization. He wrote several books on various occult subjects and edited a number of others. A Miss Loraine Follette was listed as General Secretary at the same address.

Dr. Cummings, of Syracuse, one of our Fraters did some checking on this group and found no remnants of the group left. Every building at the Genesee St. address had been torn down for now nothing is to be found between 1716 and 1722 W. Genessee St. Checking of old directories and telephone books gives no clue to the persons mentioned in the publications of the Order. Without question this was another of the book-selling bodies which were abounding at the period of this Order's existence. Grumbine, himself, had a very checkered career. At the time of the appearance of this so-called Order he was living in Chicago and later bobbed up in Kansas City, Mo., and still later in parts of California, posing as some sort of a "mental healer."

Order of the White Shrine of Jerusalem: A woman's organization, which was organized in Chicago, Ill., September 23, 1894, incorporated under a charter granted by the State of Illinois, October 23, 1894; later it was deemed best to accept a new charter, which was granted October 25, 1904. Membership was restricted to members of the Eastern Star and Master Masons in good standing; recently the requirement relative to Eastern Star membership has been rescinded.

It has but one degree—*White Shrine of Jerusalem*—based on the biblical account of the birth of Jesus. Its teachings are scriptural and its object is to practice the simple gospel of Christ and his philosophy of peace and good will on earth.

The Supreme Shrine was formed at Grand Rapids, Mich., in 1897; it now has subordinate Shrines in every State, except Florida, and in all the provinces of Canada, a total of 720. Membership of the Order in 1952, was 190,000.

When the organization was first established, it was planned to serve as "an

125

advanced degree or degrees in Adoptive Masonry, to follow the degree of the Order of the Eastern Star." Due to some adverse legislation, passed by the Eastern Star, this declaration was later abolished. Court trouble prevented the growth of the organization from 1897 to 1909, when there were at least two Supreme bodies; in the latter year a consolidation was effected.

Local bodies are designated Shrines, with a Worthy High Priestess presiding. The National Organization has as its head a Supreme Worthy High Priestess.

Order of Wisdom: (See Order of Knight Templar Priests.)

Order of York Cross of Honour: (See Knights of the York Cross of Honour.)

Order of Zuzumites: (See Zuzumites, Ancient Order of.)

Orient, Grand Commander of the: The 43° Rite of Mizraim.

Oriental Shrine of North America: (See Ladies Oriental Shrine of North America.)

Osiris, Legend of: Several Masonic degrees have their origin in the legend of Osiris. Osiris was the husband of Isis. Here enters Typhon, the villain, who surreptitiously took the measurements of Osiris and made a magnificent chest of fir; he arranged to get Osiris into the chest, fastened the lid down tight, and placed it in the Nile River. Isis went forth in search, in full mourning, finding the body at the foot of a tamarisk tree; she found the chest, but Typhon had divided the body into twenty-four parts. Osiris was resurrected. The tamarisk is the original of the acacia plant.

Overseer, or Surveyor: A degree of the Helvetic Rite, involving a general inspection of the Temple by the candidate.

Oxford Working: One of the ritual forms in use in England for working the Craft degrees; other workings are "Stability," "Emulation," "Oxford," etc.

Palestine, Knight of; Palestine, Knight of St. John: (See Chevalier d'Palestine.)

Palestine, Mystical Order of: A mystical Order of Palestine is referred to by Baron Tschoudy in his "Etoile Flamboyante," but details are lacking.

Palestine, Order of: (See Chevalier d'Palestine.)

Palladium, Order of: (See Rite of Palladium.)

Palm and Shell: (See Order of Palm and Shell.)

Palm Tree, Knights of the Masonic Order of: (See Order Knights of Palm Tree.)

Particular Lodge: Subordinate or private lodges are sometimes given this designation.

Passed Masters: A term used by early English lodges to describe the conferring of the degree of Past Master. In 1733, a lodge at Bath, listed four "Pass'd Masters." Carlile, in his expose, describes the signs and words which are substantially those in use today.

Past Master: Freemasonry recognizes two types of Past Masters; the actual Past Master who has been elected and installed as a Master of a regular Craft lodge; a virtual Past Master, who has been elected and installed, but serves only long enough to qualify him for advancement in Royal Arch Masonry. There are records of this procedure as far back as 1768 at Bolton, England.

Past Master Degree: The 2° in the Royal Arch Chapter series of the

American Rite, and the 5° of the American Rite. At one time it was generally worked by lodges, and even today, in a few jurisdictions, the degree is conferred under grand lodge direction. Chapters do not recognize Past Masters made in lodges of the Craft degrees. In England, and some other countries, the degree is called "Installed Master." The degree is interesting because of its explanation of the duties of a Master, and stresses justice, toleration and moderation.

Patmos, Knight of: The 3° of the Knight Templar Priests; it was a part of the Irish system.

Patriarch of the Crusades: The 29° of the A.A.S.R.; also the Grand Scottish Knight of St. Andrew. (See Knight of St. Andrew.)

Patriarch, Grand: The 20° of the Council of Emperors of the East and West.

Patriarch of Isis: The 27° of the Ancient and Primitive Rite; it begins the seventh class; the ceremonial instructs the Neophyte upon the trials and morality of the Ancient Mysteries, after which he is admitted to the Temple of Symbols and taught the significance of the statutes, obelisks and emblems. The charge is a history of the Mysteries.

Patriarch of Memphis: The 28° of the Ancient and Primitive Rite; the candidate represents Osiris and ceremonially passes through what Herodotus termed "a representation of His sufferings." The charge is an application of this ceremony to that of Master Mason.

Patriarch Noachite: The 21° of the A.A.S.R. The degree is also called "Noachite" or "Prussian Knight." It teachers that arrogance is an offense to God and will be punished.

Patriarch of the Planispheres: The 25° of the Ancient and Primitive Rite; the candidate is instructed in the Masonic bearing of the planispheres, the origins of the signs of the Zodiac, and those elaborate myths drawn from the firmament.

Patriarch of the Sacred Vedas: The 26° of the Ancient and Primitive Rite; the degree is based on the sublime philosophy of the Ancient Brahmins, and represents a ceremonial conference upon the Vedas, the Rules of Buddha and the Zend Avesta of Zoroaster. It has given rise to degrees in the present A.A.S.R. system.

Patriarch of Truth: The 24° of the Ancient and Primitive Rite; the meeting place represents the Great Pyramid of Cheops; in it are seven columns representing the Seven Great Gods of the people, which are explained as the esoteric emblems of the One Supreme Being. The charge is an explanation of the origin and symbolism of the Great Pyramid.

Pattos-Manuel: The name given to a Masonic authority existing at one time at Oporto, Portugal.

Peep-of-Day-Boys: A Protestant society formed in Ireland which became, in 1795, the Orange Society. (See Orange Society.)

Pelican, Knight of the: The name is sometimes applied to the 18°, or Rose Croix, of the A.A.S. Rite.

Perfect Happiness: (See Felicitares.)

Perfect Initiates of Egypt: Rebold says it was formed in 1776.

Perfect Knight: The 5° of the Ancient Egyptian Reformed Rite; a degree of the Adonhiramite Rite; 5° of the A.A.S.R.; a degree in the Rite, Elect of Truth—(Elus du Verite).

Perfect Master: (See Expert Master.)

Perfect Master of the Pelican: A degree in the Order of the Temple.

Perfect Mistress: The 4° Rite of Adoption. The hangings are of crimson cloth, the throne dais seat of the same with gold lace and fringe. The Chapter represents the interior of the Tabernacle which Moses constructed in the Wilderness. Below and a little in front of the throne are two twisted columns. That on the side of Africa represents the column of fire which led the Israelites by night. It is hollow and made luminous. The column on the side of America represents the cloud which protected the Israelites during the day. These columns are so constructed as to appear to be lost at the ceiling in waves of light, an image of the heavens, and the summits appear to be joined by an arched rainbow under which is the dais. At one angle is the Altar of Fire, the Emblem of Truth, upon which are several antique vases; in the middle is a brazier of perfume and before it a plate to receive the offerings. Upon a bench at the side are a mallet and chisel as in the third degree, but instead of a heart is a tablet with these words thereon Amana (Emenoth), Hur, Cana, or the Greek word Eullos (Truth, Liberty, Zeal, Prudence). On the floor is the Tableau or Painting on which is: 1. Pharoah's dream of the seven fat and seven lean kine. 2. Joseph reconciled to his brethren. 3. Several men with trowels to cut the earth for brick. 4. Moses exposed in a basket with Pharoah's daughter drawing him out. 5. (in front) Moses and Aaron at the head of the Israelites at the time when the Egyptian army was submerged in the Red Sea. The clothing of Wor. Master and Senior Warden is the dress of a High Priest. The Brothers and Sisters as in the Third Degree. The Sisters have each a wand. The jewel is a golden mallet. Each Sister receives a ring on which is engraved the S.W. The garters are of white taffeta, or blue satin, upon which is embroidered a heart in gold with the device upon one "Virtue unites us" on the other "Heaven recompenses us."

Also a degree in the Order of the Temple.

Perfect Observance, Lodge of: One of the two lodges chartered by the Lodge of Antiquity in London, when it broke away from the Mother Grand Lodge and set up its own. The new Grand Lodge received authority (?) from York Grand Lodge to organize.

Perfect Phreemason: The same as "Red Brother." The 6° of the Primitive and Original Rite.

Perfect Venerable Adonaite Mistress: The 11° of the Rite of Adoption. In the 10° Rite of Adoption, the Perfect Mistress underwent the trials of the place of Lenito; the cavern of the dead, the descent into Hell, and the Sanctuary of Resurrection. This grade is the interpretive recapitulation of it. The Apron ond Sash are same as in the 10°. The Jewel is a butterfly of celestial blue and gold. The ring of profession bears the crux ansata. Various emblems are painted to which explanation is given in the ceremonial work.

Perfection, Degree (or Rite): The 14° of the A.A.S.R. which at first was termed "Grand, Elect, Perfect and Sublime Mason," or "Grand Scotch Mason of Perfection of the Sacred Vault of James VI." It is said to be the "ultimate" in Masonic rites. It is the last of the ineffable degrees which refer to the Temple of Solomon. (See Rite of Perfection.)

Persian Knight: The 20° of the Ancient Egyptian Reformed Rite.

Persian Rite: (See Rite, Persian.)

Phi Omega Phi (Achoth): A Greek letter sorority open to members of

128

the Eastern Star; it was organized at Lincoln, Nebr., in 1910, and at one time had Chapters at several state universities. It began as "Achoth," but later changed its name to Phi Omega Phi, in order to compete with Greek letter sororities.

Phallic Rite: (See Rite, Phallic.)

Philadelphians of Narbonne: (See Rite, Philadelphians of Narbonne.)

Philalethes, The: (See Rite of Philalethes.)

Philalethes, Searcher After Truth: (See Rite of Philalethes.)

Philalethes Society: The Philalethes Society is an organization confined largely to Masonic students, or those who are interested in the philosophy of Freemasonry. It was formed in 1928 by George H. Imbrie, editor of a Masonic newspaper in Kansas City, Mo., Robert I. Clegg of Chicago, Ill., connected with a Masonic book concern, Cyrus Field Willard of San Diego, Calif., Masonic writer and student, Albert H. Moorhouse of Boston, Mass., Henry F. Evans of Denver, Colo., William C. Rapp of Chicago, Ill. The latter three were publishers of Masonic newspapers. The Society confers no degrees, but has forty active Fellows who are entitled to use the initials F.P.S. (Fellow of the Philalethes Society). New Fellows are elected when vacancies occur among the general membership, which is unlimited in number.

The organization became defunct in 1953, but efforts to resuscitate it have been successful and, in 1955, it began the reissue of its monthly magazine—the Philalethes. There are no annual meetings and during its lifetime was run by the four principal officers. From March, 1946, until 1953, the Society issued a twelve page magazine, which was sent to all members. The Society has no connection with the Ancient Rite of Philalethes.

Philoclesian Host: (See Order—Consecrated Order of Philoclesian Host.)

Philosopher's Degree: The 6° of the Melesino Rite (Russian).

Philosopher Mage (Magi): The 9° of the Illuminati, following that of Illuminated Prince; little is known as to the character of the degree; most of the Illuminati degrees were not in reality degrees, but "dignities."

Philosophic Scotch Rite: (See Rite, Philosophical Scotch.)

Philosophical Rite: A Hermetic Rite founded at Paris by Dr. Boileay, which dealt with alchemy, and which consisted of six degrees. The last degree was "Knight of the Golden Fleece." Members were known as "Philosophical Masons and Knights Kadosh." It was also known as the "Persian Rite." (See Rite, Philosophical; see Persian Rite.)

Philosophus: The 4° of the Societas Rosicruciana.

Philosophy Sublime: The 48° of the Rite of Mizraim.

Pilgrim, The: A degree of the Early Grand Rite in Scotland.

Pledge Degree: A degree which resembles more an obligation of secrecy than a degree, taken by one who is later to assume other obligations. (See Chief Craftsman in the Order of the Golden Key.)

Pontiff, Grand: The 19° of the A.A.S.R. The title may be traced to the early days of Ancient Rome when the college of priests was established with the Pontifex Maximus, or Grand Pontiff, at its head; they were the ecclesiastical court at Rome and had control over all persons in the matter of religion and ceremonial law; they had the government of the Vestal Virgins. Present day recipients of the degree have none of these powers (or pleasures), but occupy themselves in a study of the Apocalyptic Mysteries of the New Jerusalem.

129

Postulant of the Orders: A degree in the Order of the Temple, sometimes called "Perfect Adept of the Pelican."

Practicus: One of the grades conferred by Colleges of the Rosicruciana Society.

Preadamite: A degree of the Philosophic Scotch Rite.

Preparation: (See Illuminati.)

Presbyter: (See Illuminati.)

Priest of Eleusis: The 12° of the Knight Templar Priests. (See Knight Templar Priests, or Priestly Order of Temple.)

Priest of the Sun: A degree in the Early Grand Rite of Scotland.

Priest of the Tabernacle: The 24° of the A. A. Rite; it instructs the manner in which Moses erected the Tabernacle; this was a movable Tabernacle; this degree and the 23° are based on the official duties of the priesthood; we find here the Ark, altar, and the golden candle-sticks. The candidate represents Eleazar who succeeded Aaron in the priesthood.

Priestly Order: (See Knight Templar Priests.)

Priestly Order of the Temple: Sometimes called "White Mason"; a degree in the Early Grand Rite of Scotland.

Priests: One of three classes of the Order of the Temple of the 12th century. (See Illuminati; see Presbyter.)

Prince Adept: (See Knight of the Sun.)

Prince Hall Lodges: Prince Hall Lodges are those whose membership is made up of negroes or men of African descent. They claim authority through a charter granted by the Grand Lodge of England, September 29, 1784, to African Lodge No. 459, headed by a negro living in Massachusetts, by the name of Prince Hall; the lodge was located in Boston. In 1792, at a renumbering of lodges, it was given number "370." English records show that the last payment to the Grand Lodge was in 1797; no monies having been received after that date, the Grand Lodge erased its membership in 1813, from which time the Lodge had no official standing with the United Grand Lodge of England, the Grand Lodge of Massachusetts, in whose jurisdiction it had existed, or any other American jurisdiction.

It develops that at a much later date, the members of Prince Hall Lodge established themselves under the original African Lodge charter as a Grand Lodge, issuing charters to other groups of negroes, so that today there are thirty-eight American states with Prince Hall Negro Grand Lodges. Voorhis' list gives 4,323 negro lodges in the United States, although records show that 7,684 have been chartered; fifteen of these Grand Lodges assume the name of *Prince Hall;* five took the name of Booker T. Washington; five the name of Lincoln. The 1953 estimate placed the membership at approximately 400,000.

Prince Hall Grand Lodges: Lodges of negroes, when formed together under the name of "Prince Hall Grand Lodges" are regarded by the colored people as legitimate lodges of Freemasons. Sometimes the Grand Lodge bears the appellation "Prince Hall Affiliation" or "Prince Hall Origin." The Grand Lodges of Florida, Virginia, Mississippi and Connecticut add "Prince Hall Affiliation" to their title. The name does not always signify colored regularity, for the states mentioned do not have the name in their corporate title —for the simple reason that the bogus groups "beat them to the title."

Prince Hall Masonry: Freemasonry of the colored people, who take the name of "Prince Hall," who was a Freemason during the Revolutionary War days in Massachusetts and who formed a lodge, chartered by the Grand Lodge of England, and which consisted of colored men. The charter, or warrant, was allowed to lapse-because of inactivity; later the charter was taken up and the organization started anew, the validity of the use of this warrant is what has created differences between the white and colored groups. Discussion of the situation is always full of "dynamite." The colored people have their Blue Lodges, Chapters, Councils, Commanderies, Star, Shrine, and Supreme Council of the Scottish Rite "for the Southern and Western Jurisdictions."

Prince Mason: A degree in the Early Grand Rite of Scotland.

Prince Masons: This group, for years, controlled the degrees conferred by the A.A.S.R. up to and including the 18°. The degrees were worked independently under a Grand Council of Rites for Ireland, and all members of the 18° were termed "Prince Masons." They failed to work the 4°-16°.

Prince Masons, Chapter of: We learn that early in the Freemasonry of Ireland, there existed a degree of the A. A. Rite, similar to the 18°, but which the Irish termed a "Chapter of Prince Masons." The Supreme Council later turned over all rights to the 18° to the Chapter of Prince Masons, together with the 15°, 16° and 17°, which were worked under a "Grand Council of Rites for Ireland," the Rose Croix or 18° members known as "Prince Masons."

Prince of Babylon: Sometimes called "Suspending Cross of Babylon"; a degree in the Early Grand Rite of Scotland.

Prince of Captivity: This reference is to Zerubbabel who spent a time in captivity and who returned, when freed, to Jerusalem to lead in the rebuilding of the Temple.

Prince of Jerusalem: A degree in the Rite of Martinism. The 16° of the A.A.S.R. In England it is called "Grand Prince of Jerusalem." It refers to events which took place during the rebuilding of the Second Temple, at which time the Jews were annoyed by the attacks of neighboring nations. One scene represents Darius' court; the other the court of Zerubbabel. (Read Ezra iv.) In 1788, there was formed at Charleston, S. C., a Grand Council of this degree.

A degree of the Helvetic Rite, dealing with the discovery of the Word, much after the style of the Royal Arch degree; the Word is enclosed in a Triangle.

In an official publication of the Rite in the U.S.A. we find this description of the degree:

"The 15° and 16° are known as "Knight of the East or Sword," and "Prince of Jerusalem." These degrees are sometimes referred to as historical degrees, and constitute an allegorical narrative of a captive people "who wept beside the waters of Babylon." When liberated, they were consecrated to the task of building the Second Temple. The entire pageantry and symbolism of Freemasonry revolves about the construction of the four Temples to Jehovah, by a brotherhood dedicated to the erection of a perfect edifice at Jerusalem, and later in the hearts of men. The characters of Daniel, Joshua, Zerubbabel and his companions display the virtues of patience, courage and fortitude.

Also a degree in the Rite of Perfection, or Harodim.

Prince of Lebanon: One of the degrees of the Council of Emperors of the East and West. (See Prince of Libanus.)

Prince of the Levites Lodge: (See Rite, St. Louis des Amis.)

Prince of Libanus: The 22° of the A. A. Rite, known also as "Knight of the Royal Axe." It is said to date back to 1778, when its founder, the Marquis de Bournonville, was in command of the Island of Bourbon. The legend of the degree states that it was founded to commemorate the valuable services rendered Masonry by the mighty Cedars of Lebanon. Tradition also says that the Sidonians formed "Colleges" on Mount Libanus and always adored the G.A.O.T.U. In one apartment there is represented a workshop on Mount Lebanon; the Second Apartment represents the Council at the Round Table.

Prince of Masonry, or Memphis: The 32° of the Ancient and Primitive Rite; the historical lecture consists of a long lecture upon the morality of the Ancient Mysteries and modern Freemasonry.

Prince of Mercy: The 26° of the A. A. Rite; it is a highly philosophical degree with an impressive ritual. Moses, Aaron and Eleazar are the principal characters; the candidate represents Joshua. It is a Christian degree and alludes to various covenants made by God with Moses. Also known as "Scottish Trinitarian."

Prince of Rose Croix: The Second Class, Rite of Elected Truth; Elus de la Verite.

Prince of the Royal Secret: A degree conferred by a Council of Emperors of the East and West. The degree is also referred to as "Sublime Prince of the Royal Secret." The 31° of the A.A.S.R.

Prince of the Tabernacle: The 24° of the A. A. Rite. (See Priest of the Tabernacle.)

Prince Patriarch: The 33° of the Ancient and Primitive Rite, sometimes called "Grand Conservator." Members of this degree constitute the governing body of the Sovereign Sanctuary. The charge constitutes a recapitulation of the degrees through which the candidate has passed. It admits all races and religions and breathes the spirit of charity, pure Freemasonry, love and mutual toleration, teaching immortality and the happiness of the immortal soul.

Princesses of Sharemkhu: (See Ancient Egyptian Order of Princesses of Sharemkhu.)

Priory, Great: The name of the governing body of the Templars; there is a Great Priory of England, Scotland, Helvetia (Switzerland), and Ireland.

For more than a century, Scotland had two governing bodies of the Templar Orders; one was the Great Priory of Scotland, the other was the Grand Encampment of the Temple and Malta. They are now united in the "Great Priory of the Religious and Military Order of the Temple in Scotland and the Colonies and Dependencies of the British Crown."

In Ireland, the governing body of the Templars is the "Great Priory of Ireland," which is the successor of the "Supreme Grand Encampment of Ireland." It is said to date from 1774.

Priory of the Holy Trinity: In 1145, Queen Maud founded a Priory under the above name which she endowed by a transfer of funds from the "knighten guild" (Templars).

Professed Knight: The 7° of the Rite of Strict Observance.

Prologues: Many of the degrees of Freemasonry are preceded by "Prologues," which quite often explain the situation, historically, at the time the degree begins, or it may explain the reason for the existence of the degree. Most of these are very instructive. At one time, in London, Masonic plays were

132

presented, and most of these were preceded by a Prologue, and ended with an Epilogue; the Apprentice's and Master's Songs were sung at these times.

Promulgation, Lodge of: The existence of two rival grand lodges in England proposed quite a problem when it came to a matter of the Union of 1813, for both had strayed far from the old ritual; the Moderns felt that if the error could be traced and adjusted, the way would be cleared for a Union; accordingly, there was set up a Lodge of Promulgation, which worked from 1809 to 1811 upon "promulgating the Ancient Landmarks." This being accomplished, the matter of Union was made more simple.

Proselyte of Jerusalem: The 68° of the Metropolitan Chapter of France.

Provincial Grand Chapter of Heredom of Kilwinning: A section of the Royal Order of Scotland.

Provincial Grand Lodge of Rose Croix: The first section of the Royal Order of Scotland.

Provincial Master of the Red Cross: One of the degrees of the Clerks of Relaxed Observance.

Provost and Judge: The 7° of the Ancient and Accepted Rite; the degree was traditionally instituted by King Solomon to enable him to preserve order among the workmen; the lesson is "justice to all men." The presiding officer is Tito, the first of the 300 overseers called Harodim. Provost comes from the word praepositus (Latin) denoting "Chief"; the French is "prevot."

The degree is one of the Helvetic Rite in which Solomon honors the candidate by presenting him with the plans for the erection of the Temple.

Prussian Blue: (See Order of Prussian Blue.)

Prussian Knight: A degree of the Adonhiramite Rite; a degree of the Noachite Rite; the group was known as the "Masonic Degree of the Noachites or Prussian Knights." Frederick the Great, traditionally, was said to be Grand Master. It is the 21° of the Ancient and Accepted Rite where it is called Noachite, Prussian Knight, or Knight of St. Andrew.

Pythagoreans: The followers of Pythagoras were known as "Pythagoreans." He is mentioned in our Craft ritual as a Greek philosopher; he lived about 580-500 B.C.; he was much influenced by Egyptian culture, and it is said he traveled through various continents in search of wisdom; he studied astronomy and taught that the planets moved around the sun in regular succession; he believed in the transmigration of the soul; his followers worshipped Bacchus and Orpheus.

Queen of the South: Originally planned to serve as one of a series of the Adoptive Rite, of which the Order of the Eastern Star was a pre-requisite. (See Order of Amaranty.)

Organizations were termed Palaces; both men and women were accepted. Among the offices listed are King Solomon, Queen Bathsheba, and several other characters called Princesses. The degree commemorates the visit of the Queen of Sheba to King Solomon as recorded in the scriptures.

Queen of the Temple: An androgynous degree, originated in Virginia City, Montana. It is also known as the Queens of the Temple of the Royal Arch and its membership is limited to the relatives of Royal Arch Masons. Its ritual is dignified, yet containing some humor.

Rainbow, Order of: (See Order of Rainbow.)

Rameses: (See Order of Rameses.)

133

Reconciliation, Lodge of: When the Ancients and Moderns united, there were so many differences in their ceremonies that it became necessary to take some action in order to secure uniformity of procedure. To accomplish this, the Articles of Union set forth that the two Grand Masters should appoint nine worthy and expert Freemasons, or Past Masters from each group, to be called the "Lodge of Reconciliation" for the purpose of obligating, instructing and perfecting all members and officers in the workings of both Grand Lodges. Its minutes are still in existence.

Red Branch of Eri: The ritual of the Red Branch of Eri, worked in the U.S.A., is a verbatim copy of the liturgy used in England last century. The copy from which this ritual was printed was, in turn, copied from John Yarker's own manuscript, which contained, in addition to the ceremonies, many interesting items.

When Yarker was head of the English Revived Order of the Red Branch, there were worked five ceremonies: The three used in U. S. and also the 4° Knight Commander, and 5° Knight Grand Cross. However, when the U.S. adopted this system the last two were not included in the rituals for the reason that the investitures would be inappropriate where no subordinate bodies exist.

The Psalter of the ritual was the Major Psalter of the English Knights; their Minor Psalter consisted of the laws and rules of the Order, which would not be applicable under the Allied Masonic Degrees. In addition to these items of interest, the Yarker manuscript book contained a list of members and bodies of the English branch down to the dawn of the present century and this has historic value.

Red Brother: A degree of the Illuminated Theosophists and the Illumines of Stockholm. (See Primitive and Original Rite.)

Red Cross: (See Knight of the Red Cross.)

Red Cross Masonry: Sometime after 1857, to conform to the laws of the Supreme Grand Royal Arch Chapter of Ireland, and the Grand Encampment, Red Cross Masonry was transferred from the Royal Arch and became associated with Knight Templar Masonry.

Red Cross of Babylon: The degree is one of the series under the control of the Allied Masonic Degrees. It is a very old degree and corresponds to the 61° of the A. A. Rite; it also contains some of the incidents recounted in the Royal Order of Scotland. It is closely associated with the Royal Arch degree and the rebuilding of the Second Temple, and in Scotland is controlled by the Supreme Grand Chapter of Scotland (Royal Arch). Its outstanding feature is the passing of the bridge, symbolically passing from one state of existence to another—in the world beyond the grave—to another—a further advancement of the Soul away from earth conditions—toward God. The lesson is "Great is Truth."

Red Cross of Constantine and Rome: (See Order of Red Cross of Constantine and Rome.)

Red Cross of Daniel: There is a tradition the degree was conferred in Ireland; it is conferred in Scotland in a lodge or council; at one time it was the 33° of the Early Grand Rite of Scotland; it was also the 12° of the Royal Grand Conclave of Scotland (1819).

Red Eagle: (See Order of the Red Eagle.)

Red Masonry: A degree of the Zinnendorf Rite. The degrees of the Royal Arch Chapter are sometimes referred to as Red Masonry. (See Early Grand Rite; see Zinnendorf Rite.)

Regent: (See Illuminated Prince.)

Reigning Grand Master: The 12° of the Swedish Rite.

Representative Award: (See Order of DeMolay.)

Research, Lodges of: A "Research Lodge" is organized for the dissemination of Masonic information, particularly the history of the Craft. Failure to keep early records makes such work essential, and many of our best minds have labored to discover and preserve Masonic records. Foremost, and oldest, of these lodges is the English "Quatuor Coronati," established about 1880. The work is new in the United States, but already several such lodges are in existence. The largest is the Missouri Lodge of Research, with 850 members, of which Ex-President Harry S. Truman, has served as Master; the American Lodge of New York is growing.

Rex: (See Illuminati.)

Rigid Observers: Founded by officers of the French Grand Orient in 1819.

Rito Nacional Mexicano: A Rite of nine degrees formed in Mexico about 1834, which utilized several of the degrees of the Scottish Rite. Their original charter came from the Grand Orient of France, but Albert Pike succeeded in organizing a Supreme Council which not only ran the Rite but all of the symbolic lodges under it; it later became the Grand Lodge Valle de Mexico, out of which grew the York Grand Lodge when a schism developed in Mexico in 1911. The Rito Nacional is now an irregular group. (See Rite, Rito Nacional Mexicano.)

Rites: Mackey describes the word as meaning "a method of conferring Masonic light by a collection and distribution of degrees."

Warvelle says:

"A rite may consist of one degree, and possibly that would more correctly express its true meaning if we were to say 'a method of conferring Masonic Light.' In this sense it has been used since 1750."

We are more inclined to agree with Warvelle, but we believe a better definition is that a rite is

"an act, or series of acts, of solemn service performed according to a manner regularly used."

The latter part of the 18th century was a great day for the manufacturer of Rites. Many of those engaged in the "manufacture" were out for the money that could be made by the acquisition of some new Rite. "High falutin" names were assigned the various rites with the idea of making the necessary impression on prospective candidates. It is unfortunate that too many of our brethren, even today, are impressed more by the number of degrees than by the actual value of the rite. Today there are only two large Rites that are being worked throughout the world—the American or York Rite, known by our brethren of another continent as the English Rite—and the Ancient and Accepted Rite of the Continent, known in the U.S.A. as the Ancient and Accepted Scottish Rite, or "Scottish Rite." Both names are misnomers; the York Rite was not formed at York, nor did the Scottish Rite have birth in Scotland.

135

Rite: Adonhiramite: There are many classes of Adonhiramite Masonry. Mackey is of the opinion that the manufacturers of our early ritual were not Hebrew scholars, nor versed in biblical history and failed to distinguish between Hiram the Builder and Adoniram, who was an officer in the Court of King Solomon. This error was continued with the affixing of the title Adoniram to the name of the former, making the character Adon-Hiram or Lord Hiram, the word "Adon" meaning Lord or Master.

Adoniram is one of the chief characters in the Cryptic degrees, as well as in some of the degrees of the Scottish Rite. In the degree of Royal Master, Adoniram is one seeking to obtain the Lost Word. He is referred to in the 2d Book of Samuel, XX-24, as Adoniram, meaning the chief receiver of the taxes; he is again referred to in 1st Kings, IV-6; he was stoned to death, 1st Kings, XII-16.

Adonhiramite Masonry itself had its origin in France shortly before the Revolution. The exact date of its rise and the name of its founder, we are unable to learn. It consisted of twelve degrees, of which four—sixth, seventh, eighth and ninth—are peculiar to this rite; the others correspond with those of the same name in the Ancient and Accepted Rite.

The degrees are:

(1) Entered Apprentice; (2) Fellow-Craft; (3) Master Mason, Perfect Master; (4) First Elu, Elu of the Nine; (5) Second Elu, Perigan; (6) Third Elu, Elu of the Fifteen; (7) Minor Architect; (8) Grand Architect, Scottish Fellowcraft; (9) Scottish Master; (10) Knight of the Sword, Knight of the East and West, Knight of the Eagle; (11) Knight Rose Croix; (12) Noachite or Prussian Knight.

Rite of Adoption: Secret Societies imitating Freemasonry, for the admission of females as members, were first organized in France during the early part of the 18th century, and still exist there, and in other parts of Europe, as a distinctive Rite. By the term "Masonry of Adoption," or, "Adoptive Masonry," we imply that system of forms and ceremonies, and explanatory lectures which is communicated to certain classes of ladies who, from their relationship by blood or marriage, to Master Masons in good standing, are entitled to the respect and attention of the whole fraternity. These ladies are said to be "adopted" into the Masonic communion, because the systems of forms, ceremonies, and lectures above referred to, enable them to express their wishes and give satisfactory evidence of their claims, in a manner that no stranger to the Masonic family can do.

To the organizations thus established for the initiation of females, the French have given the name "Maconnerie d'Adoption," and the meetings are called Loges d'Adoption, because every such lodge was obliged to be adopted or placed under the guardianship of some regular lodge. As the Ancient and Primitive Rite of Masonry, from its first organization, sanctioned this Masonry of Adoption, it is deemed proper that all members of the Rite should have an opportunity of becoming acquainted with it. It is not, however, intended by this to advocate the working of the system, and at the utmost it can only be made a matter of occasional recreation at high festivals.

One of the first of these societies was the *Felicitaires, or Order of Perfect Happiness.* This society assumed a nautical character in its emblems and vocabulary; its four degrees were named: Cabin-boy, Master, Commodore and Vice Admiral. It did not long maintain its existence and gave place to the *Order of Knights and Heroines of the Anchor,* which was, however, but a refinement of the original society, and preserved its formula of initiation.

In 1747, one Beauchame, Master of one of the Paris lodges, instituted a new society which he called "L'Ordre des Fendeurs" or Woodcutters. This institution imitated the society of the Carbonari or Charcoal-burners which had been previously established in Italy. The meeting place of the Fendeurs was called the "Woodyard" and represented a forest. The president was termed Father-Master and the male and female members "Cousins." This society became at once exceedingly popular, and the most distinguished ladies and gentlemen of France joined it. It was consequently the cause of the institution of many similar societies, such as the Order of the Hatchet, of Fidelity, etc.

In consequence of the increasing popularity of the numerous Secret societies which in their external organization and secret rites attempted an imitation of Freemasonry, the Grand Orient of France, in 1774, established a new system called the "Rite of Adoption," which was placed under their control. Rules and regulations were then formed. A lodge of Adoption under these regulations was opened at Paris in May, 1775, under the patronage of the Lodge of St. Anthony, when the Duchess of Bourbon presided, and was installed as Grand Mistress of Adoption. Mention is also made of the encouragement given by the Marquise de Courtebonne, Countess de Poligniac, de Choiseul-Gouffier, and Vicomtesse de Faudnas. On March 11, 1775, the Marquis de Saisseval founded the Lodge of Candour and on the 25th a festival was given at which assisted, La Serenissime Soeur Duchesse de Bourbon; her Highness presided over a lodge in 1777 when a subscription was opened to reward a brave soldier. This example was followed by some of the greatest names in France, such as the Princess de Carignan, Marquise de Rochambeau, etc., etc. In 1780 the Princess Lamballe received in Lodge Social Contract the Viscountess d'Afrey and Narbonne. The Comtesse de Livays was initiated in 1821. On July 8, 1854, the reception of Madame Moreau as Grand Mistress is recorded in the "Franc Macon" edited by F. Dumesnil. After the installation, the reception of the beautiful Mlle. Anais G——— commenced. Before each of the brother officers were placed four boxes which she was directed to open; out of the two first she drew faded ribbons; flowers and laces, which were put in an open vessel and consumed by fire as a proof of the brief duration of such objects; conducted before the Secretary she drew from the box a scarf and apron of blue silk and a pair of gloves; from that, before the Orator, she drew a basket which contained the W.T. in silver; when it was brought before the Altar she removed the cover from a box when several birds made their escape in allusion to the words of the W.M., "Liberty is a blessing common to all the world; no one can be deprived of it without injustice."

In the United States of America many systems of Adoption have prevailed, but none has enjoyed such success as the "Eastern Star." Its theory is founded upon the Scriptures of the selection of five prominent characters illustrative of as many virtues: 1. Jephthah's daughter, illustrating the binding force of a vow; 2. Ruth, illustrating devotion to religious principles; 3. Esther, fidelity to kindred and friends; 4. Martha, undeviating faith in the hour of trial; 5. Electa, a Christian martyr, illustrating patience and submission under wrongs. The emblem is a star of five points and upon each branch is one of the five characters and her emblem; the points are blue, yellow, white, green and red. The emblems for Jephthah's daughter, sword and veil; Ruth, a sheaf; Esther, crown and sceptre; Martha, broken column; Electa, joined hands. The centre is again divided into five parts each containing an emblem, viz: 1. Open Bible; 2. Bunch of lilies; 3. Sun; 4. Lamb; 5. Lion; forming appropriate emblems of the five characters—whilst round the edges are the letters FATAL, which have a double signification. (Yarker.)

About the time the Order of the Eastern Star was being formed in the United States, a so-called Rite of Adoption was being conferred. The story of this Rite is told by the late Clarence Brain in an article appearing in Nocalore, Vol. VI, p. 243.

From the ritual it would appear that the organization was formed about 1765. The secret work involved a scene symbolical of Jacob's ladder; there was a sacred word "hoth" meaning sister; there was a password, "Hevah," the name of the mother of the human race, called in our translation of the Bible "Eve."

There were three separate obligations, the second referring to "Companion Masoness." It had a password, "Habarat," and a sacred word "Aden." The password, translated from the Hebrew, means Family, associate or Companion. The sacred word Aden means Eden or Delight.

In the third obligation there are four Hebrew words connected with the Veils of Saturn, Jupiter, Mars, and Mercury.

There are various other secret words connected with the degrees which are of no particular interest.

In the ritual of the Adonhiramite Rite (1787) there is no mention of adoptive grades, but in a ritual of two years later, there is a complete set-up of androgynous degrees:

1. Apprentice	3. Mistress
2. Companion	4. Perfect Mistress

The "Mere Loge d'Adoption de la Haute Maconnerie Egyptienne" of Cagliostro worked three grafes: In (1) the candidate as an E.A. is instructed (as the Queen of Sheba) by Solomon, in Mysteries of the Divine Religion, (2) as Companion, she cuts off the serpent's head, and (3) as Mistress the ceremony is of the Rite, involving the issuance from above of the Dove, invoking Gabriel to purify the candidate. The Grand Mistress represented the Queen of Sheba.

Rite of African Architects: The Order of *African Architects* was established by a Prussian named Baucherren, with the sanction of Frederick II. It was divided into two temples, having eleven degrees. The first temple contained the three symbolic degrees; in the second temple were Apprentice of Egyptian Secrets, Initiate in the Egyptian Secrets' Cosmopolitan Brother, Christian Philosopher, Master of Egyptian Secrets, Esquire, Soldier, Knight. The object of the institution was historical research, and the ritual was not confined to Masonry, but contained allusions to the mysteries of Christianity, and to the pursuits of alchemy and chivalry. Ragon tells us that the society possessed a large mansion for the Grand Chapter of the Order; this had an extensive library, a museum of natural history, and a perfect chemical laboratory. In their assemblies they read essays and communicated the results of their researches. They emulated the philosophers of Greece in their simple and decorous banquets, at which instructive discourses were delivered; and must affected sententious apothegems, whose meaning was sublime but concealed.

The society for some years annually decreed a gold medal, with the sum of fifty ducats, for the best memoir on the history of Masonry; many of these documents have been published, and some are of value. (How.)

Rite of Allied Masonic Degrees: The Allied Masonic Degrees is not exactly a Rite although it has under its control a number of degrees, but merely for the purpose of seeing that they are not conferred on a commercial basis.

Authority for the American organization came from Scotland, although there is a similar group in England. The formation was the direct result of a visit of the late Marquis of Ailsa to this country, accompanied by the late George A. Howell, grand secretary of the Supreme Grand Chapter of Royal Arch Masons of Scotland of which Lord Ailsa was First Grand Principal. A Dispensation was issued by Lord Ailsa in 1931 authorizing the degree of Excellent Master, which was under Allied control, to be conferred in the Grand Chapter of Royal Arch Masons of North Carolina. The degree was conferred upon 200 Royal Arch Masons on May 12, 1931, in Asheville, N. C.

Desiring to continue the use of the degree, correspondence resulted in the formation of three groups in North Carolina, with the resultant Grand Council of Allied Masonic degrees, for the control of the Excellent Master degree as well as all others in its category. A convention of representatives was held in Salisbury, N. C., April 16, 1932 and officers were elected.

In recent years the annual convention has been held in Washington, D. C., during "Masonic Week" and has been attended by a large number of representatives from all over the United States. They issue an annual publication, *"Miscellanea,"* which contains much material of value to the Masonic student, which when used with *"Collectanea"* of the Grand College of Rites, makes accessible to the student a mass of Masonic information not to be found elsewhere. The organization is incorporated under the laws of North Carolina (1933).

Under the first constitution, the following degrees were included in the list of those under their control.

1. Royal Ark Mariner.
2. Secret Monitor.
3. Knight of Constantinople.
4. Saint Lawrence the Martyr.
5. Architect.
6. Grand Architect.
7. Superintendent.
8. Grand Tyler of Solomon.
9. Master of Tyre.
10. Excellent Master.

Following the organization of A.M.D. it was discovered that a similar organization existed at Norway, Maine, and which had once been located in Richmond, Va., where it had been headed by the Rev. Hartley Carmichael and known as the Sovereign College of Allied Masonic and Christian Degrees for the Western Hemisphere, later changed to Sovereign College of Allied Masonic Degrees for America. It conferred certain academic degrees.

In its list of degrees were: Ark and Dove, Mason Elect of 27 (Grand Tylers of Solomon), Red Cross of Babylon (Babylonish Pass), Holy and Blessed Order of Wisdom (Knight Priest of the Holy Sepulchre), Grand Trinitarian Knight of St. John the Evangelist, Mediterranean Pass, Mark

Man, Knight of the Holy Cross, Knight of Rome, Knight of the Three Kings, Knight of the Holy Virgin, and Order of Priesthood. Articles of Union were effected between Sovereign College and the A.M.D. in July 1933.

Rite: American: Generally speaking, the American Rite consists of the Symbolic Lodge, Royal Arch Chapter, Council of Royal and Select Masters, and those degrees appendant to it, coupling with it the Orders conferred by a Commandery of Knights Templar. Sometimes the name of "York Rite" is erroneously given to these degrees. As a Rite, it had its beginning about 1800.

Rite: Ancien de Boullon: A ritual of this Rite is in the library of the Grand Lodge of Iowa. At one time it was owned by George Oliver and referred to as the "Oliver Ritual." It was used by him in writing his origin of the Royal Arch, and he stated it was used by the Ben Jonson Head Lodge in 1740. It is very similar to the ritual *Solomon in all His Glory,* London, 1766, which was a translation of a French original in England.

Dermott, in his Ahiman Rezon, refers to this as meeting in Pelham St., Spitalfields, which he says,

"was composed mostly of Ancient Masons, though under the Modern constitution. Some of them had been abroad, received extraordinary benefits on account of ancient Masonry; therefore they agreed to practice ancient Masonry on their third lodge night. Upon one of these nights some Modern Masons attempted to visit them, but were refused admittance. The persons so refused made a formal complaint before the Modern Grand Lodge."

An examination of this ritual shows that it contains many sections which parallel the present Royal Arch degree; it also has signs and words which are to be found in the Cryptic degrees.

Rite: Ancient and Accepted: The name given, by our British brethren, to the degrees of the Rite known in America as the Ancient and Accepted Scottish Rite.

Rite: Ancient and Accepted Scottish: The 33° system known in the United States as the Scottish Rite.

There are many stories and traditions as to how, when, and where the Scottish Rite was founded, but this we know, that May 31, 1801, at Charleston, South Carolina, the Supreme Council 33° of the Ancient & Accepted Scottish Rite of Freemasonry for the Southern Jurisdiction of the United States of America was established by John Mitchell, Frederick Dalcho, Aleander Francoise Auguste de Grasse Tilly, and Jean Baptiste Marie Dalahogue. It started as a very small group and it was not for many years that it began to acquire a place among other rites and degrees.

On August 5, 1813, Emmanuel De La Motta, assisted by six associates who were Inspectors General of the Rite, formed in New York the Supreme Council for the Northern Masonic Jurisdiction; for a time it had some competition from another group of that rite, but fortunately effected a union with them May 17, 1867.

Originally, the Rite consisted of 25 degrees, but when the Supreme Council was formed at Charleston in 1801, it was a 33° rite, eight degrees having been added to the list.

The jurisdiction of the two Supreme Councils covers the whole of the United States and the American possessions; the boundary line is the territory south of the Ohio River and east of the Mississippi, including the states of West Virginia, Maryland and the District of Columbia which is assigned to the Southern Jurisdiction; all north of this and east of the Mississippi belong to the Northern Jurisdiction.

While the Supreme Councils claim to confer the thirty-three degrees, actually they confer only twenty-nine degrees, the first three degrees being given in lodges working under grand lodges. No Scottish Rite authority in the United States or Canada would presume to exercise their right (?) to confer symbolic degrees, for it would bring them into direct contact with grand lodges, and would constitute an invasion of jurisdiction.

The 33° is reserved; it cannot be petitioned for, and is presumed to be conferred by a Supreme Council on those entitled to Scottish Rite distinction; there are in the United States, at this time, almost 9,000 brethren who have received that honor. There was a tradition at one time that one had to go to Jerusalem to receive the 33° of the Rite. This was incorrect.

There are Supreme Councils all over the world; some are very small groups, but most of the groups are in fraternal relation. The Southern Jurisdiction of the U.S.A. has served as the Mother of all the regular Supreme Councils; its See is in Washington, D. C. (or Charleston, S. C.), while that of the Northern Jurisdiction is now in Detroit, Michigan, after having been located at Boston, Mass. for many years.

There is a difference in the grouping of the degrees; in the Southern Jurisdiction, degrees from 4° to 14° are termed the Lodge of Perfection; from 15° to 18°, a Chapter of Rose Croix; from 19° to 30°, a Council of Kadosh; and from 31° to 32°, a Consistory. In the Northern Jurisdiction, the 15° and 16° constitute a Council of Princes of Jerusalem; the 17° and 18° the Chapter of Rose Croix, and the 19° to 32° the Consistory.

The government of the Rite is from the top down, in contrast to the York (or American) Rite, which is from the bottom up; for the head of each Supreme Council is a Sovereign Grand Commander who holds office for life, or until he resigns; he is assisted in each state by an Inspector General, or by a Deputy, each of whom holds a life position. In the Northern Jurisdiction, an election is held each six years for Sovereign Grand Commander; instead of having one Inspector General in a State, there are usually three, and these "Actives" hold state conferences which are called Councils of Deliberation.

The Southern Jurisdiction awards the distinction of Knight Commander Court of Honor, which is not a degree, but an Investiture. The Northern Jurisdiction confers the Gourgas Medal on those who have distinguished themselves, and the list includes: Ex-President Truman, Melvin M. Johnson, King Gustavus V. of Sweden, and Kaufman T. Keller. The Southern Jurisdiction also confers the Grade of Knight Grand Cross for exceptional service.

In the British Isles there are three Supreme Councils, Scotland, Ireland, and England; little attention is paid there to the conferring of the higher grades; usually, the Rose Croix is the last of the degrees conferred except by the Supreme Council itself. In England only those advance who have served as Wise Master of a Rose Croix Chapter; in all of these countries, the Rite has a decidedly Christian character.

The names of the degrees may differ in different jurisdictions:

4° Secret Master
5° Perfect Master
6° Intimate Secretary

7° Provost and Judge
8° Superintendent of Buildings (English)
    Intendant of the Building, S.M.J.
    Intendant of the Buildings, N.M.J.
9° Elect of Nine (English)
    Elu of the Nine (S.M.J.)
    Elect of Nine (N.M.J.)
10° Elect of 15 (English)
    Elu of the 15 (S.M.J.)
    Knight Elect of the 15 (N.M.J.)
11° Sublime Elect (English)
    Elu of the 12 (S.M.J.)
    Sublime Knight Elected (N.M.J.)
12° Grand Master Architect (English)
    Master Architect (S.M.J.)
    Grand Master Architect (N.M.J.)
13° Royal Arch of Enoch (English)
    Royal Arch of Solomon (S.M.J.)
    Royal Arch of Enoch (N.M.J.)
14° Scotch Knight of Perfection (English)
    Perfect Elu (S.M.J.)
    Grand, Elect, Perfect and Sublime Master Mason (N.M.J.)
15° Knight of the Sword (English)
    Knight of the East (S.M.J.)
    Knight of the East or Sword (N.M.J.)
16° Prince of Jerusalem (English) (S.M.J.) and (N.M.J.)
17° Knight of the East and West
18° Knight of the Eagle and Pelican, and Sovereign Prince Rose Croix
    of Heredom (English)
    Knight Rose Croix (S.M.J.)
    Knight of the Rose Croix de Heredom (N.M.J.)
19° Grand Pontiff (England)
    Pontiff (S.M.J.)
    Grand Pontiff (N.M.J.)
20° Venerable Grand Master (English)
    Master of the Symbolic Lodge (S.M.J.)
    Grand Master of all Symbolic Lodges (N.M.J.)
21° Patriarch Noachite (England)
    Noachite of Prussian Knight (S.M.J.)
    Noachite of Prussian Knight (N.M.J.)
22° Prince of Libanus (England)
    Knight of the Royal Axe, or Prince Libanus (S.M.J.)
    Knight of the Royal Axe (N.M.J.)
23° Chief of the Tabernacle
24° Prince of the Tabernacle
25° Knight of the Brazen Serpent
26° Prince of Mercy
27° Commander of the Temple (English and N.M.J.)
    Knight Commander of the Temple (S.M.J.)
28° Knight of the Sun (England and N.M.J.)
    Knight of the Sun, or Prince Adept (S.M.J.)
29° Knight of St. Andrew (England and N.M.J.)
    Scottish Knight of St. Andrew (S.M.J.)
30° Grand Elected Knight Kadosh, Knight of the Black and White Eagle
    (England)
    Knight Kadosh (S.M.J.)
    Knight of Kadosh (N.M.J.)
31° Grand Inspector, Inquisitor Commander (England)
    Inspector Inquisitor (S.M.J.)
    Grand Inspector Inquisitor Commander (N.M.J.)

32° Sublime Prince of the Royal Secret (England)
    Master of the Royal Secret (S.M.J.)
    Sublime Prince of the Royal Secret (N.M.J.)
33° Sovereign Grand Inspector General (England) (S.M.J.) and (N.M.J.)

The rituals of the degrees vary in different Supreme Councils; the majority use Pike's Recession, first issued about 1867. There is a greater variation after leaving the first series of degrees (4°-14°), and especially in the Northern Jurisdiction where accent has been placed on the drama and the teaching, rather than on the philosophic side which was a hobby of Albert Pike. There are intense advocates of both methods.

We have read the rituals of both Southern and Northern Jurisdictions; we shall not refer to the character of the rituals, but since a description of the English degrees appears in a published monitor, on sale to the public, we shall add here a synopsis of the degrees as it appears there:

4° SECRET MASTER

In it is explained the mystic signification of those things which are contained in the Sanctum Sanctorum of the Tabernacle and the Temple; viz., the altar of incense, the golden candlestick, and the table of shewbread; and also within the second veil, the ark of testimony, and its lid and cover, called "the mercy-seat." For the forms of these holy things we have, besides the lucid description in the twenty-fifth chapter of Exodus, the authority of a bas-relief on the Arch of Titus at Rome, which was doubtless copied from the originals taken to that city by the triumphant army of the conqueror, after the destruction of Jerusalem; and although the ornaments which adorned the Temple of Solomon became a prey to the Chaldeans—if they were not, as is highly probable, all restored by Cyrus on the return of the Jews to their native land, it is certain that those used in the service of the second Temple were of a like pattern. The Master in this degree, as in the symbolic, represents Solomon, who now comes to the Temple to elect seven experts, or skilful practised Masons, to replace the loss of an illustrious character. The Master is styled Most Powerful; there is one Warden, who represents Adoniram, the overseer of the workmen on Mount Lebanon, and who was the first Secret Master. The Lodge is clothed in black, and illuminated by eighty-one lights, usually represented by nine lights, arranged in threes. The badge is white, with a black edging, having a blue flap, on which an all-seeing eye is placed. The jewel of the degree is an ivory key, suspended from a white ribbon edged with black; on the key is engraved the letter Z, referring to Zadoc, who was the high priest in the reigns of David and Solomon.

5° PERFECT MASTER

The Fifth Degree is that of Perfect Master, and may be said to be a continuation of the preceding, being a tribute of respect to the worthy departed brother. In this the Right Worshipful Master represents Adoniram; he has also but one Warden, who is called "Inspector." The Deacon, or "Conductor" as he is called, represents Zabdiel, who was the father of Jashobeam, the first captain of the guards (1 Chron. xxvii. 2). The Hebrew of the Second Book of Samuel which speaks of Jashobeam, runs literally thus: "He who sat in the throne of wisdom, the head of the three, Adino of Ezni, who

143

lifted up his spear against three hundred, whom he slew at one time." The badge is white, in the centre of which is embroidered within three circles a square stone or cube on which the letter "J" is placed; the flap of the apron is green, symbolically to remind the Perfect Master that, being dead in vice, he must hope to revive in virtue. The jewel is a compass, extended to sixty degrees, to teach him to act within measure, and ever pay due regard to justice and equity. The Perfect Master's Degree is founded on this traditional event. At the death of Hiram, the widow's son, Solomon, being desirous of paying a tribute of respect to his friend, requested Adoniram, the Grand Inspector, to make arrangements for his interment. The latter erected a superb tomb and obelisk of black and white marble, which he finished in nine days. The entrance to the tomb was between two pillars, supporting a square stone surrounded by three circles, on which was engraved the letter "J." The heart of the deceased was enclosed in a golden urn, to the side of which a triangular stone was fixed, inscribed with the letters "J.M.B." within a wreath of cassia. The urn was placed on the top of the obelisk. Three days after the interment, Solomon visited the tomb, and with solemn ceremonies, in the presence of the brethren, offered up a prayer, and with hands and eyes elevated to heaven, exclaimed, "It is accomplished!"

6° INTIMATE SECRETARY

The Sixth Degree is the Intimate Secretary; in this there are only three officers, who represent Solomon, King of Israel, Hiram of Tyre, and a captain of the guards. The ceremonial and legend are intended to preserve the remembrance of an instance of unlawful curiosity, the due punishment of the offender being averted only in consideration of his previous fidelity. Our brethren will readily perceive that these three degrees are a kind of commentary upon the historical traditions of the M.M. Degree, all having some reference to the event symbolized in that degree. The collar is crimson, and apron white, with red border; on the flap is a triangle. The jewel is a triple triangle interlaced. In the degree of Intimate Secretary, the two persons who represent Solomon and Hiram of Tyre are clothed in blue mantles lined with ermine, with crowns on their heads, sceptres in their hands, and seated at a table on which are two naked swords, a roll of parchment, and a human skull. The rest of the brethren are considered only as Perfect Masters, and are termed Guards. They wear white aprons, lined and embroidered with crimson, and strings of the same, with crimson collars, to which is suspended a solid triangle. The degree relates to circumstances that occurred between Hiram and Joabert, when the fidelity of the latter was rewarded by Solomon with advancement to this rank.

The candidate is invested in open Lodge, and thus addressed by his superior:

"My brother, I receive you as an Intimate Secretary, on your promise to be faithful to the Order into which you have just been admitted, and I trust that your fidelity will be proof against every temptation. I present you with a sword as a weapon of defense against the attacks of those who may try to extort from you the secrets which I am now about to communicate."

There is a tracing-board, which is thus explained:

"The window in the clouds represents the vault of the Temple, and the letter 'J' which you see inscribed therein, indicates the Tetragrammaton, or sacred name of God. The door represents the principal entrance from the

144

palace; the tears symbolize the repentance of Joabert in Solomon's chamber of audience, and are also emblematical of the lamentations of the king in the apartment hung with black, where he used to retire to lament the unhappy fate of Hiram; and here it was he received the King of Tyre."

7° PROVOST AND JUDGE

This is the designation of the Seventh Degree. Traditional history relates its foundation by King Solomon, for the purpose of strengthening his means of preserving order among the vast number of craftsmen engaged in the construction of the Temple. The presiding officer of the Lodge represents Tito, who was the first of the three hundred overseers called Harodim, a Hebrew word which signifies "Princes" or "Provosts" (see 1 Kings v.16). In this degree there are six lights, which are so placed as to form a double triangle. The badge is white lined with red, and has a pocket; the collar is red; to it is suspended the jewel, a golden key, on the wards of which is engaged the letter "A." This degree appears out of place, as it has reference solely to the very first preparations for building the Temple; whereas those preceding it are connected with its construction and completion. Connected as these four degrees are with the historical traditions of the Third Degree, with the exception of the anachronism to which we are about to refer, they are unobjectionable and somewhat instructive. Are these traditions to be found in Preston's four sections of the Third Degree? Whence is derived the cognomen *Tito?* It is clearly Latin or Italian. *Provost* comes from Latin praepositus, which denotes the chief of any society or community; the French word *prevot* comes nearest to the form of the word, and the English expression "provost marshal," an officer attached to the army whose duty it is to seize and punish offenders against military discipline, has been adopted from the French *prevot des marechaux,* an officer who has similar functions. It has been suggested as probable that this degree was instituted among the Masonic Crusaders, as it has more especial connection with military government. The word "provost" is in England rarely used, we believe the only instances are those of the heads of certain colleges, &c.; in Scotland, it designates the chief magistrate in corporate cities, as the Lord Provost of Edinburgh, Glasgow, &c.

8° INTENDANT OF BUILDINGS

The Eighth Degree is called Intendant of Buildings, or "Master in Israel." The chief officers are a Thrice Puissant who represents King Solomon, the Senior Warden, called Inspector, representing Tito, the chief of the Harodim, and the Junior Warden, who represents Adoniram. This arrangement of the Wardens would seem anomalous, as "Adoniram was set over by the levy" of thirty-thousand men sent by Solomon to Lebanon, while the Harodim were the three hundred overseers. The historical legend of this degree also affirms that the object of its institution was to supply the loss of Hiram, the widow's son. The badge is white, bordered with green and red. On the centre is a star of nine points, and on the flap a triangle with the initial of the degree. The Lodge is illuminated by twenty-seven lights, in three groups. The most noticeable character of this degree is the metaphorical use of the five points of fellowship in conjunction with the five orders of architecture. An Intendant of Buildings, we are told, must have made "the five steps of exactness, penetrated the inmost part of the Temple, and beheld the Great Light containing

145

the three mysterious characters." The Intendant of Buildings, according to the modern acceptation of terms, is, doubtless, a most important office; but that post was filled most ably by Adoniram, and as there was but one building, the Harodim were under his control. Thus viewed, without better foundation than we are at present possessed of, the degree seems unsatisfactory.

9° ELECT OF NINE

The Ninth Degree is Elect of Nine. At this point we observe, for the first time, that the body is termed a "chapter." The chief officer is called Most Wise —he represents King Solomon; the second officer is the King of Tyre, or Most Puissant. The badge is of white satin, with a broad black border; on it are embroidered the emblems of the degree. The sash is black, bearing on it nine red roses; the jewel is a small poniard. The Lodge represents the secret chamber of King Solomon; it is illuminated by nine lights of yellow wax. The Lodge is called the Council of Nine Masters. The object of this degree is to exhibit the mode in which certain overseers, who, in order, prematurely and improperly, to obtain the knowledge of a superior degree, engaged in an execrable deed of villainy, received their punishment. It exemplifies the truth of the maxim that the punishment of crime, though sometimes slow, is ever sure; and it admonishes us, by the historical circumstances on which it is founded, of the binding nature of our Masonic obligation. The symbolic colours in the regalia are white, red and black; the white being emblematic of the purity of the knights, the red of the atrocious crime committed, and the black of grief for its results. In the Grand Orient of France this is the Fourth Degree; it requires three chambers, and in some respects has similitude to the 17° of the Ancient and Accepted Rite, being also preparatory to the Rose-Croix. It is evident that the degree is an important one, and it is evident was closely connected with the Master Mason Degree.

10° ELECT OF FIFTEEN

Or "Illustrious Elect of Fifteen," the 10°, also holds its meetings under the designation of "Chapters," and in this the historical tradition, comprising the continuation and conclusion of the punishment inflicted on the traitors who, just before the completion of the Temple, had committed a crime of the most atrocious character, is more completely developed. The three principal officers are a Most Illustrious Master, an Inspector, and the Introducter. The symbolic color of the badge and collar is black strewed with tears.

11° SUBLIME ELECT

The Eleventh Degree is that of Sublime Elect, sometimes called "Twelve Illustrious Knights." This would appear to designate a new era in Masonry; as, after vengeance had been taken upon the traitors mentioned in the preceding degrees, Solomon, to reward those who had remained faithful to their trust as well as to make room for the exaltation of others to the degree of Elect of Fifteen, appointed twelve of these latter, chosen by their companions, to constitute a new degree, on which he bestowed the name of Sublime Elect, and endowed them with a certain command over the workmen, who were, in imitation of the tribes of Israel, divided into twelve companies. The Sublime Elect rendered to Solomon daily an account of the work that was done in the Temple by their respective companies, and received payment for them. The

146

assembly is called a "Grand Chapter"; the presiding officer represents King Solomon, whose name he bears as Thrice Puissant; his two chief officers are a Grand Inspector and a Grand Master of Ceremonies. The apron is white, with a black border and lining, and on the flap is a red cross; there is also a black sash suspended from the right shoulder to the left hip, having on it three hearts in flames, and a sword or poniard hanging from it. The costume resembles very closely that of the Knights Templar, differing only in the emblem. The room or place of meeting, which is called a Grand Chapter, is hung with black. We believe this degree is included with two others in the fourth of the French Rite. The title of Knights naturally suggests the idea that this degree could not have been formed before the Christian era, and is favorable to the suggestion that it was instituted by the Military Orders in Palestine. This degree in some form appears in different rites, and as three words belonging to it were adopted by the framers of the present H.R.A., there is every reason to suppose it was an important step in the high grades.

12° GRAND MASTER ARCHITECT

The denomination of the Twelfth Degree. In this the principles of Operative Masonry become prominent; it is a purely scientific degree, in which the rules of architecture and the connection of the liberal arts with Masonry are dwelt upon. Although the lectures on the Fellow-Craft Degree illustrate architecture from the same point of view, the subject is susceptible of great extension, and under the "Grand Master Architect" numerous details illustrative of the Temple dedicated to the Most High by the wise King might be worked out. In the absence of distinct information upon many points, there is some exercise for the imagination in furnishing a complete description of the Temple of Solomon, which we must conclude was an astonishing and magnificent work for the time in which it was built; and it seems to have been distinguished from all other temples of remote antiquity by its sumptuousness of detail. The officers of this degree are the Master, who is denominated Most Powerful, and two wardens. The Chapter is decorated with red and white hangings; the ornaments are the columns of the five orders of architecture, and a case of mathematical instruments. The jewel is a gold medal, on one side of which, in high relief, the five orders are represented; on the other a cube, with triangle and other appropriate devices; this is suspended by a blue ribbon.

We think that every Mason who carefully studies the subject, will agree with us that this degree ought not to be laid aside. If it is not in its present state so full of interest as might be desired, the works of Josephus, Strabo, Calmet, and others afford abundance of illustrative materials of which the compilers of the Fellow-Craft lecture have made no use. The degree might also become a useful school of instruction in practical architecture, and by diffusing a correct taste among the fraternity, and through them among the world at large, prevent the execution of unsightly structures and confusion of styles. But we must remark that the degree, so far as we can learn, never has been practiced.

13° MASTER OF THE NINTH ARCH

The Thirteenth Degree is denominated the Master of the Ninth Arch, and sometimes, the "Ancient Royal Arch of Enoch." The historical traditions of this degree are represented as affording copious information on certain points in which the sacred volume is not entirely free from obscurity, and these have reference to the mode in which Enoch, notwithstanding the destruction caused by the deluge and the lapse of ages, was enabled to preserve important secrets that eventually were to be communicated to the first possessors of this degree. The *Book of Enoch* is one of the Hebrew scriptures designated apocryphal, that is, hidden books, from the fact that after the destruction of the Temple at Jerusalem by the Romans, the Jews, having established their sacred archives at Tiberias, hid there in a cell such books as it was considered expedient to withdraw from public inspection. The Scriptures, now known as canonical, were deposited in a new chest, or ark of the covenant; but those holy books which were not included in this receptacle, and which at the close of the first century were suppressed by the Jews, and thus concealed, were called "the Apocrypha." The motive for this proceeding is said to be, that the predictions of the Messiah's advent and reign on earth contained in the Book of Enoch are so direct and incontrovertible, that it was on this account concealed. The Book of Enoch appears to have been read by both Jews and Christians in the Apostolic age; and this is seen in that passage of St. Jude's writings in which he says: "And Enoch also, the seventh from Adam, prophesied of these, saying, Behold, the Lord cometh with ten thousand of His saints, to execute judgment upon all, and to convince all that are ungodly among them of all their ungodly deeds which they have ungodly committed, and of all their hard speeches which ungodly sinners have spoken against Him." The Book of Enoch existed until the eighth century, when it unaccountably disappeared, save some fragments, until, in 1774, Bruce brought from Abyssinia three complete and beautiful copies of what was asserted to be the long-lost book. One of these he presented to the Bodleian library, and from this, in 1826, *Dr. Lawrence,* Professor of Hebrew, afterwards Archbishop of Cashel, produced a complete translation. The subject-matter of the book consists chiefly of relations of Enoch's prophetical and celestial visions, in the most remarkable of which the angel Uriel shows to the prophet various mysterious scenes in heaven, including a survey and explanation of the solar and lunar revolutions, according to the ancient astrological theory. *Eusebius* tells us that the Babylonians acknowledged Enoch as the inventor of astrology, and that he is the Atlas of the Greeks, who communicated to that people the knowledge of astronomy and the celestial globe. *Tertullian* endeavours to show that the Book of Enoch was preserved by Noah during the deluge. There have been many treatises by the learned on this book, but it must be allowed that although occasionally religious and moral precepts are enjoined, all sense of propriety is shocked by such preposterous combinations as continually appear in what is presented to us as the Book of Enoch; so that in comparison, even the metamorphoses of the pagan mythology appear to be rational. This explanation we consider necessary, as, although the Thirteenth Degree is represented as most interesting and impressive, yet if its ritual be based upon the authority of the work described, English Masons cannot admit it to be of any great value.

The officers of this degree (which in France is called *Royale Arche)* are a Thrice Puissant Grand Master who represents King Solomon; Hiram, King of Tyre, is also represented, attired as a traveler; there is a Grand Treasurer, representing Gibulum; a Grand Secretary, representing Joabert; and a

Grand Inspector, who represents Stolkin;—who these worthies were, we are unable to learn. The badge is white, with purple border. The jewel, a triangle, has in the centre a representation of two people letting down a third through a square opening into an arch.

14° GRAND SCOTCH KNIGHT or LODGE OF PERFECTION

This is the denomination now given in England to the 14°, but it appears to have been first called in the Scotch Rite, "Grand, Elect, Perfect and Sublime Mason"; in the United States it is designed "Perfection"; in France it is called "Grand Scotch Mason of Perfection of the Sacred Vault of James VI." The degree is considered to be the Ultimate Rite of Ancient Masonry, as it is the last of the Ineffable Degrees that refer to the first Temple; its officers are a Thrice Potent Master, who represents King Solomon, Hiram, King of Tyre (his deputy), two Wardens, Keeper of the Seals, a Treasurer, Secretary, Master of Ceremonies, and Captain of the Guards. The apron is white, with red flames, bordered with blue, and bearing the jewel on the flap. The jewel is a pair of compasses extended on an arc of ninety degrees, surmounted by a crown, with a sun in the centre.

Brother Mackey gives the following history of this degree:

"By the completion of the Temple, the Masons who had been employed in constructing it acquired immortal honour. Their Order became more uniformly established and regulated than it had previously been. Their caution and reserve in admitting new members produced respect, and merit alone was required of the candidate. With these principles instilled into their minds, many of the Grand Elect left the Temple after its dedication, and dispersing themselves among the neighboring nations, instructed all who applied and were found worthy in the Sublime Degrees of ancient Craft Masonry. The Temple was completed in the year of the World 3000. Thus far the wise King of Israel had proved worthy of his great office, and gained universal admiration, but in process of time, when he had advanced in years, his understanding became impaired; he grew deaf to the voice of the Lord, and was strangely irregular in his conduct. The Lord, who had appeared to Solomon in a dream after the dedication of the Temple, assured him He had accepted the building to be His house of sacrifice. He promised to bless him and his posterity if they were constant in His worship; if they did not remain faithful, He would certainly punish them, and destroy the sacred edifice. The reign of Solomon was most prosperous; peace and plenty blessed the land; he extended the commerce of the country, and fitted out a fleet with which, aided by mariners from Tyre, he traded to Ophir for valuable commodities and the precious metals. His extended power and influence at length corrupted his virtue; he plunged into all manner of licentiousness, and the latter actions of his life inflicted a deep disgrace on his character; he took wives and concubines from among the idolatrous nations around him, who perverted his heart so that he worshipped Astoreth of the Sidonians, Moloch of the Ammonites, and Chemosh of the Moabites, to whom he built temples on the Mount of Olives; and the people, following his example, soon neglected the worship of the true God for that of idols. The Grand Elect and Perfect Masons saw this, and were sorely grieved, afraid that his apostasy would end in some dreadful consequences, and bring upon them those enemies whom Solomon had before defied. The day of the vengeance of the Most High did come; Jeroboam headed a rebellion against the king, and thirty years after the completion of the Temple Solomon died, and Rehoboam, his son by one of his Ammonite wives, succeeded; ten of the tribes revolted, and Shishak, King of Egypt, came with an army, carried off the treasures of the Lord's house and all the king's gold and silver, laying waste the whole country. After the lapse of

149

four centuries from the death of Solomon, Nebuchadnezzar, the king of Babylon, sent his general, Nebuzaradan, with an army which desolated Judea with fire and sword; they took and sacked Jerusalem, razed the wall of the city, and destroyed the Temple. The conquerors carried the people captives to Babylon, leaving only a remnant of the lower class to till the land. The holy things of the Temple, its gold and silver vessels, were borne away."

All the degrees which we have thus described are conferred by name in a body called the Lodge of Perfection. It is scarcely necessary for us to mention that the Royal Arch Degree, as such, forms no part of the Ancient and Accepted Rite, but its principles are doubtless to be found in the Thirteenth and Fourteenth Degrees; and although the present ritual differs very much from that in use previous to 1813, the Royal Arch, as far as we can discover, has for a very long period formed part of Masonic ceremonial in Great Britain.

In the Degree of Perfection which is practised in the United States, among the decorations of the Lodgeroom is a transparency, placed behind the chair of the Master, representing a burning bush enveloping a triangle, and the letters JHVH (in Hebrew) in the centre of the fire. In the west is a pillar of Beauty. The pedestal is formed from the fragments of Enoch's pillar, which, being found in the ruins, were put together for that purpose. On a table is placed bread and wine and a gold ring for the newly admitted brother. The position of the companions when seated forms a triangle; and the twenty-four lights are placed three and five in the west, seven in the north, and nine in the south.

The so-called historical lecture of this degree contains the following passages:

"At the death of Solomon, his kingdom was rent asunder, and ten of the tribes severed from the dominion of his son. But the evil did not rest here; for the fascinations and pleasures of the latitudinarian system which had so long prevailed under the influence of Solomon's pernicious example had become so agreeable to his subjects, that the whole ten tribes soon became confirmed idolaters; nor did Judah and Benjamin escape the infection. . . . When the time arrived that the Christian princes determined to free the Holy Land from the infidels, virtuous Masons voluntarily offered their services, on condition that they should have a chief of their own election, which was granted. The valour and fortitude of those Elected Knights was such, that they were admired by all the princes of Jerusalem, who, believing that these mysteries inspired them with courage and virtue, were desirous of being initiated The Masons complied with their request; and thus the royal Art became popular and honourable, was diffused throughout these various dominions, and has continued to spread through a succession of ages to the present time. . . . Whenever a Lodge of Perfection was held, nine Knights of the Ninth Arch tiled the nine arches which led to the Sacred Vault, and so on in regular progression, the youngest taking his station at the first arch, which was near the apartment of Solomon. None were suffered to pass without giving the passwords of the different arches. There were living at that time several ancient Masters, who, excited by jealousy at the honours conferred upon the twenty-five brethren, deputed some of their number to wait upon Solomon, and request that they might participate in those honours. The king answered that the twenty-five Masters were justly entitled to the honours conferred on them, because they were zealous and faithful, and gave them also hopes that one day they would be rewarded according to their merits. This answer was not satisfactory, and one of the deputies warmly observed: "What occasion have we for a higher degree? We know that the word has been changed, but we can still

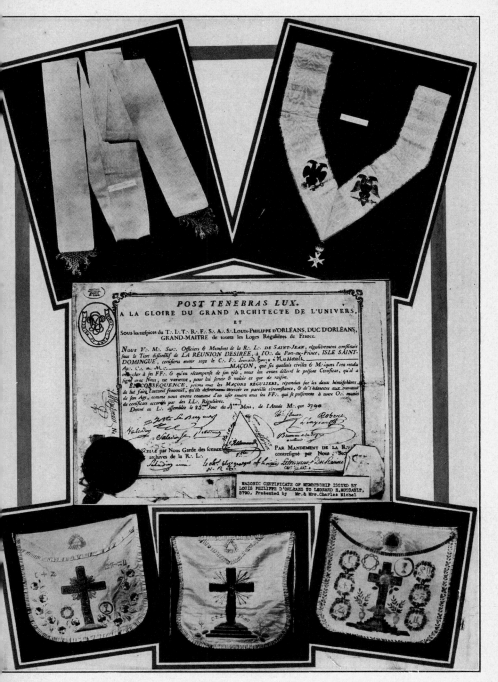

Masonic sashes, aprons, and diploma, in Jefferson Memorial Library (St. Louis, Mo.) Collection.

travel as Masters, and receive a Master Mason's wages." Solomon mildly replied, that those whom he had advanced to the Degree of Perfection had wrought in the difficult and dangerous work of the ancient ruins, had penetrated the bowels of the earth, and brought thence treasures to enrich and adorn the Temple of God; and desired the petitioners to go in peace, and aspire to perfection by good works. The deputies returned and reported their reception to the Masters. These Masters, displeased at the refusal, unanimously determined to go to the ancient ruins and search in the bowels of the earth, that they might have a good pretext for making re-application to Solomon for the required honours. The very next morning they removed the cubical stone, and descended into the cavern with a ladder of ropes by the light of torches; but no sooner had they all arrived at the bottom than the whole nine arches fell in upon them. The king, hearing of this accident, sent Joabert, Giblim, and Stolkin to make inquiries into the circumstance. At break of day they went to the place, but saw no remains of the arches, nor could they learn that any one of those who had descended had escaped to tell the tale. They carefully examined the spot, but found nothing except a few pieces of marble inscribed with hieroglyphics, by which Solomon discovered that these fragments formed a part of one of the pillars of Enoch."

The two oldest Lodges of Perfection in America were, one at Albany, constituted December 20, 1767, by the Thrice Puissant Brother Henry Andrew Francken, D.G. Inspector-General, from Kingston in Jamaica, and the other at Holmes' Hole, Martha's Vineyard, Mass.

We think we know the source of the 14°, and as its contriver's name is rather conspicuous in the Masonic history, the introduction here of a notice of a remarkable individual will not appear out of place. The *Chevalier Ramsay* was born at Ayr, in Scotland, in 1686, and in early life went to France, where he became the intimate friend and associate of the celebrated Fenelon. He is said to have been a man of most extensive erudition, and to have cultivated most of the known sciences. Being of a restless and ambitious disposition, he engaged actively in political intrigues, and particularly devoted himself to the cause of the exiled princes of the house of Stuart, and conceived the idea of making use of the Masonic association to subserve the interests of their party. With this end in view he endeavoured to obviate the objections of the French noblesse to the mechanical origin of the institution at which their pride revolted, by asserting that it arose in the Holy Land during the Crusades as an order of chivalry. His theory was that the first Freemasons were a society of knights, whose business it was to rebuild the churches which had been destroyed by the Saracens; that the infidels, with the view of preventing the execution of this pious design, sent emissaries among them, who, disguised as Christians, became confounded with the builders and paralyzed their efforts; that the knights, having discovered the existence of these spies, became in future more careful, and instituted signs and words for the purpose of detection; and that, as many of their workmen were newly-converted Christians, they adopted symbolic ceremonies with a view of instructing their proselytes more readily in the new religion. Finally, upon the Saracens gaining the upper hand, the Knights-Masons were compelled to abandon their original occupation; but being invited by the King of England to remove into his dominions, they had accepted the offer, and in this secure retreat devoted themselves to the cultivation and encouragement of architecture, sculpture, painting and music.

In 1728, Ramsay attempted to lay the foundation of this new, and, according to his idea, improved, system of Masonry, and proposed to the Grand Lodge of England to substitute, in place of the three ancient degrees, others of his own invention, but which he asserted had been practised from time immemorial in the Lodge of St. Andrew at Edinburgh (It is right to state that there is no record in the Records of the Grand Lodge of such a proposition, and many well-known Masonic historians reject this version of the degree in toto). His views being rejected in London, he carried them to Paris, where his degrees were adopted, not indeed as a substitute for, but as an addition to, ancient Craft Masonry. These degrees became popular, and in a short time gave birth to numerous others on the Continent of Europe, the splendor of the decorations, and the gorgeous manner in which the ceremonials were conducted, captivating the senses. Ere long they fell into oblivion, except so far as thus preserved.

15° KNIGHT OF THE SWORD AND THE EAST

This especially refers to those valiant Masons who, with trowels in hand and swords by their sides, were ever ready and prepared to construct and defend the Holy City and Sanctuary, would appear to be one of very considerable interest, as it is founded on the circumstance of the assistance rendered by Darius to the Jews, who, liberated from their captivity, had been prevented by their enemies, after death of Cyrus, from achieving their purpose of rebuilding the Temple. In this degree the meetings are designated "councils," and an important change takes place in the symbolic colors adopted; the hangings of the council-chamber are water-green, in allusion to a circumstance hereafter referred to. The chamber is illuminated by seventy lights, in memory of the seventy years captivity. The sash is a green watered ribbon, bordered with gold fringe, worn across the body from the right shoulder to the left hip, the figure of a bridge being in the front, having on it the letters "Y" and "H"; there are also sometimes other emblems painted on the ribbon. The apron is white, lined with red and bordered with green, and has on it emblems of war and its consequences. From Scripture and tradition is derived the following legend of this degree:

The Knights of the East derive their origin from the captivity, when the whole land was "a desolation and an astonishment," and the nation did "serve the King of Babylon seventy years." And when the seventy years were accomplished, the Israelites were restored to liberty by Cyrus, in fulfillment of the prophecy of Jeremiah. This prophecy was very remarkable, for it not only fixed the date for the return of the Hebrew people to their own land, but also for the overthrow of the Babylonian monarchy. "It shall come to pass, when the seventy years are accomplished, that I will punish the King of Babylon, and that nation saith the Lord, for their iniquity, and the land of the Chaldeans, and will make it a perpetual desolation." And the last words of the prophet declare—"Thus shall Babylon sink, and shall not rise from the evil that I will bring upon her."

But to return to the historical events said to be connected with this degree. Cyrus permitted the Jews to return to Jerusalem for the purpose of rebuilding the Temple, and he caused all the holy vessels and ornaments which had been carried away by Nebuzaradan to "be restored, and brought again unto the Temple which is at Jerusalem, every one to his place, and place

153

them in the house of God." (Ezra vi.5). The King committed the charge of the holy vessels, as well as of the returning captives, to Sheshbazzar, the prince of Judah; this is the Babylonian name of Zerubbabel, who was of the royal line of David, and a direct ancestor of our Lord Jesus Christ. When the Israelitish captives were assembled they numbered 42,360, exclusive of slaves and servants amounting to 7,337.

This traditional history relates that Zerubbabel, for the protection of his people, armed 7,000 Masons, and placed them in the van to repel such as should oppose their march to Judea. Their march was unimpeded as far as the banks of the Euphrates, where they found an armed force opposed to their passage. A conflict ensued, and the enemy was cut to pieces or drowned at the passage of the bridge. The emblematic color of the degree is in allusion to this circumstance. The journey occupied four months, and in seven days from their arrival the work of restoring the Temple was commenced. The workmen were divided into classes, over each of which a chief, with two assistants, was placed. Every degree of each class was paid according to its rank, and each class had its distinctive modes of recognition. The works had scarcely commenced, before the workmen were disturbed by the neighbouring Samaritans, who were determined to oppose the reconstruction of the edifice. Zerubbabel therefore ordered, as a measure of precaution, that the Masons should work with a sword in one hand and a trowel in the other, that they might be able at any moment to defend themselves from the attacks of their enemies. The second Temple occupied forty-six years in its construction, and was consecrated in a like manner to that of the Temple of Solomon. Those Masons who constructed it were created by Cyrus Knights of the East, and hence the title of this degree.

This appears in both the French Rites; in the Grand Orient it is the 6°; in both it is termed Knight of the East. The assembly is called a Council. Everything bears a Hebrew character; there are the candlesticks with seven branches, the brazen sea, and the table of shewbread, &c. There are seventy lights, in memory of the seventy years capitivity. The Chief of the Council is designated Sovereign, and represents Cyrus, King of Persia. The second officer is Nehemiah the Chancellor, Esdras is the Grand Orator, Mithridates the Grand Treasurer, and there is also a Grand General. Zerubbabel and two others appear to receive the authority from the King of Persia to rebuild the Holy City and Sanctuary. The sash, which is worn from right to left, is water-green, and on it are embroidered the symbols of the degree; to it is attached a small poniard. The apron is white satin with green border. The green color has reference to the river Euphrates.

16° GRAND PRINCE OF JERUSALEM

This degree is founded on certain incidents which took place during the rebuilding of the second Temple, at which time the Jews were much annoyed by the attacks of the neighboring nations, as mentioned in the legend of the Fifteenth Degree.

The assembly is called the Grand Council, and the apartment should be separated into two parts. In the first is represented Darius the King, seated on a blue dais; this part represents the city of Babylon, and it should be hung with red. The other part represents the City of Jerusalem, where Zerubbabel presides, and it should be hung with orange.

154

In this degree the fact of the Valiant Masons who, at the building of the second Temple, were armed with sword and shield to protect the workmen, is especially referred to.

The rooms are illuminated by twenty-five candles in groups of five.

We find the following passage in Ezra iv: "The people of the land weakened the hands of the people of Judah, and troubled them in building." It goes on to say that these enemies obtained a letter from King Artaxerxes saying, "Give ye now commandment to cause these men to cease, and that this city be not builded until another commandment shall be given from me." And "So it ceased until the second year of the reign of King Darius," when the Israelites sent an embassy to that potentate to implore his protection and permission to resume the work, and succeeded in gaining the object of their petition.

The emblematic color of the degree is yellow; the apron is red, lined and bordered with pink; the flap is yellow, having on it a balance on which are the letters D and Z. The jewel is a gold medal with a like emblem and on the reverse a two-edged sword and five stars.

The first Grand Council of Princes of Jerusalem of which we find any record was formed at Charleston, in the United States, which took the control of all subordinate degrees up to the fifteenth.

17° KNIGHT OF THE EAST AND WEST

The Seventeenth Degree is entirely chivalric and, as far as can be at present discovered, makes no pretense in its history to ancient Freemasonry. Its inventors asserted that it was organized by the Knights engaged in the Crusades; that in 1118—the same year that the Order of the Temple was instituted—eleven Knights took the vows of secrecy, friendship, and discretion, between the hands of Birinus, the patriarch of Jerusalem. The presiding officer is called Most Equitable Sovereign Prince Master, the other officers being High Priest, two Wardens, Keeper of the Seals and Archives, Treasurer, Master of the Ceremonies, Master of the Entrances, and Tyler. The badge is yellow bordered with red, having for its emblem a two-edged sword. The jewel is a heptagon of silver, having at each angle a golden star; in the centre is a lamb on a book with seven seals; the reverse has a two-edged sword between the scales of a balance; it is suspended from a blue ribbon.

As somewhat more deference is paid by the Supreme Council to this degree than any which precede it, and as it is distinctly conferred by an authoritative body, and forms a portion of the ceremonial of the 18°, it is necessary that we should give some explanation of it. The practice in conferring the degree of Rose-Croix, is to give, first, the degrees by name from the fourth to the fourteenth inclusive, in a Lodge of Perfection; then to declare a Grand Lodge of Princes of Jerusalem opened, and confer the fifteenth and sixteenth degrees, also by name; having closed that, a Grand lodge of Knights of the East and West is opened, and that degree is given by name, accompanied by secrets and password; thus we perceive that some importance is attached to the degree. From the following description it will be seen that were this degree practised in accordance with the ritual, the grand council chamber of the Order would have a most gorgeous appearance. It must be hung with red, spangled with golden stars; in the east, under a canopy, is placed a throne elevated on seven steps, supported

155

by the figures of four lions and four eagles, between which is placed an angel with six wings. On one side of the throne is displayed a transparency of the meridian sun, on the other, of the lustrous orb of night. In the east also are two vases, one containing water and the other perfume. On the south and north sides are canopies for the Ancients; while in the west are two seats with canopies, raised five steps, for the Venerable Wardens, who in conjunction with the Most Puissant act as the Grand Council. Twenty-four Knights are necessary to form a full council. On a pedestal in the east is placed a large Bible, from which are suspended seven seals. The covering of the floor displays a heptagon within a circle, over the angles of which appear certain initials; in the centre is the figure of a man clothed in a white robe, with a golden girdle around his waist; his right hand, which is extended, is surmounted by seven stars; he wears a long white beard; his head is surrounded with glory, and from his mouth issues a two-edged sword. Seven candlesticks stand around him, bearing the mysterious initials. The seven stars by which his hand is surmounted, are explained to signify the seven qualities which ought to distinguish a Freemason, viz., friendship, union, submission, dscretion, fidelity, prudence and temperance. But there is a higher meaning attached to the symbol of the seven stars, derived from passages in the Old Testament; they represent the seven eyes mentiond by Zechariah, which typify the care of Divine Providence, ever watchful to promote the welfare of his creatures; and the seven lamps of the Apocalypse, which symbolize the Holy Spirit of God, whence are also derived the seven spiritual gifts of a Christian man.

The candidate being in possession of the password of the 17°, then presents himself for admission to the Rose-Croix Chapter.

18° SOVEREIGN PRINCE OF ROSE CROIX HEREDOM (OR KNIGHT ROSE-CROIX, OF THE EAGLE, OR THE PELICAN)

The Eighteenth Degree is the most ancient and most generally practised of the historical degrees of Masonry. It is found in all the principal rites, and where (like the Royal Arch) it does not exist by name, its place is supplied by others whose symbols do not differ materially from it. To those who have not gone beyond the symbolic degrees, the name is perhaps more familiarly known than any other of the higher degrees. Of its origin, nothing satisfactory is known; one writer supposes it to have been instituted by the Knights Templar in Palestine, in the twelfth century, and asserts that Prince Edward, afterwards King Edward I, was there admitted into the Order; he also says that the Order was derived from an Egyptian priest converted to Christianity. *Ragon,* in his treatise entitled "Orthodoxie Maconnique," has most· elaborately investigated the subject, and attributes its origin to a pious monk, named John Valentine Andrea, who flourished in the early part of the seventeenth century, and wrote, among other works, two treatises, one entitled "Judicorum de Fraternitate R. C."; the other, "Noces Chimiques de Rozen Crutz." Ragon says that Andrea, grieved at seeing the principles of Christianity forgotten in idle and vain disputes, and that science was made subservient to the pride of man instead of contributing to his happiness, passed his days in devising what he supposed to be the most appropriate means of restoring each to its legitimate moral and benevolent tendency. *Clavel* absurdly affirms that

156

the degree was founded by the Jesuits, for the purpose of counter-acting the insidious attacks of freethinkers upon the Romish faith, but offers no evidence in support of his assertion; when in fact they were the great enemies of Masonry, and so far from supporting it, wrote treatises against the Order. Many of the Rosicrucians were amongst the reformers of the age, and hence the hostility of the Romish Church. The almost universal recognition of this degree in all countries would favour the theory of its being of long standing.

Hurd in his "Treatise on Religions," speaks of the Brethren of the Rose, or *Ne plus Ultra.* "They were to declare openly that the Pope was Antichrist, and that the time would come when they should pull down his triple crown. They rejected and condemned the doctrines of the Papacy and of Mahomet, calling the one and the other the blasphemies of the East and the West. They called their association the *Fraternity of the Holy Ghost.* They claimed a right of naming their successors, and bequeathing to them all their privileges; to keep the devil in a state of subjection; and that their confraternity could not be destroyed, because God always opposed an impenetrable cloud to screen them from their enemies.

Rosetti, in his work on the "Antipapal Spirit of Italy," asserts similar statements with regard to this and other societies connected with Freemasonry. I knew Rosetti when he resided in England, and although I do not know whether he belonged to our Order, he was accustomed to speak (as well as write) of his certainty that the Templars were Masons, and that the Rose-Croix originated with them. This was from information he derived from Italian works unknown in this country. He says, speaking of the higher degrees, "The rites which, hastily considered, may seem absurdities, will, when maturely judged, be found otherwise."

The ceremonies of the degree are of the most imposing and impressive character, and it is eminently a Christian degree. Its ritual is remarkable for elegance of diction, while the symbolic teaching is not only pleasing, but consistent with the Christian faith, figuratively expressing the passage of man through the valley of the shadow of death, accompanied and sustained by the Masonic virtues—faith, hope and charity—and his final reception into the abode of light, life, and immortality.

Officers of a Rose-Croix Chapter are, the Most Wise Sovereign, a High Prelate, the First General, the Second General, who may be assimilated to Wardens; a Grand Marshal, who presents the candidates for admission; Raphael, their conductor during the ceremony, and the Captain of the Guard, who has charge of the entrance. The candidate, previous to his admission, if he has not already done so, must sign a declaration of fealty and allegiance to the Supreme Council; and on his admission, prior to the ceremonial, he promises this more fully in the presence of the Chapter. To give this degree in the full perfection of its ceremonies, several chambers are required, and the aid of solemn music; the rooms must also be large and lofty. There are two badges worn in this degree, or rather one, which is reversible; the first may be called the badge of mourning, and is of black silk, having in its centre the passion cross; the other side of white satin, on which the cross with roses is worked in embroidery richly ornamented; it has a rose-coloured border; the collar is of rose-coloured satin, richly embroidered. The jewel includes the most important symbols of the degree; it is a golden compass, extended

157

on an arc to twenty-two and a half degrees, or the sixteenth part of a circle; the head of the compass is surmounted by a crown with seven emerald points; it encloses a cross of Calvary, formed of rubies or garnets, having on its centre a full-blown rose, whose stem twines round the lower limb of the cross. At the foot of the cross is a pelican wounding her breast to feed her young, which are in a nest beneath. On the reverse, instead of a pelican, there is a figure of an eagle. On the arc of the circle is engraven in cypher the password of the degree. The symbols of which the jewel is composed will satisfy our readers of the Christian character of the degree.

When the Rose-Croix Degree is conferred, the recipient is created and constituted "a Knight of the Pelican and Eagle, and Prince of the Order of Rose-Croix." The Degree of Knight of the Eagle and Pelican appears to be the name by which the Rose-Croix is elsewhere known, its ritual and legend being somewhat similar; but in the Council of the Ancient and Accepted Rite in England and Wales, both pass as one degree. The eagle on the jewel, it is ingeniously suggested, is a symbol of Christ, in His divine character, bearing the children of His adoption on His wings, teaching them with unequalled love and tenderness to spread their new-fledged wings, and soar from the dull corruptions of earth to a higher and holier sphere.

In Deuteronomy xxxii, 11, there is a beautiful comparison of the care and paternal affection of the Deity for His people with the natural tenderness of the eagle for her young:

> "As the eagle stirreth up her nest,
> Fluttereth over her young,
> Expandeth her plumes, taketh them,
> Beareth them upon her wings;
> So Jehovah alone did lead him,
> And there was no strange god with him."

The pelican is appropriately adopted as an emblem of the Saviour who shed His blood for the salvation of the human race, from the custom attributed by the poets to this bird of tearing open its breast to feed its offspring with its own blood. Ragon says that in the hieroglyphic monuments of the ancients the eagle was the symbol of a wise, and the pelican of a benevolent man; he therefore considers the eagle and pelican of this degree to be intended to symbolize perfect wisdom and perfect charity. The 102nd Psalm, which was written towards the end of the captivity, alludes to the lonely situation of the pelican in the wilderness, as illustrative of the poignancy of the writer's grief at witnessing the desolation of his country and the prostration of her sacred altars. In this view the pelican is a fitting symbol for the degree.

The cross was from the earliest ages, with the Egyptians, a symbol of eternal life; but since the crucifixion it has been peculiarly adopted as an emblem of Him who suffered on it; in this latter signification only it is adopted as an emblem in this degree—and hence its form. The rose, in Scripture, is applied as a figurative appellation of Christ; in the Canticles He is called "the Rose of Sharon." The cross alludes to His death; the rose on the cross is, therefore, an emblem of the death of the Saviour for the sins of mankind.

The rose, in ancient mythology, was consecrated to Harpocrates, the god of silence, and in the mysteries the hierophant wore a crown of roses, as emblems of silence and secrecy. Following this idea, Ragon suggests that as the cross

158

was, in Egypt, an emblem of immortality, and the rose of secrecy, the rose followed by the cross was the simplest mode of writing "the secret of immortality."

Another theory of the origin of Freemasonry assigns to the union of the rose and the cross this explanation—that as the rose was the emblem of the female principle, and the cross or triple phallus of the male, the two together, like the Indian lingam, symbolized universal generation. Without entering upon the question of the age of our institution, we may notice the undoubted fact that both the rose and the cross were used as symbols from the most remote antiquity.

Whatever may have been the origin of the Rose-Croix Degree, it now bears in most countries an entirely Christian character; it is, indeed, a bold attempt to christianize Freemasonry, and to apply the rites, symbols, and traditions of ancient Masonry to the last and greatest dispensation; to add to the Temples of Solomon and Zerubbabel a third—that to which Christ alluded when He said, "Destroy this temple, and in three days I will raise it up." Many commentators on our institution insist that *all* degrees of Freemasonry allude to the religion of Christianity. If this be granted, it may certainly be asserted that the light on the subject becomes clearer in each succeeding degree, and displays its full effulgence in the exquisite mysteries of the Rose-Croix. Jehovah says, "I am come down to deliver My people"; He is said to come down in the person of Jesus Christ; in this degree the divine glory is symbolically asserted to have been manifested at the period when the word was recovered, the cubical stone being changed into the mystical rose, attended with the appearance of a blazing star, dispelling darkness, restoring the true light, and making the new law visible in our works. The brother who is admitted to the Rose-Croix will observe that the great discovery made in the early degrees of Masonry ceases to be of any value in this degree; for the Wisdom, Strength and Beauty which supported the Temple of Solomon are replaced by the Christian pillars of Faith, Hope and Charity; the three great lights of the Royal Arch of course remain, but the three lesser give place to thirty others, which, added to the three greater lights, allude to the years of the Messiah's sojourn upon earth. In short, from beginning to end, everything bears the impress of Christianity. At its meetings the brethren break bread and eat salt with one another, and on the goblet of fraternal affection invoke the blessing of Him who is the Rose of Sharon, to aid on earth their progress to that state of perfection which will enable them, when bursting from the tomb, to join their Great Emmanuel in the skies, and be there united in a happy eternity.

To this degree has been attached the significant designation of *Ne plus Ultra*. In the original form of the Order of Knights Templar in this country it was the next step taken about the simple Templar Degree, and was followed by that of the Kadosh. All encampments being qualified to give those degrees, the emblems of all are engraved on the certificates issued prior to 1851, and the seal confirms the grant. The "Ne plus Ultra" is at the top of the Masonic ladder; the "K.D.S.H." uniting the whole structure. The Rose-Croix Degree possesses similar characteristics to the Templar; the object in both degrees is the same; the Templar, perhaps, confining itself more to fact, while the Rose-Croix displays more of the allegory; hence in the latter was afforded a better opportunity of interweaving the symbols of Craft Masonry with an

159

emblem of the Christian faith. The older Masons are united in the opinion that these degrees ought never to have been separated. The high consideration in which the Rose Croix is held is shown in the circumstance that its ritual has met with universal acceptance; the Symbolic Degrees are in all countries identical, so also is the Rose-Croix—and this cannot be said of any other degree.

We can nowhere find a satisfactory explanation of the word *Heredom.* *Ragon,* in the second edition of his "Orthodoxie Maconnique," says it was invented by the Stuart party, and is a corruption of the Mediaeval Latin word *haeredium,* which signified "a piece of ground fallen by inheritance." *Mackey* observes that, in an old MS. of the Scotch Rites, he has discovered the following explanation—that *Heroden* is the name of a mountain situate in the northwest of Scotland, where the first or Metropolitan Lodge of Europe was held, and supposes that the present orthography may be the French mode of spelling it. Dr. *Oliver* calls the H.R.D.M. and R.S.Y.C.S. two degrees, as worked in the "Royal Order of Scotland"; he states that the Royal Order of Heredom was founded on the dissolution of the Order of the Knights Templar, A.D. 1314, and that the Rose-Croix was, by the Grand Chapter of the former degree, added in 1736. It is not impossible, however, that the word *Heredom* has some esoteric connection with the often quoted word *Harodim,* of which we have already spoken at length in the former part of this account of the Rite.

In connection with the R.C. degree it may be observed that the initials of the Latin inscription placed on the cross, I.N.R.I., representing *Jesus Nazarenus Rex Judaeorum,* were by the Rosicrucians used as the initials of one of their Hermetic secrets: *Igne Natura Renovatur Integra*—by fire nature is perfectly renewed. They also adopted them to express the names of their three elementary principles, salt, sulphur, and mercury, by making them the initials of the sentence *Igne Nitrum Roris Invenitur.* A learned Mason finds in the equivalent Hebrew letters the initials of the Hebrew names of the ancient elements, *Iaminim,* water; *Nour,* fire; *Ruach,* air; and *Iebschah,* earth.

In the first part of the ceremony, on the floor is a painting representing seven circles in white on a black ground, and in the centre a pelican, the circles representing the seven periods of the world's existence, through which the aspirant for honours has to pass. This symbol is doubtless of long date, for we learn from a traveler in the Island of Ceylon, that in the ancient·city of Amurajapura, there is in the sacred enclosure of a Dagobah, or Temple, a circular slab of dark bluish granite, and on it are sculptured seven concentric rings; within each of these are different sacred emblems, and in the seventh, or innermost, are a cow, a lion, a horse, and an elephant, also a peculiar long narrow leaf. The centre is occupied by .·. which forms the letter I of the Lath alphabet.

The second part symbolizes the passage through trials and difficulties, and the Valley of the Shadow of Death. The third chamber introduces the neophyte into light and immortality.

The antiquity of this degree is shown in Rosetti's work on the secret societies which preceded the Reformation, especially in the extract which follows:

"St. Paul, in the second chapter of his Epistle to the Galatians, calls the three Apostles—who attended their Divine Master in His most divine moments, and who witnessed His transfiguration on Mount Tabor, and His devotion in the garden—pillars; and following that passage of the Apostle, the Paulicians (the Paulicians, who are generally considered to be a branch of the Manichaeans, first appeared in Armenia in the seventh century) made then three pillars, emblematic of the three theological virtues: St. Peter was *faith;* St. James, *hope;* and St. John, *charity.* In a rite which is supposed to have descended from the Albigenses, three pillars appear, with the names of those virtues on them. The candidate is obliged to travel for thirty-three years (thus they call the thirty-three turns he takes, in allusion to the age of our Lord), to learn the beauties of the *new law.* His leader takes him round the three columns, repeating successively the name of each virtue, and afterwards asks him what he has learnt in his pilgrimage; to which he answers that he has learnt the three virtues of faith, hope, and charity, and that by them he intends to govern himself. The Master assures him that they are the principles and *pillars* of the new *mystery.* In these same rites of the pilgrimage undertaken by the candidate who is thirty-three years of age, which extends through thrirty-three years, the tragedy of Good Friday and the events of the following days are rehearsed, and Christ dies and rises again under his eyes. This new mystery, or new law, is the essence of *Dante's Vita Nuova.* In the Paradise we find this rite described exactly. Before the last vision, St. Peter examines him on faith, St. James on hope, and St. John on charity; relating to the three pilgrimages—of the palmers, or Templars, to St. John of Jerusalem; of the pilgrims, or Albigenses, to St. James in Gallicia; and of the Romei, or Ghibbelines, to St. Peter's in Rome; and at the examination presides Beatrice, who, by a far-fetched comparison, is likened to Christ, when transfigured before the eyes of His three Apostles."

"Wishing to let us know that these things are all mystical, he says in the Convito, 'There is one thing which should be very attentively observed by readers, for their own and the pupils' benefit; we read that when Christ went up into the mount to be transfigured, He took only three Apostles with Him out of the twelve; and by that we are to understand that, in *very* secret things, we should have but few companions.' "—*Rosetti.*

The Rose Croix Degree is alluded to in the works of Henry Cornelius Agrippa, a man of great learning and talent, of a noble family at Cologne, born 1486. His works were printed at Leyden in 1550. He practised as a physician and astrologer, and by the ignorance of the age was considered to be addicted to magical arts. He visited England in 1510.

Amongst the earliest known to have belonged to the Rosicrucian Brotherhood, was John Gower, the friend of Chaucer, whose sumptuous monument in St. Mary Overies' Church, or, as it is now called, St. Saviour's, Southwark, shows the recognition of the degree in the purple and gold band with fillets of roses which encircles his head; in Gower's works also the degree may be traced. The initiated in the Rose-Croix Degree will, by careful study, find allusions to it in the poems of Chaucer.

St. Saviour's Church is perhaps one of the least known in the great metropolis; it is well deserving of a visit. England does not contain a more elegant Gothic structure, and there are many memorials of interest to Masons; an effigy of a cross-legged Knight Templar; the stone effigy of an emaciated man wrapped in a shroud, which is drawn up in a very curious manner, at the back of the head, into a projecting knot; in the window of the south transept is, in beautiful stone tracery, the double triangle; and now placed upon the organ are the shields of Templars.

19° GRAND PONTIFF (OR SUBLIME ECOSSAIS)

Grand Pontiff is the denomination of the 19°, and an appellation more decidedly papal could scarcely be found. Except in this and some other

Masonic degrees, the modern title of pontiff would appear to be applied exclusively to the head of the Romish Church. Yet it can be undoubtedly traced to the early days of ancient Rome, when Numa Pompilius (B.C. 710-672) founded the college of priests, and instituted the office of *Pontifex Maximus*. The pontiffs stood in the place of an ecclesiastical court at Rome, having superintendence and power over all persons in matters connected with religion and ceremonial laws; and amongst their numerous duties were the government of the vestal virgins, and the superintendence of their moral conduct; the brethren who reach this Masonic degree, however, are not, as we are advised, possessed of any of these extraordinary powers, but are occupied in an examination of the Apocalyptic mysteries of the New Jerusalem, as set forth in Revelation xxi and xxii. There are two chief officers: a Thrice Puissant in the east, who is seated on a throne under a canopy of blue, wearing a white satin robe, and the Warden in the west, who bears a staff of gold. All the members are clothed in white, and wear blue fillets embroidered with twelve golden stars. The decorations or hangings of the Lodge represent the vault of heaven—celestial blue, with stars of gold. The sash is crimson with golden stars; to it is suspended the jewel, a square, on one side of which is Alpha, and on the other Omega.

20° GRAND MASTER AD VITAM, OR GRAND MASTER OF ALL THE SYMBOLIC LODGES

This is the imposing name bestowed on the 20°. Here the brother is again led to temple-building. The historical lecture refers to the period of the destruction of the third Temple by Titus, A.D. 70. The Christian Freemasons then in the Holy Land, filled with sorrow, departed from their home with the determination of erecting a fourth Temple—a spiritual edifice; and dividing themselves into different Lodges, dispersed over the various countries in Europe. A considerable number went to Scotland, and made choice of the village of Kilwinning, where they established a Lodge and built an abbey, in which the records of the Order were deposited; we are not informed where these worthy brethren were traveling during the period between A.D. 70 and 1140, when this magnificent abbey was founded, in which we have tolerably good proof that a Masonic Lodge was founded by the builders engaged in constructing the edifice. The presiding officer is styled Venerable Grand Master, and represents Cyrus Artaxerxes. Who is the personage meant we are at a loss to imagine; the younger Cyrus was the younger brother of Artaxerxes, second king of Persia of that name, and died in his twenty-fourth year, B.C. 358. Taylor says, on the suggestion of Prideaux, that the period of Artaxerxes Longimanus, who died B.C. 358, corresponds with the Ahasuerus of Scripture, mentioned in the Book of Esther, whose wife was the daughter of Cyrus I. This is one of those numerous instances of anachronism in dates and persons that occur in the traditional history of the symbolic and historical degrees, and perplex the inquirer in his researches; they have arisen through the superficial acquaintance the framers had with ancient history, and could easily be set right. The names of Cyrus and Artaxerxes did not belong to the same individual. The Lodge, when perfect, is composed of nine Grand Masters; they all wear collars of yellow and blue. The jewel is a triangle, on which is engraved initials of the words.

162

21° NOACHITE, OR PRUSSIAN KNIGHT

The Very Ancient Order of Noachites is the 21°. We now find the traditional history carried back to an earlier date than in any other degree in Masonry, either symbolical or historical, for it commemorates the destruction of the Tower of Babel. It is stated that the meetings in this degree are holden only on the night of the full moon, and that no other light is permitted than what is derived from that luminary. The meeting is called a Chapter, and it is presided over by a Knight Commander Lieutenant, who represents Frederick II, King of Prussia. The other officers of the degree are five knights—the first being called Knight of Introduction; the second, of Eloquence; the third, of Finances; the fourth, of Chancery; and the fifth, of Defence. The badge is white satin with a yellow border. The Knights wear a black sash from right to left, and on the front is the jewel, an equilateral triangle crossed by an arrow.

The Noachites profess to be descendants of Peleg, who, they say, was the chief architect of the "tower whose top was to reach to heaven." This is a gratuitous assumption, for all that Moses tells us is, "that his father named him Peleg (division) for (or, because) in his days the earth was divided." This Order of the Noachites was first established in Prussia in 1755. There must have been formerly in English Masonry some matters connecting the name of the survivor of the deluge with its traditional history (probably "the Ark and Mark," and "Ark and Dove" Degrees, were then used), for we find in *Ahiman Rezon,* published in 1764, by Lawrence Dermott, the first of the old charges which is as follows:

"CONCERNING GOD AND RELIGION:—A Mason is obliged by his tenure to observe the moral law as a true *Noachida* (son of Noah, the first name of Freemasons) ; and if he rightly understand the Craft, he never will be a stupid atheist, nor an irreligious libertine, nor act against conscience. In ancient times, the Christian Masons were charged to comply with the Christian usages of each country where they traveled or worked; being found in all nations, even of divers religions. They are generally charged to adhere to that religion in which all men agree (leaving each brother to his own particular opinion), that is, to be good men and true, men of honour and honesty, by whatever names, religions, or persuasions they may be distinguished; for they all agree in the three great articles of *Noah,* enough to preserve the cement of the Lodge. Thus Masonry is the centre of their union, and the happy means of conciliating persons that otherwise must have remained at a perpetual distance."

It is to be observed that in the genealogical table of Jesus Christ, as given by St. Luke, Phaleg is called Phalec; there may be some further reference to him, on that account, in the historical traditions of the degree. Our ancient brethren evidently called themselves Noachidae, or sons of Noah, and his precepts were preserved among them, the three first of which are : 1. Renounce all idols. 2. Worship the only true God. 3. Commit no murder. On this head Brother Oliver says, "The spurious Masons of antiquity, in all their mysteries, commemorated the descent of Noah into the ark, and his subsequent exodus. The entrance into initiation was symbolic of his entrance into the vessel of his salvation; his detention in the ark was represented by the darkness and the *pastos* (coffers, or couch) in which the aspirant was placed; and the exit of Noah, after the forty days of deluge, was seen in the manifestation of the candidate, when, being fully tried and proved, he was admitted to full light, amid the surrounding initiates, who received him in the *sacellum* or holy place."

It is not improbable that the ancient Masons, real or spurious, derived the connection of "our father Noah" from the Egyptian mysteries; as, according to Bishop Cumberland, Mizraim, the son of Cham, grandson of Noah, was the first king of Egypt, and the name Osiris was his appropriated title, signifying "prince."

22° PRINCE OF LEBANON, OR KNIGHT OF THE ROYAL AXE

The 22°, *Thory* asserts, was instituted by Pierre Riel, Marquis de Bournonville, who, when in command of the island of Bourbon in 1778, was there elected Grand Master of all the Franch Lodges in India. The legend of this degree states that it was instituted to record the memorable services rendered to Masonry by the mighty cedars of Lebanon, as the Sidonian architects cut down the cypress for the construction of Noah's ark. (The best authorities consider that the descriptive term gopher wood agrees with the cypress; shittim wood, from Jerome's description, is doubtless the black acacia, which is very common about Mount Sinai, and on the mountains that border the Red Sea.) Our ancient brethren, indeed, do not tell us how the Israelites had the wood conveyed to them from the land of promise to the mountains in the wilderness. They further say, that the descendants of the Sidonians were employed in the same offices, and in the same place, in obtaining materials for the construction of the ark of the covenant; and also, in later years, for building Solomon's Temple; and lastly, that Zerubbabel employed labourers of the same people in cutting cedars of Lebanon for the use of the second Temple. The tradition adds that the Sidonians formed colleges on Mount Libanus, and always adored the G.A.O.T.U. Sidon was one of the most ancient cities of the world, and even in the time of Homer, the Sidonians were celebrated for their trade and commerce, their wealth and prosperity. But their worship was not that of the true and living God, for medals are in existence bearing the inscription "to the Sidonian goddess," and this agrees with the appellation in 1 Kings xi. "Ashtoreth, goddess of the Sidonians." The allusion to the "colleges" on Mount Libanus may have some reference to the secret sect of the Druses, who still exist in that country, and whose mysterious ceremonies, travellers affirm, have considerable affinity to Freemasonry.

There are two apartments; the first representing a workshop at Lebanon, with axes, saws, mallets, wedges, and such like implements; the Master is Most Wise, his Wardens, Wise Princes. This apartment is hung in blue and lighted by eleven lamps, and this assembly is a "college." Each brother is armed with an axe. The second apartment represents the council of the Round Table; the presiding officer is Grand Patriarch, and the others Patriarchs; the room is hung with red; a round table, in the centre, has on it the square, compass, and other mathematical instruments; each Patriarch is armed with a sword.

The collar belonging to this degree is celestial blue, lined and bordered with stars; the badge, which is white, has on it represented a table, upon which are laid several architectural plans and mathematical instruments. The jewel is an axe, crowned in gold.

23° CHIEF OF THE TABERNACLE

The 23° commemorates the institution of the Order of Priesthood in Aaron and his sons Eleazar and Ithamar; and the ceremonial was in some degree founded on the instruction delivered to Moses in Exodus xxix and xl. In many rites the degree of High Priest is to be found; in the old ritual of the Holy Royal Arch, the High Priest was the chief officer, and we still retain in that portion of English Masonry, as well as in the Master Mason's Degree, reference to him who only had the privilege of entering the sanctuary once in the year, on the day of solemn expiation, to make atonement for the sins of the whole people; so that doubtless this was a genuine Masonic degree, and not unworthy of practice at the present day. The installation of the Third Principal of a Royal Arch Chapter has undoubtedly been derived from this or some similar ceremonial. In the United States the order of High Priest, conferred on the immediate Past First Principal, somewhat resembles that of Past Master of a Lodge; the ceremony, when duly performed, is exceedingly impressive—when celebrated in ample form, the presence of at least nine High Priests is required. In America, as was formerly the case in England, High Priest is the title given to the First Principal.

In this degree there are three chief officers, viz: a Sovereign Grand Sacrificer and two High Priests, and the members are called Levites. They wear a white badge, lined with scarlet, and bordered with a tri-coloured ribbon—red, purple and blue; in the centre is embroidered a representation of the "candlestick of pure gold, with three branches on the one side, and three branches on the other side," and on the flap a violet-coloured myrtle. The jewel, which is a thurible, or censer, is suspended from a broad sash of four colours—yellow, purple, blue, and scarlet—and worn from the left shoulder to the right hip.

The Lodge is hung with white, ornamented with columns of red and black, ranged in pairs at equal distances; the Holy Place is separated by a railing and curtain. There is a red altar, on it the Book of Wisdom and a poniard; the throne is elevated on seven steps. There is the altar of burnt offering and the incense; also two chandeliers of five lights each. There is the obscure chamber, which is hung with black; it has one lamp, an altar, and a stool on which are three skulls, also a skeleton with this inscription: "If you are fearful, go from hence; it is not permitted for men who cannot brave danger without abandoning virtue."

The Grand Sacrificer wears a long red robe over a yellow tunic, which is without sleeves; on his head is a mitre of cloth of gold. He wears a black scarf with silver fringe. The Levites wear white robes with red scarfs.

In the prophecy of Zechariah there is an account of the splendid and significant emblem used in this degree, presented in a vision which will abundantly reward an attentive examination; the principal object that met the eyes of the prophet was a "candlestick all of gold, with a bowl on the top of it and seven lamps." The image is evidently taken from the candlestick in the tabernacle. This candlestick is the scriptural symbol of the universal Church.

24° PRINCE OF THE TABERNACLE

The name which is given to the 24°, is intended to illustrate the directions for constructing the tabernacle which Moses built for God by His express command, partly to be a palace of His presence as the King of Israel, and partly to be the locality of that most solemn worship which the people were to pay to Him. This was a movable chapel, if we may so call it, so contrived as to be taken to pieces and put together at pleasure, for the convenience of carrying it from place to place, during the wanderings of the Israelites in the wilderness for forty years. This movable fabric, which may properly be called the sacred tent, was nevertheless built with extraordinary magnificence and at a prodigious expense, that it might be in some measure suitable to the dignity of the King whose palace it was, and to the value of those spiritual and eternal blessings of which it was designed as a type or emblem. The value of the gold and silver alone, used for the work, amounted, according to Bishop Cumberland's estimate, in English money, to £35,359 7s.6d. sterling. The Lodge is called a "hierarchy," and its officers are a Most Powerful Chief Prince, representing Moses, and three Wardens whose style is Powerful, and who respectively represent Aaron, Bezaleel, and Aholiab. There are two apartments necessary for this degree; the first, or vestibule, is decorated with the various attributes of Masonry; the second, which is of circular form, is hung with tapestry, representing a colonnade. The sun is represented on the Masonic pavement, and in the centre is the chandelier with seven branches.

The members wear short cloaks of blue taffeta, edged with gold embroidery, and a robe of cloth of gold. They have a coronet environed by stars and surmounted by a luminous triangle. The badge is white, lined with scarlet, and bordered with green; in the centre is embroidered a representation of the tabernacle; the flap is sky-blue.

The 23° and 24°, it will be seen, have been based upon the official duties of the priests. In the former we find the ark, altar, and golden candlestick; the Wardens are styled High Priests, and the presiding officer Grand Sovereign Sacrificer. In the latter degree there are three Wardens, placed in the south, west, and north. The officers represent Moses, the lawgiver; Aaron, the High Priest, Bezaleel and Aholiab, the cunning artists under whose direction the tabernacle was constructed. The candidate represents Eleazar, who succeeded Aaron in the priesthood. The brother who is admitted to the degree of High Priesthood is thus addressed: "The station you are called upon to fulfil is important, not only as it respects the correct practice of our rites and ceremonies, and the internal economy of the Chapter over which you are called upon to preside; but the public reputation of the institution will generally be found to rise or fall, according to the skill, fidelity, and discretion with which its concerns are managed, and in proportion as the conduct and character of its principal officers are estimable or censurable.

In the first degree of Scotch Knighthood, the adept is informed that he has been elevated to the degree of High Priest, which entitles him to receive the following information: That in future he has to adore the Deity under the name of Jehovah, which is much more expressive than the word Adonai; that in this degree he receives the Masonic science as descended from Solomon and revived by the Templars. In the Second Degree the Royal Art is traced to the creation, from which period it has been transmitted through Noah, Abraham, Moses, Solomon, and other worthies, down to Hugo de Payens, founder of the Knights Templar, and Jaques de Molay, their last Grand Master. In the next degree the *great word* is revealed to him, discovered by the Knights Templar when building a church at Jerusalem. It is related that in digging under the spot whereon had been placed the holy of holies, in the bosom of Mount Moriah, they discovered three stones, on one of which was this word engraven. The Templars, on leaving the Holy Land, carried with them these relics, and on their arrival in Scotland, deposited them, on St. Andrew's day, as the foundation-stones of their first Lodge, whence they assumed the name of Knights of St. Andrew. The tradition adds that their successors, being entrusted with this secret, are Perfect Masters of Freemasonry at the present day, and High Priests of Jehovah.

Our Royal Arch brethren will readily trace in this legend a resemblance to certain parts of the ceremonial belonging to that Supreme Degree; and in reference to the place in which the discovery was made, it is to be observed that Josephus speaks of some vaulted chambers that existed on the holy spot in his time. The old traveler *Maundrell* also says that in a garden situate at the foot of Mount Moriah he was shown several large vaults running at least fifty yards underground; they were built in two aisles arched at the top with a huge firm stone, and sustained by two pillars, each consisting of a single stone two yards in diameter.

25° KNIGHT OF THE BRAZEN SERPENT

The 25° is of long standing, and founded upon the events described in the Book of Numbers xxi. 6-9: "And the Lord sent fiery serpents among the people, and they bit the people; and much people of Israel died. Therefore the people came to Moses, and said, We have sinned, for we have spoken against the Lord, and against thee; pray unto the Lord, that he take away the serpents from us. And Moses prayed for the people. And the Lord said unto Moses, Make thee a fiery serpent, and set upon a pole; and it shall come to pass, that every one that is bitten, when he looketh upon it, shall live. And Moses made a serpent of brass, and put it upon a pole, and it came to pass, that if a serpent had bitten any man, when he beheld the serpent of brass, he lived."

The ritual says that Moses, in obedience to the divine command, placed the brazen serpent upon the *tau,* and every one who looked upon it was directed to pronounce the word *hatathi,* "I have sinned"; and having done this, he was immediately healed. Commentators regard the word rendered "pole" in our translation to mean *standard,* and the earliest form of the standard of which we have a representation, the Persian, is the figure of the tau. The hangings of the Lodge are red and blue. A transparency, representing the burning bush, with the Incommunicable Name in the centre, is placed over the throne. There is only one light; in the centre of the apartment there is a mount accessible by five steps; upon the summit is placed the symbol of the degree. The Lodge is named the "Court of Sinai." The presiding officer is styled Most Powerful Grand Master, and represents Moses; the Wardens are called Ministers, and represent Aaron and Joshua; the Orator is styled Pontiff, the Secretary Grand Graver, and the Candidate "a Traveller." The jewel, which is suspended by a red ribbon, is a serpent entwined around a tau cross standing on a triangle.

The legend states that this degree was founded in the time of the Crusades, by John Ralph, who established it in the Holy Land as a military and monastic

167

order, and gave it the name it bears, in allusion to the healing and saving virtues of the brazen serpent among the Israelites in the wilderness—it being part of the obligation of the knights to receive and gratuitously nurse sick travellers, protect them against the attacks of the infidels, and escort them safely through Palestine.

The brazen serpent which Moses set up was preserved as a memorial of this miracle till the time of Hezekiah—more than 700 years—who, in extirpating idolatry, "removed the high places, and brake the images, and cut down the groves, and brake in pieces the brazen serpent that Moses had made; for until those days the children of Israel did burn incense to it." This was a bold measure; for some kings, however, bent on the extirpation of idolatry, would have hesitated at the destruction of that which was certainly in itself an interesting memorial of a remarkable manifestation of the power of God.

It is not improbable that the influence of the example of the Egyptians, combined with the remembrance of the benefits derived from this particular brazen serpent, induced the Israelites to adopt the practice of serpent-worship. In the wilderness their fathers had been directed to look on it and live— they did so and lived. And this direction and its consequence, misunderstood and perverted, may have formed the foundation of the idolatry into which they fell. In what manner they worshipped the serpent does not appear, but it is most probable that, with a recollection of its origin, they regarded it as symbolizing the divine healing power, and as such burned incense before it when attacked with disease, much in the same manner as the classical ancients resorted on similar occasions to the serpent-symbol of the healing god.

The worship of the serpent is supposed by *Bryant* to have commenced in Chaldea, and to have been the first variation from the purer Zabaison. That it was intimately connected with Zabaism cannot be doubted, for the most prevailing emblem of the solar god was the serpent; and wherever the Zabaean idolatry was the religion, the serpent was the sacred symbol. But the universality of serpent-worship, and the strong traces which it has left in astronomical mythology, seem to attest an origin coeval with Zabaism itself. The earliest authentic record of serpent-worship is to be found in the astronomy of Chaldea and China; but the extensive diffusion of this remarkable superstition through the remaining regions of the globe, where Chinese wisdom never penetrated, and Chaldean philosophy was but feebly reflected, authorized the inference that neither China nor Chaldea was the mother, but that both were the children of this idolatry.

Few ancient nations of any celebrity will be found which have not, at some time or other, admitted the serpent into their religion, either as a symbol of divinity, or a charm, or an oracle, or a god.

Diodorus informs us that in the Temple of Bel or Belus, in Babylon, "was an image of the goddess of Rhea, sitting on a golden throne; at her knees stood two lions, and near her very large serpents of silver, thirty talents each in weight. There was also an image of Juno, holding in her right hand the head of a serpent."

Herodotus says: "In the vicinity of Thebes there are sacred serpents, not at all troublesome to men; they are very small, but have two horns on the top of their head. When they die they are buried in the Temple of Jupiter, to whom they are said to belong."

In his notice of the Egyptian mythology, *Bryant* says, "The symbolical worship of the serpent was in the first ages very extensive, and was introduced into all the mysteries wherever celebrated. It is remarkable that wherever the Ammonians founded any places of worship, there was generally some story of a serpent."

Serpent-worship, under some form or other, was one of the most widely diffused modes of idolatry of the ancient world; it was the deified symbol of something good and beneficent. Among the Greeks and Romans it symbolized the good genius, and their worship of the healing power (the god Aesculapius), under the same figure, was but an extention of the same general idea. In various points of view Aesculapius corresponds to the Egyptian deities Serapis and Horus. In the monuments upon which these divinities are figured, they bear serpents as the emblems of health, and carry the chalice or salutary cup of nature surrounded by serpents.

There was a remarkable superstition in regard to a serpent of enormous bulk, which girded the world, current in the mythology of almost every nation where ophiolatria prevailed. This idea perhaps originated in the early consecration of the serpent to the sun, and the subsequent conversion of a serpent biting his tail into an emblem of the sun's path. This hierogram was again considered as *typical of eternity,* partly from the perfect figure of *a circle* thus formed, *without beginning or end;* and partly from an opinion of the *eternity of matter.*

Remains of this superstition were observed by *Bishop Pococke,* when he visited the banks of the Nile.

"The next day we came to Raigny, where the religious sheikh of the famous serpent, Heredy, was at the side of the river to meet us. He went with us to the grotto of the serpent. He said it had been there ever since the time of Mahomet. He comes out of the grotto only during the four summer months, and it is said they sacrifice to it."

In the ancient Persian mysteries the status of Mithra stood erect on a globe, out of which issued a serpent, the emblem of life, which, twining in numerous folds around the body of the deity, marked the convolutions of his orb, and the cycles of revolving time. When the honours of initiation were conferred on the candidate, a golden serpent was placed in his bosom, as an emblem of his being regenerated and made a disciple of Mithra; for this animal, renewing its vigour in the spring of every year by casting its skin, was not only considered as an apt symbol of renovated and reviviscent virtue, but of the sun himself, whose genial heat is annually renewed when he revisits the vernal signs.

26° THE PRINCE OF MERCY

Or "Scotch Trinitarian," is the name given to the 26°, which, of course, clearly designates its character and intention. It is a highly philosophical degree, and its ritual very impressive. The assembly is styled the Thrice Heavenly Lodge; the Chief Prince, whose title is Most Excellent, represents Moses; the Senior Warden represents Aaron; the Junior, Eleazar; and the candidate, Joshua. The Lodge is hung in green, and decorated with nine columns, alternately red and white. At each column is a candelabra of nine stars, giving 81 lights, which can be reduced to 27, as in the following degree. The jewel is a gold equilateral triangle, within which is a heart, also of gold, inscribed

169

with a Hebrew letter, one of the symbols of the tetragrammaton; it is suspended from a tricoloured ribbon of green, white and red. The apron is red, bordered with white fringe, and has a blue flap; on the flap is embroidered the jewel.

This is a Christian degree, and its ritual speaks of the triple alliance which the Eternal has made with man, and alludes in the first place to the covenant entered into with Abraham by circumcision; secondly, to that with His people in the wilderness through Moses; and thirdly, to that which He made with mankind by the mediation of His Son Jesus Christ.

With regard to the word "covenant," we may notice that *Mr. Taylor,* in his edition of Calumet's Dictionary, says, the word *testamentum* is often used in Latin to express the Hebrew, *berith,* which signifies "covenant"; whence the titles *Old and New Testament* are used improperly to denote the *Old and New Covenant.* Without discussing the doctrine advance in the ritual of this degree, we may remark that the first covenant between God and man was made with Adam at his creation, when he was prohibited to eat a certain fruit. A second covenant God made with man, after his fall, promising not only forgiveness on his repentance, but also a Messiah, who should redeem the human race from the death of sin and from the second death. A third covenant was with Noah, when the Lord directed him to build the ark, and which was renewed. These covenants were general; but that made with Abraham was limited; the seal or confirmation was the circumcision of all the males in Abraham's family. The affects of this covenant appear throughout the Old Testament; the coming of the Messiah is the consummation and end of it. The covenant of God with Adam forms what we call a state of nature; that with Abraham, explained further under Moses, constitutes the law; that ratified through the mediation of Jesus Christ is the kingdom of grace. In common discourse, we usually say the Old and New Testaments; the covenant between God and the posterity of Abraham, and that which He has made with believers by Jesus Christ; because these two covenants contain eminently all the rest. The most solemn and perfect of the covenants of God with men, is that made through the mediation of our Redeemer, which must subsist to the end of time. The Son of God is the guarantee of it, it is confirmed with His blood; the end and object of it is eternal life, and its constitution and laws are infinitely more exalted than those of the former covenant.

27° KNIGHT GRAND COMMANDER OF THE TEMPLE

The assemblage is called a "Court," and altogether the degree has a character dissimilar to every other that precedes it; everything about it is of the chivalric and military class. The presiding officer is styled Most Puissant, the Wardens are Sovereign Grand Commanders, and even the Knights are designated Commanders. The chamber is hung with red, having black columns surmounted by torches; on an altar is placed the Book of the Evangelists, with a sceptre and naked sword; on a pedestal is placed a lustre bearing twenty-seven lights. The members ought to be placed in a circle, and if there is no reception, at a round table. The badge is red satin, lined and edged with black; with a Teutonic cross encircled by a wreath of laurel, and a key, all embroidered in black, upon the flap. The scarf is red, bordered with black, hanging from the right shoulder to the left hip, and bears on it a Teutonic cross

170

in gold enamel. The jewel is a golden triangle, on which is engraved the Ineffable Name in Hebrew; it is suspended from a white collar bound with red, and embroidered with four Teutonic crosses. The accounts we have from the French writers all concur in connecting this degree with the Knights Templar, and it certainly has much of the character of that Order. It is generally considered to have been intended to supply the Templar Degree under this rite, but as we shall fully enter into the subject under its proper head, as a distinct rite, it is not necessary to say more in this place.

28° KNIGHT OF THE SUN

This degree is highly philosophical; it also bears other names, being sometimes called Prince of the Sun, Prince Adept, and Key of Masonry, or Chaos Disentangled. *Ragon,* who in his "Cours Philosophique" speaks disparagingly of the high degrees, says this is not a modern invention, but is of the highest antiquity, and was, in fact, the last degree of perfect initiation, teaching, as it did, the doctrines of natural religion, which formed an essential part of the ancient mysteries. The ceremonies and lecture, which are of great length, furnish a history of all the preceding degrees, and explain in the fullest manner the various Masonic emblems. The great object of this degree is the inculcation of truth, and as this virtue is one of the three great tenets of Masonry, we need scarcely say it deserves commendation. To be true and trusty is one of the first lessons in which the aspirant is instructed—it is the prime essential of the Master. All mortal affairs are transitory, but truth alone is immutable and eternal; it is the attribute of Him in whom there is no variableness nor shadow of changing. This might with propriety be called the Degree of Perfection; for truth, like a substance or reality, is opposed to typical representations, which are but as shadows; the law was given by Moses, but the grace and truth—the reality of the promised blessings—came by Jesus Christ. Every man should speak truth to his neighbor; that is—honestly, sincerely, with integrity. Truth on the part of God is united with mercy and goodness, because fidelity to promises being one great test of truth, and goodness and mercy being implied in the divine promises, when God realized any special good, He did but show Himself faithful and true, fulfilling the desires, or acting for the advantage of those who confided in Him and in His word. The love of truth is one of the noblest characteristics of the Christian, or truly pious man of any creed; and as genuine piety, wherever it prevails, will banish falsehood, so we find a real love of truth, and the conformity of a man's conduct with the regulations of truth, to be always the most desirable—the most favourable—the most decisive proofs of genuine religion; which, being itself a system of truth, delights in nothing more than in truth, whether of heart, discourse, or conduct.

The principal officers of this degree are styled Thrice Perfect Father Adam and Brother Truth; there are seven subordinate officers, who are named after the seven chief angels—Zaphiel, Camael, Anael, Michael, Gabriel, Raphael, Zaphriel.

Four apartments are requisite for the due ceremonial of this degree. The first represents a grotto; in the centre is a column, to which is attached a chain; on one side is a table, having on it a Bible and a small lamp. Over the entrance to the next apartment is inscribed, "You who have not power to subdue your passions, flee this sanctuary." This chamber is hung with black, and lighted by three candles in the east, west, and south. The fourth chamber is hung with red, and is illuminated by eleven candles. The last chamber is azure blue, and has but one light, which is very powerful, being a large illuminated glass globe, representing the sun—the symbol of the Great All, from whom flow all philosophical principles. The collar is white, having on it a chain suspending the jewel, a triangle of gold, with an eye in the centre. The Master wears a red robe and yellow tunic; he has a sceptre with golden globe on the top. The badge represents a sun, with an eye upon the flap.

The historical legend describes the seven cherubim, whose names are written in the circle of the first heaven, to represent the corporal plasures of this life which the Eternal presented to man at the Creation, when He taught him to enjoy and to obey; these are—seeing, hearing, smelling, tasting, feeling, tranquility, and thought.

In the Holy Scriptures we frequently read of missions and appearances of angels, sent to declare the will of God, to correct, teach, reprove, or comfort. Reference to these angelic missions is made in this degree, and we will describe those to which the allusion applies. In the apocryphal book of Tobit, Raphael tells Tobias that he is one of the seven angels who attend in the presence of God. The holy St. John saw seven angels standing before the Lord (Rev. viii.2); and that sublime and mysterious book, the Apocalypse, we find the number seven ever prominent. "The seven stars are the angels of the seven churches; and the seven candlesticks are the seven churches."

The number seven, among all nations, has been considered as a sacred number, and in every system of antiquity we find a frequent reference to it. In one of the lectures of the high degrees, it is stated that the different Masonic grades originally were seven in number, from the example of the G.A.O.T.U. who created all things in six days and rested on the seventh. Enoch, it is said, employed six days in constructing the arches, and on the seventh, having deposited the secret treasure in the lowest arch, was translated to the abode of the blessed. Solomon, who had been employed somewhat more than six years in building the Temple, celebrated its dedication in the seventh, with every solemnity that was due to the Divine Being in whose honour it had been erected. The Pythagoreans called this a venerable number, because it referred to the creation, and because it made up the two perfect figures— the triangle and the square. The radical meaning is "sufficiency," or "fullness," and the number seven was thus denominated, because it was on the seventh day that God completed His work of creation; and hence, says *Parkhurst,* seven was, both among believers and heathens, the number of sufficiency or completion. In Freemasonry, seven is an essential and important number, and throughout the whole system the septenary influence extends itself in a thousand different ways.

This degree was worked by the Kent Lodge. We think it very probable that it was some knowledge of this degree which induced Rosetti to connect the theology of Swedenborg with Freemasonry. The degree is noticed by him in illustration of the Purgatory of Dante. It was formerly in extensive practice; and one of those preserved by the Ancient Masons in England, as already mentioned. Many consider Pernetti the inventor.

29° GRAND SCOTTISH KNIGHT OF ST. ANDREW

The 29° is the preparation for the "Kadosh." This degree has also been called "Patriarch of the Crusades," in allusion to its supposed origin during those wars, and it had also the name of "Grand Master of Light." There are a Master and two Wardens. The Lodge, as in the degree of Secret Master, is illuminated by eighty-one lights arranged by nine times nine, but the hangings of the room are red. The assembly is called Grand Lodge, the Grand Master is called Patriarch, the other officers Worshipful Masters. The Master and officers are attired in scarlet robes with scarfs of purple, from which is suspended the jewel, a triple triangle, having in its centre the compasses, beneath it a square reversed; in the angle is a poniard. The Knights wear purple collars, to which the jewel, a cross of St. Andrew, is attached; they also wear a white sash with gold fringe. The Grand Master and his two officers are on thrones covered with red drapery with gold fringe; above that of the Master is a transparency of a luminous triangle, bearing within emblems of the degree.

This is the first of the degrees which Ramsay proposed to substitute in place of the ancient Symbolic Degrees, and as a full explanation of his theory has been already given, under the degree of the Grand Scotch Knight, it is unnecessary to do more here than remark the inconsistency of this system. We have here, placed within four degrees of the pinnacle of his fabric, a degree intended to supersede the very first step in Freemasonry.

A *hierogram,* in this degree, is thus explained. The triangle or delta is the mysterious figure of the Eternal. The three letters which you see signify as follows: G at the top of the triangle refers to the *Grand Cause* of the Ma-  sons, S on the left hand the *submission* to the same order, and U at the right hand to the *Union* that ought to reign among the brethren; which all together make but one body, or equal figure in all its parts. This is the triangle called equilateral. The G placed in the centre of the triangle signifies the Great Architect of the Universe, who is God; and in this ineffable name is found all the divine attributes. The letter is placed in the centre of the triangle that we may understand the imperative requirement for every true Mason to bear it profoundly impressed upon his heart. The hierogram, though thus explained in the ritual, means in reality, *God, the Grand Superintendent of the Universe.* When we compare this clumsy contrivance with the beautiful simplicity of the ancient Symbolic Degrees—in which the Mason is gradually advanced step by step in knowledge, being taught the whole duty of man to God, his neighbour, and himself, before he is plunged into the mysteries of triangles and other geometrical symbols—and examine the system which Ramsay proposed to set up in its place, we can but conclude that those degrees in the rite he put forward, which really possess merit, were not devised by himself, but gathered from other systems.

30° GRAND ELECTED KNIGHT KADOSH

Also called Knight of the Black and White Eagle. The 30° is acknowledged to be very important, being found in many rites. Previously to the adoption of the Ancient and Accepted Rite, the Kadosh Degree formed, we believe, a part of the ceremonial of the Knights Templar. *Ragon* mentions the Kadosh as having been established at Jerusalem in 1118, in which case it must, of course, have belonged to the Templars.

The word from which this degree takes its name has been a considerable

173

difficulty with all commentators—its first appearance in the volume of the Sacred Law is where we read that "God blessed the seventh day and sanctified it." (Gen. ii.3.) He separated and distinguished it from the days of the week, setting it apart for the purposes of a Sabbath agreeably to the primary meaning of the word which is here made use of, *kodesh,* signifying "separated" or "consecrated." In the law, as delivered by Moses, we find the following precept concerning the feasts and sacred assemblings: "Six days' work shall be done; but the seventh day is a Sabbath of rest, a holy convocation; *mikra-kodesh.* (Lev. xxiii.3.) Mr. Taylor says, the word *kadesh,* as he writes it (the word is differently rendered by translators) signifies "holy" or "holiness," and is equivalent to the Greek "sacred." The name is also applied to certain places, where, probably there had been a divine appearance, as Meribah in Kadesh (Num. xxvii.14), and Meribah-Kadesh (Deut. xxxii.51); and in Ezekiel xlvii.19, it is used in the plural, Meriboth-Kadesh. In its application to this degree, we must consider it to be derived from the appointments of the priestly office. Exodus xxviii 36-38: "And thou shalt make a plate of pure gold and grave upon it, like the engravings of a signet, *Holiness to the Lord.* And thou shalt put it on a blue lace, that it may be upon the mitre; upon the forefront of the mitre it shall be. And it shall be upon Aaron's forehead, that Aaron may bear the iniquity of the holy things, which the children of Israel shall hallow in all their holy gifts; and it shall always be upon his forehead, that they may be accepted before the Lord." This plate had engraven on it, *kodesh-laihovah,* which is rendered in our translation, and agreeably to the ancient versions, "Holiness to the Lord." The size and form are not defined by Moses, but the Jewish doctors say it was two fingers broad, and made in a circular form, adapted to the shape of the head, and so long that it reached from ear to ear, and was fastened by a blue lace or ribbon, which was tied behind the head.

The mitre was a turban of fine linen, furnished in front with a plate of pure gold, bearing the inscription we have mentioned. In chapter xxxix this ornament is called *nezer,* from a root signifying "to separate"; hence it denotes a crown, as a mark of separation or distinction.

It was formerly the custom in English Royal Arch Chapters for the Third Principal to wear a mitre of this description, and also a similar head-plate, as well as the breast-plate ordained to be worn by the High Priest. These two ornaments—the head-piece and the breast-plate, as worn by that officer in the Mount Sion Chapter (the oldest in London) are now in possession of a Past Principal; their use, as well as of some other regalia, has been discontinued. Prior to 1833, the High Priest was the First Principal of a Royal Arch Chapter, and is still according to the American working.

We are induced to believe that in the Kadosh was formerly comprised the degree—if it may be so called—of High Priest; and that it is not unlikely to have been adopted by the military and religious orders in Palestine, and conferred on the principal clerical members of those orders. We can suggest no better theory for the connection of priestly and knightly rank in the degrees of chivalry.

We are told by *Pluche,* that in the East, a person preferred to honours bore a sceptre, and sometimes a plate of gold on the forehead, called a *kadosh,* to apprise the people that the bearer of these marks of distinction possessed the privilege of entering into hostile camps without fear of losing his personal liberty.

We have already observed that the Kadosh Degree—prior to the establishment of the Supreme Council of the Ancient and Accepted Rite in England was always conferred in encampments of Knights Templar; the preamble of the certificates issued up to the year 1851 runs thus: "Royal and exalted Religious and Military Order of H.R.D.M., Grand Elected Masonic Knights Templar, K.D.O.S.H. of St. John of Jerusalem, Palestine, &c." By this title the Order would also appear to assume a derivation from the Hospitallers. The ritual, however, connects the degree with the Knights Templar, and furnished the history of the destruction of the Knights by the atrocious Philip of France and his minion Clement V. The Knights' costume should be black, worn as an emblem of mourning for the death of the illustrious Jacques de Molay, the martyred Grand Master. These remarks are not strictly applicable to the present practice in England, as no reference is made to the death of Jacques de Molay.

When the ritual is duly celebrated in ample form, three chambers are required, besides an ante-room for the reception of the candidate. According to the mode prescribed, and, we believe, adopted in France, the first room is hung with white drapery, and display neither dais nor altar; at the bottom of the apartment is seen a statute of Wisdom, dimly visible by the pale light of a spirit-lamp placed over a chafing-dish. In England the chamber is hung with black; the Grand Sacrificator here receives the candidate and his conductor. The second chamber, which is called the "Areopagus," is hung with black; at the farther end of the room is a table, covered with blue cloth, behind which are placed the two Lieutenants and an officer called the Orator; these three form the "Council of the Areopagus." The first Lieutenant, seated in the centre, presides, holding a golden sceptre; the other Lieutenant, on his right, bears the golden scales of justice, while the Orator, who is on the left, displays a sword; on either side of the room are ranged the seats of the Knights; three yellow candles light this chamber. The third hall, which is called the "Senate," is hung with red; in the east is the dais, on which is placed the throne, bearing on its canopy the double-headed eagle, crowned, and holding a poniard in his claws; a drapery of red and black, interspersed with red crosses, descends from the wings of the eagle, and forms a pavilion. On each side of the throne are placed the standards of the cross: One, white, with a green cross, bears the motto "God wills it"; the other black, with a shield charged on one side with a red cross, and on the other a double-headed eagle, has the motto "Conquer or die." The hall of the Senate is illuminated by eighty-one lights, which are dispersed in a peculiar way; here is placed the mysterious ladder, which is symbolic of virtue and science; one of the supports is dedicated to the love of God, and the other to the love of our neighbour; the steps represent justice, candour, truth, wisdom, patience, and prudence; the platform is the *ne plus ultra;* the descending steps are grammar, rhetoric, logic, arithmetic, geometry, music, and astronomy. This symbol of the Order appears also on the old Knight Templar certificates.

The Knights wear a broad black sash, suspended from the left shoulder,

175

the point fringed with silver bullion; on it are embroidered the emblems of the degree. The jewel is a Teutonic cross of red enamel, in the centre of which is the number 30. Some adopt the Eagle of the superior degrees, distinguished by the extremities being tipped with gold.

We may here observe, that in the practice of our French brethren, this is the last of the degrees which has its teaching engraved on the cubical stone, which is divided into eighty-one points—the square of nine, and the pyramid bearing the initials N.P.U., i.e., *ne plus ultra,* which is variously applied to this and the 18°.

It is to be observed that the description of the ceremonial is derived from a French MS. of the middle of the last century, some portions differing in England.

We cannot but think the degree is of high antiquity, though not perhaps in its present form, for, as now practised, there appears a want of unity of design. Thus we find the emblematic ladder prominent in the Symbolic Degrees as well as in the Rose-Croix; while the admixture of the military and religious ceremonies is more conspicuous in this than in any other degree. In its present form it bears evident traces of Teutonic origin; and most probably it was devised by the German knights. One standard used in this rite bears a green cross, which designated that nation in the Holy Land; the motto is the same as was borne by the pilgrims in the first crusade. The red cross belonged to the Templars, and was assumed by the two other orders on the extermination of the Templars. To this ceremonial additions were made in the 18th century, when the degrees now concentrated in the Ancient and Accepted Rite were establishd.

Although much importance is attached to the degree, it suffers by comparison with the Rose Croix. There are several inconsistencies which strike us upon examining this degree—we may, for instance, inquire why the second chamber is named after the celebrated seat of justice at Athens. That court took cognizance of all crime and immortality, and idleness as the cause of vice; it heard causes in the darkness of night, that its members might not be prepossessed in favour of either plaintiff or defendant by their appearance; it allows only a plain statement of facts, and hence its decisions were most just and impartial. We can see no possible connection between the degree and the Greek tribunal. Again, the third chamber bears a Roman name, and one not applicable to a body which acknowledges a superior council. Other anachronisms might be noticed, but these are sufficient to illustrate the weak points of the degree.

It will be seen from the preceding remarks that the philosophical part of the degree is alone retained, and all reference to Jacques de Molay discarded; but the results of research into this and the Temple Degree prove that, if not identical, they are intimately connected. The allegory of the three days is more in harmony with the Rose-Croix; hence some desire that the Templar Degree should be brought into the Ancient and Accepted Rite, which it appears might be accomplished if the 30° were restored to its original fullness.

All degrees beyond the Rose-Croix are designated *Philosophical,* as they are particularly directed to the philosophical explanation of the Masonic system, which in all the inferior degrees receives a moral signification.

176

31° THE SOVEREIGN TRIBUNAL OF THE THIRTY-FIRST DEGREE, OR GRAND INQUISITOR COMMANDER

It is not an historical degree, but is simply administrative in its character; the duties of the members being to examine and regulate the proceedings of the subordinate lodges and chapters. The meeting is designated a "Sovereign Tribunal," and is composed of nine officers, viz. A Most Perfect President, a Chancellor, a Treasurer, and six Inquisitors—one being elected to perform the functions of Inspecting Inquisitor. The decoration of the Lodge is white, with eight golden columns; on the dais above the presiding officer's throne are the letters J.E.; there is also an altar covered with white drapery. In the east, on a low seat, is placed a case containing the archives of the Order covered with blue drapery, having on its front a large red cross; on the right of the altar is the table of the Chancellor; on the left, that of the Treasurer. The floor of the Sovereign Tribunal is covered by a painting, the centre of which represents a cross, encompassing all the attributes of Masonry. As regalia, the members wear a white collar, on which are embroidered the emblems of the Order; the jewel is a Teutonic cross surmounted by a celestial crown, and having the number 31 in the centre. In France the regulations direct a white apron, with *aurore* (yellow) flap, embroidered with the attributes of the degree.

32° SUBLIME PRINCE OF THE ROYAL SECRET

The Lodge is styled a "Grand Consistory," and should be held in a building of two stories. We first enter the chamber of the Guards, and next, a room for preparing the candidates. The third, in which the Lodge is held, is hung with black; on the draperies are represented skeletons, tears, and emblems of mortality, embroidered in silver. In the east is a throne, elevated on seven steps, which is the seat of the President; the throne, also, is draped with black satin, bearing similar emblems to the hangings; on a table covered with black satin are the actual emblems of mortality; the covering has the letters J.M., in memory of Jacques de Molay. It is somewhat remarkable that, with the numerous references to the chivalric orders in this and the other degrees, the Rite ignores, as such, the Templar Degrees.

The seats of the two principal officers are covered with crimson satin, bordered with black, and strewn with tears of silver; in front are embroidered certain letters.

There is represented a camp of the Crusaders. The form of the camp is thus explained: It is composed of an nonagon, within which is inscribed a heptagon, within that a pentagon, and in the centre an equilateral triangle, within which is a circle. Between the heptagon and pentagon are placed five standards, in the designs of which we find five letters, which form a particular word. On the first standard is emblazoned the Ark of the Covenant, with a palm tree on each side; the ark has the motto *Laus Deo*. On the second is a lion of gold, holding in his mouth a golden key, with a collar of the same metal; the ground is blue, and on it is the device, *Ad Majorem Dei Gloriam*. The third standard displays a heart in flames, with two wings; it is surmounted by a crown of laurels; the field is silver. The next bears a double-headed eagle crowned, holding a sword in his right claw, and a bleeding

177

heart in his left; the field is a water-green. The last bears a black ox on a field of gold. On the sides of the nonagon are nine tents; the colours are distinguished by numbers. On the tents are certain letters, which form the secret word. The tents are designed to represent the different degrees of Masonry as follows: 1. Esdras typifies the Three First Degrees; with blue streamer. 2. Joshua, Perfect Master; green flag. 3. Aholiab represents the Sixth and Eighth Degrees; has a red and green flag; 4. Joiada, the Seventh Degree; has a red and black flag. 5. Peleg, the Ninth and Twelfth Degrees; has a black flag. 6. Joakim, a black and red flag, represents the Tenth and Eleventh Degrees. 7. Nehemiah, for the Fourteenth Degree, a red flag. 8. Zerubbabel, a flag of bright green, represents the Knight of the East, the Sword, or the Fifteenth Degree. 9. Malachi represents the Rose-Croix, as well as the Sixteenth and Seventeenth Degrees; it has a white flag with red stripes.

THIRTY-THIRD DEGREE, OR SOVEREIGN GRAND INSPECTOR-GENERAL

From its members is selected the "Supreme Council," which is the Chief Tribunal in this Rite; not more than one Supreme Council can exist in any one nation which must be composed of nine members, not less than three of whom constitute a quorum, for the transaction of business.

The Lodge is hung with purple draperies, displaying representations of emblems of mortality. In the east is the dais, having in its rear a transparency bearing the Sacred Name, in Hebrew characters. In the centre of the chamber is a square pedestal, covered with crimson, supporting a Bible, upon which a sword is laid across. In the north is another pedestal, displaying a skeleton which holds a poniard in the right hand, and the drapery of the Order in the left. In the west is a throne, elevated with three steps, before which is a triangular altar, covered with crimson. Over the entrance door is inscribed, in letters of gold, the motto of the Order, *Deus meumque jus*. The chamber is illuminated by eleven lights, five in the east, two in the south, three in the west, and one in the north.

The sash is white, four inches broad, edged with gold fringe, and embroidered in gold with the emblems of the Degree. The jewel as for collar jewel 32°, but with number 33.

We have already noticed the ingenious proceedings of the Chevalier Ramsay, and the theory which he set up respecting the rite of which we are treating; but it appears that as early as 1715, on raising the standard of revolt in Scotland, the adherents of the House of Stuart made many efforts to enlist Freemasonry as an auxiliary to their cause. The better to carry out this purpose, it was affirmed that the great legend of the Order alluded to the violent death of Charles I, and that Cromwell, Bradshaw, and Ireton were alluded to as the traitors the Masons were to condemn. New degeees were invented in furtherance of the project, named Irish Master, Perfect Irish Master, &c., and all had a political bias. They doubtless were favourably received by those of the Fraternity who were attached to the Jacobite cause; and if they did not give Ramsay the idea, must have furnished him the materials to set his scheme on foot.

Rite: Ancient Free and Accepted Architects: This Rite is based on a geometrical system evolved by a student brother, the late Henry P. H. Bromwell, of Colorado, who spent a large part of his life in Illinois, where

178

he became Grand Master in 1865. In his research he discovered many things which he regarded as important, and which should be disseminated to the craft, which he proceeded to do through a series of three degrees known as "Select Architects, Most Excellent Architect, and Royal Architects." The Order was founded March 1, 1862, at Charleston, Ill., and at one time had several lodges located in that area, in California and in Colorado. With his death, the Order became defunct. A revival was attempted in Denver in 1905. Much of Bromwell's material is contained in his book, "Restorations of Masonic Geometry and Symbolry," sold by the Grand Lodge of Colorado. What Bromwell did was to take the three degrees of Craft Masonry and amplify the usual instruction found in them; the degrees are valuable only to the student of Freemasonry who wishes to know more of Craft symbolism.

Rite of Ancient Craft Masonry: The Mother Grand Lodge of England set forth, in 1813, that Ancient Craft Masonry consisted of the three degrees of Entered Apprentice, Fellow Craft, and Master Mason, together with the Holy Order of the Royal Arch. It is generally accepted that the Rite consists of those degrees having to do with the loss, recovery, and preservation of the Word, which would include lodge, chapter, and council.

Rite: Ancient and Egyptian Reformed: On December 11, 1879, "the Most Serene Grand Orient of Naples; Supreme Council Grand Orient, Mother-Power of the Egyptian Rite" sent out its printed statutes and regulations. With it went a statement that the rituals of the different degrees, of which the Rite was composed, were being issued in which it was said: "You will find it more easy to convince yourself that we do not dispense with one point of the general principles of the world-wide Masonic Order."

The Grand Orient above mentioned was at one time provisionally located at Catania, but in August, 1877, removed to Naples, its secular and historic home. It had in its obedience a Supreme Consistory Chamber of the Rite, 32°; a Grand Chamber of Justice, 31°; a Sovereign Council of Knights of the Eagle, 30°; a Sovereign Chapter General Knights of the Pelican, 18°. There was a National Grand Symbolic Lodge, with one Areopagus, two Chapters, and six Symbolic Lodges in Naples; and three Areopagi, six Chapters, and eighteen Symbolic Lodges elsewhere in Italian Territory.

The degrees worked under this Rite were given as:

1°, Apprentice; 2°, Companion; 3°, Master; 4°, Knight of the Secret; 5°, Perfect Knight; 6°, Confidential Knight; 7°, Egyptian Knight; 8°, Knight of Israel; 9°, Knight of the Elect; 10°, Knight of Fifteen Elect; 11°, Unknown Knight; 12°, Knight Architect; 13°, Knight of the Secret Vault; 14°, Knight of the Alliance; 15°, Knight of the Sword; 16°, Knight of Jerusalem; 17°, Knight of the Crusades; 18°, Knight of the Pelican; 19°, Knight of the Bridge; 20°, Persian Knight; 21°, Knight Noachite; 22°, Knight of Libanus; 23°, Knight of the Temple; 24°, Knight of the Light; 25°, Knight of the Serpent of Sinai; 26°, Knight of the Sacred Delta; 27°, Knight of the Sacred Fire; 28°, Knight of the Sun; 29°, Knight of the Propaganda; 30°, Knight of the Eagle; 31°, Grand Inquisitor; 32°, Grand Inspector-General; 33°, Grand Patriarch of the Order.

Rite: Ancient and Primitive: A complete history of this Order would necessarily involve an account of most of the Rites prevalent last century which devoted themselves to Templary, Theosophic, Hermetic and Occult research. Suffice it for this article to give the reader a general impression upon the more important points of the Rite.

The leading fact is, that prior to 1721 some of the English Masons of the York Rite, which was once known as a Templar Rite of Seven Degrees, were well acquainted with the ancient mystical language of those occult fraternities who boasted the *gnosis,* or wisdom of old Egypt, and were then, in 1721, addressed as the "higher class" of Masons. The Continental brethren developed this Hermetic element to an almost incredible extent. Martinez Paschalis, who was a German, of poor parents, born about 1700, after having acquired a knowledge of Greek and Latin at the age of sixteen, journeyed to Turkey, Arabia and Damascus, and obtaining initiation into the *Temple Mysteries of the Easter,* upon his return, established a particular *Order of Rose-Croix,* or *Elected Cohens,* which influenced greatly all the Masonry of his century, and especially some of the Orders from which the *Rite of Memphis* drew its inspiration.

The basis of the Antient and Primitive Rite, or Order of Memphis, for they are one and the same, is to be found in the *"Rite of Philalethes,"* or *Lovers of Truth,* an Order promulgated about 1773, and identical in its principles with the *"Primitive Philadelphes,"* or *Lovers of Mankind.* On this, as a groundwork, was established, in 1814, at Montauban, France, by the Brothers Samuel Honis, of Cairo, Gabriel Mathieu Marconis de Negre, the Baron Duman, the Marquis de Laroque, Hypolite Labrunie, and J. Petit, a Grand Lodge of the Disciples of Memphis. In the same year was published at the "Orient of Memphis" the Hieroglyphic of Master of Masters, which claimed for the Oriental, or Egyptian Rite, that it was the only true system of Masonry, and fortified by unquestionable authenticity. Whatever was the aim of the authors of this pamphlet, it is noteworthy that the Rite employed its language and philosophy almost verbally in its ceremonies.

The Disciples of Memphis continued work at Montauban for a short time until the Grand Lodge fell into abeyance, and was then revived at Paris in 1839, as one of the subordinate bodies of the recently constituted Sovereign Sanctuary and Grand Orient of the Antient and Primitive Rite of Memphis, which had published its statutes, and extended to Marseilles and Brussels in 1838, flourishing, with various vicissitudes, until now, in 1857 Jacques Etienne Marconis, Grand Hierophant (son of Gabriel Mathieu Marconis), inaugurated the Rite in person at New York, with David M'Clellan as Grand Master, and afterwards, in the year 1862 (when he had united his privileges with the Grand Lodge of France), chartered it as a Sovereign Sanctuary, with the sanction of the said Grand Lodge, the Patent being *vised* by the Grand Master Marshal Magnan, and sealed with the seals of the said Grand Lodge, Harry J. Seymour being appointed Grand Master General. On June 3, 1872, the said Sovereign Sanctuary 33°, in and for the United Kingdom of Great Britain and Ireland was installed.

This body, in 1875, sanctioned the conferment of the Rite of Mizraim upon members of the Rite of Memphis, the former having no separate governing body in England.

The Rite is divided into three series, and subdivided into seven classes, which form the schools which are to teach the Masonic knowledge, physics, and philosophies which have an influence upon the happiness and moral and material well-being of temporal man.

The *First Series* teaches morality; that study of himself which endows the Mason with the beautiful name of philosopher, or lover of wisdom, by which is understood that triumph over the passions which represents the union of virtue with justice and liberty. The neophyte is taught the signification of symbols, emblems, and allegories; he is impressed with that need of mutual assistance which nature has wisely willed that we should relatively hold to each other, and the extension to others of that mutual love and tolerance which forms the true and stable basis of all society.

The *Second Series* teaches the natural sciences, philosophy, and history, practically giving an explanation of the poetic myths of antiquity, and the state of nature most convenient to man.

The *Third Series* makes known the complement of the historic part of philosophy, including the immortal elements of the human mind, with those divisions of science which are named occult or secret; it develops the *mystic* and transcendant part of Masonry, and admits the most advanced Theosophical speculations.

Each of these Three Series is divided into two classes; thus constituting, with Craft Masonry, or the Lodge, seven classes. The *Second Class,* or *College,* explains the Masonry of the first Temple. The *Third Class,* or *Chapter,* that of the second Temple. The *Fourth Class,* or *Senate,* develops Hermetic or Rosicrucian Masonry. The *Fifth Class,* or *Areopagus,* Templar Masonry. The *Sixth Class,* or *Consistory,* is a school for instruction in the ancient myths, dogmas, and faiths. The *Seventh Class,* or *Council,* teaches the religious mysteries of ancient Egypt.

Originally these three series, of Seven Classes, were a collection of ninety degrees drawn from all known Masonic Rites, of which the first thirty-three were identical with those of the Ancient and Accepted Scottish Rite in 1865, the Grand Lodge of France, in order to simplify the working, reduced them to thirty working degrees, of which the first twenty ceremonies are similar to degrees of the A. and A. Scottish Rite, and the remaining ten ceremonies are practically selected from the subsequent fifty-seven degrees of the old Rite of Memphis.

A short description of these thirty-three degrees will convey all the knowledge which we are permitted to give in a work of this character. There is the less reason to extend this condensation as the attentive student will gather from our ample description of other Rites whatever is applicable to this Order.

FIRST SERIES (CHAPTER)

The first to the third degree are not conferred by the Rite, but the aspirant for the higher degrees must be a Master Mason under some constitutional and regular Grand Lodge.

DISCREET MASTER 4°

This is the name of the fourth degree, and commences the second class. The Most Wise represents Solomon; the Knight Senior Warden, Hiram of Tyre; the Knight J.W., Zabud; the other officers represent Zadok; Stolkin; Benaiah; Zobah; Jehosaphat; Adonhiram; Ahishar. The cordon is white, broidered with black, and the jewel an ivory key, with the letter Z in the centre.

The ceremonial refers to the deposit in the *sanctum sanctorum* of the "heart of truth," and the aspirant is admitted to the rank of Levite, as one of the seven selected to fill the place of H.A.B. The instruction is as to the relationship of man to God.

SUBLIME MASTER 5°

The name of the fifth degree. The Chapter is divided into two apartments, representing King Solomon's Chamber of Audience, and the mausoleum of

H.A.B. The cordon is crimson, edged with gold lace, and the jewel is three triangles interlaced.

The ceremonial refers to the interment of the heart of H.A.B. in a tomb secretly erected for that purpose, upon which the aspirant, as Johaben, intrudes. The instruction refers to the intimacy which exists between divine and human nature.

KNIGHT OF THE SACRED ARCH 6°

The name of the Sixth Degree. The Chapter represents the Audience Chamber of King Solomon. In the East is suspended the sacred delta, to right and left are two pillars supporting an arch, on which are painted nine signs of the Zodiac. In the second apartment are nine arches, with certain Hebrew inscriptions, and in the midst is a delta, resembling that suspended in the Orient. The cordon is purple, edged with gold lace, and the jewel a double triangle, with a triple tau at the bottom of it.

The ceremonial refers to the preparation for Solomon's Temple, when the workmen discovered the temple of nine arches erected by Enoch before the flood. Reference to this tradition will be found in the "Book of Enoch," brought by the traveller Bruce from Abyssinia, and translated by the Archbishop of Cashel; this is curious, as the degree is without question far more ancient than the rediscovery of the lost Book of Enoch. The degree also explains the assistance which King Solomon received from the Mysteries of Egypt. The moral is, that labour in the Nine Mystic Arches of the Great Cause is necessary to those who would know truth.

KNIGHT OF THE SECRET VAULT 7°

The seventh degree. The Most Wise represents Gedaliah; the Knight S.W., Seraiah; the Knight J.W., Zephaniah; the other officers represent Jeremiah; Shealtiel; Iddo; Jozadak. The cordon is crimson fringed with gold, and the jewel a golden compass open upon the quarter circle.

The ceremonial refers to the concealment of the sacred delta in the secret vault, and the death of Gedaliah in its defence, who is impersonated by the candidate. Instruction is given in the cabalistical knowledge of the sacred name as a portion of the Master's secrets.

KNIGHT OF THE SWORD 8°

The eighth degree, and opens the Third Class. The degree is elsewhere known as Knight of the East, Red Cross of Babylon, or of Palestine. The Most Wise represents Cyrus; the Knight S.W., Sissines; the Knight J.W., Sathrabuzanes; the other officers represent Danie; Abazar; Snabazar; Ratim; Semetius; Mithridates. The cordon is water green, with emblems of mortality in gold, and the letters L.D.P., and the jewel is a sabre.

The ceremonial has reference to the return of Zerubbabel from the Court of Cyrus, as a Persian Knight, to rebuild the Second Temple. We learn from it to combat the vices and passions which dishonour humanity.

KNIGHT OF JERUSALEM 9°

The ninth degree. The Most Wise represents Nehemiah; the Knight S.W., Darius; the Knight J.W., Ezra; other officers represent Haggai; Joshua; Ananias. The cordon is sky-blue, edged with gold fringe, the jewel, a gold medal having on one side a hand holding a balance in equilibrium, and in the other a two-edged sword and two stars.

The ceremonial represents the Journey of Zerubbabel to the Court of Darius, and the famous contest as to the relative strength of wine, the king, women, and truth, after which the neophyte discovers the symbolical jewels.

KNIGHT OF THE ORIENT 10°

The tenth degree. The cordon is black edged with red, the jewel a medal in form of a heptagon.

The ceremonial refers to the period of revival of the Mysteries, and the following from the Book of Maccabees. "And Mattathias cried throughout the city with a loud voice, saying: Whoever is zealous of the law, and maintaineth the covenant, let him follow me. Then there came unto him a company of the Assideana, who were mighty men of Israel, even all such as are voluntarily devoted unto the law. And Judas Maccabeus, with nine others or thereabouts, withdrew himself into the wilderness and lived in the mountains."

KNIGHT OF THE ROSE CROIX 11°

The eleventh degree. The collar is red, embroidered in gold, the sash white, and the jewel a pelican feeding its young, between the compass, upon a quarter circle.

This well-known grade represents that period when the Temple of Jehovah was sullied and forsaken in Zion, and its members were wandering in the woods and mountains, overwhelmed with grief and the deepest sorrow; labouring for the new law of love, and terminating their work in the discovery of those three sacred principles, Faith, Hope, and Charity, which were to rule all nations under the mystic INRI, here interpreted according to universal moral principles. The history teaches that community which existed between the Egyptian and Jewish mystics. All the grades in this Rite are unsectarian.

SECOND SERIES (SENATE)

KNIGHT OF THE RED EAGLE 12°

The twelfth degree of the Rite and the first of the Senate, and commenced the Fourth Class. The cordon is black, and the jewel an eagle in red and gold.

The ceremonial is an introduction to Hermetic philosophy, and the neophyte is purified by the four elements. It bears some resemblance to the degree conferred by the modern English Rosicrucian Society, either the latter has been derived from it, or both have drawn from a more ancient source in common. The orator's discourse is a learned dissertation upon ancient initiation.

KNIGHT OF THE TEMPLE 13°

The thirteenth degree. The cordon is red, and the jewel a square and compass with the letter G on a delta.

The ceremonial teaches that moral system which Pythagoras termed "Divine Geometry," and Plato called "the Science of the Gods."

KNIGHT OF THE TABERNACLE 14°

The fourteenth degree. There are two apartments which represent the outer and inner courts of the Tabernacle. The Sublime-Grand Commander represents Aaron; the Senior Knight Interpreter, Eleazar; the Junior Knight Interpreter, Ithamar; other officers represent Moses and Joshua. The tabernacle contains the banners of the twelve tribes. The cordon is red, and the jewel a key.

The ceremonial gives the symbolical explanation of the banners, treats upon the symbolism of the Tabernacle of Moses and the Temple of Solomon, with Egyptian derivations, and refers to the disobedience and punishment of Korah, Dathan and Abiram.

KNIGHT OF THE SERPENT 15°

The fifteenth degree. The place of meeting represents the Court of Sinai. The Grand Commander represents Moses; the Senior Knight Interpreter, Eleazar; the Junior Knight Interpreter, Joshua; the Orator represents Ithamar. The interior of the Tabernacle is decorated with the banners of the twelve tribes. The cordon is red, and the jewel a brazen serpent twined round a tau cross.

The ceremonial has reference to the brazen serpent which Moses erected in the wilderness, and to the foundation of the grade by a Western Knight in the time of the Crusades. The orator's discourse is a learned exposition of serpent myths and a description of the serpent worship of ancient peoples. In America there is an immense serpentine mound, with the serpent in the act of vomiting the egg, an Egyptian symbol frequently used in this rite.

KNIGHT SAGE OF TRUTH 16°

The sixteenth degree. The Senate is hung with black, having a brazier of burning spirits in the centre. The cordon is black, and the jewel a circular medal having on one circumference the twelve names of the Egyptian months, and on the other the twelve emblems of the Zodiac.

The ceremonial teaches that God and truth are one, and man's happiness is of his own creation. The orator's discourse treats of the knowledge of the Chaldean and Egyptian Magi.

KNIGHT HERMETIC PHILOSOPHER 17°

The seventeenth degree. The Senate is hung with black. The cordon is violet, edged with broad silver lace, and the jewel the Hermetic cross.

The ceremonial embraces a description of the cross, and the cabalistic signification of the letters I N R I, to which a moral application was assigned in the degree of Rose-Croix. The lecture is an Hermetic exposition of nature's mysteries.

KNIGHT KADOSH 18°

The eighteenth degree, and commences the Fifth Class. There are three apartments; the first, of Reflection, is hung with black; the second, or Senate, is red; the third, or Areopagus, is decorated with the banners of the Rite and a symbolical statue of Justice. The cordon is black, and the jewel a double-headed eagle with the Hermetic cross on the breast.

The ceremonial is here a Templar grade, but some of the old English Conclaves of Templars, and the "Early Grand" Templars of Scotland, confer it as their Commander's ceremony, and this was the old system as applied to the Rose-Croix. The orator's discourse is an elaborate history of the Templars.

KNIGHT OF THE ROYAL MYSTERY 19°

The nineteenth degree. There are in the Senate nine banners of the principal faiths of the world in form of a camp. The cordon is black, and the jewel is a medal representing a camp, in the form of a nonagon.

The ceremonial represents a Knight Kadosh, or Templar, in search of truth, who undergoes initiation into the nine principal faiths of the world, from which he learns tolerance, and that there is truth to be found in all systems. The Orator's discourse is an exposition of the principles of ancient initiation.

KNIGHT GRAND INSPECTOR 20°

The twentieth degree. Three apartments are used, and it is the last and chief grade of the Senate. The collar is violet, scarf black, and the jewel, enclosed within a circle represented by a serpent with its tail in its mouth, is the double-headed eagle, having the Hermetic cross on its breast.

During his travels the Aspirant takes five O.B.'s. First, to the flag of his country, and is crowned with the civic crown; second, to the banners of the rite, and undergoes the test of molten lead; third, fidelity to secrets, and is crowned with a wreath of cypress; fourth, duty to his brothers, and is refreshed; lastly, he takes the O.B. of general duty, and is crowned with roses, and proclaimed. The Orator's discourse is an eulogy upon ancient and modern Masonry, and the blessings it has conferred on mankind.

THIRD SERIES (COUNCIL)
GRAND INSTALLER 21°

The twenty-first degree of the Rite, and the first of the Council, and commences the Sixth Class. The scarf of all the following grades is white, and the jewel a winged egg within a triangle; the emblem engraved thereon varying with the degree, but in these following, the double-headed eagle and Hermetic cross.

The Aspirant is entrusted with the Ritual used in installing the officers of the lower grades, and is taught symbolism.

GRAND CONSECRATOR 22°

The twenty-second degree. The Aspirant is entrusted with the Ritual used in consecrating Masonic Temples, and is taught the mysteries of the Mystic Temple—Saphenath Pancah.

GRAND EULOGIST 23°

The twenty-third degree. The Aspirant is entrusted with the Ritual used at interments; and has the doctrine of the immortality of the soul strongly impressed upon him, with the Egyptian opinions thereon.

These last three grades are official or ceremonial.

PATRIARCH OF TRUTH 24°

The twenty-fourth degree. The scarf is white, and the emblem engraved upon the Kneph jewel, a pyramid surmounted by a sun. The Chamber of this degree represents the Great Pyramid of Cheops; in it are seven columns representing the seven great gods of the people, which are explained as the esoteric emblems of the one Supreme Being. There is a revelation of the Fountain of Perfect Light, and the same scientifically considered. The Orator's Charge is a learned explanation of the origin and Masonic symbolism of the Great Pyramid.

PATRIARCH OF THE PLANISPHERES 25°

The twenty-fifth degree. The Neophyte is instructed in the Masonic bearing of the Planispheres; the origin of the signs of the Zodiac; and the elaborate myths of the ancients drawn from the firmament.

PATRIARCH OF THE SACRED VEDAS 26°

The twenty-sixth degree. This degree is a ceremonial conference upon the Vedas, the Rules of Buddha, and the Zend Avesta of Zoroaster; especially is the sublime philosophy of the ancient Brahmins developed, and the sweet maxims of the gentle Buddha.

These three grades are schools of instruction.

PATRIARCH OF ISIS 27°

The twenty-seventh degree, and commences the seventh class. The scarf is white, and the emblem upon the Kneph jewel is a serpent coiled around a lion; the triangle is engraved, as indicated in the ceremony. In this class three apartments are necessary, and are splendidly decorated. The ceremonial instructs the Neophyte upon the trials and morality of the ancient Mysteries, after which he is admitted to the Temple of Symbols, and is taught the signification of the statutes, obelisks and emblems of the class. The Orator's Charge is a history of the Mysteries.

PATRIARCH OF MEMPHIS 28°

The twenty-eighth degree. The Neophyte represents Osiris, and ceremonially passes through what Herodotus terms "a representation of His sufferings."

185

The Orator's Charge is an application of this to the ceremony of Master Mason.

ELECT OF THE MYSTIC CITY 29°

The twenty-ninth degree. This is preparatory to the next degree, and the Neophyte learns three grand secrets—how to enjoy long life, wealth, and genius; he undergoes certain trials, and is then consecrated as an Elect who has attained the Apex of the Mystic Egyptian Delta. The Orator's Charge is a general history of the Mysteries, and the Neophyte receives instruction as to various Eastern associations which have a bearing upon Moral, Occult, and Theosophical Masonry, and learns something of all the existing Masonic Rites.

SUBLIME MASTER OF THE GREAT WORK 30°

The thirtieth degree constituted the nineteenth of the old Rite. The Temple is cubical, and represents Nature; it is superbly decorated with emblems and symbols, and is hung with celestial blue sprinkled with silver stars. There are nine banners of the zodiacal signs. On the right of a throne, ascended by seven steps, is a statue holding a golden sceptre, and on the left a female statue with a serpent. Each of the seven principal dignitaries has before him a chandelier of three branches with red tapers. The President of the Council is termed Sublime Dai, and represents Osiris; the second officer is termed First Mystagogue, and represents Seraphis; the third officer is termed Second Mystagogue, and represents Horus; and the complete officers allude to the twelve great gods of the Egyptians. The collar (embroidered in gold with the radiated eye in a triangle) and the scarf are white, edged with gold lace, and the jewel a winged-egg, having on it two squares, in the centre of which is a radiated triangle, and Masonic emblems of the degrees, and the figures 30. Swords, with red sword-belts, are worn in all the grades.

When fully worked, the ceremonial of this grade represents the great Egyptian Judgment, as found in the Book of the Dead, and transferred traditionally to Christianity. The continuity and consistency is thorough from the moment the Neophyte enters the *Pronaos* to make his demand, and overruns the *Sanctuary of Spirits,* until triumphantly received and crowned in the *Temple of Truth* as an adept who, by the practice of virtue, has rendered himself eternal, a demi-god.

GRAND DEFENDER 31°

The thirty-first degree. The collar is black with a white stripe, embroidered with emblems; scarf and waist-sash white; jewel, the double-headed eagle—"31." The grade is conferred *ex officio* upon the second and third officers of a Chapter, Senate and Council, and constitutes a Grand Tribunal, whose proceedings are regulated by the Constitutions. The Orator's discourse is principally a lecture upon justice.

PRINCE OF MEMPHIS, OR, OF MASONRY 32°

The thirty-second degree. The collar is purple, with the emblems; the scarf and waist-sash white; the jewel as last degree, but with the figure "32." The grade is conferred *ex officio* on the President of a Chapter, Senate, or Council. The members constitute a Mystic Temple or Provincial Grand Lodge. The Orator's Discourse is a lengthy essay upon the morality of the ancient mysteries and modern Masonry.

PRINCE PATRIARCH GRAND CONSERVATOR 33°

The thirty-third degree. The collar and scarf is of golden colour, with an embroidered Kneph edged with silver lace; waist-sash celestial blue, edged with gold lace; the jewel as last, but with "33." The grade is conferred *ex officio* upon the Presidency of the Mystic Temple (32°); and the members form the governing body or Sovereign Sanctuary of Great Britain and Ireland. The Orator's Discourse is a summary of the degrees through which the candidate has passed before reaching this exalted rank. The degree is very sparingly conferred, but the only qualification is that the recipient should show zeal in promoting the Rite.

In conclusion, we may add that although all these thirty-three degrees have a full Ritual which admit of being easily worked in three sectional divisions, with the same officers for each division, yet in actual practice it seems easy to reduce them to a few triplets, without in the least impairing the design of the Rite, as follows:

6°—Sacred Arch)	
8°—Knight of the Sword)	An application of the Ancient Mysteries to
11°—Rose Croix)	the Mystic schools of the Jews.
12°—Red Eagle)	
16°—Sage of Truth)	The same, as applied to the Rosicrucian
17°—Hermetic Philosopher)	Schools.
18°—Knight Kadosh)	
19°—Royal Mystery)	The same, as applied to the Order of
20°—Grand Inspector)	Templars.
27°—Patriarch of Isis)	
28°—Patriarch of Memphis)	The primitive Mysteries from which the
30°—Sub. Mas. Gt. Work)	lower triplets are derived.

The Sovereign Sanctuary rewarded merit by five decorations: First, that of the Grand Star of Sirius; second, that of the Alidee; third, that of the third series; fourth, the Lybic Chain; fifth, of Eleusis. It added a bronze decoration for the reward of merit and bravery in Masons and non-Masons. It recognized the legitimate degrees of all other Rites, and extended the hand of fellowship to all alike. It admitted the Hindoo, Parsee, Jew, Mohammedan, Trinitarian and Unitarian, breathing pure Masonry, charity, love, and mutual tolerance; adoring T.S.A.O.T.U., and teaching the immortality and happiness of the immortal soul. It relied upon Masonic worth, ability and learning, rather than social standing and pecuniary qualifications, and sought to extend Masonic knowledge, justice and morality. It levied only a small capitation fee upon the members admitted to its thirty degrees. It admitted only Master Masons in good standing under some constitutional Grand Lodge, and prohibited all interference with Craft Masonry. (How)

So far as we know the Rite is not now practiced in the United States.

Rite: Ancient Reformed: It is reported that such a Rite has been practiced in Holland in recent years.

Rite Ancient Toltec: The membership of this "Rite" is almost exclusively made up of residents, or former residents, of Kansas. There is but one Council of the Rite, and that is located in Topeka, Kansas. The "Lady Secretary" informs us that

Ours is the only Council ever chartered, and so far the Grand Council has not seen fit to organize others. It is an Order composed of Knights Templars and Thirty-two degree Masons, their wives, widows, daughters, and sisters. We hold two *Reunions* each year—spring and fall.

No one makes application for membership; the election must come complimentary through some friend. There are three beautiful degrees.

The jewel of the Order, or Rite, is a Passion Cross superimposed on the Double Eagle, symbolizing the restriction of membership to those of the American or Scottish Rite.

The Degrees are known as:
1. The Cloister Degree.
2. The Chapter Degree.
3. The Council Degree.

The emblems of (1) is a Trowel suspended by a Chain; on the handle of the Trowel is the All-Seeing Eye; of (2) an Arrow, and of (3) the Passion Cross. An examination of the list of Officers shows an Excellent High Priest and an Excellent High Priestess, with Sisters Hope and Faith, Custodians of the "Treasure House," Inscribers of the Codices; in the Chapter degree we find the same two principal officers with Priestess of Mercy, and Princess of Justice; characters taking part in this section of the work are those appearing in the Merchant of Venice—Portia, Shylock, Antonio, Salerio, Bassanio, Gratiano, and others. The last degree is probably more ceremonial than the other two; it is presided over by a Knight Commander and a Lady Superior, while there are Lady Ciencia (Science), and Lady Natura (Nature).

Male members are called "Knights," while female members are "Ladies."

Rite: Bahrdt's: At the close of the last century Bahrdt opened a Lodge at Halle, in Saxony, under the name of the "German Union," and succeeded in securing the protection of the Prince of Anhaldt-Bernburg, and the cooperation of twenty persons of rank. The Rite had six degrees: The Youth; the Man; the Old Man; the Mesopolyte; the Diocesan; the Superior. The Grand Lodge of the State, however, dissolved the fraternity.

Rite of Baptism: Although we have rites and ceremonies sufficient to task the powers of memory in the best-constructed brain, our continental brethren are ever at work to contrive some novelty for the Masonic institution. In France has been instituted an order for the Baptism of the sons of Masons, which has been also adopted by the *Foyer Maconnique Lodge* in New Orleans, and the first opening of their proceedings occurred in 1859. These, however, do not appear to have any very remarkable characteristic. The sponsors make promises of good order and moral conduct, and the neophyte's left hand is dipped into the water by the W.M. To the mother is given a gold alliance-ring with this injunction; "May this ring recall to you, as to us, your future steps in the Masonic Temple; always remember what you have seen and heard. Henceforth Masonry can have no secrets for you; you know her laws and obligations. Be then satisfied, dear sister, for this name, which it gives us pleasure to bestow on you, makes us feel that there cannot exist true fraternity and happiness unless accompanied by the presence of woman."

Rite: Brazilian: (See Brazil, Grand Orient of.)

Rite: Capitular Masonry: The term applied to those degrees conferred by a Chapter, usually a Chapter of Royal Arch Masons. (See Royal Arch Masonry.)

Rite: Chapter of Clermont: (See Chapter of Clermont.)

Rite: Circle of Light: (See Circle of Light, Rite of.)

Rite: Clerks of Strict Observance: (See Rite of Strict Observance.)

Rite of Consecrated Philoclesian Host: (See Consecrated Philoclesian Host.)

Rite: Council of Emperors of East and West: This was a Union of the Chapter of Clermont and the Knights of the East; its degrees included: *First Grades:* Entered Apprentice; Fellow Craft; Master Mason. *Second Grades:* Petit Elu; Inconnu Elu; Elu de Quinze. *Third Grades:* Architect; Provost

188

and Judge; Grand Architect. *Fourth Grade:* Royal Arch. *Fifth Grades:* Knight of the East; Grand Commander; Prince of Jerusalem. *Sixth Grade:* Knight of the Eagle Rose Croix. *Seventh Grades:* Knight of the East and West; Knight of the Triple Croix; Knight of Palestine; Templars; Knight of the Sun; Physical; Moral College of Heredom (Kadosh) or (Black Eagle).

Rite: Council of Trinity: It is said in Mackey's Lexicon to be an independent Masonic jurisdiction, in which are conferred the degrees: (1), Knight of the Christian Mark and Guard of the Conclave; (2) Knight of the Holy Sepulchre; (3) The Holy and Thrice Illustrious Order of the Holy Cross. They are, as it will be readily seen, all Christian degrees, and conferred only on Knights Templars.

(1) This degree is said to have been organized by Pope Alexander IV (who authorized the distinguishing attire of the Knights to be a red tunic with a white cross), for the defence of his person, selecting for the purpose a body of Knights of St. John. The officers are an Invincible Knight, Senior and Junior Knights, Recorder, Treasurer, Conductor, and Guard. The ritual is composed from passages in the Books of Ezekiel and Jeremiah. The jewel is a triangular plate of gold with the letter "G" within a five-pointed star. (2) This degree was instituted by St. Helena, the mother of Constantine, A.D. 326, when, on her visit to Jerusalem, she is said to have discovered the true cross. During the War of the Crusades, the Knights of the Holy Sepulchre were eminent for their valour. Upon the loss of the Holy Land they took refuge in Perugia and afterwards were incorporated with the Knights of Rhodes. Curzon, in his "Visits to the Mountains in the Levant," says: "The Order is still continued in Jerusalem, but conferred only on Roman Catholics of noble birth, by the superior of the Franciscan College, and that the accolade is bestowed with the sword of Godfrey de Bouillon, which, with his spurs, is preserved in the sacristy of the Church of the Holy Sepulchre." The presiding officer in America is called the Right Reverend Prelate. It is now appended to the Constantine degree. (3) This, we presume, is the governing council.

Rite: Dead Rites in Masonry: Of the many hundred Rites, Orders and Degrees, very few have survived the test of time. Many rites were organized for the purpose of making money for their founders; such organizations cannot last. It is unfortunate that we have more than one rite in all Masonry; as it is, our labors are divided among several loyalties and much competition.

Rite: Early Grand Rite of Scotland: In 1779, Mother Kilwinning Lodge No. 0 issued a charter to form a Lodge in Dublin, Ireland, under the name of *"High Knight Templars Lodge of Ireland,"* from which doubtless sprang the Early Grand Encampments of High Knights Templar in that country. Indications also show that those Encampments worked the Holy Royal Arch and many other Grades connected with Masonry.

Strange though it appears, the Irish Templars—deriving originally, as indicated, from Scotland, reintroduced the Order into Scotland by issuing several charters for Encampments of High Knights Templar in the city of Edinburgh and other cities. The first of these was granted in 1795 (Kilmarnock No. 22), the last in 822 (Stewarton No. 51). One of these Encampments (No. 31) was located in Edinburgh and, under the leadership of Alexander Deuchar, afterwards became the foundation upon which was built the Grand Conclave of Knights Templar of 1812, later becoming the Grand Priory of

1832, and finally the Convent General of 1854. From that source sprang also the Supreme Grand Royal Arch Chapter of Scotland and the resuscitated Grand Lodge of the Royal Order of Scotland.

The faithful Encampments of High Knights Templar in Scotland continued under their Irish Charters until the year 1822, when they received a Charter of Renunciation from Ireland, creating them into an independent jurisdiction. As before, the Scottish Grand Encampment continued to work all Grades above the Craft. However, in 1884, a division was made in the Body, resulting from the Early Grand Encampment of Scotland discontinuing all Grades save the regular Knightly Orders. From this division sprang the Early Grand Royal Arch Chapter of Scotland and also the Grand Council of Rites. This whole System was termed the *Early Grand Rite of Scotland*.

From 1822, there existed in Scotland two Templar Bodies; both claiming sovereignty and priority, both working the Order of the Temple. It was not until 1909 that the Early Grand Encampment of the Temple and Malta in Scotland and the Great Priory of Scotland united.

Likewise, it was not until 1895 that the Early Grand Royal Arch Chapter and the Supreme Grand Royal Chapter of Scotland united. During all those years there were two Bodies conferring the same basic Grades. Today, Freemasonry in Scotland is united and prosperous in all branches.

The Early Grand Rite was, for nearly the duration of the 19th century, an active factor in the Masonic life of Scotland. The whole System was one of perpetuation, amalgamation, and adoption—but it cannot be said of it that it was an originating Body, as regards Grades.

The Grades of the Early Grand were forty-seven in number; divided into the following divisions: *Blue Series,* comprising the Grades above the Craft, and predicating its Membership thereupon, the governing Body of which was the Lodge—it worked the Funeral Master, Fellow Craft Mark, Marked Master, Architect, Grand Architect, Master of the Blue and Master of All Symbolic Lodges; the *Red Series* worked the Royal Ark Mariner, Fugitive Mark, Link and Chain, Sublime Master, Order of the Scarlet Cord, Order of Brotherly Love, Royal Master, Select Master, Most Excellent Master, Excellent Mason, Super Excellent Mason, and the Holy Royal Arch; the *Black Series* worked the Red Cross of Rome and Constantine, Knights of the Holy Sepulchre, Knights of St. John, Knights of the Christian Mark, Holy and Illustrious Order of the Cross, The Pilgrim, Knight Templar, Knights of St. Paul, or Mediterranean Pass, and Knights of Malta; the *Green Series* comprised the Prince of Babylon, sometimes called Suspending Cross of Babylon, The Prince Mason, Knight of the Black Cross, Knight of the White Cross, Knight of Patmos, Knight of Death, Knight of the Rosy Cross of St. Andrew, Heredom of Kilwinning, and Knight of the Black and White Eagle; the *White Series* was composed of the Priestly Order of the Temple, or White Mason, Priest of the Sun, Priest of Eleusis, and The Mother Word, or Royal Secret; and the *Purple Series,* which was official, Knights Companions, Knights Commanders, and Knights Grand Cross.

FOURTH DEGREE, called FUNERAL MASTER

This degree was originally and may still be conferred upon any Master Mason, without fee, for the purpose of opening a Funeral Lodge, and when thus conferred, is fully recognized by the Early Grand. It is the Degree upon

190

which Funeral Lodges, or Lodges of Sorrow should be held, and no one should be allowed to take part on these occasions who has not taken this Degree. When the Degree is conferred as part of the Early Grand Rite, it is done in a Lodge of "Masters of all Symbolic Lodges."

NINTH DEGREE, called MASTER OF THE BLUE

The Ninth degree of the E.G. Rite is called Master of Blue, sometimes called Knights of the Blue, or Knights of Solomon. The emblem is a beehive. The degree is conferred in a Lodge of P. Masters.

TENTH DEGREE, called MASTER OF ALL SYMBOLIC LODGES

The Tenth Degree of the E.G. Rite is called, in the modern classification, Master of all Symbolic Lodges. In what is erroneously called the "York Rite" it is called Past Master. The original name of the degree, and preserved by us, is the Chair Degree. When the degree is to be conferred, a Lodge of F.C. Marks-men is opened, the candidate being present.

THE RED SERIES

THIRTEENTH DEGREE, called LINK AND CHAIN

The Thirteenth Degree of the Early Grand Rite, called the Link and Chain amongst our older Brethren, formed one of a series called Ark, Mark, Link and Wrestle, and before the classification of the Degree in regular sequence, was conferred in a Royal Arch Chapter upon deserving Companions. Preparation to working this Degree, the Lodge being opened on the XI Degree, and all Officers and Brethren being properly seated, the presiding officer requests all not XIII Degree to retire.

FOURTEENTH DEGREE, called SUBLIME MASTER

The Fourteenth Degree is called Sublime Master, from Israel having as a man struggled with God, and prevailed. It was more familiarly known to our older Brethren as the Wrestler or Jacob's Wrestle. The Jewel is the letters H. and P. crossed.

With this degree is completed the Series known to the Brethren as the Ark, Mark, Link and Wrestle, degrees interesting to the Masonic student and antiquarian, but which, owing to the ephemeral character of the various bodies at different times claiming jurisdiction over the High Grades, have been all but lost, and, were it not for their preservation in the Early Grand Rite, would be known only by the names occurring in some old list, or being mentioned in an encyclopedia.

FIFTEENTH DEGREE, called ORDER OF THE SCARLET CORD

The Fifteenth Degree of the Early Grand Rite is called the Order of the Scarlet Cord. The emblem of the degree is a lattice window, with a loop of scarlet cord hanging from it. In conferring this degree there is no special ceremony observed. The candidate is dressed as an Ark Mariner, and the degree is conferred in an Ark Lodge, which is raised for the purpose of conferring the degree, exactly as in the last degree, with the difference of signs. The introduction is the same also, except that instead of reading from Genesis, the reading is from the second Chapter of Joshua, and the penalty of the Obligation is that you may meet the fate from which the spies were saved by Rahab.

TWENTIETH DEGREE, called EXCELLENT MASON

The Twentieth Degree of the Early Grand Rite is called the Excellent Mason. It is held under a Royal Arch Chapter and is one of the Royal Arch Degrees proper under the ancient System of working, although now it is only worked in Scotland and Ireland. The Lodge represents the Grand Lodge of Babylon, when those wishing to return to assist in the building of the Second Temple were examined before obtaining passports to the Sanhedrim at Jerusalem. The Lodge is termed a Council.

TWENTY-FIRST DEGREE, called THE SUPER EXCELLENT MASTER

The Twenty-first Degree of the Early Grand Rite, called the Super-Excellent Mason, was founded at the same time and for the same purpose as the Excellent Mason, the ceremonies of both being founded on the incidents of the Exodus, the first treating of the leadership of Moses, the second of the leadership of Joshua. Unlike the preceding degrees, which can be given separately for the purpose of preparing a candidate for the Royal Arch. (Miscellanea.)

Rite: Eclectic: The Baron von Knigge, in 1783, established at Frankfurt, Germany, an Order or Rite which he called *Eclectic Masonry,* having for its object the abolition of the high grades or philosophical degrees. Hence Eclectic Masonry only acknowledged the three symbolic degrees, but permitted any Lodge to select at its own option any of the higher degrees, provided they did not interfere with the uniformity of the first three. It is clear the Baron did not succeed in his endeavors, as the degrees he reprobated are in high esteem, and nothing is heard now of his system.

Rites: Ecossais Rectifie: On April 25, 1777, a code was drawn up for this Rite, which was later adopted at Wilhelmsbad; this put an end to the Rite of Strict Observance, introducing a Reformed Rite of five or seven degrees. It eliminated every reference to vengeance, murder, or brute force. It was ordered that "the brethren will communicate (The W.M.), without ceremony, and free of charge, to all who have received the Ecossais, the high degrees current before the reform and known as Chevalier d'Orient (Knight of the East), Rose Croix, &c." (See Rite of Strict Observance.)

Rite: Egyptian of Cagliostro: This was the child of Count Cagliostro's imagination; he served the Order as Grand Copht; with his death the supposedly mythical Order passed from favor. It worked three grades, as in the Craft, but with much different ritual; there were adoptive grades for women.

Rite: Elect of Truth: *Elect of Truth,* or *Lodge of Perfect Union,* was the name given to a rite adopted in 1776 in a Lodge of Rennes, France, and for a time extended to other cities. It was divided into three classes, which contained fourteen degrees. The first class comprising the Entered Apprentice, Fellow Craft, Master, Perfect Master; the second class, the Elect of Nine, Elect of Fifteen, Master Elect, Minor Architect, Second Architect, Grand Architect, Knight of the East, Rose Croix; and the third class, the Knight Adept, and Elect of Truth. This rite has ceased to exist.

Rite of Elected Cohens: The *Rite of Elected Cohens,* or *Priests,* was founded sometime between 1754 and 1760 by Martinez Paschalis, by whom it was introduced into the Lodges of Bordeaux, Marseilles and Toulouse. Of its

192

principles very little is known, but it is said to have been divided into two classes, in the first of which was represented the fall of man from virtue and happiness, and in the second his final restoration. It consisted of nine degrees: Entered Apprentice; Fellow-Craft; Master Mason; Grand Elect; Apprentice Cohen; Fellow-Craft Cohen; Master Cohen; Grand Architect; Knight Commander. Clavel tells us this rite was rather popular among the literateurs of Paris for a short time, but it has now ceased to exist.

Rite of Emperors of East and West: (See Emperors of East and West.)

Rite of Fessler: It is well known that during the panic created by the French Revolution, Masonry, as well as most other beneficent institutions, declined, and the Lodges were generally closed, and only met occasionally under circumstances of great difficulty; but so soon as order was restored and Masonry began to revive, Professor Fessler, Grand Master of the Grand Lodge "Royal York Friendship," at Berlin, revised the statutes and regulated the proceedings of the lodges under jurisdiction. He also created, or perhaps more properly speaking, selected nine degrees for this rite; they were: Entered Apprentice; Fellow-Craft; Master; Holy of Holies; Justification; Celebration; Knight of the Passage; Fatherland; Perfection. The ritual was drawn from the "Golden Rose-Croix," the "Strict Observance," and the "Chapter of Clermont." Clavel says it was the most abstrusely learned and philosophical of all the degrees in Masonry. It was abandoned with the intention of bringing the Ancient York Rite into unison with the Constitutions of England.

We may here remark that degrees in Prussia were not passed through with the same rapidity as in some other countries, twelve months at least being requisite between each of the symbolic degrees.

Rite of Foundation: For many years it has been the custom for the Masonic Fraternity, being a society of Freemasons, to lay the cornerstones of public buildings. As a result of this custom a ceremony, or rite, has grown up, for the laying of these cornerstones. The ceremony is dignified and impressive, and it is too bad that in some sections of the country it is not being given.

Rite: French (Modern): The *French* or *Modern Rite* was established by the Grand Orient of France about 1786, to preserve the high degrees and for the purpose of simplifying the system, the number was reduced to seven: Entered Apprentice, Fellow-Craft, Master Mason, Elect, or First Order of Rose-Croix, Scotch Order, or Second Order of Rose-Croix, Knight of the East, or Third Order of Rose-Croix, and the Rose Croix, or *Ne Plus Ultra*.

The peculiar signs and secrets of the first two symbolical degrees under this rite are in reverse of those adopted by the Grand Lodge, or Supreme Council of the Ancient and Accepted Rite of France, in which the practice is the same as in our own Grand Lodge. In the Third Degree the Lodge has a very solemn appearance, being hung with black drapery, and displaying many sombre and awe-inspiring emblems. The Master is designated *Tres Respectable* (Very Worshipful), and the members Venerable Masters; all the brethren appear covered. In the Fourth Degree there are three chambers—the Room of Preparation, the Council Chamber, and the Cavern. The lesson inculcated in this degree is intended forcibly to imprint on the mind of its recipient the certainty with which punishment will follow crime. The Fifth Degree requires also three chambers, the second of which is most elaborately furnished and decorated with various Masonic attributes; in the east is a triangular pedestal, on which is placed the cubical stone; in the centre of the chamber is a column, and by it a table, having upon it the corn, wine and oil; and in the north is a sacrificial altar. The lodge is illuminated by twenty-seven lights, in three groups of nine each; it represents the Temple completed, and its whole appearance is most gorgeous. The Lodge is denominated Sublime; the presiding officer is *Tres Grand* (Very Great), and the brethren are Sublime Masters. In this degree the passwords correspond with those of our Royal Arch. The Sixth Degree also requires three chambers; the second, which is called the Hall of the East, represents the council of Cyrus at Babylon, and is described —in somewhat inconsistent terms—as being composed of that prince, seven principal officers, and other *knights*. The decoration is green, and requires many lights. Behind the throne is a transparency, representing the vision of Cyrus, in which he received the injunction, "Restore liberty to the captives." The candidate, in passing from the second to the third chamber, has to cross a bridge of timber over a stream choked with corpses and rubbish; and having at length arrived at the last, or western chamber, he perceives the Masons reposing among the ruins of Jerusalem. The room is hung with red, and illuminated by ten groups of candles of seven each. In the centre is the representation of the ruined Temple. The Sovereign Master represents Cyrus; the Chief Officer, Daniel the Prophet. The badge is of white satin, bordered with green; the sash, of water green, is worn from left to right; the jewel is the triple triangle, crossed by two swords. The Seventh Degree resembles the 18° of A. & A. and A. & P. (Ragon, in his "Cours Philosophique," says the symbolism of this rite is entirely astronomical. This is erroneous, as the first six degrees have all reference to the Old Testament history; the Seventh Degree partakes of a Hermetic and Chivalric nature.)

A rite, slightly differing from the preceding, and called the *Ancient Reformed Rite,* we are told, is now practiced in Holland and Belgium. (How.)

Rite: French Noachites: (See Noachites; see Prussian Knight.)

Rite of Freres Pontiff: (See Freres Pontives.)

Rite: Grand Chapter of Heredom: (See Heredom.)

Rite: Grand College of Rites: The Grand College of Rites of the United States of America is the governing body for one of the student groups which are doing so much to promote the study of Freemasonry. The Grand College specializes in the study of old rituals, many of which are printed in their publication, "Collectanea." It does not print any of the rituals current in the United States. It is a plan conceived by some of the leaders in our Fraternity to prevent the use of old rituals by those who would seek to commercialize on them by public sale of degrees as in the Thomson fraud.

The American group was formed in 1932 and has held annual convocations since that date, most of them being in Washington during "Masonic Week" in February.

The Fellowship was limited to 100 members, but honorary fellowship is offered to any interested Master Mason; the insignia is a special adaptation of the Cross, containing a Circle, a Square, a Triangle, a Pentagon, and the Seal of Solomon.

The fraternity is under obligations to our brethren of the Grand College of Rites for making available such rituals as the Rite of Memphis, Rite of Adonhiramite, Swedenborg Rite, and many others; while they have no value

194

as degrees they at least supply us with information as to what rituals were being used by some of our Masonic ancestors.

Rites over which the American College has control are:

(1) Order of Martinists; (2) Rite of Schroeder; (3) Swedenborgian Rite; (4) French Rite; (5) Adonhiramite Rite; (6) Swedish Rite; (7) Ancient and Primitive; (8) Rite of Misraim; (9) Rite of Memphis; (10) Crata Reposa; (11) Fratres Lucis; (12) Ancient Reformed Rite; (13) Brazilian Rite; (14) Order of the Marquis de St. Martin; (15) Ancient Order of Zuzemites; (16) Reformed Scottish Rite.

Rite: Grand Lodge of the Three Globes of Berlin: In his "Historical Landmarks," Brother Oliver says: "At this time (about 1775) the increasing innovations," as our account of these varied rites shows, "covered pure Masonry with disgrace"; and with a view of applying a remedy, Lord Petre, the English Grand Master (from 1772 to 1777), entered into negotiation with the Prince of Hesse Darmstadt, Grand Master of Germany, which resulted in a mutual compact being formed, which confirmed to the Grand Lodge at Berlin the sole authority in Germany, thus annihilating the "Strict Observance" of Baron Hunde. This compact was further confirmed by the King of Prussia, who erected the Grand Lodge at Berlin into a body corporate. The three ancient symbolic degrees are under the control of the Grand Lodge, but the higher degrees—seven only being practised—are governed by the Internal Supreme Orient, which council is appointed by the Grand Lodge. This rite is practiced to a very great extent throughout Germany.

Rite of Heredom: (See Heredom, Royal Order of; see Order of Heredom.) (See Haradom; see Rite of Perfection of Heredom.)

Rite: High Priests or Cohens: (See Rite of Elected Cohens.)

Rite: Illuminati: About 1775 or 1776, Adam Weishaupt, a professor of canon law in the University of Ingolstadt, in Bavaria, in conjunction with a few other men of high position and intellectual attainments, formed a secret society of a more singular nature than modern times had ever known. Of this association the most extraordinary accounts have been given at various periods, in which the romantic element has combined with malicious exaggeration to distort the few facts which are really known concerning it. We are told that the design of the institution was to accomplish the overthrow of all civil and religious government—the throne and the altar were equally destined to annihilation, and society was to have been completely disorganized. Weishaupt himself is said, by the opponents of his system, to have been an extremely political reformer, and an infidel. But little is known of this person; the meagre accounts that we have of him have been written under the influence of strong prejudice; and there is great reason to doubt whether he or the society which he established deserved the bad character which has been attached to them.

Freemasonry has been frequently accused of a connection with the much-dreaded, but little known, institution of the Illuminati; and the world at large has been led to believe that the French Revolution, and all the horrors that followed, were, in a great degree, the result of conspiracies hatched under their united auspices.

The idea of connecting his institution with Freemasonry did not exist in Weishaupt's mind at its formation, for it will be seen that the first steps have

195

no Masonic bearing whatever; but it seems that imagining that union with an ancient and honored institution would be favorable to the promulgation of his scheme, he became a member of a Lodge in Munich, and in a short time his persuasive arguments induced many Masons to enlist into the new Order. He then contrived to interweave the three ancient symbolic degrees with Illuminism, the better by their means to get over the scruples of the more enlightened of those who became his followers. By his adversaries it is said that as soon as the Masons witnessed the development of his "high degrees," they saw their error, and one and all retreated; while some, who had left the society in disgust at witnessing the disloyal and infidel precepts that were broached, betrayed its principles.

Upon learning the political tenets taught in its assemblies, the Elector of Bavaria ordered a judicial examination into the charges made against the Order, and the result was that meetings were forbidden, and the society extinguished in his dominions. It, however, spread into other parts of Germany, and was introduced into France in 1787; the state of the public feeling in France at this period was favorable to the tenets of an institution like Illuminism, and it made rapid progress.

Although Professor Robison and others have endeavoured to connect the Illuminati with Freemasonry, certainly nowhere has it been established that there was ever any specific union or connection with our noble Order. Events which occurred in France during the fever of the French Revolution cannot be received in evidence, all society and order having been overturned in that convulsion. It is clear that the institution had but a very brief existence in the country of its birth, and that throughout Germany the Masonic Lodges were closed against its founder; indeed, several dissolved themselves, as it was said Lodges might by possibility harbor conspirators, and therefore they must remain closed till quieter times.

Weishaupt himself, in recommending his scheme, speaks disparagingly of all Masonry, but says he has contrived a system, "inviting to Christians of every communion, which gradually frees them from all religious prejudices, and which animates them by a great, a feasible, and speedy prospect of universal happiness, in a state of liberty, free from the obstacles which society, rank, and riches continually throw in our way." Certainly Freemasonry teaches nothing of this sort. Doctrines even more alarming to the minds of those who reverence "the right divine for kings to govern wrong," were promulgated in France, and the causes of the Revolution may at this day be traced, not to such institutions as the Illuminati, but to the deplorable corruption of the national morals, and the exhaustion of its resources.

The wasteful wars of Louis XIV, his stupendous public works, the splendid edifices erected by him, and the pomp of his magnificent court, although supported by the most oppressive taxation, had at least the effect of flattering the national vanity; but the wanton prodigality of Louis XV produced a different result upon the national mind. The habit of lavishing the public money in profligate expenditure was firmly fixed in the court, and the corrupt system of government too deeply rooted to be easily eradicated, and when Louis XVI ascended the throne he succeeded to an empty treasury and a debt of four million livres. The young king's virtuous attempts at reform were opposed by the clergy and noblesse, and at the period of which we are treating, the smouldering fire of public indignation was ready to break into flame.

196

Accounts of an institution holding tenets like those attributed to the *Illumines* would naturally increase the alarm of the upper classes, who saw on every hand signs that their days of public plunder were approaching an end. A work entitled *Essai sur la Secte des Illumines,* which was published anonymously, but has since been ascertained to have been the production of the Marquis de Luchet, made its appearance in 1788; and the pretended disclosures which were therein made increased the prevailing excitement.

The Illuminati, says our author, began by excluding the New Testament, and every reference to Christianity, altogether from their Lodges; no part of their system, however, from his account, appears to bear the slightest resemblance to symbolic Masonry. The sect had two classes, which were subdivided into lesser degrees, their first class containing the following: Novices; Illuminatus Minor; Illuminatus Major. In the second class were attained the mysteries; this was divided into two degrees, lesser and greater: The lesser comprehended the degrees styled "Priests" and "Regents, or Princes"; in the greater are comprehended those of "Magus" and "Rex." Between these two classes were afterwards interwoven the three symbolic degrees of Masonry, with those of Scotch Novice and Scotch Knight. From the last class were chosen the "Elect," who were the supreme council, and the "Areopagites." The operations of the sect depended in every degree on the tact of one single brother, designated the Brother Inquisitor, whose office was to make proselytes, and to prepare the minds of the newly initiated for the part they intended to act.

It has been said that Illuminism found its way into Britain, but the statement is without foundation, and there is no record of any one of our countrymen having embraced its principles. As all we know of the institution is derived from hostile writers, it is quite possible that Illuminism is wrongly judged. (How.)

Rite: Illuminati of Avignon: The *Illuminati of Avignon* was a species of Masonry together with some ideas taken from Swedenborg, somewhere about 1760, by Pernetti (who had been a Benedictine monk) and the Baron Gabrianca, a Polish nobleman. Very little is known of the institution, and it might have been forgotten but for the Marquis de Thome, in 1783, taking up the system that had been adopted in the Avignon Lodge, and from it framing what is now known as Swedenborg's Rite.

Rite: Illuminated Theosophists: Out of the Illuminated Theosophists came the Swedenborg Rite.

Rite: Illuminees of Stockholm: (See Swedenborg Rite.)

Rite: International Rite, or Co-Masonry: The International Mixed Rite was founded January 14, 1882, and admits women to its lodges. Naturally, it is irregular and unrecognized.

Rite: Jacobitism: (See Jacobitism.)

Rite of Kilwinning: There is no doubt as to whether the Freemasonry which existed at Kilwinning is entitled to the claim of "Rite." That the Lodge at Kilwinning served as a "mother lodge" and gave warrants to form new lodges cannot be denied, but it was not a grand lodge, nor did it function as a rite. (See Kilwinning Masonry.)

Rite: Knights Beneficent of the Holy City: (See Knights Beneficent of the Holy City.)

Rite of Christ: (See Christ, Rite of Knights of.)

Rite: Knights of Malta: (See Knights of Malta.)

Rite of Martinists: The *Rite of St. Martin,* or *Martinism,* was instituted by the Marquis de St. Martin, a disciple of Paschalis, sometime after 1775, whose system was said to be a reform. There were in this novelty two classes, embodying ten degrees. After the three first degrees, followed the first Temple, as it was termed by De St. Martin, comprising those degrees of Ancient Master, Elect, Grand Architect, and Master of the Secret. The degrees of the Second Temple were Prince of Jerusalem, Knight of Palestine, and Knight Kadosh. It was first brought out at Lyons, but in time extended to the principal cities of France and Germany. This rite most likely perished when all the Continental Lodges were closed, during the panic produced by the French Revolution. (See Order of Martinists.)

Rite of Masonic Baptism: (See Baptism, Rite of.)

Rite: Melesino: (See Melesino Rite.)

Rite of Memphis: *"The Rite of Memphis,* or *Oriental Rite,* was brought to Europe by Ormus, a priest and sage of Alexandria, Egypt, who was converted by St. Mark in 46 A.D., and who purified the Egyptian doctrines according to Christian principles."

Such was the legendary story offered by the founders of the Rite (Ed.).

The actual truth is that the Rite was founded in Paris in 1813, by the Brothers Bedarride. Those who care to delve further into its history should consult Marc Bedarride's "De l'Ordre Maconnique de Misraim," Paris, 1845.

The Ancient Mysteries were divided into two classes—the greater and the lesser mysteries. The latter had for its object the instruction of the initiates in the "Humanities"; the sacred doctrine was restricted to the later stages of initiation, and this was called the great manifestation of the "Light." Between the instruction in the "Humanites" and the sacred doctrine were several symbolic degrees. All the Mysteries were arranged on three points—the Moral, the Scientific, and the Sacred. From the first point one passed to the second without further instruction, but on arriving at the second part of the initiation a long preparation was necessary before passing three other symbolic degrees; the first of these completed the Lesser Mysteries, and the two others were the commencement of the Greater Mysteries. It was not until one arrived at the first symbolic degree, that the legends are given, and in the other two degrees one attempted to understand the meaning of these legends, and so become fit to receive the full power or manifestation of the Light.

The general division of the Rite comprised the preparations, the voyages, and the symbols, and the autopsy. The preparations were divided into two classes—the first has as its symbolic title the name "Wisdom," and its object was Morality; the initiates were called "Thalmedimites" or disciples. The second preparation had as its title "Force," and its object was the "Humanities": The initiates of this second degree were called "Heberemites"; or associates.

The voyages and the symbols were divided into three classes. In the first, called the "Obsequies," the initiates were known as "Mouzehemites." In the second, called "Vengeance," they were "Bheremites," and in the third, called "Deliverance," they were called "Nescherites."

The "Autopsy" was the final stage of the initiation, the completion of the edifice, the keystone of the whole structure. The following table shows the status of the system:

198

Lesser Mysteries

1° Thalmedimites ....Wisdom
2° Heberemites ....Force   Preparation
3° Mouzenhemites ....Obsequies

Greater Mysteries

4° Bheremites ....Vengeance   Voyages
5° Nescherites ....Freedom   &
6° Grand Initiates ....Autopsy   Symbols

The dogma of Monotheism—that is to say—there is only *one* God—was taught to the Grand Initiates. The dogma of rewards and penalties in another life was taught in the Lesser Mysteries. Pantheism had been the religion of the ancients; the word "Pantheism" comes from two Greek words, the one meaning "all," and the other "God"—that is, "God is All."

The last Constitution available shows 92° in the Rite of Memphis, although there is evidence to show that it grew to 97°, and later reduced to 33° in order to compete with another Rite.

The 92° system was divided into three Series, as follows:

First Series

1° Apprentice
2° Companion
3° Master
4° Discreet Master
5° Master Architect
6° Sublime Master
7° Just and Perfect Master
8° Knight of the Elect
9° Elected Knight of the Nine
10° Elected Knight of the Fifteen
11° Sublime Elected Knight
12° Knight of the G.M. Architect
13° Knight of the Royal Arch
14° Knight of the Sacred Vault
15° Knight of the Sword
16° Knight of Jerusalem
17° Knight of the Orient
18° Knight Prince Rose Croix of Heredom
19° Knight Prince of the Orient
20° Knight of the Grand Pontiff of Jerusalem
21° Knight of the G.M. of the Temple of Wisdom
22° Knight Noachite, or of the Tower
23° Knight of Liban
24° Knight of the Tabernacle
25° Knight of the Red Eagle
26° Knight of the Serpent of Airain
27° Knight of the Holy City
28° Knight of the Temple
29° Knight of Johan, or of the Sun
30° Knight of St. Andrew
31° Knight Grand Kadosh
32° Grand Inquisitor Commander
33° Sovereign Prince of the Royal Mystery
34° Knight Grand Inspector
35° Grand Knight of the Temple

The above named degrees are said to teach morality, explain the various

199

Order of Silver Trowel

Philalethes Society

Order of Red Cross

Knight Templar Priest

Order of Constructor Masons

Knight Masons of Ireland

Menorah-7-Branch Candlestick

Societas Rosicruciana

Rosicrucian Emblem

Knights Beneficent of
the Holy City

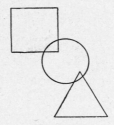

R. & S. Masters

Order of High
Priesthood

Knights of Malta

Society of Blue Friars

Allied Masonic
Degrees

Mark Master

Cryptic Rite

Royal Order of Scotland

201

Masonic symbols, cultivate philanthropy, and teach the early history of the Order.

Second Series

This Series comprises the 36°-68°, and teaches natural science, philosophy and history, and explains the poetic myth of antiquity. Its aim is to incite members to seek for the origins and causes, and to develop a humanitarian and sympathetic outlook.

36° Knight Philalethes
37° Doctor of the Planispheres
38° Wise Sivaist
39° Prince of the Zodiac
40° Sublime Hermetic Philosopher
41° Knight of the Seven Stars
42° Knight of the Arc of Seven Colours
43° Knight Supreme Commander of the Stars
44° Sublime Pontiff of Isis
45° Shepherd King of the Hutz
46° Prince of the Holy Hill
47° Sage of the Pyramids
48° Philosopher of Samothrace
49° Titan of Caucasus
50° Infant of the Harp
51° Knight of the Phoenix
52° Sublime Scalde (Poet)
53° Knight of the Sphinx
54° Knight of the Pelican
55° Sublime Sage of the Labyrinth
56° Pontiff of Cadmas
57° Sublime Chief
58° Brahmin Prince
59° Pontiff of the Ogygie
60° Scandinavian Knight
61° Knight of the Temple of Truth
62° Sage of Heliopolis
63° Pontiff of Mithras
64° Guardian of the Sanctuary
65° Prince of the Truth
66° Sublime Kavi
67° Very Wise Mouni
68° Grand Architect of the Mysterious City

Third Series

This Series comprises the degrees 69°-92°. It is said to teach the remaining portion of the history of the Order, and deals with the higher philosophy, studies the religious myths of the different ages of humanity, and admits the most daring theosophical studies.

69° Sublime Prince of the Holy Curtain
70° Interpreter of the Hieroglyphics
71° Orphic Doctor
72° Guardian of the Three Fires
73° Guardian of the Uncommunicable Name
74° Supreme Master of Wisdom
75° Sovereign Prince of the Senates of the Order
76° Sovereign Grand Master of Mysteries
77° Supreme Master of the Sloaka
78° Doctor of the Sacred Fire

202

79° Doctor of the Sacred Vedas
80° Sublime Knight of the Golden Fleece
81° Sublime Knight of the Luminous Triangle
82° Sublime Knight of the Redoubtable Sadah
83° Sublime Theosophical Knight
84° Sovereign Grand Inspector of the Order
85° Grand Defender of the Order
86° Sublime Master of the Luminous Ring
87° Grand General Regulator of the Order
88° Sublime Prince of Masonry
89° Sublime Master of the Great Work
90° Sublime Knight of Knef
91° Sovereign Prince of Memphis, Chief of the Government of the Order
92° Sovereign Prince of the Chiefs of the Sanctuary of Memphis

Legionary Decorations

The Order of Memphis has three Grand Legionary Decorations, and one Symbolic Decoration, as follows:

1. The Grand Star of Sirius
2. Legion of the Knights of Eleusis
3. Legion of the Knights of the Redoubtable Sadah
4. Decoration of the Golden Fleece

It was a distinctly autocratic system, its government being under the direction of seven "Grand Dignitaries" elected for life.

THE RITE OF MEMPHIS

The story of the Rite of Memphis in the United States constitutes a story of dissension. Had it not been for the machinations of one Harry J. Seymour, the story of the Rite of Memphis in the United States might have been entirely different, for a Rite of more than 90° would have had a mighty numerical appeal to brethren who aspired to "higher" degrees.

In 1852, the Lodges of the Rite in France were closed by civil authority, but in 1862, Marconis, the foremost exponent of the Rite, secured recognition from the Grand Orient of France, which very promptly put the degrees "on a shelf as Masonic curiosities."

The Grand Secretary of the Grand Orient said:

Afterward, and in consequence of the bad faith of Bro. Marconis de Negre, who pretended he had ceded this Rite to the Grand Orient of France for France alone, Bro. Harry Seymour assumed the title of Grand Master of the Rite of Memphis in America and founded a Sovereign Sanctuary in New York . . . when the Grand Orient learned that this power went beyond the three symbolic degrees and that its confidence had been broken, it broke off all connection with Seymour."

Dr. R. Ramsay of Ontario, Canada, one time Grand Master of the Rite, said of it:

The Rite actually possesses ninety-five rituals *in extenso,* embracing the principal features and the more prominent dogmas of not only the Ancient Mysteries, but of every Masonic rite at the present time in existence.

Bro. Longley, in the Canadian Craftsman, 1878, described the thirty-three degrees to which it had been reduced:

4° *Discreet Master:* The duties are to guard the furniture of the Temple. Teaches through Solomon the reverence we owe to God; corresponding degrees—Royal Arch Mason; 4° A.A.S.R.; 4° Rite of Memphis, and 4° Rite of Mizraim.

6° *Sacred Arch:* Alludes to the concealment of the Ineffable Name of God as given to the Patriarch Enoch, and discovery by the Sojourners. Corresponding degrees—Royal Arch; 13° A.A.S.R.; 13° Rite of Memphis; and 11° Rite of Mizraim.

7° *Secret Vault:* Professes to reveal pronunciation of the Sacred Name. Corresponding degrees: Royal and Select Master; 14° A.A.S.R.; 14° Rite of Memphis; 20° Rite of Mizraim.

11° *Rose Croix:* In this degree the candidate becomes a Disciple of the Great Benefactor of our race; is instructed in the virtues of Faith, Hope and Charity, and ascent to Elysium. Corresponding degrees: Knight Templar; 18° A.A.S.R.; 18° Rite of Memphis, and 46° Rite of Mizraim; Royal Order of Scotland.

16° *Knight of Kadosh:* Traces the descent of the Knights Templar from the Builders of the Ancient Temple at Jerusalem through the Knights of the Dawn and Palestine. Corresponding degrees—Knights Templar; 30° A.A.S.R.; 30° Rite of Memphis; 65° Rite of Mizraim.

17° *Knight of the Royal Mystery:* Third degree is here explained by Christian Allegory, and the leading tenets of the nine principal religions of the world are described. Corresponding degrees—Knight Templar Priest; 32° A.A.S.R.; 32° Rite of Memphis; 48° Rite of Mizraim.

18° *Grand Inspector:* Inculcates a spirit of toleration, of love, and of charity, especially addressed to those who are, or may become rulers in Masonry. Corresponding degrees—33° A.A.S.R.; 33° Rite of Memphis; 77° Rite of Misraim.

By the above quotations it is very easy to see and comprehend that the Supreme Rite of Memphis actually embraces within its series of degrees, the above most important grades of the York Rite, the Chivalric Orders, the Cryptic degrees, the Royal Order of Scotland, and the Ancient and Accepted Scottish Rite, including even the exclusive thirty-third. . . .

I will now briefly glance at the present position (1878) of the Egyptian Rites, by which I mean

1. The Oriental Rite of Mizraim, 90°, and its condensation.

2. The Reformed Egyptian Rite, 33°; the Supreme Rite of Memphis, 96°; and the Ancient and Primitive Rite, 33°.

These Rites, in all essentials, are the same, although the Rite of Mizraim has a tradition of the tragedy peculiar to itself.

The Oriental Rite of Mizraim and Reformed Rite (Egyptian), principally under the Sovereign Sanctuary of Italy, on account of its organization at so early date as 1717, assumes the title of Mother Grand Council of the World.

Marconis was elected Grand Hierophant of France in 1838 but the closing of the Lodges made them dormant until March 5, 1848 when the Rite was revived and continued until 1862 when its authority was turned over to the Grand Orient of Italy who at once reduced the number of degrees to 33.

The Rite was brought to the United States in 1856 when Marconis in person established an organization in New York City. H. J. Seymour obtained in 1862 a patent to found a Sovereign Sanctuary. It became decidedly popular. Its death was decreed when it reduced the number of degrees from 96 to 33 for then it came in competition with another Rite offering the same amount of Masonic knowledge. Little has been heard of it in recent years, although one of the student groups reproduced its rituals a few years ago. (See Rite of Mizraim.)

Rite: Mexican National: (See Rito Nacional Mexicano.)

Rite of Misraim: (See Misraim; Mizraim.)

Rite: Mixed: (See International Rite or Co-Masonry.) Any group which accepts members from both sexes is said to be a Mixed Rite.

Rite of Mizraim (Misraim): The *Rite of Mizraim* was first promulgated in Italy—we believe at Milan, in 1805—and was said to have been brought from Egypt by a learned philosopher of that country, named Ananiah. It is said that its founders were some Masons who had been refused admission into the Supreme Council of the Scotch Rite then organized in Milan. It was established in France in 1814, and is continued in some lodges in Paris at the present time, but the Grand Orient of France has never recognized it. It consists of ninety degrees, which are divided into four series—symbolic, philosophic, mystical and cabalistic; and in each series are seventeen classes. The names of the degrees in this more than any other of the rites, prove that the founders must have sorely tested their inventive faculties. They appear indeed to have been driven to their wits' end, for the forty-ninth and fiftieth bear the very expressive titles of "Chaos the First and Second," while the fifty-second rejoices in the somewhat profane designation of "Supreme Commander of the Stars!" At the fifty-fifth and fifty-sixth the comic element predominates; they are the "Washer and Bellow-blower!" Many of the degrees pretend to be founded upon and borrowed from the rites of ancient Egypt, but allowing that the rite may have in many degrees an eminently philosophical character, it is altogether too complicated and diffused ever to be practiced. One of its chiefs, Marc Bedarride, in 1835, published an elaborate work, exponent of its principles, under the title of "De l'Ordre Maconnique de Mizraim," from which we learn that the legend of the Third Degree is abolished in this rite.

H.A.B. is said to have returned to his family, after the completion of the Temple and to have passed the remainder of his days in peace and opulence. The legend substituted for that admitted by all the other rites, is carried back to the days of Lamech, whose son Jubal, under the name of Hario-Jubal-Abi, is reported to have been slain by three traitors, Hagava, Hakima, and Haremda! (HOW)

Rite of Misraim

One thing Bro. Bedarride does not explain. The omission on his part leaves us with a very feeble comprehension of the matter, and it is, that Adam, or the "All-powerful," baptized this Order with the name of an Egyptian king, who, if we take the commonly received Hebraic Genesis for authority, "was born eight hundred years after Adam appeared upon the earth, and others, from the fear of perjuring themselves, or of impairing in any manner the sublime heritage which they had been delegated to transmit to their disciples in all their purity. But if these celebrated Grand Conservators (names are not given) our predecessors, have not performed the sacred duty, they have not failed to leave their successors the traditions of our mysteries in hieroglyphic characters in a manner intelligible to none but the initiated, and thus these documents have been preserved from all profane indiscretion." Commencing in this manner, Bro. Bedarride goes on to speak of the venerable Order, traversing by forced marches whole series of centuries, and stopping every two or three hundred years to indicate the existence of some Grand Conservators, without designating where, how, or by what means they were initiated.

He pursues this romance until the beginning of the present century, when he begins to make a little history; but even of this his recital is so much mutilated that he fails in his search to discover the truth, though he attempts to ascent to the sources of his facts. It is generally believed in the Masonic world that the brothers Mark and Michael Bedarride, who were the chiefs of this Rite, also were its inventors; but it has recently been discovered that they were but its propagators. We say here that this Rite is composed of an aggregation of monstrous legends stolen from all Rites, including those taken from the Scottish, Martinist, and Hermetic Rites. We will add, that after the sixty-seventh degree, it runs upon wheels supplied by Bible subject, and that so purely Israelitish are its bearings, that it could, with more correctness, be called the "Jewish" than the "Egyptian Rite." We also find that this collection of degrees is divided into four series, in manner similar with the Rite called Egyptian, which had been created by Joseph Balsamo, surnamed Cagliostro, professed by the Mother-Lodge, "Wisdom Triumphant," founded by him at Lyons in 1782. We will say that this curious man was born at Palermo in 1743. He acquired a celebrity rarely obtained by impostors. Arrested at Rome on the 25th of December, 1789, he was condemned to death by the Holy Office on the 21st of March, 1791, but Pope Pius VI commuted his punishment to perpetual imprisonment in the Castle of St. Angelo, where he died.

This Egyptian Rite had but an ephemeral existence, and it is probable enough that some of Cagliostro's rituals have served to complete the deplorable work of the Rite of Misraim, whose author was the Brother Lechangeur, of Milan, as we shall endeavor to demonstrate. (We would here say that Cagliostro, in a voyage that he made to London, brought a manuscript which belonged to a man named G. Coston, in which he found the plan of a Masonry founded upon a system which was magical—part cabalistic, and part superstitious. From this work he arranged his plan of the Egyptian work.)

A Grand Orient of Italy had been founded in Milan shortly after the organization of that at Naples, and the Prince Eugene Beauharnois had been invested with the dignity of Grand Master. Some superior officers, resident at Milan, who had been installed at Paris in the High Degrees of the Scottish Rite (32°), resolved to establish a Supreme Council of that Rite, at the suggestion of brethren in Paris. A person named Lechangeur, an officer of an operative lodge at Milan, demanded to become a party in this arrangement, and his demand was complied with. They gave him certain degrees, but refused to give him the Superior degrees; but, having some good reason for keeping him out of their Supreme Council, he obtained no others. Vexed at this refusal, Lechangeur informed the members of this Supreme Council that he would get the better of them in creating a Rite of ninety degrees, into which he would not admit them. He accomplished his threat, in fact, and it is to him that is to be attributed the creation of this self-styled Oriental Rite.

The first thing that Lechangeur did, after having elaborated his Rite, was to elevate himself to the highest office recognized by it—in this respect imitating all other fabricators of Rites—that of "Superior Grand Conservator of the Order of Misraim," and in this capacity to deliver Patents of authority to all who offered to propagate this new Rite to his profit.

These delegates being thus authorized, were confined in their operations to the organization of Chapters in the cities of the Italian peninsula, more particularly to Naples; and those Chapters should, in their turn, create Delegates, and deliver to them Patents of authority to their profit.

We should call this an "elegant illumination," and it no doubt was, for "somebody's pockets." We shall now try to explain how, and by whom, this Rite of Misraim, was first introduced in France.

Bro. Michael Bedarride, a native of Cavaillon, in the Department of Vaucluse, and belonging to the Jewish religion, was initiated in Freemasonry on the 5th of July, 1802, in the Lodge "Candor," at Cezena, in Italy, and affiliated in the year 1805 with the Lodge "Mars and Themis," in Paris, which conferred upon him, as it did also upon his brother, Mark Bedarride, the Degree of Master. Michael Bedarride, who was a merchant in Naples, obtained the position of Commissary of Subsistence in the Italian army, upon the staff of which army his Brother Mark had a position. During their sojourn in Italy the two brothers had affiliated with several lodges in that country. On the 3d of December, 1810, through the intervention of one of the patentees of Lechangeur, Michael Bedarride obtained a similar Patent, authorizing him to confer the degrees of the Misraimites up to the 73°. Subsequently, at Milan, he received of the Brother Lechangeur himself an increase of degrees, and a Patent dated 25th of June, 1811, conferring upon him the degree of "Grand Hazsid," or 77°, with the right of conferring all the degrees to that point. A similar Patent had already been delivered on the 3d January, 1810, by Lechangeur to Mark Bedarride. It seems that for some reason, which we do not know, the Brother Lechangeur did not wish the Brother Bedarride to possess the degree of "Grand Conservator," or 90° of his Rite; but, notwithstanding, the possession of this degree became absolutely necessary to enable him to succeed in their projects.

With this object Michael Bedarride addressed a man named Polack, an Israelite resident at Venice, who, usurping the right claimed by Lechangeur, had proclaimed himself Superior Grand Conservator, or Independent Grand Master, and obtained of this person, on September 1, 1812, a Patent conferring upon him the title he so greatly desired. This document, however, did not appear to be sufficiently authoritative for his purpose, as it bore but one signature, and consequently lacked evidences of authenticity, for, immediately after the death of Lechangeur, he sought at the hands of the Brother Theodore Gerber, of Milan, to whom Lechangeur had bequeathed the powers he had given to himself another Patent. The application was successful, and on the 12th of October, 1812, Michael Bedarride procured this new authority, signed by Theodore Gerber, and conferring upon Michael Bedarride the title of Superior Grand Conservator of the Order of Misraim, in Italy. Besides the signature of Gerber, this document bore also the signatures of Mark Bedarride, who, as we have shown, had not then obtained the 77°, and seven or eight other brethren, who were reputed to compose the "Sovereign Grand Council of the Ninetieth Degree of the Grand Master Absolute"; and it is by virtue of the powers that they have arrogated to themselves, in concert with the Chief of this Rite, that they delegated to Michael Bedarride the same powers and all their supreme rights as therein expressed by this Patent, to create, form, regulate, dissolve, whenever desirable, Lodges, Chapters, Colleges, Directories, Synods, Tribunals, Consistories, Councils, and General Councils of the Order of Misraim—prerogative that this Brother, as therein expressed, has merited by "the most profound study of the sciences, and the most sublime practice of every virtue that is known to but a very small number of the elect (?) inviting all Brethren, of every Degree and every Rite, to assist the Puissant and Venerable Grand Conservator, Michael Bedarride, with their counsel, their credit, and their fortune, him and the rejected of his race," etc., etc.

It is by virtue of this curious document, which we consider it unnecessary further to explain, that the Brother Michael Bedarride, through the organ of his brother Mark, announced himself in Paris Chief of this self-styled Oriental, Ancient and Sublime Order, which he says is the stem of all Masonic Rites in existence; although he must have suspected by whom it had been fabricated. When the Brother Mark Bedarride, then a retired officer of the army of Italy, arrived in Paris in 1813, and where he was joined shortly afterward by his brothers, Michael and Joseph Bedarride, the latter of whom had also, at Naples, received some Patents from a Delegate, patented by Lechangeur; these three brothers found four others—two of whom were named respectively Joly and Gaborea—who had likewise procured in Italy some Patents which conferred upon them also the right of creating Lodges, Councils, etc., up to the 90°, while the other two named respectively Garcia and Decollet, bore Patents giving them authority to the 77°.

We spoke of a certain number of brethren who resolved to create a new Power founded upon the plenary powers which Brother Joly had received in Milan.

Now let us see what they did. In September, 1816, this new organization requested permission to rank under the jurisdiction of the Grand Orient, and, to allow them to do so, proposed to abandon the administration of the first two series of the Rite, comprising sixty-six degrees, and reserve to themselves but the power to control those from sixty-seven to ninety. Some commissioners were named on the part of each body to arrange the particulars; but the Grand Orient, though at first very well disposed to conclude the arrangement, after a more mature examination of it, rejected the proposition on the 14th January, 1817, and on the 27th of the following December addressed to the Lodges of its correspondence a circular, by the terms of which it prohibited them from receiving the members of the Rite of Misraim in their assemblies.

Unlike the generality of such documents as are issued by the Grand Orient, the motives expressed in the edict were for once logical. It stated the patentees had not furnished the titles required to authenticate the original and the authenticity of the Rite of Misraim, that the assertion of its introduction into Italy under the pontificate of Leo X, in the 16th century, by Jambilicus, a platonic philosopher, who lived in the 4th century, eleven hundred years before Leo X, was destructive in the nature of dates; that the Rite was never practiced at Alexandria nor at Cairo, as it pretended to be, etc., etc.; for these reasons this Rite could not be admitted in the Grand Orient.

The Grand Orient having thus brought to public notice the irregularity of the power claimed by the brothers Bedarride, the latter sought, as much as it was possible, to destroy the doubts thus engendered. Michael Bedarride had, on the 3d of May, 1816, exhibited, signed by seven brethren, which detailed all the Masonic titles he had obtained, that is, the dates of his receipt of them in Italy; but this document though in it he was named "Superior Grand Conservator," gave him no legal power, and to meet this contingency it was necessary to produce another document. This latter soon appeared, signed by thirteen brethren of the Rite, and among them the Count de Grasse-Tilly, founder of the Supreme Council of the Scottish (33°) Rite at Paris, the Count Muraire, the Count Lallemand, the Duke of St. Aignan, the Chevalier Lacoste, and, we believe, several others. These brethren in this patent styled themselves "Sovereign Grand Masters absolute of the Rite of Misraim," a title which had been conferred by Michael Bedarride, after he had organized his Grand Council of 90°; and it was by virtue of the powers which this title conferred, and with which they had been invested by Michael Bedarride, that they, in their turn, by means of this patent, bestowed upon him the title and powers of Supreme Grand Conservator of the Order for France.

The new patent which we have just mentioned was dated the 7th of September, 1817; but, unlike the other, it bore no mark of having been produced at Milan, and this fact somewhat invalidated its use at Paris; nevertheless, as the brothers Bedarride had the whole world to operate in, this circumstance merely induced them to change slightly the field of their operations. In 1818, Joseph turned up at Brussels, and Michael in Holland. It would appear, however, that the means which they employed were not the most laudable; for, upon the 18th of November, 1818, the Prince Frederick, Grand Master of the Netherland Lodges, addressed a circular to all the lodges of that country, pointing out the brothers Bedarride, who by that time were running about the Kingdom, as dishonorable men, who, to obtain their objects, had recourse to very reprehensible tricks and means unworthy of true Masons, and which had already brought them into discredit at Paris. This circular wound up its charges with interdicting the exercise of the Rite of Mizraim in all the lodges under his authority, and supported this interdiction wth the reasons advanced by the Grand Orient of France on 29th of December, 1817, and which we have mentioned. Notwithstanding these prohibitions, notwithstanding these difficulties which opposed them, the brothers Bedarride succeeded in establishing in Paris, beside the lodges "Rainbow" and "Disciples of Zoroaster," four other lodges namely, "The Twelve Tribes," "Disciples of Misraim," "The Burning Bush," and "The Children of Apollo," all of which were in active operation toward the close of the year 1818.

This increase of lodges permitted them to give, on the 19th of January, 1819, a brilliant Feast of Adoption, which was presided over by the Count Muraire and the Countess Fouchecourt. Notwithstanding their seeming success, the brothers Bedarride were constantly at war with their own lodges, who complained of their administration, and demanded an account of the funds. The brothers responded to these demands by expelling the most clamourous of the claimants. It was thus that, by the decision of a self-styled Council, which the brothers Bedarride directed as they wished, bearing date of 15th of August, the Brethren Marie, Richard, Chasserian, Beaurepaire, Ragon, Meslet and Joly were expelled from the Rite. But this despotism but increased the indignation. The Lodge "Disciples of Zoroaster" separated itself from the Rite of Mizraim by an unanimous decision, date 30th April, 1819. In the minutes of this occasion, and which this Lodge published at that time, the motive for separation is thus expressed:

1st. They had vainly called for the correction of many articles contained in the general regulations in consequence of their despotic and unsatisfactory character; and

2d. The suppression of the word "absolute" in connection with the title of "Sovereign Grand Master," as, in the present century, such distinction is a usurpation and an offence to free men.

3d. In nearly all of the general regulations the Grand Conservator has arrogated to himself powers as obscure as they are arbitrary.

4th. And, finally, according to a judgment of the Tribunal of Commerce of the Seine, the firm of Joseph Bedarride & Co. (the brothers Mark and Michael were the associates not named), living in Moon Street, at No. 37, was in a condition of open bankruptcy. This proceeding was signed by the W. Master and by all the officers of the Lodge, to the number of twenty. The supreme power confined itself to striking the W. Master, and, by an edict dated 11th June, 1819, Dr. Ganal was expelled. The Mother Lodge, "Rainbow," also revolted against the administration of the Grand Conservators, which its members unanimously declared to be most deplorable, and brought the declaration before the Chiefs of the Order, in the hope that they would require the Brothers Bedarride to render an account of the receipts and expenses. In the position in which they found themselves, the brothers Bedarride could not satisfy the demands which were addressed to them in connection with the finances, because the revenues of all kinds which they received through their connection with the Rite, were necessary to pay their debts and support their personal expenses. They, in consequence, made use of their omnipotence to declare all the members of the Lodge of "Rainbow" who had taken part in the revolt against them, as disturbers of the peace of the Order; and this done, they dissolved the Lodge for the purpose of reconstructing it with non-dissenting materials and its President, Count Lallemand, sharing the fortunes of the opposing members, by an edict of the Grand Council of 7th July, 1810, was expelled. (Bulletin, S. C., S.M.J. Vol. VII.)

Rite: Moderne French: (See Rite, French.)

Rite of Palladium: This Rite is attributed to Fenelon (p. 16). Note: The Order of the Palladium claimed to have been of great antiquity; fell into decay; was revived by Fenelon, Archbishop of Canbray; organized into the mentioned Rite at Paris in 1737, all of which is mythical. Two grades were worked (the legend continues) in this androgynous group; Adelph and Companion Ulysses, the latter changed its title to Companion of Penelope when taken by a female.

Rite of Perfect Initiates: Also known as the Perfect Initiates of Egypt. The Rite comprised seven degrees and was formed at Lyons, France, from a copy of "Crata Repoa," of which Bailleul, in 1821, has given us a translation from the original German. Mackey says that Cagliostro's Egyptian Rite was termed the "Rite of Perfect Initiates" when it was first introduced at Lyons, by its founder.

Rite of Perfection: The Rite of Perfection. We have already referred to the rite denominated "Chapter of Clermont." The Chevalier de Bonneville is said to have taken a prominent part in its establishment, about 1753-56, to do honour to Louis of Bourbon, Prince of Clermont, who was at that period the Grand Master of the Freemasons of France. The leading principle in this rite is to establish the connection of the Knights Templar with Freemasonry. It bore also the name of the *Rite of Heredom,* and consisted of twenty-five degrees, most of them being the same as those of the Ancient and Accepted Rite:

210

1. Entered Apprentice; 2. Fellow-Craft; 3. Master Mason; 4. Secret Master; 5. Perfect Master; 6. Intimate Secretary; 7. Intendant of Buildings; 8. Provost and Judge; 9. Elect of Nine; 10. Elect of Fifteen; 11. Illustrious Elect; 12. Chief of the Twelve Tribes; 13. Royal Arch; 14. Grand Elect Perfect Ancient Master; 15. Knight of the Sword; 16. Prince of Jerusalem; 17. Knight of the East and West; 18. Rose-Croix Knight; 19. Grand Pontiff; 20. Grand Patriarch; 21. Grand Master of the Key of Masonry; 22. Prince of Libanus; 23. Sovereign Prince Adept, Chief of the Grand Consistory; 24. Illustrious Knight Commander of the Black and White Eagle; 25. Most Illustrous Sovereign Prince of Masonry, Grand Knight, Sublime Commander of the Royal Secret.

This rite was in practice for a few years in Paris, and possibly is still in existence. It will be seen that the names of some of the degrees which differ from the first formation of the Ancient and Accepted Rite are the same as those adopted by the Supreme Council in England. The *Primitive Scotch Rite* was founded on the Rite of Perfection by Marchot, an advocate at Namur, but we cannot learn that it was adopted in any other place. There are thirty-three degrees in this rite, and they are similar to the Scotch Rite; but in this the Rose Croix is the twenty-second and the Kadosh the twenty-eighth degree.

In the historical part of the lecture in this rite, we are told that the Masons who were employed in constructing the first Temple acquired immortal honor; and the world-wide fame of that stately edifice caused the Order to become more uniformly established and regulated than before. Their scrupulousness in admitting new members into the Order brought it to a high degree of respect—merit alone being regarded in the admission of candidates. With these principles instilled into their minds, many of the Grand Elect left the Temple after its dedication, and dispersed themselves among the neighbouring kingdoms, instructing all who applied and were found worthy in the sublime degrees of ancient Craft Masonry. (See Rite of Perfection of Heredom; see Heredom.)

Rite of Perfection of Heredom: The Rite comprised 25 degrees, of which the first 81 were identical with those of the A.A.S.R. (See Heredom; see Rite of Perfection.)

Rite of Pernetty: The *Rite of Pernetty,* or the *Illuminati of Avignon,* was established in 1779 and transported, in 1778 (sic), at Montpellier, under title of the "Academy of True Masons." A. E. Waite says: "The Rite of the Illuminati at Avignon is said, as we have found, to have been instituted in 1760, and was known as Brethren of the Rite of Pernetty. When the headquarters were removed to Montpellier, it assumed the name of Academy of True Masons.

Rite: Persian: (See Persian Philosophic Rite.)

Rite: Persian Philosophic: Formed in France about 1819. It was not much encouraged, and has now ceased to exist. Little is known of its ritual, and whether the three symbolic degrees were essential to its members, or whether they are included in the fanciful names of the degrees adopted, we are unable to learn. It consisted of seven degrees: (1) Listening Apprentice; (2) Fellow-Craft Adept, Esquire of Benevolence; (3) Master, Knight of the Sun; (4) Architect of all Rites, Knight of the Philosophy of the Heart; (5) Knight of Eclecticism and Truth; (6) Master, Good Shepherd; (7) Venerable Grand Elect.

Rite: Phallic: In the story of Osiris and Isis, we learn that Isis found all the parts of Osiris body except the phallus; so she made another, which she consecrated and honored in an annual festival. Phallic worship is mentioned in Ezekiel XVI-17. The Phallus was the symbol of the male generative organs and was universally respected among the ancient races. Rites which deal with the phallus are termed "Phallic Rites."

Rite: Philadelphians: (of Narbonne) Rite: The *Primitive Rite,* or the *Rite of the Philadelphians of Narbonne,* established in that City April 19, 1780, and reunited to the Grand Orient of France in 1786. The list of members was printed in 1790 under the title of the First Lodge of the Primitive Rite in France—which appears to have been much in common with the Rite of Memphis or Oriental Rite. It is formed of three classes of Masons, who receive 10 degrees of instruction; these degrees or classes do not represent so many grades but merely denominate the number of phases necessary to pass through before entering upon an infinite number of grades.

The first Chapter of the Rose-Croix possessed teaching, which in several rites is venerated by numerous eminent brethren; the second Chapter of the R.C. consists of a number of historical documents; the third Chapter deals with all the Masonic teachings, both physical and philosophical, which influence the well being and the happiness of mankind—in short with all the sciences which may be termed occult or secret, their special object being the re-integration of man to his original rights.

The Rite was divided into three classes:

A. Symbolic Freemasonry; B. The second class worked: 1. Perfect Master, 2. Sublime Master, 3. Knight of the Sword; and C. The Third Class contained four Chapters of Rose-Croix Masonry: (a) Subject matter of the ritual; (b) Masonic history; (c) Masonic philosophy and morals, and (d) Pursuit of occult sciences.

(See Rite: Primitive of Narbonne.)

Rite of Philalethes: The *Rite of Philalethes,* or *Searchers after Truth,* which was drawn from the speculations of the theosophists St. Martin and Paschalis, is said to have been invented by Savalette de Langes, keeper of the royal treasury, and was first adopted in the Lodge of Amis Reunis at Paris, about the year 1775. It consisted of twelve degrees: Apprentice; Fellow-Craft; Master; Elect; Scotch Master; Knight of the East; Rose Croix; Knight of the Temple; Unknown Philosopher; Sublime Philosopher; Initiated; Philalethes or searcher after Truth. At the death of the founder of the rite, the Lodge of Amis Reunis was dissolved; and the rite, not having extended further, ceased to exist. An attempt to revive a rite bearing this name was at one time made in London.

Rite: Philosophic Scotch: The *Philosophic Scotch Rite* was established in Paris, and adopted by the Grand Lodge in 1776. Some few years previously, a Mason, named Pernetty, founded a rite, to which he gave the name of *"Hermetic, or Sublime Masters of the Luminous Ring,"* the object of the contriver being to instruct his disciples, not only in the higher degrees of Masonry, but also in the art of transmuting metals and preparing the elixir of life. Pernetty had for a pupil a physician named Boileau, who did away with the alchemy, and made it more purely Masonic, and then gave this reformed rite the name above affixed to it.

This rite, which Clavel says is still practised in France, has twelve degrees,

212

the three degrees of ancient Craft Masonry being necessary pre-requisites, though they do not form a part of the rite. The degrees:

One, 2, and 3, Knight of the Black Eagle or Rose-Croix, divided into three parts; 4, Knight of the Phoenix; 5, Knight of the Sun; 6, Knight of Iris; 7, Freemason or True Mason; 8, Knight of the Argonauts; 9, Knight of the Golden Fleece; 10, Grand Inspector, Perfect Initiate; 11, Grand Inspector, Grand Scotch Mason; 12, Sublime Master of the Luminous Ring.

The doctrine taught in this rite was, that Freemasonry was founded by Pythagoras; and the lectures consisted of an explanation of the philosophy and peculiar doctrines of the Samian sage, asserting, for instance, that the symbols he adopted in his secret instruction were chiefly derived from geometry; thus, the right angle was an emblem of morality and justice; the equilateral triangle was a symbol of God, the essence of light and truth; the square referred to the Divine mind; the cube was the symbol of the mind of man after it had been purified by acts of piety and devotion, and thus prepared for mingling with the celestial beings. The point within a circle, and the dodecahedron or figure of twelve sides, were symbols of the universe; the triple triangle was an emblem of health; and the letter y a representation of the course of human life, in which there were two diverging paths, the one of virtue leading to happiness, and the other of vice conducting to misery. Pythagoras, in pursuit of knowledge, traveled into Chaldea and Egypt, and is said to have been instructed in the sacred lore of the Hebrews, either by the Prophet Ezekiel or Daniel. Dr. Oliver asserts that he was initiated into the Jewish system of Freemasonry, and that "his mysteries were the most perfect approximation to the original science of Freemasonry which could be accomplished by a philosopher bereft of the aid of revelation." Iamblicus relates, as evidence of their brotherly love and of their means of mutual recognition, the following incident: A Pythagorean traveling in a distant country, fell sick and died at a public inn. Previously, however, to his death, being unable to compensate the landlord for the kindness and attention with which he had been treated, he directed a tablet, on which he had traced some enigmatical characters, to be exposed on the public road. Sometime after another disciple of Pythagoras passed that way, perceived the tablet, and learning from the inscription that a brother had been there sick and in distress, and that he had been treated with kindness, he stopped and reimbursed the innkeeper for his trouble and expense.

Rite of Platonic Academy: Founded in 1482 under Laurent of Medici by Marsilius Ficinus: Note: The assumption that the Platonic Academy presumably founded by Marsilius Ficinus at Florence in 1480, under the patronage of Lorenzo de Medicis, was Masonic, is based upon the statement that the hall in which they met contained Masonic emblems. Naturally the Academy would not be Masonic; the appearance of emblems which were adopted by the fraternity in various parts of the world, has led many Masonic writers afield and into error. Yarker, in his "Arcane Schools," refers this organization to Rome; both Mackey and Clavel make mention of it with effort to connect it with the Craft, the latter most earnestly, but erroneously.

Rite: Primitive: (See Swedenborg Rite.)

Rite: Primitive and Original (or Swedenborgian Rite): We draw our information respecting this rite chiefly from Brother Samuel Beswick, of

213

Strathroy, Canada, who is author of a work upon the Swedenborgian Rite, and a pamphlet determining the length of the two Egyptian cubits by careful measurement of the Great Pyramid. He asserts that Emanuel Swedenborg was initiated at Lund, in Sweden, in 1706, and progressed to the higher degrees of Templar as practiced in Sweden; that this rite (sometimes called Illuminati of Stockholm) was well known to the higher class of Swedish Masons at the middle of last century, but was supplanted by Zinnendorf's Rite, which made a spurious use of the information obtained from it. It may still be practised there amongst a select few. It must not, however, be confounded with those rites of the French Theosophists, which drew much of their doctrine from the Swedish Philosopher. The rite was, last century, introduced into England by the Brothers Chastannier, Springer (Swedish Consul), C. F. and Aug. Nordenskjold, and others, who were members of the first Swedenborgian Society in London, known as the "Theosophical Society of the New Jerusalem." For a long time the degrees were privately practised without charters. Their archaic character is pre 1717.

The rite requires all its members to be Master Masons; but it is not necessary that they should belong to the Swedenborgian Church; and the ceremonies are, as will be seen, necessarily of an unsectarian character. To the three degrees of Craft Masonry it adds the following:

4° Enlightened Phremason or Green Brother.
5° Sublime Phremason or Blue Brother.
6° Perfect Phremason or Red Brother.

The jewel is a carbuncle, set and radiated in gold, in the form of a sun, and having the sacred name upon the face in Hebrew letters of gold, above it the square and compasses. The ribbon for the jewel and apron is for Grand Officers, purple, bordered with gold; Past Masters, blue and gold; W. Masters, blue and silver; Members, plain blue.

Of the ceremonies we are permitted to say but little; they are intended to indicate what Freemasonry was ceremonially before the days of King Solomon, who could not have been initiated under the present Craft Rite; and it is the only Order which has succeeded in showing how the Masonic theories of the learned Brother, Doctor Oliver, may be reconciled with facts; indeed, it is most probable that he was acquainted with the rite, and better instructed than Masons have given him credit for.

The bearing of the three grades is astronomical, and their similes are drawn from the Heavenly Temple of the Great Master Builder, lit by the lamps of the firmament. By certain signs, known to all Freemasons, and considered as emblematical of the position of the constellations at the period when Masonry was established, the ceremonials and institution of the Masonic Order are assigned to the year 5876 B.C., and then embodied in a well-known Chaldean, Egyptian and Jewish emblem.

Rosetti, in his "Essay on the Anti-papal Spirit of Secret Societies," asserts that an expert Mason would find much of the institution of Freemasonry in the writings of Swedenborg; but excepting some principles general to Christians as well as Masons, we have not been able to discover any absolute proof that Swedenborg was a Freemason (the most reliable thing is that in 1787 Col. Baltzer Wedemar asserted in a Swedish Lodge lecture that Swedenborg was a Mason, and that he had seen his signature at the Lodge at Lund. King

214

Gustavus III confirmed these assertions). Swedenborg, for fifty-eight years of his life, devoted himself to the cultivation of science, and produced a great number of works, in which he broached some novel and ingenious theories, one of which consists in applying positive science to all; for instance, one of his rather incomprehensible rules runs thus: "The beginning of nature is the same as the beginning of geometry; thus natural particles arise from mathematical points, precisely as the lines and forms of geometry; and this, because everything in nature is geometric." His scientific labors are forgotten, but his theological labors, which occupied the latter part of his life, resulted in the establishment of a sect, or new church, designated by his name, in England, the United States, Sweden, and Germany. He was a most methodical man, and laid down these rules for the guidance of his life:

1. Often to read and meditate upon the Word of God.
2. To submit everything to the will of Divine Providence.
3. To observe in everything a propriety of behavior, and always to keep the conscience clear.
4. To discharge with fidelity the functions of his employment, and the duties of his office, and to render himself in all things useful to society.

The tenets inculcated in his writings and adopted by his followers are:

1. There is one God; that there is in Him a Divine Trinity, and that He is the Lord and Saviour Jesus Christ.
2. That having faith consists in believing in Him.
3. That evil actions ought not to be done, because they are of the devil and from the devil.
4. That good actions ought to be done, because they are of God and from God.
5. And that they should be done by man himself, as of himself; nevertheless, under the belief that they are from the Lord, operating in him and by him.

(See Swedenborg Rite.)

Rite: Primitive and Original Rite of Symbolic Phremasonry: There have been at least two systems of Freemasonry which claimed the title of *The Swedenborgian Rite:* The first is referable to London, and one Benedict Chastanier, circa 1784, based on the Order of Illuminated Theosophists, established there by him in 1767; the second is the more modern and is the object of this study.

In 1870, Samuel Beswick published a book entitled "Swedenborg Rite and the Great Masonic Leaders of the 18th Century," otherwise "Swedenborg and Phremasonry." The book was especially written for those who were, or desired to be, members of the Swedenborgian Rite. Aside from one or two minor points of interest, the book is of little interest and of no historical value, due to its many erroneous statements and its general lack of authenticity.

In examining the claims of Beswick one must cautiously weigh every statement made, since few of them are true—or even near true. The book gives us, at least, one fact—in 1869 (the year in which the book was written), we know that the Swedenborgian Rite was in existence in America.

Beswick declares that the Rite was revived in America by members of the Swedenborg New Church (which is most likely true) in 1859 (which is possible, but problematic). The Swedenborgians who founded the Rite, he

215

continues, were Masons of the "higher degrees" and were initiated in the Swedenborgian Lodges. "A Lodge, called Menei Temple No. 1, was organized and began work, February, 1859, in the old Kane Lodge Room, Broadway, New York City. From thence it was removed to the Egyptian Room, Odd Fellows Hall, and worked from May, 1861-1862. A few meetings were subsequently held in the Montauk Lodge Room, Brooklyn, Long Island." (P. 167, Swedenborg Rite and the Great Masonic Leaders of the 18th Century.)

A Balustre of 1902 tells us: The Rite consists of Three Degrees to which Craft Masons in lawful and regular possession of Symbolical Masonry can alone be admitted. It makes no pretense to supersede any other Rite but is independent and self-contained, offering philosophical explanations of Masonic science of deep significance, the doctrines contained in certain sections of the Arcana Coelestia of Emanuel Swedenberg, after whom the Rite is named.

The Rite consisted of six grades: the first three were not worked as they were the same as the Craft degrees of the York Rite. The others were:

4° Enlightened Phremason, or Green Brother.
5° Sublime Phremason, or Blue Brother.
6° Perfect Phremason, or Red Brother.

The three degrees as above are no more than amplification of the three Craft degrees.

From external evidence, it appears very likely that the Swedenborgian Rite, of the 19th century, was manufactured in America; I would be bold enough to state that it appears the product of Beswick and his colleagues of the New Church. I cannot believe, as did the late Dr. Carr (The Freemason, Oct. 3, 1925), and referred to by Dudley Wright (P. 862, The Master Mason), that the Rite was founded by the Marquis de Thome in 1783, as a modification of the Illuminati of Avignon, and is the germ from which the modern Rite sprang. No evidence of the Rite can be found during the 19th century, save the American organization, which indicates the new Rite was known or worked anywhere or at any time, save as coming from America; and, as a fact, the American Rituals do not bear earmarks of revision of another older liturgy. Truly, the American Rituals contain too much of American Craft Ritual to be anything similar to the older system which was supposedly theosophic and Swedenborgian in content.

The system we now study was introduced, presumably from New York, into Canada, say circa 1875. In 1876 there was a Supreme Grand Lodge and Temple of Canada, with only two subordinates, and Colonel W. J. B. McLeod Moore was its Supreme Grand Master. The third subordinate, as may be seen from records hereafter produced, was warranted in England and from that seed sprang the Supreme Grand Lodge and Temple for the United Kingdom of Great Britain and Ireland, with John Yarker as its head. The original Emanuel Lodge and Temple No. 3 (Canada), at Bristol, became No. 1 on the English registry and divided its membership into two additional bodies: Egyptian, No. 2, at Manchester, and St. John's No. 3, at Baildon.

John Yarker credits the introduction of the Rite into Canada and Great Britain to Samuel Beswick (P. 490, The Arcane Schools) and this is very good evidence of the facts in the case. While it is unfortunate that we cannot, offhand, find records of the parent American body, or any of its subordinates, we do know that Canada was alive and active, for the time being at least, in 1876.

The Rite took temporary root in English soil and spread out from thence, although a few years later we hear nothing further from the Rite and may assume it died a natural death in Great Britain, as it did in Canada and the United States.

Rite: Primitive of Narbonne: Established in that city in 1780. The degrees were selected from other rites, and were chiefly of a philosophical character, assuming as their object the reformation of intellectual man, and his restoration to his primitive rank of purity and perfection. (See Rite, Philadelphians of Narbonne.)

Rite: Primitive Philadelphes: (See Ancient and Primitive Rite.)

Rite: Primitive Scottish: The Rite was founded in 1781 and practiced in France and Belgium; it has thirty-three degrees, which differ somewhat from the Ancient and Accepted Rite; it also has some of the Philosophical Scottish Rite of fifteen degrees.

Rite: Ramsays: (See Jacobitism.)

Rite: Rectified: (See "Martinism.")

Rite: Rectified Rite of the Scottish Rule: "Rectified" refers to the riddance from Freemasonry of all alchemic, cabalistic, and other "alloys" borrowed from the Order of the Temple. The system and traditions of the Strict Observance were examined at the Assembly of Lyons, 1778; from this meeting came forth the "Masonic Code of the United and Rectified Lodges of France." The first part of the Act embraces the three degrees of St. John, and the degree of Scottish Master; the second, the rule of the Benevolent Knights of the Holy City. Such was the title the Knights of the Chapter declared they would take in the future, in preference to the Templar; here we have the origin of the Scottish Rule of the Rectified Rite, the object of which is Benevolence in its widest sense, and the improvement of Man by Christianity in its primitive purity; it follows that the whole system, in all its parts, is calculated to make in the simplest way possible, and by means peculiar to the Masonic institution, true and faithful Christians, free from the spirit of sectarianism. The Code of the Rectified Lodges, and that of the Benevolent Knights, as drawn up at Lyons in 1778, were approved in 1782 at the Assembly at Wilhelmsbad.

The essential difference between the two Scottish systems is: Whereas the Ancient system professed especially to believe that the Masonic Brotherhood had been imagined by the Templars themselves to perpetuate their Order secretly until the moment of its public reestablishment, the New Order, renouncing all secular and worldly claims, is attached only to the spiritual and Christian parts of the ancient chivalric religious societies. The Temple to be rebuilt mystically, remains therefore the same to the end, and finally becomes the Holy City, and it is in this sense that all the ramifications made in the rituals and ceremonies of the degrees are carried on.

The Rectified Rite of Scottish Rule had for its object: To maintain and strengthen in the bosom of Masonic Lodges, the principles which are at its base; attachment to the spirit of Christianity and faith in a Supreme Power, the G.A.O.T.U.; Devotion to Country; Improvement of the individual, quell passions, correct faults, advance intellectual faculties; the exercise of Benevolence towards all men, whatever their nationality, political or religious opinions, or social status.

It was stated: "The Rectified Rite responds to the aspirations of many Freemasons, who hold to the traditions of pure Freemasonry, and desire to associate themselves with the glorious principles of the Freemasonry of 1717."

The Rectified Rite of the Scottish Rule consisted of: (a) Symbolic Lodges of the Masonry of St. John, comprising the three degrees of Entered Apprentice, Fellow Craft and Master Mason; (b) The Symbolic degrees of St. Andrew; (c) The Prefectures, which comprise two classes; Novice Esquires and Benevolent Knights of the Holy City.

It is divided into the following sections: (a) The Helvetic Grand Chapter; (b) The Grand Prior; (c) The Directory; (d) The Prefectures.

Rite: Rectified Rose Croix: (See Rose Croix.)

Rite Reformed: The *Reformed Rite* was an emendation of the *"Rite of Strict Observance,"* rejecting the connection which the latter rite had with the Knights Templar; and was established by an assembly of Masons who met at Wilhelmsbad, under Ferdinand, Duke of Brunswick, in 1782, assuming in the first instance the title of the *"Order of Charitable Knights of the Holy City."* M. de St. Martin's system was merged in this; and Clavel says the Lodges that had adopted Martinism, adopted the Reformed Rite. Novelties charm the gay and versatile French, and the rite soon spread over the country. Clavel further states it to be in practice in France and Switzerland.

The rite had what were called five degrees, but as the last had three sections, there were really seven in all: Apprentice, Fellow-Craft, Master, Scotch Master, Charitable Knight of the Holy City; the three sections of the last were named—Novice, Professed Brother, and Knight.

Presumed to have been a reformation of the older Rite of Strict Observance. (See Rite of Strict Observance; see French Rite.)

Rite: Reformed Helvetic: The *Reformed Helvetic Rite* was the name given to the Reformed Rite, when introduced into Poland in 1784, by Brother Glayre, of Lausanne (minister of State to Stanislaus, King of Poland), who had been the Provincial Grand Master of this rite in Switzerland. Clavel says that several alterations were made in the rite, and hence the addition to its name. The Grand Orient of Poland adopted it.

Rite of Rigid Observance: (See Rite of Strict Observance.)

Rite: Rito Nacional Mexicano: The full name of the Rite is Benemerito Rito Nacional Mexicano; it was, and is, an irregular Mexican group which pretends to confer the three symbolic degrees of Freemasonry. Article 6a of their 1936 Constitution and By-Laws refers to the initiation of women, which law in itself wou'd prevent its recognition by regular Freemasonry. The headquarters of this irregular group is in Mexico City, Mexico. (See Mexican National Rite.)

Rite: Rosaic: The name given by its institutor, M. Rosa, a Lutheran minister in Germany. It was for a short time highly patronized and exceedingly popular, but was superseded by the Rite of Strict Observance. We have no information as to the ritual or practice.

Rite: Rose Croix: (See Rose Croix; see Knights Rose Croix.)

Rite: Rosicrucian: (See Rosicrucians.)

Rite: Royal Masonic for the U.S.A.: (See Rite of Mizraim.)

Rite: Royal York of Berlin: This Grand Lodge conferred a series of degrees which are referred to as the "Royal York Lodge of Berlin Rite."

Rite: Russian: (See Melesino Rite.)

Rite: St. Louis des Amis: There are to be found a number of instances in which this lodge conferred other than Symbolic Craft degrees.

Rite of St. Martin: (See Martinism.)

Rite of Schroeder: Invented by a person of that name, and besides the three degrees of Ancient Craft Masonry, had many others containing a mixture of alchemy magic, and theosophy. It was first practised in a lodge at Sarreburg.

Rite of Seven Degrees: Union Lodge No. 270 and Loge St. George de l'Observance in London worked in the French language; both practiced the "higher degrees" through a College of Rites which adopted a series of seven degrees, and appears to have combined the Templar traditions with the Ecossais Rite, as well as with some others. The Baldwyn Rite (Encampment) may have adopted some of its ritual. Most of these London lodges were Moderns. Lintot was the recognized leader of this Rite.

The degrees conferred were the three degrees of the Craft series; the 4° was an Elu degree, which numbered sections included such as: Architect, Provost and Judge, Grand Architect, Companion of the Royal Arch, Grand Elu, Sublime Master, and Perfect Ecossais. The 5° was Knight of the East and West, in which passing the bridge played an important part. The 6° was Knight of the Eagle, Pelican, Rose Croix of St. Andrew of Heredom, Triple Cross, or Knight Rose Croix. The 7°, and last degree, was Knight Kadosh. In some instances the Royal Arch was referred to as the 5°; and the degrees of Petit Elu Inconnu, Knight of the Sun, Knight de l'Epee of the East, and Grand Commander of the East are frequently mentioned.

The origin of the system is thought to be the Chapter of Clermont in France (1754); this body conferred the degrees of 4° Ecossais; 5° Knight of the Eagle, 6° Illustrious Knight Templar, and 7° Sublime Illustrious Knight. And in the body "Knights of the East" (1756-67) we find a series of seven degrees very similar to the Rite of Seven Degrees. The Clermont body and the Knights of the East united into a "Council of Emperors of the East and West, etc." and their system bore many resemblances to this Seven Degree Rite.

Rite: Societas Rosicruciana: (See Roscrucians.)

Rite of Strict Observance: The Rite of Strict Observance was founded in Germany by Baron Hunde, in 1754; and, according to *Clavel,* it was based on the Order of the Knights Templar. It comprises seven degrees: Entered Apprentice, Fellow-Craft, Master Mason, Scotch Master, Novice, Templar, and Professed Knight. The legend of the rite thus narrated its origin. On the murder of Jacques de Molay, the Grand Master of the Templars, Pierre d'Aumont, Grand Prior of Auvergne, with two Commanders and five Knights, escaped from France, and sought safety in Scotland under the disguise of operative Masons. Soon after their arrival they were so fortunate as to discover one George Harris, a Grand Commander, with some other Templars; a Chapter of all the Knights was held on St. John's day, 1313, and Pierre d'Aumont was elected Grand Master. To avoid the persecution which still pursued their own body, they met as a Lodge of Freemasons, that Order being tolerated at the period of the Templar persecution. In 1361 the chief seat of the Order was established at Old Aberdeen; and, under the veil of Masonry, in this rite the Templar Order was diffused from Scotland to various parts of the Continent. Some of the degrees embody the practice of alchemy, magic, and other now obsolete pseudo-scientific delusions.

We have no knowledge of this rite being now anywhere practised. The rite nevertheless attained considerable influence at one period; proof of which is found in the schism that was created among its members, and resulted in an order called the *Clerks of Relaxed Observance,* which offset claimed pre-eminence, not only over the parent rite, but over the whole brotherhood of Masons. For admission into this association it was imperative that the candidate should be a member of the Catholic Church of Rome, and that he should have taken all the degrees of the Rite of Strict Observance. The new rite had ten degrees: Apprentice, Fellow-Craft, Master Mason, African Brother, Knight of St. Andrew, Knight of the Eagle, Scotch Master, Sovereign Magus, Provincial Master of the Red Cross, and Knight of Light; the last degree was divided into five sections, and it required seven years for completion. Alchemy and magic were the objects of this rite. *Clavel* says its members boasted that they had possession of the true philosopher's stone, the elixir of life, the command of spirits, and a method of discovering the hidden treasures of the Temple.

Rite: Sublime Masters of the Luminous Ring: Founded in France in 1780 by Grant. This gave new life to the Pythagorean cult. Note: Mackey concurs in this statement, as does MacKenzie, that Baron Grant of Blaerfindy was the founder, the place, France; the year, 1780. However, the more accurate Waite does not commit himself on the matter in the absence of authentic data.

Rite: Swedenborg: (See Primitive and Original Rite.)

Rite: Swedish: Swedish Freemasonry of the eighteenth century presented a peculiar combination of the three Symbolic Masonic degrees with Templar and Rosicrucian grades. Each of these factors—Symbolic Masonry, Templar Degrees, and Rosicrucian—helped to shape it, and each introduced into the Swedish system its peculiar doctrines and ideals;

Symbolic Masonry: the attainment of the "golden age of Astrea" through moral improvement of each individual brother.
Templar Masonry: a struggle with the enemies of Christianity and virtue acquired in the first degrees.
Rosicrucianism: the mysticism of esoteric Christianity.

Under this scheme, the Masonic program was:

(a) Moral self-improvement and strengthening of Christian virtues in individual members.
(b) Active fight for Christianity and virtue against the forces of evil.
(c) Mystical attainment, through perseverance in the first two stages of approach to Christ himself in His Inner Church.

In this system the Symbolic degrees followed the generally accepted English pattern of dignity and simplicity but the Templar degrees were accompanied by elaborate ceremonial reminiscent of mediaeval days, and gorgeous acces-

220

sories. This is practically the Masonic pattern in the Scandinavian countries to this day. A Study of Theosophy and Alchemy is a reminder of the influence of the Rosicrucianism.

The Swedish system claims that it has its origin in the Order of Knights Templar and the mysteries which they practiced; the Rite is characterized by its autocracy; it is a hierarchy of degrees and rank; its higher officials cannot be changed; the brethren of lower grades must render full and complete obedience to their superiors. Grand Masters are, as a rule, selected from members of the Royal Family or nobility. The local situation changes from time to time, due to local conditions, as may be noted in Norway, and more recently in Denmark.

The degrees of the system are divided into Three Classes or Grades:

First Class (St. John's Lodges): Apprentice, Fellow-Craft, Master.
Second Class (St. Andrew's Degrees) St. Andrew's or Scottish Lodges: Scottish Apprentice-Fellow, Scottish Master.
Third Class (Knightly Degrees in Chapters): (To form a Chapter required as a basis, three St. John's Lodges and one Scottish Lodge of the Second Class; it required 27 Knights to constitute a quorum making it "legal." If 49 were present it was "ordinary," and "perfect" if the full 81 were present.)
6. Steward brethren or Knights of East and Jerusalem.
7. Brethren Elect of King Solomon, or Knights of the Temple (also called Knights of the West, or of the Key.)
8. Confidants of St. John, or Brethren of the White Ribbon.
9. Confidants of St. Andrew, or Brethren of the Purple Ribbon.
10. Brethren of the Rosy Cross.

The brethren of the latter, or tenth degree, were sub-divided into three classes, which are nothing more than official grades:

1. Members of the Ruling Chapter, not occupying office.
2. Grand Officers of the Chapter.
3. The Grand Ruling Master (usually the King). He also bears the title "Vicar of Solomon."

It will be seen that the brethren of the 10th degree govern the organization; they are formed into a "Chapter" ruled by a Grand Master and his Grand Officers.

Four degrees are not actually degrees, but apparently civil orders; these consist of 10° Member of Chapter; 11° Dignitary of the Chapter; 12° Vicar of Solomon. The latter is only an office and is held by the King who is perpetual Grand Master. None are admitted to the 11° unless they can show four quarterings of nobility. The first nine degrees essentially compose the Rite. The 13° is the *Order of Charles XIII.* The latter Order was instituted by Charles XIII, May 27, 1811, and is a civil Order conferred upon Freemasons only by the King

"to incite his subjects to the practice of charity, and to perpetuate the memory of the devotion of the Masonic Order to his person while it was under his protection and to give proof of his royal benevolence to those he had so long embraced and cherished under the name of Freemasons." (The Order usually consists of the King, Princes of the Royal Family, twenty-seven lay brethren, and three ecclesiastical brethren all of whom are equal in rank in the Order.)

Rite: Templar: (See Knights Templar.)
Rite of True Masons: (See Order of True Masons.)

221

Rite of Universal Harmony: This Rite was instituted in 1782 by Mesner. (Note: Mackey concurs in this.)

Rite: York: The *York Rite,* the most ancient, has existed from time immemorial, and, according to tradition, originated in the City of York, where the first Grand Lodge of England was held, A.D. 926. In this, the parent Lodge of Pure Masonry, it is said only the three primitive degrees of Ancient Craft Masonry were in the first instance acknowledged, and since 1813 that of the Royal Arch. To them, in the United States, &c., have been added four other degrees, viz: Mark Master; Past Master; Most Excellent Master; Sublime Degree of the Holy Royal Arch. Thus this Rite consists of four and seven degrees; but in the United States, where it is still practised, two have been annexed, those of Royal Master and Select Master. But, as mentioned in the account of the Ancient and Accepted Rite, the Ancient York Masons in England in the last century practiced other degrees. The York Rite, as a matter of fact, died out in the early part of the last century; full information as to this point is obtainable in the "History of Freemasonry at York," by Brother Hughan, so that no Mason now can fairly be said to practice the York Rite.

Rite of Zinnendorf: The *Rite of Zinnendorf* was a modification of the Illuminism of Avignon, with additions from the Swedenborgian, and combining also several selections from the Scotch and other rites. Its promulgator was Count Zinnendorf. The system consisted of seven degrees, divided into three sections, the first of which is entitled St. John's Masonry, and comprises: 1, Entered Apprentice; 2, Fellow-Craft; 3, Master Mason. The second section, or Red Masonry, contains the Scotch Apprentice, and Fellow-Craft, and the Scotch Master; the third, called Capitular Masonry, embraces the Favourite of St. John and Elected Brother. We understand this is the Masonic system of Denmark.

Rite of Zuzumites: (See Zuzumites.)

Rite of Xerophagistes: The Rite of Xerophagistes was founded in Italy in 1746. Note: If indeed such a Rite ever existed, it would doubtless trace its origin to the Bull of Pope Clement XII (dated April 28, 1748), and would doubtless contain the Craft grades under the nom de plume of "Xerophagists" (from two Greek words signifying "eaters of dry food"). Both Mackey and Thory make mention of the body.

Roman Eagle: This is not a degree as might be inferred from the expression "more ancient than . . . the Roman Eagle," but it is an emblem of the Roman Empire. A Latin Lodge was organized, in 1784, by Dr. John Brown, of Edinburgh, under the title of the *Roman Eagle Lodge,* the whole ritual being in Latin. It had a brief existence.

Rosaic Rite: (See Rite, Rosaic.)

Rose Croix: The Rose Croix is one of the best known of Masonic degrees, appearing in many Masonic Rites; in its present arrangement it constitutes the 18° of the Ancient and Accepted Rite, where it and the 17° constitute the Philosophical and Doctrinal degrees of that Rite; they are conferred in a Chapter of Rose Croix and open a new development of Masonic teaching, and constitute a departure from the symbolism and teaching of the symbolic lodge degrees.

Wherever you turn in studying Masonic degrees, you find mention of the Rose Croix degree. It may not always be in that form but whatever the name may be, it is one and the same. We find: "Knight Rose Croix," "Sovereign Princes of Rose Croix," "Prince of Rose Croix de Heredom," as well as reference to it under the name of "Knight of the Eagle and Pelican," although it is not now, and never was an Order of Knighthood.

The first known ritual of the degree is dated 1767, and was called Les plus secrets Mysteres des Hauts Grade de la Maconnerie devoiles, or le Vrai Rose-Croix. (The greater secrets of the mysteries of the high degrees, called the True Rose-Croix.) Several editions of this ritual were issued. We know as a matter of fact that the degree antedates the date of the printed ritual.

It appears in the so-called Morin ritual of about 1765, from which it would appear that it was being exploited by our Hebrew brethren, which is quite extra-ordinary since the degree deals with Christian legends and traditions; it was listed as the 18° of that rite and is still the 18° of the Ancient and Accepted Scottish Rite. The degree emphasizes the Christian virtues of Faith, Hope and Charity.

Just where the name Rose Croix came from we do not know; some attribute it to the legendary Christian Rosenkreutz, said to have been the founder of the Rosicrucian Society; others claim the name to have been derived from a combination of figures—the Rose and the Cross—hence, the Rosae-Crucis. Then we have the RSYCS of the Royal Order of Scotland which differs materially from the Rose Croix of the A.A.S.R.

Dr. William L. Cummings says:

The cross, as a symbol of eternal life was used long before the days of Moses; in ancient mythology, the rose was consecrated to Hypocrates, the God of Silence, and hence became the emblem of Secrecy. Ragon suggests the combination of the rose and cross as a mode of writing "the secret of immortality."

Albert Pike said of the degree:

the beginning of a course of instruction which will fully unveil to you the heart and inner mysteries of Masonry . . . in all time, Truth has been hidden under symbols, and often under a succession of allegories; where veil after veil had to be penetrated before the true Light was reached, and the essential Truth stood revealed.

Brother Ronald W. Meier says the degree

demonstrates the lessons of the Rite: Good against Evil; Light against Darkness; Intelligence against Ignorance; Education against Superstition; Toleration against Fanaticism . . . a complete revelation of that which was promised—all moving forward to the Unity and Goodness of God, the Immortality of the Soul, the Ultimate defeat of Evil, Wrong and Sorrow by a Redeemer yet to come, if he has not already appeared, and the Reign of the New Law, the Law of Love and Charity among all men.

These degrees deal with the first Temple and the attempt to restore and maintain the old worship in a second temple reared upon the ruins of the first. Neither endured. The degree is designated in the N.M.J. as the 18° Knight of the Eagle and Pelican. There we find that Man had to have a new Temple, a New Law, a new Word. The degree sets forth a law of the heart, a law of warm and intimate human virtues, which the simplest and humblest may practice. It symbolizes the perfect life which every man can understand and take for his guide and inspiration.

223

There are many Rose Croix degrees, most of which employ the same symbolism. In October, 1845, there was formed in London, as the 18° of the Ancient and Accepted Rite, the "perfect degree of Rose Croix of Heredom" apparently derived from the Royal Order of Scotland. The degree was brought to Bristol, England by French refugees in 1800; there in France, chapters worked under the Grand Orient.

Wherever the degree is found, it will be seen that it is tinged with occultism, Rosicrucianism, Christianity, and alchemy. It is called Rose Croix, according to one writer, because in the early days of the fraternity, operative Masons in Scotland, caused medals to be struck, whereon was a symbol which serves as a veil for this grade: a Rose upon a Cross, because Jesus Christ, by his exemplary conduct has been compared to the Rose of the Gospel. Some of these medals passed into the hands of ignorant Masons, who adopted the name of Rose Croix to distinguish themselves, and kept the title "Knight."

The Rt. Hon. Gerald Fitzgibbon, head of the Prince Masons of Ireland, 1909, said the Rose Croix came from France to the Templars, through Pierre Laurent, and Emmanuel Zimmerman, Jan. 20, 1782, and ever since had been "rigorously reserved for the Templars." In 1796 a Sublime Council was opened in Dublin to work the "higher" degrees; On June 1, 1802, under French Warrant, the "Metropolitan College of Heredom of Ireland" was opened, which governed the Rite of Perfection until 1824. About 1908 the degree came under the Supreme Council of Ireland, A.A. Rite.

There is a "Magnetic Rose Croix" which is the 38° of the Rite of Mizraim; the Rose Croix of Heredom is the 1° of the Royal Order of Scotland; the Rose Croix of the Grand Rosary is the 4° of the Rose Croix Primitive Rite; the Philosophic Rose Croix appears in the German Hermetic Rite and the Philosophical Scottish Rite; there is a Rectified Rose Croix.

Rose Croix:
The 11° of the Rite of Memphis.
A degree in the Rite of Philalethes.
A degree in the Modern French Rite.
A degree in the Rite of Elect of Truth.
A degree in the female Rite. (See Honourable Fraternity of Ancient Freemasons.)

Rose Croix Knight: A degree in the Rite of Perfection; also of the Adonhiramite Rite.

Rose, Order of the: An androgynous degree formed in Berlin in 1778.

Rosicrucians, The: The secret society of the Rosicrucians was one of the great mysteries of mediaeval days. Sir Bulwer Lytton's novel "Zanoni" is an attempt to portray the Rosicrucian mysteries. The sect derives its name from one Christian Rosenkreuz, who is said to have prolonged life by his researches in alchemy; he died at the age of 106. The volume "Fama Fraternitas" is almost a text-book; it exerted much influence on Freemasonry. Rebold says the society was founded by Valentine Andrea in 1616, and resuscitated with Masonic forms about 1767.

This cult declared that in accordance with the Mosaic account of creation, not to be taken literally, that two original principles in the beginning preceded from the Divine Father—Light and Darkness. They taught that there are three ascending Angels, divided into nine orders. They held that all things visible and invisible have been produced by the contention of light with darkness, and the earth has a denseness in its innumerable heavy concomitants downwards; that they contain less and less of the original divine light as they thicken and solidify the grosser and heavier matter. The modern day order does not claim any direct connection with the ancient one.

The Rosicrucian Society, in its modern Robes of Glory, is traceable to 1865, when the plan was first projected by Robert Wentworth Little, the Society being started the subsequent year, in London, England ("History of the Societas Rosicruciana in Anglia," 1900, and "Data of the History of the Rosicrucians," 1910, by Dr. W. W. Westcott). The early champion of the Society, however, was Frater Kenneth Mackenzie, who had resided in Germany. He gave of his time and energies to the Society, which has "made itself most useful to Freemasons by the publication of papers upon occult and abstruse subjects, of a superior kind (P. 491, "The Arcane Schools" 1909, by John Yarker).

The Society was based upon the symbolism and traditions of a still earlier Society known as the Rosy Cross, which in turn, claimed origin from that immortal character—real or mythical—Christian Rosenkreuz, known by the familiar initials C.R.C. In building upon the ancient Order, the modern Societas Rosicruciana has not departed from precedence. The birth of the Society, in thus building upon an ancient Order, whose titles and insignia have been borrowed, very closely resembles Freemasonry, which has built upon the ruins of a still earlier Society, and from which the symbols, tools, titles and framework were borrowed for a Craft Masonic, yet Speculative. Were we to be, as some have been, critical of the birth of the Rosicrucian Society, then we should, by the same token, criticize the birth of the Speculative branch of Freemasonry.

"The Societas Rosicruciana in Anglia," as the Society is termed in England, mothered several other similar Societies in different nations: Scotland, America, Ireland, and Greece. Today, however, there are only three High Councils in the world: Societas Rosicruciana in Anglia, Scotia and U.S., the others being at present considered very dormant.

The Society in the United States owes its origin to the High Council of Scotia, who, in 1879 (December), established a College for the State of Pennsylvania and, in 1880, for the purpose of establishing a High Council in the United States, chartered a College (in April) in the State of New York. These two Colleges met in 1880 and formed a High Council for the United States. During the same year, however, they having previously applied for Charters, Colleges were established by Scotland in Massachusetts (May 9, 1880) and Maryland (May 10, 1880) (P. 10, "Constitution of the High Council S.R.I.U.S."). While the formation of High Council in April, 1880, was legal in every sense of the word, yet another assembly was convened on September 21, of the same year, at which representatives from all four Colleges attended, and the Founding of High Council was formally ratified and an Act of affirmation unanimously passed. Thus, was High Council born. At the meeting of that date, or rather the day following (Sept. 22), Frater George O. Tyler, of Burlington, Vermont, was admitted and at some later date a Charter was granted for a College at Burlington. Likewise a Charter was subsequently issued for a College at Duluth, Minn.; plans were also made for the formation of a College in New Orleans, but no Charter was ever issued ("Publication No. 1," New Jersey College, S.R.I.U.S.).

During the process of formation of the American High Council, the Supreme Magus of Canada, Frater W. J. B. McLeod Moore, issued authority to Frater Albert Pike for the formation of a College in Washington, D. C., but as the authority was dated after the actual formation of High Council, it was withdrawn and amounted to nothing.

The very nature of this paper disallows a more complete historical sketch of the Society in the United States, although much data is now available on the lean years that came upon the Society; the entrance of outside influences upon a dormant Body and an attempt to revive a legal organization upon contrary principles—which failed—and a number of so-called Rosicrucian organizations in America, which are neither Masonic nor Rosicrucian.

Having lightly treated of the historical phase of the Society of Rosicrucians, we may now consider its objects, grades, et cetera.

"Its purpose is the scientific and literary, historical and archaeological investigation of the occult wisdom of the ancients, the origin of the mysteries, of secret societies, and of the lost sciences and arts of alchemy, astrology, the Kabbalah, the hieroglyphic literature of Egypt, etc. Essays are read at the meetings, discussion is invited, and old and curious books, pictures, etc., are exhibited." (P. 54, Vol. I, A.Q.C.)

The grades of the Society are nine in number, which are grouped in three Orders: The First Order consists of I°, Zelator; II°, Theoricus; III°, Practicus; and IV°, Philosophus. The Second Order consists of V°, Adeptus Junior; VI°, Adeptus Senior; VII°, Adeptus Exemptus. These two Orders are worked by Colleges; however, the Third Order is worked only by High Council, and consists of: VIII°, Magister Temple, which is an Official Grade and is held by Secretaries and Treasurers of American Colleges, by virtue of their offices; X°, Chief Adept, which is held by virtue of an appointment ad vitam, of the Magi of High Council.

Societas Rosicruciana in Civitatibus Foederatis

The Societas Rosicruciana in Civitatibus Foederatis (the Rosicrucian Society in the United States) was organized in 1879. It was descended from the first organzed body of its kind which was established in England in 1866 and in Scotland a few years later, although the roots of the organization appear to have been in Scotland. Membership in the Society is predicated on the aspirant being a Freemason, the members being selected by invitation.

The objects of the Society are as follows:

1. To consider, examine and record all such matters as may come within the purview of the philosophy of Freemasonry, and those sciences embraced in it, as also those sciences which are akin thereto, with the purpose of obtaining verified truth in place of traditional error, of reconciling any apparent discrepancies between History, Myths, Legends, Philosophy, and Sciences, as embraced in the study of Freemasonry.
2. To facilitate the study of the system of Philosophy founded upon the Kabalah and the doctrines of Hermes Trismegistus, and to investigate the meaning and symbolism of all that now remains of the wisdom, art, and literature of the ancient world.
3. To create a base for the collection and deposit of archaeological and historical subjects pertaining to Freemasonry and Secret Societies, and other interesting matter.
4. To draw within a common bond men of scientific inclination, and authors who have been engaged in these investigations, and, as well, those

226

interested in them, with the view of strengthening their exertions by association, and of placing in juxtaposition the results of their labors for comparison, that Freemasonry may be rendered free from the apparently gross contraditions within itself, its sciences and historical myths.

5. To promote generally true Science and the principles of philosophy proper, to the end that the members and those within their influence may be enlightened by the results of these investigations, either by published papers on subjects read and discussed within the Society, or by lectures, delivered under its sanction or auspices.

6. To revive the good of the life labors of that class of scientists and scholars whose aim and study was what the name of the Society implies.

The Society in any country is governed by a High Council, presided over by a Supreme Magus, IX°, elected for life. The membership groups are known as *Colleges* and, in the United States, presided over by a Chief Adept, IX°, who becomes a titular Provincial Officer appointed for life. Membership is restricted to seventy-two active members. Colleges have power to confer the following grades:

First Order: First Grade, Zelator; Second Grade, Theoricus; Third Grade, Practicus; Fourth Grade, Philosophus.

Second Order: Fifth Grade, Adeptus Junior; Sixth Grade, Adeptus Major; Seventh Grade, Adeptus Exemptus.

The Eighth Grade, Magister Templi, is an Official Grade and the Ninth Grade, Chief Adept, a Provincial Grade. They are both conferred by the High Council only, and constitute the Third Order.

The usual practice, in the United States, is to confer the First Order on the Aspirant and advance into the Second Order Grades by recognition of literary effort or services to the Society.

There are eighteen officers in High Council and a corresponding number of officers in each College. Those of the Colleges are elected and appointed annually. Those of High Council each three years.

Aspirants of a College are required to submit a Latin motto and a statement that they are not a member of any society using the name "Rosicrucian" or considered a Rosicrucian organization, as a matter of ethics.

The Society is not primarily interested in increasing its membership, but is always happy to add to its numbers such brethren whose interest in the Society's aims is sincere and whom it considers to be in sympathy with the movement.

In 1878, 1879 and 1880 five Colleges were chartered by the High Council of Scotland in the United States. One of these was never active (Illinois), but the others met in Boston and formed a High Council in 1880, and rechartered Pennsylvania, Massachusetts, Maryland and New York Colleges on September 21 of that year. A College in Vermont was chartered the following day, but was never active. Minnesota had a College chartered in 1912, but this charter was finally returned to High Council. Texas had a College chartered in 1918 and this was revoked in 1935. There was a military College in 1933 under dispensation, but it was finally recalled in 1940. Illinois College chartered in 1934, was withdrawn in 1947. The Colleges in Pennsylvania, Maryland and New York only worked a few years.

Present Colleges (1954) are: Massachusetts (1880); New Jersey (1932); North Carolina (1932); Virginia (1934); Colorado (1935); Long Island (1935); Nova Scotia (1936); Ontario (1937). The membership is slightly over two hundred Fratres in the United States.

In the nearly seventy years of the Society in the United States there have been but thirty-nine who have attained the Ninth Grade IX°. Of these the following have served as Supreme Magus:

1, Charles E. Meyer (Pa.) April 21, 1880; 2, Thomas J. Shryock (Md.), October 7, 1908; 3, Eugene A. Holton (Mass.), February 3, 1918; 4, Frederick W. Harimton (Mass.), March 21, 1927; 5, Arthur D. Prince (Mass.), May 28, 1940.

At the time of the formation of the Society in the United States, the following High Councils were in existence:

England—William Robert Woodman, IX°—Supreme Magus.
Scotland—The Earl of Kintore, IX°—Supreme Magus.
Greece—Prince Rhodocanakis, IX°—Supreme Magus.
Canada—William J. B. McLeod Moore, IX°—Supreme Magus.

The Societies in Greece and Canada became defunct so that those in England, Scotland and the United States are the sole organizations now operating in the world. These three High Councils have entered into a concordat that provides for the same ritual to be used in the "work" or grades of the three societies. In England and Scotland only the three presiding Magi of the High Councils receive the Active Ninth Degree grade, so that in these countries there are only three IX° members at any one time. (See Societas Rosicrucians.) (See Rosicrucian Rite.)

Rosy Cross: The degree, or Order, is, traditionally, supposed to have been established by the Scotch hero, Robert le Bruce, 1314, after the Battle of Bannockburn; in the beginning it was limited to Royal Arch Masons. The "Rosy Cross" is said to have been, originally, the Cross of Christ, sprinkled with His Blood. (See Order of Heredom.) The 2° of the Royal Order of Scotland.

Roughmasons: In the 15th century, there were three classes of Masons: Freemasons, Roughmasons, and Handhewers—or in some instances only Freemasons and Roughmasons. The word Rough Mason seemed to be synonymous with Layer.

Round Table, Knight of the: (See Knight of the Round Table.)

Royal Arch: The Royal Arch is without doubt the most talked of, and written about, degree of Freemasonry. The United Grand Lodge of England, in 1813, set it out as the *ultimate of the Craft system* when it included it in the degrees of the Craft-referring to it as the "Holy Order of the Royal Arch."

And the degree appears in other Rites, although not under the same name; it constituted the 4th Grade of the Councils of the Emperors of the East and West, but there it was not the degree which we know as the Royal Arch; its traditions are unknown, but they displayed the Delta prominently, and the candidate represented one who had discovered the lost architect, receiving as his reward the position of Chief Architect, and carrying on the work of building. In the obligation was a promise to obey the statutes of "the Grand Lodge South of the River Trent."

A degree similar in character to the Royal Arch of the American or English Rite, is that of the 13° of the Ancient & Accepted Rite; but it differs in character from that we are accustomed to.

228

The degree was first heard of about 1740; meetings were termed "Chapters." At one time, in England, it was divided into two branches, just as were the two grand lodges; later they united into one Grand Chapter—that which exists at this time.

In the U.S.A., the degree marks the culmination of the Chapter series of degrees known as Royal Arch Masonry, and there it constitutes the 7° of the Rite. Chapters join to form a Grand Chapter, and representatives of Grand Chapters make up the General Grand Chapter, established in 1797, and which is the parent body of most Royal Arch Masons in the Western Hemisphere.

Royal Arch (Other Groups): The "Grand Royal Arch" was the 31° of the Mizraim Rite; the Royal Arch of Solomon is the 13° of the A.A.S. Rite; the Royal Arch of Zerubbabel is the 7° of the American or English Rite; the Royal Arch Super Excellent is the Irish degree.

The legend of the Royal Arch is the story of the return from captivity of a group of Jewish captives, under Zerubbabel, whose object was to Rebuild the Temple. While engaged in the rebuilding, they discovered a vault, which proved to be one especially constructed to contain secrets belonging to the First Temple. Further investigation resulted in the finding of the long lost Word. In the American Rite the vault is entered from above; in the Arch of Solomon or Enoch, there are nine arches. The Irish legend concerns the *repair* of the Temple; the English legend deals with the *rebuilding* of the Temple. One is known as the *Jeshua* legend; the other the *Zerubbabel* legend.

In the Irish degree of the Royal Arch Super Excellent there were four candles on the altar, one unlighted; the three lighted candles represented the three Grand Masters; the unlit one, the profane—thus: *Light shining in Darkness and the Darkness Comprehended it Not.* This expression appears in many of the Irish Patents. When Dublin Freemasons changed the name of the Super Excellent Degree, and adopted the name of "Red Cross Masons, they adopted the symbol of the Four Triangles joined at their apexes. This may have been the origin of the Templar unlit candle.

Royal Arch Degree: That great Masonic Historian, Dr. W. J. Chetwoode-Crawley, in his Camentaria Hibernica, 1885, said of this degree:

The Royal Arch is not a separate entity, but the completing part of a Masonic legend, a constituent ever present in the compound body, even before it developed into a degree . . . if the Royal Arch fell into desuetude the copestone would be removed, and the building left obviously incomplete.

And Dr. Hopkins, in his lectures on Freemasonry, said:

I would urge everyone, having made himself acquainted with our ordinary Craft ceremonies, and having undergone the necessary probation, to proceed to that sublime and exalted degree by which alone the cravings for Masonic lore can be satisfied, his doubts explained, and the completeness of the system be fully developed.

And Dr. William F. Kuhn of our country said:

the degree is an unfolding into a second volume the history of that which was lost to its final recovery. Without the Royal Arch, the Master's degree is like a song half sung, a tale partly told, or a promise unfilled, for it is the complement of the Master's degree.

Even Carlile, in his exposure, referred to the degree as

a species of Masonic Knighthood.

229

And Morin, in his ritual of 1765, lists a "Knight of the Royal Arch," a degree which bears close resemblance to the present day ritual.

And our early day companions believed it to be intimately connected with the Craft system, for in the beginning it was conferred under the questionable authority of a Lodge Warrant, and the minutes transcribed in the lodge records, until finally prohibited by Grand Lodge. There was a Royale Arche which was the 13° of the twenty-five degree system, which remained there when extended to the 33° system. The degree also appeared as the 31° Grande Royale Arche of the 90° Rite.

And the greatest historian of them all, William J. Hughan, says that

it is probable that Royal Arch Mason was the first ceremony associated with the Craft degrees, though there are minutes of other degrees before that of the Royal Arch, yet references of 1743-4 place it in the position of being one of the earliest known of the additional ceremonies.

Royal Arch of Enoch: Also referred to as "Sublime Elect" is one of the degrees of the Helvetic Rite; it resembles the Royal Arch of the English system.

Royal Arch Excellent: A quaint degree of the Helvetic Rite which embodies elements of the Royal Arch as we have it in the U.S.A., some of the Templar ceremonies, and even the Order of High Priesthood. Members were referred to as "frere Compagnon" or brother companion.

Royal Arch of Jerusalem: A degree of the Helvetic system which bears a close affinity to the second section of the Royal Arch as conferred in the United States.

Royal Arch Mason: One who has received the degree of Royal Arch Mason in a regular Chapter of Royal Arch Masons. (See Royal Arch.)

Royal Arch Masonry: Sometimes referred to as "Chapter Masonry." As a rule, the term implies all of those degrees which are conferred as a part of the Chapter system; this would include the degrees of Mark Master, Past Master (Installed Master in England), Most Excellent Master, Royal Arch Mason, and the Order of High Priesthood.

Royal Arch of Solomon: The 13° of the Ancient and Accepted Rite. (See Royal Arch.)

Royal Arch Super Excellent: (See Royal Arch.)

Royal Arch Widow: A degree put on for the entertainment of wives of Royal Arch Masons. It had its origin in Cut Bank, Mont.; the ritual was transplanted eastward, where it was used, with some additions, by Chapters of Royal Arch Masons in Iowa, Missouri and Wisconsin. The Grand Chapter of Royal Arch Masons of Missouri, after adding certain features, printed the ritual and permitted its sale by the Educational Bureau of the General Grand Chapter, R. A. Masons, where it has been found of service in creating interest in Chapter Masonry. Officers in the degree represent King Solomon and his Royal Household; the degree is entirely humorous, but the conclusion is dignified and explanatory of the objectives of Freemasonry.

Royal Arch of Zerubbabel: The 7° of the American, or English, Rite, known as the "Royal Arch Degree." (See Royal Arch.)

Royal Architect: (See Ancient Free and Accepted Architects.)

Royal Ark Mariners: In his Constitutions of 1733, Dr. James Anderson mentioned that we should all conduct ourselves as sons of Noah (or Noachidae). There are many who assume that this is a reference to an Ark ceremony, but this study is neutral. It is possible, though hardly probable; the question depends upon what might be termed the date of the speculative Grades.

Further, in some quarters it is a more or less accepted theory that the Ark and Anchor with which we are so familiar in the Craft are but indications of an ancient Ark ceremony of yesteryears. It is assumed that an ancient Grade relating to the Deluge was discontinued and the symbols thereof incorporated into the lectures of the Craft. This theory, likewise, is possible, but the present study does not either accept or deny the possibility of such a theory.

At page 108, Vol. VI A.Q.C., Brother W. J. Hughan mentions two very old brasses of the "Ancient Stirling Lodge," of Scotland. Opposite this page is reproduced one of the brasses, at the top of which appears (reverse side) a crude Ark and Dove, under which is "Redd Cros or Ark"; below this drawing are other drawings, illustrating "Knights of Malta" and "Night Templer," and probably the Royal Arch. While these brasses have been assigned a date so early as the 17th century, Brother Hughan does not concur therein; he suggests that they are mid-eighteenth century, which appears more reasonable. Thus, without dates, some evidence is indicated of an early working of the Ark ceremony. The mention of the Ark Grade in intimate connection with the old Red Cross appears to have been quite usual in the 18th century.

On a certificate issued from "the High Priest of the Grand Chapter of Knights of the Red Cross and Noachidas," held under sanction of Lodge 271 (I.C.), is "dated in Limerick 27th February, 1790, and of the Order of the Red Cross, 2326°."

In the "History and Description of the Town and Borough of Ipswich," G. R. Clarke, 1830, we find (Pages 116-117) a paragraph quoted under the date of 17th of June 1790. We reproduce in part: " . . . a person of the name of Noah Sibley, a man of some parts and oratory, established a club or society, at a house in St. Clement's, purporting to be a particular branch of Freemasonry, called the Good Samaritan, or the Ark Masons . . . their public exhibitions were attended with much ceremony in their various processions through the different streets of the town, when a model of Noah's Ark, and a variety of insignia and banners were displayed."

Another early reference to the Grade is found in the "Freemason's Magazine," for 1794 (Vol. iii, p. 147) :

"Aug. 16, Being the birthday of His Royal Highness the Duke of York, it was celebrated with all the honours of Masonry by the Order of Knights Templars resident at London, united with the Society of Antient Masons of the Diluvian Order, or Royal Ark and Mark Mariners, assembled at the Surry Tavern in the Strand, by summons from Thomas Dunckerley, Esq., Grand Master and Grand Commander of those United Orders."

Perhaps the most interesting account of the early Grade is to be found in an open letter to the editor of the "Monthly Magazine," for 1798 (Vol. vi, p. 425) :

"As a proof of this, I shall now present you with a faithful account of one of the new degrees in Free Masonry, and which has not, I believe, been noticed by any writer on that subject.

231

"The brothers of this institution are distinguished by the high-sounding appellations of The Fraternity of the Royal Ark Mariners, Mark, Mark-Master, Elected of Nine, Unknown, Fifteen, Architect, Excellent, and Super-Excellent Masons, etc., etc.

"You must observe that they profess themselves to be followers of Noah (and in ONE respect they doubtless are so. Vide Genesis IX. 21) ; therefore they call themselves Noachidae or Sons of Noah. Hence their president, who at present is Thomas Boothby Parkyns Lord Rancliffe, is dignified with the venerable title of GRAND NOAH, and the lodge where they assemble is called the Royal Ark Vessel.

"These brother mariners wear in lodge time a broad sash ribbon, representing a rain-boy, with an apron fancifully embellished with an ark, dove, etc.

"Among the other rules of this society, one is, 'That no brother shall be admitted to enter as a mariner on board a Royal Ark Vessel, for any less sum than ten shillings and six-pence for his entrance; of which sum three shillings and six-pence shall be paid to the Grand and Royal Ark Vessel for his registry, and the residue be disposed of at the discretion of the officers of the vessel.'

"Their principal place of meeting in London, is at the Surry Tavern, Surry-street, in the Strand. It is not in my power to entertain your readers with extracts from their elegant, learned, and scientific lectures. If they have any traditionary notices respecting the antediluvian state, the primitive language, or the original peopling of the different regions of the earth, it is a thousand pities they do not communicate such inestimable treasures to the world, for the clearing up of perplexing doubts and difficulties which attend those recondite subjects."

Opposite page 98, Vol. xxiv, A.Q.C., is a reproduction of the Warrant issued to Charles Sinclair in 1796, authorizing him to convene the Vessel at the Surry Tavern.

Another early reference (A.Q.C., xvii, 89) is "1790, William Boyce took all the degrees of ye Red Cross, also Royal Ark Mariners." This is from the records of the Preceptory at Bath.

There are also early references in America, but these we omit.

The Grade of Royal Ark Mariner is today worked under two authorities, other than in this country: (1) In Scotland the Grade is worked in a Lodge attached to a Royal Arch Chapter under control of Supreme Grand Royal Arch Chapter, and (2) in England it is worked in a Lodge, attached to a Mark Lodge, and under the Grand Lodge of M.M.M. of that country.

The Ritual of the Grade used by the Grand Council of The United States of America, is the same as that worked today in Scotland. The legend is of the Deluge and it is both beautiful and instructive.

The Jewel of the Grade is a Rainbow, its ends descending into water upon which rests the Ark. At the top of the rainbow is a Dove, bearing an olive-branch. The Jewel is suspended from a ribbon containing the colors of the Rainbow.

This was the 11° of the Early Grand Rite, and is sometimes known as the Knights of the Ark, the Ark and Dove, and other similar names. It is the first degree of the Series, known as the "Red" or "Royal Arch" series. With it was coupled the degrees of Fugitive Mark, Link and Chain, Wrestle, Scarlet Cord, and Brotherly Love. The three principal officers represent Noah, Papheth, and Shem. The legend is built around Noah and the Ark of Refuge, the signs, words, and grips all having some connection with that event.

This degree is well known in the British Isles, where it is under the control of recognized Masonic bodies. It appears to be a remnant of the old "operative" work, probably built up about the 18th century by genuine operative Masons in the north of England, who were anxious to have some method of distinguishing the operative from the speculative Mason. The Ark Mariner relates to the deluge and the subject matter is taken direct from the Holy Bible.

One of the features of the degree is the use of a stone instead of the V.S.L. on which the obligation is taken. There is no deep teaching in the degree, although it is a beautiful degree. It was formerly taken under the wing of the Grand Mark Lodge of England, June 21, 1871. The degree was not inherent in the Mark at the time of the formation of Grand Mark Lodge, but it was worked continuously in certain Mark Lodges during the whole life of the Grand Mark Lodge, consequently we find the Mark degree associated with the Royal Ark Mariner degree in a separate lodge opened for the purpose of conferring it. In Scotland, the degree is closely allied with the Cryptic degrees, and in the United States it is under the control of the Grand Council Allied Masonic Degrees. At one time the degree was under the control of a Sovereign College in the United States, which chartered six lodges of Royal Ark Mariners; two of these still remain, one in Maine, the other in New York, but both are now under control of the Grand Council of Allied Masonic Degrees.

Royal Companion: The 2° of the True Kindred: (See Hero or Heroine of Jericho; see True Kindred.)

Royal Court: A degree of the Tall Cedars of Lebanon.

Royal, Exalted and Religious Military Order of Masonic Knights Templar: (See United Religious and Military Orders of the Temple and of St. John of Jerusalem, Palestine, Rhodes and Malta.)

Royal Grand Conclave of Scotland: From its foundation in 1810, it claimed jurisdiction over ALL the HIGHER degrees worked in Scotland. When the Supreme Grand Chapter of Scotland was formed in 1817, it divided jurisdiction as follows:

Supreme Grand Royal Arch Chapter: Master Past the Chair, Excellent Master, Super Excellent Master, Royal Arch, Mark Mason, Ark Mason, Link and Wrestle, Babylonian Pass or Red Cross of Daniel, Royal Order of Prussian Blue, and High Priest.

Knight Templar: Black Mark, Mediterranean Pass, Knight of Malta, Knight of the Holy Grave, Knight of Patmos, Knight of the Red Cross of Constantine, Knight Templar.

Royal Master: The 1° of the Cryptic system, 8° of the American Rite. It is very popular in the United States because of its beautiful Craft symbolism and some very fine passages of ritual. It was 17° of the Early Grand Rite and conferred in a lodge of Excellent Masons; some of the test questions are those used in the American Royal Master; the candidate represents Adoniram; the legend is that of the *American* Royal Master.

The degree is also found in the English system where its teaching and ritual are quite similar to American working, from whence it originally came. The degree is here controlled by the Grand Councils of the Cryptic degrees. The apron of the degree is black, edged with red.

233

Royal Order of Heredom: (See Heredom, Royal Order of.)

Royal Order of Heredom and the Rosy Cross: (See Order, Royal Order of Heredom and Rosy Cross.)

Royal Order of Jesters: (See Jesters, Royal Order of.)

Royal Order or Prussian Blue: Due to the Irish Freemasons, and the Early Grand Encampment at Dublin; these degrees attained popularity in Scotland; they were an illogical association of Red Cross Masonry with Templarism, a situation which prevails even in our own United States.

The words "Libertas" and "Veritas" are often engraved above or below the Cross which appears on their seals. It must have been called the "Red Cross of Daniel" because, as the ritual says, "Daniel was an instrument in God's hands, by which Cyrus was urged to the restoration of the Jews, and the rebuilding of the Temple at Jerusalem."

Royal Order of Scotland: (See Order: Royal Order of Scotland.)

Royal Priest: The 5° of the Initiated Brothers of Asia.

Royal Secret: (See Sublime Prince of the Royal Secret; see "Mother Word" of the Early Grand Rite of Scotland.)

Royal Society: Not a Masonic Society, but composed of many active Freemasons. Out of the study of Alchemy and the Science, there came such organizations as the Alchemists and the Rosicrucians. One of these groups carried a somewhat more dignified title, yet carried on the same studies; it was called the "Royal Society," and was established by Charles II for the improvement of natural science. Many of its earlier members were Freemasons, including Dr. Desaguliers, Martin Clare, and shall we add Sir Christopher Wren?

Russian Rite: (See Melesino Rite.)

Sacred Arch: The 6° of the Rite of Memphis.

Sacred Arch, Knight of the: (See Knight of the Sacred Arch.)

Sacred Temple: (See Order of the Sacred Temple.)

Sage of Truth, Knight of: (See Knight of Sage of Truth.)

Sages, Academy of: A Swedish Order of about 1770, founded by Ashmole in London.

Sanctified Authorities: The 3° of the Druid Order; also known as the "Druids."

Scald Miserable Masons: Opponents of Freemasonry during its early history, attempted to deride Masonic processions by holding "mock" processions, dressing themselves in ridiculous costumes, and parading the principal streets. There are several old prints which show the character of these mock processions. The last procession was in 1745, for in the meantime the Grand Lodge prohibited public procession, so that today, in England, a procession of Freemasons is rarely seen.

Scandinavian Knights: Of this society we have been unable to find information.

Scandinavian Rite: Rebold refers to this Rite, founded in 1772, which was probably a term applied to the Hermetic Rite.

Scarlet Cord, Order of: There is a sister organization of the degree of Secret Monitor; it is called the "Royal Order of the Scarlet Cord," and it is said to have been "discovered in a book printed in Amsterdam in 1770." Its meetings are "conclaves," held quarterly at the time the sun enters the constellations of Aquarius, Taurus, Leo, and Scorpio.

234

Schroeder's Rite: (See Rite of Schroeder.)

Sciots: (See Ancient Egyptian Order of Sciots.)

Scotch Apprentice: A degree of the Zinnendorf Rite.

Scotch Knight: The sixth step in the Order of the Illuminati; this with the Scotch Novice completed the whole of the "interior edifice" which was revealed to those who were not permitted to go beyond the "concealed degrees." (See Illuminati.)

Scotch Knight of Perfection: The 14° of the A. & A. Rite in England.

Scotch Ladies of Mt. Tabor: An androgynous French Order, founded in 1810, using a quasi-Masonic ritual; it had a Grand Master and a Grand Mistress; it dissolved at the time of the French Revolution.

Scotch Master: The degree appears in several Masonic systems; it is in the Adonhiramite Rite; the Clerks of Relaxed Observance; the Philalethes; the Reformed Rite, and doubtless in others. In the Rite of Melesino was a Scotch Master degree, also termed the "Knight's Degree"; it was the 5° of the Rite.

Scotch Novice: The fifth step in the Order of the Illuminati; this, with the Scotch Knight degree, completed the whole of the "interior edifice," which was conferred upon all, and which was generally regarded (by those who did not know) as the ne plus ultra of Illuminatism. (See Illuminati.)

Scotch Order, or Second Order of Rose Croix: A degree of the Modern French Rite.

Scotch Philosophical Rite: This was a Hermetic Order, founded at Paris by Dr. Boileau. Rebold says it was practiced by some of the lodges in Belgium; it was founded about 1776 and had six degrees, the last of which was the Knight of the Golden Fleece. (See Rite: Philosophic Scotch.)

Scotland: (See Early Grand Rite of Scotland; see Royal Order of Scotland.)

Scottish Elder Master: The ritual is one of the earliest Scotch Master ceremonies we have record of (circa 1810) and, while the Ramsay reference is to be disregarded as concerning a myth long since exploded, the Grade does belong to the Rectified Rite and survives today under the Great Priory of Helvetia, where it consists of two ceremonies. The two Saint Andrew's Grades are also worked by the *Maitres Ecossais de Saint-Andre "Renovation, Chapitre No. 1,"* under the *Grande Lodge Nationale Independente et Reguliere pour la France et les Colonies Francaises.* The Deputy Grand Master has command over the Grades, which were secured from Switzerland sometime ago.

Scottish Master Ecossais: (See Ecossais.)

Scottish Master of St. Andrew and Perfect Master of St. Andrew: One of the degrees of the C.B.C.S. (See Knights Beneficent of the Holy City.)

Scottish Master of the Sacred Vault of James VI: This degree resembles that of the Select Master (the old form of the Royal Arch of Enoch), and has now become the 13° of the Scottish Rite. The Stuart dynasty adopted the Masonic emblem of the Beehive, as the symbol of resurrection. Our English brethren dropped the emblem because of its Stuart connection, but it has been retained in the American system as a symbol of Industry.

Scottish Masters: Tradition tells us that superior workmen from the group at York made frequent journeys to Scotland, where they deliberated with others, and because of the knowledge which they received on these occasions, were termed Masters of the "Valle" or Scottish Masters. They were regarded as the most learned members of the fraternity.

Scottish Rite: The term commonly applied in the United States to the degrees of the Ancient and Accepted Scottish Rite; these include the 4°-33°. While the Rite has its three symbolic degrees of Entered Apprentice, Fellow Craft, and Master Mason, they are forbidden by Grand Lodges of the United States and Canada, to practice them; they are quite different in general character from those of the American or York Rite, or those in England. The 33° is conferred only upon the recommendation of the active head, or heads of the organization in each state. In the British Isles, the Rite is referred to by the name "Ancient and Accepted Rite." The word "Scottish" is a misnomer for the degrees, for they are not of Scottish origin, but probably French. The Rite is popular in the Latin American countries because there is little competition from other Rites.

Scottish Trinitarian: (See Prince of Mercy.)

Searcher After Truth: Also known as "Seekers After Truth." It was founded in 1773 and was a mixture of the Swedenborg system with that of Paschalis' Rite of High Priests; it had two classes—lower and higher. (See Philalethes.)

Second Architect: A degree in the Rite Elect of Truth.

Second Chapter of Rose Croix: It is said to consist of "a number of historical documents."

Secret Master: The 4° of the Ancient and Accepted Rite; a degree of the Rite of Perfection; one of the degrees of the Helvetic Rite, in which the candidate is replaced for the missing craftsman, being selected from his twelve associates.

Secret Monitor: The degree is similar to the 1° of the Secret Monitor as worked by the Grand Conclave, and is associated with the story of David and Jonathan. It bears witness to the split which occurred during the early days of the organization of the Grand Conclave of the Secret Monitor. It is the only degree in English Freemasonry under control of two bodies. The jewel is the Hackle, suspended from a Crown; on the ribbon, above the jewel, is a bow.

The Order works under a Grand Conclave of the Order, in contrast to the degree worked by the Allied Masonic Degrees. Only Master Masons are admitted; there are two degrees and a Chair Degree. Attached to the Order is the Order of the Scarlet Cord which has no less than seven degrees. It is very popular in England; it is said to have had an American origin.

As early as 1778 there was a society in Holland known as the Order of Jonathan and David, which probably furnished the germ for the origin of the American Grade now known as Secret Monitor. In his "Catalogue," Kloss gives the title of a book published in 1778 at Amsterdam which gives the statutes and formula of reception of the early Dutch society. This Dutch society became Masonic, no doubt, as there is mention of it in connection with Freemasonry in that country at a date just later than the above mentioned. At page 162, Vol. v, A.Q.C., there is, in addition to other Dutch Masonic data, the following statement: "From the foregoing documents it is not possible to determine whence they issued or derived their authority. The names, however, of De La Garde, Bergh, Dalmencourt, De Consalvin, are to be found on old documents and certificates issued by a Chapter named "Jesus," and another called "Jonathan and David," of Avignon, France, in 1788.

"The Bro. Bolt who was thus authorized to erect Chapters of the Rosy Cross, was also empowered to constitute Chapters of the United Orders of Jonathan and David, and Jesus Christ, by a document of which the following is a part:

"'Les Grand-Maitres plenipotentiares des ordres fraternals et confederes de Jonathan et David et Jesus Christ, au nom et sous l'auspice et la tolerance mysterieuse de Sa Saintete, Pius Pontife Souverain! Magistre Supreme at Oecumenique! Serviteurs de Dieu! par la clemence divine. . . .'"

The birth of the Masonic Grade of Secret Monitor appears to have occurred in the United States, where it was worked for many years under various titles—"Brotherly Love," "Jonathan and David" and finally "Secret Monitor." Its first appearance seems to have been just after the conclusion of the War between the States—say 1866 circa.

There is a tradition that the Grade was created by two Freemasons, during the War, whose Masonic membership brought them together and saved the life of one of them. One was a soldier of the Union and the other of the Confederacy. However, facts are wanting and this tradition cannot be authenticated.

The Grade was one of the many so-called "side degrees" which were worked throughout America during the last half of the 19th century. It was usually conferred—by communication—by one Mason upon another, without fee and no record being made of the event. Too, many Lecturers conferred the Grade and thus it spread into most of the States.

Sometime near the close of the 19th century, Dr. Issachar Zacharie carried the Grade from America over to England. There, a Body was created to administer over the Grade, termed a Supreme Council. The Grade was rearranged into three ceremonies: (1) That of Induction, (2) The Assembly of Princes, (3) The Installation of a Supreme Ruler.

Early records of the working of the Grade are scarce in this country, due to the fact that it was worked as a "side degree" and no Minutes were kept. However, in Scotland, the Early Grand Rite secured a version of this American Grade and incorporated it into their multifarious System. It there formed the 16th degree and was worked under the title "Order of Brotherly Love." A copy of the Ritual of that Rite (dated 1890), in the Archives of the Grand Council of the Allied Masonic Degrees of the United States of America, shows a very weak and insignificant Ritual-ceremony, hardly worthy of consideration.

The ritual now employed by the Grand Council in this country is an original text which was used here in 1896. It is a very instructive ceremony and based, for the most part, upon the love which we are taught existed between Jonathan and David. It teaches a beautiful lesson in friendship and fidelity.

The Jewel of the Grade is a hackle surmounted by a crown, in gold. This is worn suspended from a ribbon, black in the centre, bordered on either side with white, the ribbon being surmounted by a gold bow.

The apron of the Grade is black, edged with white border. In the centre a hackle is embroidered in white while on the flap is an ear, likewise embroidered in white.

237

When a Collar is worn, it should be of purple silk, approximately four inches in width. However, in this country the Collar, or the Apron, are never worn, save when a Council is fully exemplifying the Grade.

With the Secret Monitor is allied the Royal Masonic Order of Masonic Knights of the Scarlet Cord, in which there are said ot be seven degrees. Only those who have attained the three degrees of Secret Monitor are eligible.

Secret Societies: Freemasonry does not class itself as a secret society, but as a society with secrets; There were at one time, and may be some now, whose *membership* is secret—these are *secret* societies, but today the names of all members are known to those who care to know; and the secrets consist only in some words and grips which are only of use to members in making themselves known.

Secret Vault: The 7° of the Rite of Memphis.

Secular Templars: (See Rite of Strict Observance.)

Select Architect: (See Ancient Free and Accepted Architects.)

Select Mason of 27: One of the degrees listed by Moses Cohen in his capacity as Grand Inspector General in a certificate issued him, November 9, 1790, by Abraham Jacobs in Jamaica. The degree has much in common with the degree of Select Master of the Cryptic Rite—9°. The Select Master was also a degree in the Early Grand Rite of Scotland. The degree closely resembles a degree of the Scottish Rite, that of Intimate Secretary, the legend being the same.

Select Master: The 18° of the Early Grand Rite, worked in a lodge of Excellent Masons; the candidate represents Izabud (Zabud). The legend is that of its American counterpart and includes the deposit.

Sepulchre, Order of: There are several Masonic rites which include the Order of the Holy Sepulchre; the Roman Church also has its Order of the Holy Sepulchre—not connected in any way with the Masonic Order.

The proceedings of the Red Cross of Constantine, U.S.A., 1913, contains an article taken from the Westminster (England) Gazette:

What is the oldest order in existence? The claim is made for that of the Holy Sepulchre, the Grand Officership of which has just been conferred by the Pope on a member of the Irish Nationalist Party, Sir Thomas Grattan Esmond. It appears that no date, or the name of the Founder can be assigned to the Order of the Holy Sepulchre although there is a legendary tradition that traces its origin to the time of Charlemagne.

In the midst of the last century, however, when the Latin Patriarchate of Jerusalem was re-established, the office of Grand Master of the Order was transferred to it by Pope Pius IX, who for many years later, in 1868, created by statute three ranks of the Order, (1) Grand Cross, (2) Commander, and (3) Knight. The costume is a white cloak with the Cross of Jerusalem in red enamel.

The Pope is Grand Master of the Order.

The Duke of Kent, in 1811, granted authority for the establishment of a "Conclave of the Knights of the Holy Temple and Sepulchre" in Scotland, by virtue of his being the Grand Master of Knights Templar in England. (See Knight of Holy Sepulchre.)

Seraphim, Order of Swedish: This Order, formed in Sweden in 1334, was resuscitated about 1748, limiting its membership to 24 knights, not including members of the Royal Family, who are to be considered members without petitioning.

238

Serpent, Knight of the: (See Knight of the Serpent.)

Serpent, Knight of the Brazen: (See Knight of the Brazen Serpent.)

Service to Masonry: (See Order of Service to Masonry.)

Serving Brethren: One of the Classes in the Order of the Temple (12°). In some of the continental bodies, there are admitted a limited number of brethren, called "serving brethren" who do the menial tasks connected with the operation of the building and the conferring of the degrees.

Seven Golden Candlesticks: A side degree, worked in the U.S.A. about 1870. (See Rite of Seven Degrees.)

Sharemkhu, Princesses of: (See Ancient Egyptian Order Princesses of Sharemkhu.)

Shrine: (See Ancient Accepted Order of Nobles of the Mystic Shrine.)

Side Degrees: The name given to degrees once conferred in lodges and chapters, after a lodge had been closed, and which had nothing to do with Masonic Rites or Degrees; they taught nothing not found in legitimate Freemasonry; some of them were humorous, although they professed to teach a good lesson. Their obligations required little but secrecy, when it was apparent little secrecy was required. They proved to be Masonic parasites and most of them have disappeared. In some instances, one or more of these degrees has been made the principal feature of a group not connected with Freemasonry, but national in character.

Some of these degrees, and we do not intend to list all, are: Belief and Confidence; Eureka Hiatus; Knights of Three Kings; Cedars of Lebanon; Seven Golden Candlesticks; The Cable-Tow; Order of the Yellow Dog; Missouri Hound Dog.

Sidonian: A degree of the Tall Cedars of Lebanon.

Sigma Mu Sigma: Sigma Mu Sigma was established at Tri-State College, Angelo, Ind., on Good Friday, 1921, by three Knights Templar who, with nine other Master Masons, had received a charter of incorporation from the State of Indiana. When a national Council of Sigma Mu Sigma was formed in 1924 it acquired a charter from the United States Government in the District of Columbia, and during the five years which followed, nine collegiate chapters were established. In 1928, the fraternity was admitted to Junior membership in the National Interfraternity Conference, having achieved the highest interfraternity scholastic rating. In 1929, membership requirements were changed so as to include sons and brothers of Master Masons, but with the depression which followed, like the Square and Compass Club, it was found impossible to maintain its chapters even with the broadened membership requirement.

Then came, on August 3, 1952, the union of Square and Compass and Sigma Mu Sigma, the consolidation taking place at the Masonic Temple, Angelo, Ind. The late Dr. Harry K. Eversull was elected the first Grand President, and Dr. William Moseley Brown, of Virginia, the first Grand Secretary.

There is a ritual which attempts to inculcate a complete understanding of the purpose of initiation and the various rites and degrees conferred by the Masonic fraternity. The governing order of the fraternity is the Grand Chapter, which meets in annual convocation and is made up of representatives from each active and alumni chapter, all of whom are required to be Master Masons. There is an official magazine—The Azureor. There is also an esoteric publication—The Sigma Mu Sigma.

Dr. Brown writes us that the organization "now admits DeMolays and others not necessarily members of the Masonic fraternity, but they have to be sponsored and recommended by Master Masons in good standing."

Silver Head: The Fifth Order of Melchizedek.

Silver Trowel: (See Order of the Silver Trowel.)

Siri: An Egyptian Secret society; it means "secret," or "magic." It is found in the Sudan and Senegambia. It has for its object the study of the occult, and was introduced into Africa by the Arabs. It contains many of the mysteries of the Hebrews (Cabalistic) and touches upon Astronomy. (See A.Q.C. XII 66-93.)

Sisters of the Guild: An androgynous order of 1820.

Social Mason: The degree is referred to in Miscellanea Vol. I, p. 203.

Societas Rosicruciana in Anglia (Also Scotia, and U.S.A.): (See Rosicrucian Society.)

Societas Rosicruciana in Civitatibus Foederatis: (See Rosicrucian Society.)

Society of Blue Friars: (See Blue Friars, Society of.)

Society of the Trowel, or Societa della Cucchiara: A non-Masonic organization established at Florence, Italy, about 1512. It was composed of many learned inhabitants of that city—although not Masonic.

Society of United Irishmen: This organization was prohibited from meeting as an open political society in Ireland about 1790, and it became a secret society in many places, particularly Northern Ireland, where its members concealed their gatherings under the cloak of meeting as lodges of Freemasons, because Freemasonry had a name for not engaging in plots, and in politics, and such meetings had been free from Military and Civic intervention.

Socius: The 6° of the Rite of Strict Observance.

Socrates, Order of: In 1766, the Order of Socrates was founded in Paris by one Chastanien, Master of a lodge in that city; a similar organization was organized in London, but it seems to have been succeeded by a newer and more popular rite—The Rite of Swedenborg.

Sojourners' Club: To be distinguished from the National Sojourners (a military society of Freemasons), for this was a club formed in New Mexico to give assistance to military forces who were Freemasons.

Sojourners, National: (See National Sojourners.)

Solar Spiritual Order of the Silver Head and Golden Star: The Fifth Order of Melchizedek.

Soldier: A degree of the Rite of African Architects.

Soldiers of the Crucifixion: (See Militia Ecclesia Evangelica.)

Solomon Order of 11: The name given to one of the trade guilds in France; members were known as "compagnons" (companions), which is the same as the French 2° of Freemasonry.

Sons of Noah: (See Allied Masonic Degrees.)

Sons of Solomon: The group existed as early as 1640; it is said to have contained the legend of the builder, later introduced into Freemasonry in France.

Sophists, Holy Order of: Rebold refers to the Rite, which he says was founded in 1801 by Covelier of Treues.

Sovereign College of Allied Masonic Degrees: The original organization of the Allied Degrees in the United States. It was founded at Richmond,

Va., in 1890, and later removed to Norway, Maine; and still later its head-quarters have been wherever the secretarial officer lives.

It controls the Ark Mariner, Secret Monitor, St. Lawrence the Martyr, Tyler of Solomon, Knight of Constantinople, Holy and Blessed Order of Wisdom, Trinitarian Degree of St. John of Patmos, and has authority to confer an academic degree—Doctor of Universal Freemasonry. It was organized for the purpose of uniting under one Masonic government a number of side degrees (see Side Degrees) hitherto unorganized. Its object was two-fold—to work with proper rituals such degrees as were, from their importance or beauty, worthy of propagation; and to lay on the shelf such degrees possessed by it, as were merely absurdities. It merged with the Grand Council of A.M.D. July 18, 1933. (See Allied Masonic Degrees.)

Sovereign Commander of the Temple: The 27° of the A.A.S.R.; 44° of the Rite of Mizraim.

Sovereign Fellow: An honor conferred by the Sovereign College of Allied Masonic Degrees.

Sovereign Grand Commander of the Temple: A degree required for admission into the Sublime Degrees of Sovereign of Sovereigns.

Sovereign Grand Inspector General: The 33° of the Scottish Rite; there are two types—active and honorary. The actives control the government of the Rite.

The 33° symbolizes the number of years spent by the Saviour on earth; it has few historical allusions, being more administrative; its jewel is the black, double-headed Eagle of Prussia. It is the only degree conferred by the American Supreme Councils. Originally the Rite was a system of 25°, but extended by the Supreme Council formed at Charleston, S. C., in 1801, to a 33° system, although the degree was said to have been instituted in 1786.

Sovereign Magus: A degree of the Rite, Clerks of Relaxed Observance.

Sovereign Mistress: The 12° of the Rite of Adoption. (See Mistress.)

Sovereign Prince Adept, Chief of the Grand Consistory: A degree in the Rite of Perfection.

Sovereign Prince Rose-Croix: The 18° of the Rite of Perfection or Harodim.

Sovereign Sanctuary of America: In 1862, Marconis instituted the Sovereign Sanctuary out of the Ancient and Primitive Rite, reducing the system to a 33° system.

Speculative Masonry: "Speculative" Masonry became synonomous with Freemasonry in the 18th century; it is used, in a sense, as the opposite of "operative," or "practical" Masonry. It is a system of morals veiled in allegory and illustrated by symbols. The original society was composed of operative Masons, men who worked at the building trade. By a natural infiltration, those who were not active workmen began to acquire membership, and, later, control. Those who worked only in a "speculative capacity" were termed Speculative Masons.

Spiritual Knighthood: The 7° and last of the Melesino Rite, which was also called the "Grand Priest or Spiritual Knighthood."

Square and Compass: The Square and Compass originated as a club of Master Masons at Washington-Lee University, Lexington, Va., in 1897. They were incorporated by the State of Virginia May 12, 1917, as the "Square and Compass Fraternity." During the next eleven years there were formed fifty-seven collegiate squares (chapters) and had initiated more than 5,000 members. Because of the depression following World War I, many of the Squares became inactive.

In December, 1950, a convention was held in Richmond, Va., at which time the name Square and Compass-Sigma Alpha Chi was adopted and charters were issued to four Squares. On August 3, 1952, the group was united with the Sigma Mu Sigma Fraternity at a meeting held in the Masonic Temple in Angelo, Ind. (See Sigma Mu Sigma.)

Square Clubs: There are to be found in industry, the professions, and schools, organizations known as "Square Clubs," which is another method of referring to groups of Freemasons, who have not assumed the name "Masonic," which, in some jurisdictions, is forbidden.

Square Hams: An association made up of Freemasons who operate radio stations; radio amateurs.

Squire Novice: A degree of the Knights Beneficent of the Holy City.

St. Andrew: Apprentice and Fellow of St. Andrews is the 4° of the Swedish Rite; it is identical with the Secret Elu of the French Rite. Favorite of St. Andrew is the 9° of that Rite, known as Knight of the Purple Collar. The Grand Scottish Knight of St. Andrew is discussed under Knight of St. Andrew.

St. John the Evangelist: There are several "St. John" degrees. One by the above name is to be found in the Red Cross of Constantine; the 8° of the Swedish Rite is "Favorite Brother of St. John"; St. John of Jerusalem is the Knight of St. John.

St. John of Jerusalem is the name given the Order of the Templars in Scotland; its official title was "Conclave of the Knights of the Holy Temple and Sepulchre, and of St. John of Jerusalem." Its head, in 1811, was the Duke of Kent, who, at the same time, was Supreme Grand Master of the English Templars.

And there is a Catholic Order of St. John of Jerusalem and Malta, which refers to itself as "The Roman Catholic and Aristocratic Order, etc."

The Zinnendorf Rite referred to itself as "St. John's Masonry."

St. Lawrence (Laurence) the Martyr: One of the degrees under the control of the Allied Masonic Degrees; the legend of the degree has nothing to do with Freemasonry, but is well known to every student of the mediaeval legends of the Saints. The lesson taught is Fortitude. It appears to be a piece of operative ritual brought from Lancashire, and originally worked into a degree to enable a "genuine operative" to be distinguished from a "speculative." The jewel is a gridiron—and here we have the expression of placing one on the "grid."

The Grade, so we are informed, was worked in England two centuries ago and was an operative working which was perpetuated. Little of an authentic nature can be said concerning this. Extremely rare indeed are records of the Grade and as yet no real early Minute has appeared. How old the Grade is, no one appears to know. In 1884, when the Grand Council of the Allied Masonic Degrees of England and Wales was formed, it was taken under their control. Naturally, it was worked sometime before that date, as it came into this country prior to 1884, by way of England. The legend relates the martyrdom of Saint Lawrence, who was afterwards canonized for his fidelity and Christian attributes.

While the ceremony relates neither to the First nor Second Temple, nor to Masonic Chivalry, it is interesting in its simplicity and has a little-heard-of-legend, which is pleasing to examine and has merit. The very peculiarity of the Grade marks it as different and is perhaps the ground upon which the operative origin is claimed. If this Grade was really worked in Lancashire, which was near to Grand Lodge activity, it does seem that records would be available and something a bit more definite obtainable.

The Jewel of the Grade is a silver Gridiron, suspended from a ribbon, orange in the centre and royal blue on either side.

St. Paul, Knight of: One of the Orders, or degrees, conferred by the Order of Templars in Scotland; it was the first of the Templar system.

Stability Ritual: One of the rituals permitted in England which appears to be very popular.

Steinmetzen, The: The guild system started in Germany about the 11th century, and by the beginning of the 13th century had become so strong that two of the successive emperors decreed the total suppression of all such bodies. The decrees were not obeyed. Emperor Rudolph reinstated the guilds. The earliest copy of their Laws dates from 1459; they were in the custody of the Masters, and it was forbidden to copy them. They had a benevolent fund from which unemployed, or sick, might draw, but they had to return the funds when able to resume work. There were three classes: Masters, Fellows, and Apprentices. An Apprentice served five years; then he became a Fellow or Journeyman and spent a year traveling. On setting forth he was provided with a Mark. There were two types of Steinmetzen. One had only passwords and signs, or grips; the other had written indentures, and were known as "Word Masons" or "Writing Masons."

In erecting the great cathedral at Wurzburg, they erected two large pillars at the front, named as those in front of Solomon's Temple.

Stone-Cutters of Strasburg: An organization of German workmen, formed on Masonic lines. It had five "grand lodges," located at Cologne, Strasburg, Vienna, Zurich, and Magdeburg; it had subordinates in France, Hesse, Swabia, Thuringia, Franconia, and Bavaria. Their laws were revised in 1459 and printed in 1464.

Strict Observance: A schismatic group of the Rite of Strict Observance was called "Clerks of the Strict Observance." The Rite had seven degrees. (See Rite of Strict Observance.)

Sublime Degree of Sovereign of Sovereigns: Listed as a part, if not a full degree, in the Order of the Temple of Christ. Candidates were required to have had the degrees of "Triple Cross of Kadosh," "Grand Inquisitor or Elected of Truth," "Prince of the Royal Secret," "Grand Inspector 33°," and "Sovereign Grand Commander of the Temple." Initiation consisted of "journeys." It was one of the "vengeance" degrees, involving as characters, Philip, Pope Clement, and DeMolay.

Sublime Degrees: There are many degrees which bear the title "Sublime" as a portion of their titles.

The 3° of the regular Masonic Rite is referred to as the "Sublime Degree of Master Mason." In the Royal Arch degree, we find candidates "exalted to the Most Sublime degree of the Royal Arch."

Sublime Ecossais Mason: The grade of the *Heavenly Jerusalem* in the Illumines of Stockholm.

Sublime Elect: The 5° Rite of Adoption. Two apartments are necessary for receptions, or the hangings are disposed so as to be able to change the colors promptly either by turning the panels or the drapery. For the first point of reception the hangings are green sprinkled with golden stars, with gold lace and fringe. There are nine lights, of which seven are together and two separate; to these are added three lamps having three beaks, suspended, two in Asia, one in Europe, on the side of Africa. For the second point the usual hangings are poppy red with gold lace and fringe. Upon the altar is a vase burning spirits of wine. The Tableau or painting represents Bethulia with its High Priest and scattered dwellings; Judith going to the Camp with her servant who carries a sack; Judith cutting off the head of Holophernes (strong captain) in his tent. The clothing of the President, or High Priest, is a long white robe; large red and green girdle going twice around, the ends of the left side reaching the ground, but whilst at labor, thrown over the left shoulder. On the breast is a gold plate having upon it D.V. (discretion and verity); it is suspended by four chains which pass over the neck and under the arms. On the forehead is a white linen cloth, with a yellow band inscribed "Kadosh Adonai" (consecrated to the Lord). The apron is white, doubled with poppy red and green border. It may be embroidered with attributes, as Chisel for Mistress; Globe for Sublime Elect; Sword, Lance, Dissevered Head and Sack. The Sash for Sisters is of red moire, scarfwise from left to right, suspended to which is a sword with a green rosette, over the breast are five stars of five points and on the shoulder is a white rosette. The jewel is a chisel and mallet, sword and trowel with gold wedding ring suspended from the left breast by a blue ribbon.

The 11° of the A.A.S. Rite, where the avengers were given their reward.

Sublime Elect of Truth: The 4° of the Order of Christ.

Sublime Knight Elected: The 8° of the Lodge of Perfection, Scotch Masonry, and the 11° in the catalog of that system; it is termed "Twelve Illustrious Knights," or "Master in Israel." The lesson is that the faithful brother shall be rewarded.

Sublime Master: The 14° of the Early Grand Rite of Scotland; the degree is also known as the "Wrestler," or "Jacob's Wrestle." During the degree Chapter xxxii, 24-32 of Genesis is read; the degree consists of little but an obligation.

The 5° of the Ancient and Accepted Rite. The ceremonial of the degree has reference to the entombment of the architect, erected secretly for the purpose.

Sublime Master of the Great Work: The 30° of the Ancient and Primitive Rite, or the 90° of the original Rite. The degree, when fully worked, represents the great Egyptian Judgment as found in the Book of the Dead, and is the source of Albert Pike's 31° of the A.A.S. Rite. The candidate concludes the degree by being triumphantly received in the Temple of Truth, as an Adept, who by the practice of virtue, has rendered himself eternal, a demi-God.

Sublime Masters, Circle of Light: (See Circle of Light.)

Sublime Masters of the Luminous Ring: The 10° of the Philosophic Scotch Rite.

Sublime Phreemasons: The 5° of the Primitive and Original Rite. (See Blue Brothers.)

Sublime Philosopher: A degree in the Philalethes.

244

Sublime Prince of the Royal Secret: The 32° of the Ancient and Accepted Scottish Rite; the lesson conveyed in one jurisdiction of the Rite is "Fidelity" even unto death. In another jurisdiction we find the degree entirely philosophic, placing bfore the candidate the better part of the teachings of the ancient religions, dwelling particularly upon the fact that each religion had within itself a secret doctrine which was not taught the public at large; now is explained the great Camp of Masonry, and the duties of all Masonic groups in carrying on the Crusade for Light, Toleration and Brotherhood.

The story in the former jurisdiction is somewhat different where it develops into a drama, or an allegorical representation of the actual ceremonies of the mediaeval ages carried out at the elevation of an aspirant for knighthood; proof of the valor and fidelity of the candidate was required.

Super Excellent Mason: The 21° of the Early Grand Rite. The degree is a preparation for the Royal Arch degree and is founded on incidents connected with the leadership of Moses and the second leadership of Joshua; it was formed according to tradition to enable those entitled to share in the work of rebuilding the Temple, the signs and words admitting them to the Sanhedrin at Jerusalem, the signs and words being those given at the Veils.

One of the Helvetic Rite degrees, closely akin to that of the Royal Arch, and particularly the first section, which is like the work found in American chapters. It closely followed that of Excellent Masons.

In England the degree is controlled by the Council of Cryptic Degrees which "brings the story of the first Temple down to the time of the threatened destruction." The jewel of the degree is a white enameled triangle with the point downward—the triangle of the Preserver—which the Rite is.

Super Excellent Master: This is the third of the Council of Royal and Select Master series (Cryptic Rite) and the 10° of the American Rite system. During the early history of Freemasonry in the United States, the name was given to a section which preceded the Royal Arch degree and which involved the passing of the Veils, a ceremony still in use in Scotland.

The degree has little connection in symbolism with the degrees of Royal Master and Select Master with which it is associated; it has been revised in recent years and has become one of the most dramatic rituals of Freemasonry. Its legend tells the story of the faithless Zedekiah, his contempt for Jeremiah, the prophet of God; his arraignment before Nebuchadnezzar, and his final punishment. It teaches that when men forget God, they invariably reap the results of those who sin, and who labor not in the cause of Truth.

Super Fellow Erector: A degree of the old operative Rite. The candidate is taught to place his own mark upon the stone, also a constructional mark, so that the Erector may know where it is to be placed and in what direction.

Superimposed Upon the Craft: Such degrees are those of the First Class of the Rite of Elected Truth; the Knights Adept; and the Perfect Master.

Superintendent of Buildings: The 8° of the Ancient and Accepted Rite.

Superior: A degree in Bahrdt's Rite.

Supreme Conclave True Kindred: Controls the three degrees of Hero or Heroine of Jericho (Royal Companion); Good Samaritan (Knight of the Lady of the Cross). (See Order of True Kindred.)

Supreme Councils of Sovereign Grand Inspectors General: Governing bodies for the degrees of the Scottish Rite.

In Ireland, the Supreme Council 33°, was formed in 1824. The Grand

245

Chapter of Prince Masons of Ireland is more or less under the control of this Supreme Council, since all candidates for the Rose Croix must have their names submitted to the Supreme Council. The only degrees conferred are: Knight of the Sun; Philosophical Mason (Knight Kadosh 30°); Grand Inspector 31°; Prince of the Royal Secret 32°; Grand Inspector General 33°.

In the United States there are two Supreme Councils, denominated "Southern" and "Northern." The former constitutes all the States of the Union lying south of the Ohio and west of the Mississippi Rivers. There are nine or ten spurious organizations claiming to be Supreme Councils in the U.S.A.

Suspending Cross of Babylon: A degree in the Early Grand Rite of Scotland. (See Prince of Babylon.)

Swedenborg Rite: The Rite was established in Paris in 1783 by the Marquis de Thome; he named it the Rite of Swedenborg, presumably because some of Swedenborg's religious ideas were incorporated in it. (See Primitive and Original Rite.)

Swedish Rite: (See Rite: Swedish.)

Sweet Brier: Mentioned in the "Ladies' Friend" (Mich.), 1866. An adoptive degree, better known as the "Three Buds of the Sweet Brier." Its recipients were the wives, widows, mothers, sisters and daughters of Master Masons. Its emblem was the sweet-brier.

Sword of Bunker Hill: Illinois is the home of an organization known as Sword of Bunker Hill, which is acquiring a rapid growth throughout the Middle West. It was established in 1912 in Oregon, Ill., by Brother Frank G. Taylor, who was, at the time, superintendent of schools at that place. From their official publications we learn the object of the organization:

"To promote the interest of Masonry by encouraging a more regular attendance at its meetings. To form a social and fraternal organization to perpetuate the principles of American liberty. To instill into the minds of each generation the sacrifices of our Masonic forefathers in forming our great republic. To forever inspire patriotism and loyalty by administering to every candidate for our Order the oath of allegiance to state and nation. To provide a time and place for good clean fun. To further cement our friendship and brotherly love by providing social entertainment. To contribute a portion of our initiation fee to a worthy Masonic charity."

Taylor died at Saratoga, N. Y., July 21, 1949. Before his death he had served as High Priest and District Inspector in the Grand Chapter and as Master of his Council. The first charter was issued October 15, 1912, to Liberty Hill Order, at Oregon, Ill.; next came Lincoln Park Order No. 2, in Chicago, the Orders being connected with Royal Arch Chapters. Later the requirements were changed to permit Master Masons to become members. Recent reports show that the majority of the Orders are located in Illinois, although there are others in Arkansas, Indiana, Louisiana, Missouri, New Jersey, New York, Tennessee, Wisconsin. All members are regarded as life members. The average number of initiates in recent years has been 3,000.

There is but one degree—The Order of the Sword. Local bodies are termed Orders; the national organization is termed Grand Order Sword of Bunker Hill, and it holds one meeting annually. The ritual is patriotic in character and brings to the attention of the candidate patriotic service rendered by famous Americans.

Tabernacle, Chief of the: (See Chief of Tabernacle; see Prince of Tabernacle.)

246

Table Lodge: When our ancient brethren held their meetings around the dining table, the lodge was duly opened; the Master sat at the head of a U-shaped table, with his two Wardens at the ends of the "U." The program was educational and instructive. These table lodges are still held in various parts of the country as a means of getting away from the routine.

Tall Cedars of Lebanon: The Tall Cedars of Lebanon has confined its membership largely to the Atlantic Seaboard, its various Forests being located in New Jersey, Delaware, Pennsylvania, and the District of Columbia. It was a local group confined to New Jersey until 1902, at which time Forests were established elsewhere.

Its object is said to provide social entertainment and recreation, and to promote wider acquaintance among Freemasons. It has two degrees: (a) Royal Court; (b) Sidonian. Local groups are called Forests, presided over by a Grand Tall Cedar. The national body is Supreme Forest, presided over by a Supreme Tall Cedar. Annual sessions have been held since 1903.

Tammany Societies: Sometimes called "St. Tammany Society"; it was an outgrowth of the old Sons of Liberty. The Saint, after whom it was named, was a legendary Indian Chieftain. Washington is said to have been a member at Hampton, which had received a charter from the Grand Lodge of England, dated February 2, 1759.

Tau Kappa Epsilon: (See Order of Golden Key.)

Templar: The 6° of the Strict Observance Rite.

Templar Degrees: The Order of the Red Cross, the Order of Malta, and the Order of the Temple, constitute the Templar system in the United States, where membership in a Royal Arch Chapter is made a pre-requisite. The Red Cross Order is not in the system in the British Isles. In England and other countries the Temple Order is conferred under authority of Great Priories, rather than Grand Encampment.

Templar Priest of Holy Wisdom: When the Scottish Rite was established in England, the Templar body gave up control of the Rose Croix and Kadosh degrees; some of the encampments still retained the old degrees, and, in 1851, there was issued a revised ritual. In the old encampments, the degree of Knight Templar Priest or Holy Wisdom was conferred; it was said to have been instituted in 1786 when the so-called revival of the *Christian Order* took place. It created Chaplains, erroneously called Prelates, which means "Bishops." Many Freemasons of high social position joined the Order, and its progress for several years was rapid.

Templars, Rite of Modern: This Rite was founded in 1804 by Drs. Ledon and Fabre-Palaprat, according to Rebold, who said "the rite is now extinct in Great Britain and the U.S.A., being in those countries fitted onto the York Rite as high degrees."

Templars (Spanish): In Spain, the Templar Orders bore various names; they were founded to wage war against the Moors, as well as to protect pilgrims who were visiting the holy shrines in that country. One of these, the Order of St. Jago, 1170, was approved by Pope Alexander III. The Grand Master ranked next to the King; he had eighty-four commanderies and two hundred priories under him at one time; they took oaths of poverty, chastity and obedience.

Temple, Grand Commander of: The 58° of the Metropolitan Chapter of France; the A.A.S. Rite also has a degree by this name.

Temple Mysteries of the Easter: We are told that Martinez Paschalis, a German, 1700, journeyed to the Far East where he obtained initiation into these mysteries; returning, he set up the Rose Croix, or Elected Cohens.

Temple, Order of: The culminating degree (called an Order in U.S.A.) in the Knights Templar when conferred in the U.S.A. It is doubtful whether its ritual bears the slightest resemblance to the ritual of the Crusader Knights. It is the third of the Orders conferred in Commanderies of Knights Templar, although it was the second at one time, the Order of Malta being the last. Its members are required to believe in the practice of Christian virtues.

Teutonic Knights, Order of: (See Order of Teutonic Knights.)

Thalmedimites: The 1° of the Rite of Memphis.

Theoricus: The second grade of the Rosicrucian, U.S.A.; the 12° of the German Rose Croix.

Theosophic Apprentice: A grade in the Illumines of Stockholm.

Theosophic Companion: A grade in the Illumines of Stockholm.

Theosophic Master: A grade in the Illumines of Stockholm.

Third Chapter of Rose Croix: The degree deals with physical and philosophical, the sciences and the occult. Its special object is to regenerate Man to his original rights.

Third Degree: Our brethren sometimes refer to the degree of Master Mason as the "3d degree."

Thirty-third (33°) Degree: The last degree of the Scottish Rite system; membership is by invitation.

Thistle, Order of: (See Order of the Thistle.)

Thrice Illustrious Master: In many jurisdictions the newly elected Master of a Council of Royal and Select Masters must be installed as such in a ceremony peculiar to the Order before he is permitted to preside in a Council of such. All other brethren and companions are asked to retire during the ceremony, only those who have received the ceremony being eligible to remain. At the conclusion of the investiture, which is very brief, the companions are called back into the hall and informed that during their absence, "Comp. ...... has been regularly installed at T.I.M. of this Council."

The obligation is simple, requiring only secrecy; the candidate is seated in the chair, presented a scarlet robe and given certain words and a grip. It fills the same purpose as does the Order of the Silver Trowel, the Anointed Kings, or the T.I.M. degree in the United States, although the ceremony is not here a required one.

(See Order of the Silver Trowel.)

Titles: Masonic titles are frequently objected to as being high-sounding, exaggerated, and calculating to give an unfavorable impression to those not members. William J. MacLeod Moore, of Canada, says:

What can be more absurd than the terms "Most Wise and Perfect Master," or a group of "Sublime Princes of the Royal Secret," presided over by a "Puissant Sovereign Grand Commander, Sovereign of Sovereigns" . . . or a "Thrice Potent Grand Commander," or a "Most Equitable Sovereign Prince Grand Master"; . . . the abolition of these ridiculous and empty titles would not take away from the beauty and teaching of the degrees, and is loudly called for.

In our own country, the General Grand Council of Royal and Select Masters has a "Most Puissant General Grand Master," and the General Grand

Chapter of Royal Arch Masons has a "Most Excellent General Grand High Priest," while the Grand Encampment of Knights Templar has a "Most Eminent Grand Master" who rules a host of "Very Eminents, Right Eminents," and quite a few "ordinary" Eminents.

Tower Degree: The 2° of the Royal Order of Scotland.

Town Masons: (See Cathedral Masons.)

Triad Fraternity: A Chinese Society which bears, in some instances, a close resemblance to Masonic ceremonies. Frequent references are found to the "Square and Compass" and to "Squares" and "Circles."

Tribunal Supreme: The 71° of the Rite of Mizraim.

Trigradal System: Freemasonry, believed to have once been encompassed in one degree, later developed into a three degree system, usually referred to as a "tri-gradal" (three grades) system.

Triple Cross of Kadosh: A preliminary degree to the Sublime degree of Sovereign of Sovereigns.

True Freemason: A degree in the Philosophic Scotch Rite.

True Kindred: The degree is founded on the touching record of the piety, submission and filial tenderness of Ruth, the Gleaner, as recorded in the Book by that name. (See Order of True Kindred.)

True Kinsman: Mentioned in the Ladies' Friend (Mich. 1866).

True Mason: Same as True Freemason; the 5° of the Philosophic Scotch Rite. (See Order of the True Mason.)

True Sister: The 2° of the Order of the Sacred Temple.

Ubiquarians: One of the multitudinous societies formed in England at a time when Freemasonry was becoming most popular; its life was short.

Union Bands, Knight Templar Priests: An Irish society, formed of several lodges of a district for working the higher degrees under Craft Warrants; it existed in Ulster from the end of the 18th to the 6th decade of the 19th century. Certificates were given to members signed by the president of the Order under the name of "United Sacred Band of Templar Priests" and the motto: "Let Truth Prevail though the Universe should sink into Ruins." They worked the Priestly Order of the Temple.

Union Degree: On December 27, 1813, the two Grand Lodges of Moderns and Ancients, united into the United Grand Lodge of England; each worked a different ritual. To reconcile the members and institute a regular mode of working, the United Grand Lodge introduced a new degree (?)—the Union Degree—to be used in subordinate lodges through which all members might become acquainted with a standard working. (See Union Masters Degree.)

Union Masters Degree: When the two Grand Lodges in England united in 1813, certain ritual defects were encountered, necessitating members in both groups to become obligated through a special ceremony which was arranged by committees of each of the Grand Lodges. It is said to have been sort of a "compromise ritual." It was arranged to "obligate, instruct and perfect Masters, Past Masters, Wardens, and members of the lodges," in the craft ceremonies.

The Grand Lodge of New York was notified of this arrangement, presumably because there were lodges in this country working both rituals.

An instruction book of the times said:

"It having been ascertained that the differences existing between Ancient and Modern Masons were not essential and that the fundamental principles

249

are the same. It was agreed between the two Grand Lodges of England that these bodies should be united and form but one. . . . It was indispensable to administer an obligation to all. By every brother who has received the three degrees, either in an Ancient or Modern Lodge, a particular obligation must be taken, the manner of using the words, grips and signs, giving alarm, entering, etc., explained; but to those entered, passed and raised in a United Lodge it is only requested to make a trifling addition to the obligation appertaining to each degree at the time of its being conferred, and varying the method of using the signs."

The degree itself was a rather brief ceremony, consisting of an obligation to keep the secrets inviolate.

United Grand Lodge of Lusitania: The official title of the "once" Grand Lodge of Portugal, formed in 1819; out of this came the schismatic Grande Loja de Portugal. Freemasonry there is non-existent.

United Religious and Military Orders of the Temple and of St. John of Jerusalem, Palestine, Rhodes, and Malta: There is much difference of opinion as to the origin of this degree of the Masonic Institution, and without attempting to show that the form of conferring the degree is identical with that of the gallant and devoted soldier-monks of the Crusades, it cannot be controverted that their Institution possessed some features of similarity to Freemasonry. The connection between the Knights Templar and the Masonic Institution has been repeatedly asserted by the friends and enemies of both. Brother Lawrie says: "We know the Knights Templar not only possessed the mysteries, but performed the ceremonies, and inculcated the duties of Freemasons"; and he attributes the dissolution of the Order to the discovery of their being Freemasons, and assembling in secret to practice the rites of the Order. He endeavors to show that they were initiated into the *Order of the Druses,* a Syrian fraternity which existed at that date, and indeed now continues.

In a French MS. ritual of about 1780, in the degree of *Black and White Eagle* (30°) the transmission of Freemasonry by the Templars is most positively asserted. The history of the Templars and their persecution is minutely described in the closing address, and the Grand Commander adds:

"This is, my illustrious brother, how and by whom, Masonry is derived, and has been transmitted to us. You are now a Knight Templar, and on a level with them."

The *Order of the Temple,* in the twelfth century, was divided into three classes: Knights, Priests, and Serving Brethren. Every candidate for admission into the first class must have received the honor of knighthood in due form, and according to the laws of chivalry, and consequently the Knights Templar were all men of noble birth. The second class, or the Priests, were not originally a part of the Order, but by the bull of Pope Alexander, known as the bull *omne datum optimum,* it was ordained that they might be admitted, to enable the knights more commodiously to hear divine service, and to receive the sacraments. Serving Brothers, like the Priests, were not a part of the primitive institution. They owed their existence to the increasing prosperity and luxury of the Order.

Over this society, thus constituted, was placed a presiding officer, with the title of Grand Master. His power, though great, was limited. He was, in war, the commander-in-chief of all the forces of the Temple. In his hands was

250

placed the whole patronage of the Order, and as the vice regent of the Pope, he was the spiritual head and bishop of all the clergy belonging to the society. He was, however, much controlled and guided by the Chapter, without whose consent he was never permitted to draw out or expend the money of the Order.

The Grand Master resided originally at Jerusalem; afterwards, when that city was lost, at Acre, and finally at Cyprus. His duty always required him to be in the Holy Land; he consequently never resided in Europe. He was elected for life from among the knights in the following manner: On the death of the Grand Master, a Grand Prior was chosen to administer the affairs of the Order until a successor could be elected. When the day which had been appointed for the election arrived, the Chapter usually assembled at the chief seat of the Order; three or more of the most esteemed knights were then proposed, the Grand Prior collected the votes, and he who had received the greatest number was nominated to be the electing Prior. An Assistant was then associated with him in the person of another knight. These two remained all night in the chapel engaged in prayer. In the morning they chose two others, and these four, two more, and so on, until the number of twelve (that of the Apostles) had been selected. The twelve then selected a chaplain. The thirteen then proceeded to vote for a Grand Master, who was elected by a majority of the votes. When the election was completed, it was announced to the assembled brethren, and when all had promised obedience, the Prior, if the master-elect were present, said to him:

"In the name of God the Father, the Son, and the Holy Ghost, we have chosen, and do choose thee, Brother N., to be our Master." Then turning to the brethren he said: "Beloved sirs and brethren, give thanks unto God; Behold here our Master."

The remaining officers were a Marshal, who was charged with the execution of the military arrangements on the field of battle. The Prior of Jerusalem, called the Grand Preceptor of the Temple, was the Treasurer of the Order, and had charge of all the receipts and expenditures. The Draper had the care of the sumptuary department, and distributed the clothing to all the brethren. The Standard-bearer bore the glorious Beauceant to the field. The Turcopilier was the commander of a body of light horse called Turcopoles, who were employed as skirmishers and light cavalry. And lastly, to the Guardian of the Chapel was entrusted the care of the portable chapel, which was always carried by the Templar into the field.

Each Province of the Order had a Grand Prior, who was, in it, the representative of the Grand Master; and each House was governed by a Prior or Preceptor, who commanded its knights in time of war, and presided over its Chapter during peace.

The mode of reception into the Order is described to have been exceedingly solemn. A novitiate was enjoined by the canons, though practically it was in general dispensed with. The candidate was received in a Chapter assembled in the chapel of the Order, all strangers being rigorously excluded. The Preceptor opened the business with an address to those present, demanding if they knew of any just cause or impediment why the candidate should not be admitted. If no objection was made, the candidate was conducted into an adjacent chamber, where two or three of the knights, placing before his view the

251

rigour and austerities of the Order, demanded if he still persisted in entering it. If he persisted, he was asked if he was married or betrothed, had made a vow in any other Order, if he owed more than he could pay, if he was of sound body, without any secret infirmity, and free? If his answers proved satisfactory, they left him and returned to the Chapter, and the Preceptor again asked if anyone had anything to say against his being received. If all were silent, he asked if they were willing to receive him. On their assenting, the candidate was led in by the knights who had questioned him, and who now instructed him in the mode of asking admission. He advanced, and kneeling before the Preceptor with folded hands, said:

"Sir, I am come before God, and before you and the brethren; and I pray and beseech you, for the sake of God, and our sweet Lady, to receive me into your society and the good works of the Order, as one who, all his life long, will be the servant and slave of the Order." The Preceptor then inquired of him if he had well considered all the trials and difficulties which awaited him in the Order, adjured him on the Holy Evangelists to speak the truth, and then put to him the questions which had already been asked of him in the preparation room, further inquiring if he was a knight, and the son of a knight and gentle-woman, and if he was a priest. He then asked him the following questions: "Do you promise to God and Mary, our dear Lady, obedience as long as you live, to the Master of the Temple, and the Prior who shall be set over you? Do you promise chastity of the body? Do you further promise a strict compliance with the laudable customs and usages of the Order now in force, and such as the Master and Knights may hereafter add? Will you fight for and defend with all your might, the Holy Land of Jerusalem, and never quit the Order but with the consent of the Master and Chapter? And, lastly, do you agree that you never will see a Christian unjustly deprived of his inheritance, nor be aiding in such a deed?" The answers to all these questions being in the affirmative, the Preceptor then said: "In the name of God, and of Mary, our dear Lady, and in the name of St. Peter of Rome, and of our Father the Pope, and in the name of all the brethren of the Temple, we receive you to all the good works of the Order, which have been performed from the beginning, and will be performed to the end; you, your father, your mother, and all those of your family whom you let participate therein. So you, in like manner, receive us to all the good works which you have performed and will perform. We assure you of bread and water, the poor clothing of the Order, and labour and toil enow."

The Preceptor then took the white mantle, with its ruddy cross, placed it about his neck, and bound it fast. The Chaplain repeated the 133d Psalm:

"Behold, how good and how pleasant it is for brethren to dwell together in unity,"

and the prayer of the Holy Spirit, *"Deus qui Corda fidelium"*; each brother said a *Pater,* and the Preceptor and Chaplain kissed the candidate. He then placed himself at the feet of the Preceptor, who exhorted him to peace and charity, to chastity, obedience, humility, and piety, and so the ceremony was ended.

The secret mysteries of the Templars, most of the historians say, were celebrated on Good Friday; and what those mysteries were, we discover from those who still carry them on as their heirs, the Order as kept up in France and other countries on the Continent—not the Masonic Institution. They are accustomed in these secret rites to act over the events which took place on the Thursday, Friday and Saturday of the Holy Week, and then solemnize with great pomp the resurrection of Christ, the deliverer of mankind, out of the servitude imposed by sin.

Bartolo, in his treatise concerning the cause brought before our Lord Jesus Christ between the Virgin Mary on the one side and the Devil on the other, chose the same three days for the hearing of the cause; and on Easter Day, the day of the resurrection, he describes that Judge proclaiming mankind freed from Satan's power.

Dante also, from the opening of his sublime poem to the end of his first pilgrimage, spent the same three days in visiting the servants of Satan (in purgatory). On the third day He rose from the dead, and on Easter Day He saw the Star of Love shining before Him.

Rosetti observed, "In the *Ne plus Ultra*—a Rose-Croix Degree—there is reference to the three days, the Thursday, Friday, and Saturday of the Holy Week, during which time they represent the Last Supper with the Apostles, and the death on the Cross at Calvary."

It is to be observed that, during the persecution of the illustrious Knights of the Temple, which was set on foot by the infamous Clement, assisted by the no less infamous Philip le Bel of France, a most prominent charge against the Order was that they maintained a secret doctrine which was subversive of Christianity. The accusation of irreligion the Templars most strenuously denied, but not so the fact of their possessing certain secrets, which was true beyond all doubt—and secrets they remained (as far as the outer world is concerned) from that day to this—not the slightest information has ever been obtained concerning them from any source. This much, however, we do know, that the Templars and all the other orders of knighthood possessed certain mysteries and peculiar forms, which were confined to themselves; and the rites observed in receiving and affiliating members approached, in a remarkable degree, to the practice of Freemasonry. They had, for instance, graduations in rank, which may be taken to answer to the degrees in our Craft; some religious ceremonial was used in communicating each additional secret of the Order; and to each was attached a solemn obligation.

It has been stated by several authors, but has never been satisfactorily proved, that the Templars were a branch of the Masonic Institution, and secretly opposed to the Papacy. But the whole history of the Order is opposed to such an idea; and it was rather the great wealth and social influence exerted by this formidable body that excited the cupidity of King Philip and the jealousy of Bertrand Got, Clement V., than any actual infidelity to the Church itself on the part of the Templars. It is true that various secret associations existed from the very earliest ages of the Roman Church, having such objects, but it is not to be believed that a body of men who deliberately sacrificed their lives and fortunes to the cause of the Crusades, and to the dissemination of Papal doctrines, could, in private, combat the principles which they publicly professed. But there can be no doubt that, for purposes of security, they had a code of secret signs and passwords analogous to, although not identical with, those of Freemasonry. That they were totally different from those of the present day may be safely concluded; in fact, many Chivalric institutions existed, with a closed system of initiation, and hence they were occasionally taken for Masonic sodalities. But the whole conduct of the Knights refutes the charge of any attempt to subvert either Christianity or the Church; in fact, until the attack made upon the Templars by King Philip, the Orders of chivalry had always been considered by the Church of Rome as her strongest bulwarks.

The esteem in which they were held by the Church of Rome is amply shown in the privileges which were granted to them in every state in Europe, exempting them from all authority except that of the Pope himself, and which in course of time increased the power and pride of the Knights to an extent which could not fail to bring upon them the combined jealousy and envy of all the reigning princes of the age, and was one of the principal causes of their downfall.

The most celebrated and enduring of the ancient guilds on the Continent was the League of the Hanseatic Towns. This far-famed commercial confederacy was established during the rule, if not by the direct influence, of the *Order of Teutonic Knights*. The name is derived from the ancient German word "Hanse," signifying an association for mutual support and defence (the term has been adopted in our own tongue, and is found in two ancient charters granted by King John to the city of York, and the town of Dunwich, in Suffolk). The Hanseatic League maintained ships and soldiers at their joint expense, to protect their commerce from pirates and enemies. In 1428 they had a fleet of 248 ships, and maintained a force of 20,000 soldiers. This extraordinary association and the great Order of *Teutonic Knights* flourished at the same period; during the 200 years from 1250 to 1450 they were perhaps at their highest power, and in the most perfect organization. The Teutonic Order eventually became absorbed into the Electorate of Brandenburg; the Hanse Towns existed as free republics until 1810, when they were crushed by the despotic rule established over Europe by the first Napoleon.

The illustrious Order of the Temple has, through many vicissitudes, survived to our times; and, indeed, of late years a great, and we may say an astonishing, influence has been exercised in the Masonic Craft by this brotherhood in England, on the continent of Europe, and in the United States. Notwithstanding the persecution the Order was subjected to, consequent upon the machinations of Philip le Bel and Pope Clement, it continued to exist, if not to flourish. Jacques de Molay, the martyred Grand Master, in anticipation of his fate, appointed his successor to rule the Fraternity, and from that time to the present there has been an uninterrupted succession of Grand Masters. It is true, as years passed on and clouds arose still more ominous to the existence of the society, the Templars (we believe there is no doubt) amalgamated their body with that of their ancient brothers in arms, the *Knights of St. John,* or, as they were afterwards called (from the island that became their headquarters), the *Knights of Malta*. In the Preceptories of the Order which remained in England the secrets imparted to the newly installed brother of the Temple included, for many years, the degrees known as *Knight of St. John and Knight of Malta*. With these were also conferred the "Rose-Croix of Heredom," one of the higher degrees, which, it is said, was originally brought into this country from Scotland, and the "Kadosh," or *ne plus ultra* of Masonry. Of the Kadosh there are said to be six degrees, and, however worked, we are at liberty to say that there is little doubt that they are intimately connected with the ancient ceremonies of the Order of the Temple.

The influence of this noble Order has been widely exercised on the Continent. In France and Italy chapters of the chivalric degrees have long been

254

held, and latterly under the sanction of the Church. At Sonnenberg, in Germany, there was a *Grand Encampment of the Knights of St. John* early in the last century, where several German princes were elevated to the privileges of the Order, amongst whom were Leopold of Saxe-Coburg, the sovereign of Belgium, and Michaud, the historian of the Crusades. In Prussia the military Orders flourish, and there is good ground for tracing their preservation up to the Teutonic Order, the Knights of which were the original founders of the power of the Prussian monarchy. It is not unreasonable to conclude that a portion of the persecuted brotherhood of the Temple sought refuge with their more prosperous fellow-soldiers of the Teutonic Order, and that their secrets and ceremonies may have been thus perpetuated in the north of Europe, while the *Knights of St. John* preserved them in the south.

Frederick II, when Crown Prince of Prussia, was initiated into Masonry in secret, being much in fear of his father, and he subsequently held a Lodge at Charlottenburg, near Berlin, of which he was Master. This Lodge now exists as the Grand Lodge of the Three Globes, with a complete system of ceremonies regulated by a Council termed the *Inner Orient,* and founded upon degrees imported from France and modified by the Council. It has been claimed that Frederick II added eight degrees to the system of the Emperors of the East and West, and left a Masonic Constitution behind him, but this is an obvious mistake on the part of interested writers, as, on the contrary, the King soon withdrew himself from everything except Craft Masonry.

The Templar Degree derived its origin in England from two sources— France and Germany: The *Cross of Christ Encampment,* held at Clerkenwell, was of French origin; the *Observance* was from Germany, and presided over by Brother Burckhardt.

The *Knights Templar Degree* is highly valued in all countries. The candidate for its honors in England, must be a *Royal Arch Mason,* and a M.M. of two years standing, and as such he presents himself at the Preceptory—as the meetings are called—in the character and garb of a pilgrim, or palmer as they were designated in the Holy Land; he figuratively undergoes seven years' travel, and then seven years' warfare, when, having conducted himself courageously through his trials, he is finally admitted into the Order. It need hardly be said that this is entirely a Christian degree, and into it none but such as are professors of Christianity can be admitted. There is not a vestige of Freemasonry, as such, in the degree, save the absolute necessity of candidates having been admitted into the Royal Arch. The New Testament is, except one slight extract, exclusively used for illustration. The object of this degree is similar to that of the Rose-Croix Knight, but whereas that deals with the event of man's redemption in an allegory, this celebrates the fact. The obligation of a Masonic Knight Templar is not unlike that taken by the Soldier Monk, and he becomes by his vow a Soldier of the Cross.

In the United States, the Knights Templar are held in high esteem, numbering more than one-third million members. The membership requirements are such as to permit any Royal Arch Mason to petition, provided he is a believer in the Christian virtues.

The degrees conferred (they refer to them as Orders) are (a) the Illustrious Order of the Red Cross, (b) the Order of Malta, and (c) the Order of the Temple. The first degree is built upon the story of Zerubbabel and his

255

return to Jerusalem for the purpose of rebuilding the City and Temple; the second has as its background the historical wanderings of the Knights of Malta, while the third deals with a traditional pilgrimage during the days of the Crusades of one who wished to return to visit the Holy Sites in Jerusalem. There is no valid reason for connecting the Red Cross Order with the Christian degrees of Malta and Temple; the Templar Rite would be complete even with the one degree itself.

The Templar Rite in Canada has adopted some of the ideas from the American Grand Encampment, yet retained much of the English ritual and tradition. There the highest authority is the Supreme Priory, while in the United States it is the Grand Encampment, composed of representatives from each of the several grand commanderies (48 in number). It constitutes a representative government—yet it is not, for only those who have served as Grand Commander, or who may now be serving in a principal capacity are eligible to sit in and vote on grand encampment matters. Triennial meetings of this body are held, the last in New York in August, 1955.

Universal Harmony, Rite of: Formed by Mesner in 1782. (See Rite of Universal Harmony.)

Universal Idealist Union of Fraternity of Initiates: (See Martinist.)

Universale Freemasona Ligo: A group of Freemasons who were originally exponents of Esperanto.

Unknown Knight: The 11° of the Ancient Egyptian Reformed Rite.

Unknown Philosopher: A degree of the Philalethes Rite.

Unlawful Societies: In 1799, the English Government passed what is known as the *Unlawful Societies Act,* requiring an annual filing of membership list of each Masonic organization, as well as other societies. Secretaries of lodges have very often submitted bills for preparing and filing these lists.

Vehme Gerichte: This was a secret society for preserving peace and order in the Middle Ages. It is first heard of at Westphalia in Germany. The country was divided into districts, and these into courts, each court headed by the Lord of the Manor. There were two divisions—outer and Inner Circles. The first was not a secret society, but served as a sort of a grand jury to which all complaints might be brought. One of the degrees of the Scottish Rite is founded on an event connected with one of these Courts. Candidates were required to state that they were free-born, of German birth, and not guilty of any crime. Then, they took an obligation to preserve the secrets of the Order from "every creature upon which the sun shone, or rain fell, and from every living thing between earth and heaven." He was given a password and a grip. Sir Walter Scott has given its story in "Anne of Geierstein," Chapter XX.

Veiled Prophets of the Enchanted Realm: (See Order: Mystic Order Veiled Prophets of the Enchanted Realm.)

Veille Bru: This rite was created the year after the formation of the Chapter at Arras, in grateful memory of the reception given by the Freemasons at that place, to the military assistant of the Pretender. It was also known as "Faithful Scottish Freemasons."

Veils, Passing of: A portion of the ceremony of the Royal Arch degree as practiced in the United States; it is said to be a portion of the Excellent Master degree in Scotland, and before 1797 was referred to in this country as the Super Excellent Master.

Venerable Grand Elect: The 7° of the Persian Rite.

Venerable Grand Master: The 20° of the Ancient and Accepted Rite.

Venerable Grand Master of all Symbolic Lodges: The 20° of the A.A.S. Rite.

Veterans, Masonic: In several states there have been formed organizations of Masonic Veterans, limiting membership to Master Masons who have been members for twenty-five years or more. Assemblies are usually held during Grand Lodge communications. And there are other groups of Veterans, composed of Master Masons who have been engaged in any of the wars in which the U.S.A. has been involved. There are several Legion and V.F.W. posts made up of such members.

Vice Admiral: The 4° of the Felicitares.

Wahoo Band: (See Order of the Bath.)

White and Black Eagle: An Order founded in 1756, and which contained six degrees, regarded as the steps up a mystic ladder. It was a French organization, and from it undoubtedly came the "Emperors of the East and West," in 1735, with its 25° system, the forerunner of the A.A.S. Rite. The Mystic Ladder of the Rite may have been evolved from this degree.

White Honor Key: (See Order of DeMolay.)

White Mason: (See Priestly Order of the Temple; see Early Grand Rite of Scotland.)

White Masonry: The name given to womens adoptive degrees; the term is also used to distinguish between Freemasonry of the white and black races. (See Early Grand Rite.)

White Rose, Order of: (See Order of the White Rose.)

White Shrine of Jerusalem: (See Order of White Shrine of Jerusalem.)

Women's Lodges of Freemasons: Such organizations are clandestine and never recognized by legitimate Freemasonry; there are such organizations, however, and are usually referred to as "Co-Masonry." (See Co-Masonry.) In recent years such organizations are being formed throughout England, apparently coming from France. One such organization is located at Larkspur, Colo.

In addition to what we have termed "Co-Masonry" there are Lodges of Women Freemasons. Naturally, they are not recognized by any regular Masonic group in the world, but occasionally they break into the news; we have a copy of a newspaper article which includes pictures of their meeting places and some of the Grand Officers, clad in their "Aprons" and "Masonic?" regalia.

This particular group is an English organization, meeting in London; the article says, in part:

In the Masonic Temple of St. Ermin's, Westminster, a picturesque, and, in one respect, an extremely peculiar ceremony took place the other day. It was the enthronement of a new Grand Master, head of the Lodge for all Britain. And the new Grand Master, under the traditional regalia of royal blue and gold with its ornamentation of arcane symbols, wore a white satin evening gown. All those who witnessed the elaborate ceremony behind locked and tiled doors, wore evening dresses.

The event was a gathering of the *Honourable Fraternity of Ancient Freemasons,* an organization exclusively for women—the only women's masonic order in the world. Just as women are barred from the United Grand Lodge of England and all other Masonic lodges, so men are barred from this so-

257

ciety, of which the public generally knew nothing until the recent ceremony drew extensive attention from the press.

In 1912 this order was founded, its Grand Master, the late Brs. Boswell-Reid, a descendant of James Boswell, biographer of Samuel Johnson. It has spread since then throughout the British Empire, its largest membership including titled women, business and professional women, practitioners, of the arts and housewives. Though composed of women, it calls itself a fraternity —not a sorority; its highest officer is *Grand Master;* its members are "brothers" and not "sisters."

The feminine fraternity works the craft degrees, the Holy Royal Arch, and the Rose Croix; it publishes a magazine and maintains a masonic(?) library. The Grand Master(?) bears the title "The Most Worshipful, the Grand Master of the Honourable Fraternity of Ancient Freemasons" and "The Most Puissant Sovereign Grand Commander of the Rose Croix of H.R.D.M.," and "The Most Excellent Supreme Grand Z. of the Holy Royal Arch" and "The Most Worshipful, the Grand Master of Mark Masonry."

The article went on to say that the English "brothers" were already planning an invasion of the United States!

Woodcutters, Order of: (See Les Fendeurs, Charbonniers, etc.)

Worthy Matrons and Patrons Clubs: Organizations composed of those who have presided over the Order of the Eastern Star in the capacity of Matron and Patron. Even the husbands and wives of these officers are sometimes included in an organization known as "Trailers."

Wrestle: (See Link and Wrestle.)

Xerophagistes, Rite of: (See Rite of Xerophagistes.)

York Cross of Honour: (See Knights of York Cross of Honour.)

York Grand Lodge: Too much attention has been given the so-called Grand Lodge at York, which was about the least important of all English Grand Lodges. This was a case of a single lodge (at York) which arrogated to itself the title of "Grand Lodge of All England." It is true that an operative organization of Masons existed at York, at least as far back as 1370, when there are to be found entries in the Rolls of York Minster, of a superior body of Masons which had established rules for its craftsmen. Annual assemblies were held and in the 16th century the names of many distinguished outsiders were listed as speculative Masons. It is said that Queen Elizabeth, disturbed by reports received from York, sent officers to make an inquiry, fearing the society might be used by her rival, Mary Queen of Scots. The report was favorable. It authorized a Military Lodge in 1770, with power to confer the Royal Arch degree, although it did not, itself, confer that grade.

York Rite: The name is probably a misnomer; there was never any such Rite at York, and the degrees referred to in this country today as "York Rite" were never heard of at York, or even in England until the last century. However, the degrees usually included under the above head, are: Entered Apprentice; Fellow Craft; Master Mason; Mark Master; Past Master; Most Excellent Master; Royal Arch Mason; Royal Master; Select Master; Super Excellent Master. If the commandery could be included, we would have the degrees (they call them Orders) of Red Cross, Malta, and Temple. In this category would also be included those degrees attached to those bodies, such as the Order of High Priesthood, Silver Trowel, Past Commanders' Associations, etc. (See Rite, York.)

Youth, The: One of the degrees of Bahrdt's Rite.

Zelator: A degree of the Rosicrucian Rite in the U.S.A.

Zerubbabel Key: (See Order of DeMolay.)

Zinnendorf Rite: A rite practiced by the National Grand Lodge of Germany at Berlin; it had seven degrees and was formed in 1767. (See Rite of Zinnendorf.)

Zirkel: A club has been established in Chicago, Ill., known as Zirkel, which is said to be a Masonic social club. We have no information as to what constitutes its membership or its particular object, other than the social contact of its members.

Zoroastrians, The Eons or: Only information comes from Ragon which he says was founded on Zoroastrian teachings.

Zuzumites: (See Ancient Order of Zuzumites.)

CROSSES

The story of the Cross and the Crown is a story of two wonderful symbols which deal with human life—a story of sacrifice, punishment, worship, and hardship, with their ultimate reward. Neither of the two emblems are to be found in symbolic Masonry, but do appear in the historical and chivalric degrees; it remained for the Orders of Knighthood to bring them to our immediate attention, laying particular stress on their teaching; these Orders, however, fail to develop the symbolic side of the symbols and make use of the Cross only in connection with the martyrdom of some Holy Man.

In Gaul, the Cross was a solar symbol when it had equal arms and angles; to the Phoenecian it was an instrument of sacrifice to the God, Baal; to the Egyptian, the Crux Ansata, or Tau Cross, was the symbol of Eternal Life. With the advent of the crusades—those great excursions of the Christian World into Mohammedan territory—there came a great wave of religious fervor; this spirit expressed itself in religious symbols and heraldic devices which were interwoven into the clothing of the Christian knight; the Cross of the Crusader makes its appearance in this manner—not the Passion Cross which now appears on the breast of the modern knight, but the Cross in its various forms, depending upon the nationality of the wearer, or the period of the Crusade, for there is ample evidence that many styles of Crosses were in

use. The Cross was the common implement of punishment among the ancients; the Christians seized upon it as an emblem of their Faith.

The word "Cross" is taken from the Latin "Crux," and as such it appears in Indian inscriptions, in the cuneiform writings at Susa, and on the Temple of Serapis. No form is more common in nature than is the Cross—it is impressed on the whole of nature—it appears in the working tools of the laborer; it is a part of man himself when he raises his hands in the attitude of prayer; there is a natural Cross on every ship which sails the seas.

Today, the Cross has become the central figure in practically all the decorations awarded by kings, princes, or governments; it is awarded to those who undergo peril, danger, or suffering in behalf of their country, and as such, it still retains the old symbolism of *punishment*. While it is generally regarded as a Christian emblem, the Jewish people say of it:

As far as it is made an object of worship by Christians, it is to be treated as an idol and prohibited for use; its use is permitted if worn as an ornament without any religious object.

Many legends have been built around the Cross; one writer of antiquity (Paulinus) says of the Cross:

Those who were persons of substance were gratified by obtaining, at their full price, small pieces of the cross, set with gems; and that wonder might not pass into incredulity, the proper authorities gave the world assurance that the holy wood possessed the power of self-multiplication, and notwithstanding the innumerable pieces which had been taken from it for the pleasure and service of the faithful, remained intact and entire as at first!

Explanation of the Crosses

Annulate Cross (1). Extremities end in rings or annulets.
Archepiscopal Cross (2). A shaft intersected by two transverse pieces, upper shorter than lower. When slanted it is emblem of 33°.
Celtic Cross (3). Has a disc at juncture of two arms; may have a circle.
Chi Rho Cross (4). (See Cross of Constantine.)
Cross Avellane (5). Has form of four unhusked filberts.
Cross Botonee (24). Has a bud or button at end of trefoil.
Cross of Calvary (6). The Passion or Latin Cross; sometimes placed on three steps, emblematic of Faith, Hope, and Charity.
Cross Catoosed (7). Cross with scrolls at extremities.
Cross Comise (14). Same as Tau Cross.
Cross of Constantine (4). Monogram of the name of Christ (Greek, Chi Rho), formed by the initials of his name; the Cross said to have been seen by Constantine in his vision; the initials "X" and "P" combined.
Cross Crosslet (8). A Cross whose four extremities form Crosses.
Cross Double Cross Crosslet (9). A Cross Crosslet with two transoms crossed.

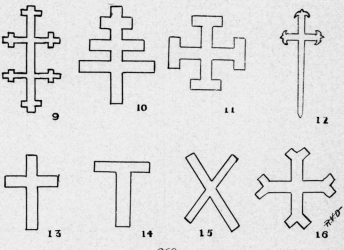

9   10   11   12

13   14   15   16

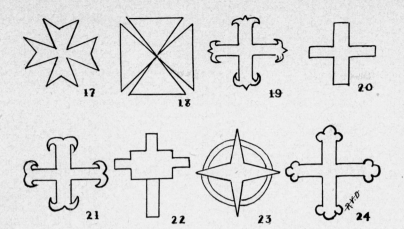

Cross *Double Parted* (22). Cross cut into four quarters, separated one from another.

Cross *Etoile* (23). Cross with four arms sharply pointed or star of four points.

Cross *Fleury* (19). Same as Cross Flory; a Cross with floriated ends.

Cross *Formee, or Patee* (18). A Cross having arms narrow at the center and expanding greatly towards the ends.

Cross *Fourchee* (16). Cross with two square ends at each extremity.

Cross *of Jerusalem* (11). Cross whose four ends are capped with a cross bar; four Tau crosses joined.

Cross *of Lorraine* (2). A Cross with two horizontal arms, the upper being shorter than the lower.

Cross *of Malta* (17) (Maltese Cross). A Cross supposed to be made up of four barbed arrow heads which meet at their points. The eight points refer to the Eight Beatitudes.

Cross *Moline* (21). A Cross whose ends are divided and curved backward.

Cross *Nowy Quadrant* (22). A Cross having each angle filled with an angular projection forming a square from which the arms radiate.

Cross *Pommee* (1). A Cross whose ends terminate with balls or protuberances.

Cross *Potent* (11). A Cross whose ends terminate in a cross head.

Cross *of St. Andrew* (15). An "X" Cross; refers to St. Andrew's Martyrdom.

Cross *of St. Anthony* (14). The Cross of St. Anthony's martyrdom; a "T" Cross.

Cross *of St. George* (20). A Greek Cross. The Red Cross.

Cross *of St. James* (12). A Latin Cross, the longest arm of which represents the blade of a sword; the opposite end, the hilt; the other two, the cross guard, the latter floriated.

Cross *Triple* (10). See Cross of Salem.

Greek Cross (20). The Cross of St. George.

Latin Cross (13). A Passion Cross, whose lower arm is longer than the three others.

Papal Cross (10). A Cross with three transoms, the smaller transoms at top.

Passion Cross (13). The Cross on which Jesus suffered crucifixion.

Patriarchal Cross (2). A double Cross; Grand Encampment insignia.

Salem Cross (10). Insignia of Grand Master Grand Encampment (See Cross of Jerusalem; the Pontifical Cross borne by the Pope).

Tau Cross (14). An Egyptian or Nile Cross; a "T" Cross.

Teutonic Cross (11). A Cross Potent, worn by Teutonic Knights; a Scottish Rite Cross.

261